HISTORY OF HINDU-CHRISTIAN ENCOUNTERS

HISTORY OF HINDU-CHRISTIAN ENCOUNTERS AD 304 TO 1996

SITA RAM GOEL

VOICE OF INDIA
NEW DELHI

First Edition, 1986
Second Revised and Enlarged Edition, 1996
Reprint, 2010
Sixth Reprint, 2020

ISBN 978-81-85990-35-4

website: www.voiceofin.com

Published by Voice of India, 2/18, Ansari Road, New Delhi – 110 002
and printed at Replika Press Pvt.Ltd.

Contents

Preface to the Second Edition

The first edition of this book, published in 1986, had 16 chapters and an appendix. This second edition has 25 chapters. The appendix — Encounter at Pondicherry — has been fitted in the chronology of encounters and forms Chapter 7 of the new edition. Chapter 14 of the old edition has been split into two chapters, 15 and 16, separating the debate on the Fundamental Right to Propagate Religion from the debate in the Constituent Assembly. Similarly, Chapter 16 of the old edition has been split into three chapters — 18,19 and 20 — separating the three subjects dealt with. Chapter 19 which formed Section II of Chapter 16 in the old edition has been expanded by incorporation of a dialogue between Ram Swarup and Bede Griffiths. Five chapters, 21 to 25, are entirely new and cover Hindu-Christian encounters that have come to my knowledge since the first edition was compiled.

The old scheme of numbering and naming the encounters serially has been given up in the new edition. I realized that there might have been Hindu-Christian encounters which had not come to my notice. The chapters have now been given headings in keeping with their contents. But the chronological order has been maintained.

The new edition has been thoroughly revised. Language has been straightened wherever necessary, and typographical errors have been removed. Footnotes have been numbered serially for each chapter, and not for each page as in the earlier edition. Some footnotes of the old edition have been expanded, and some new ones have been added. Comments at the end of Chapter 3 have been revised. A critical note regarding the role of the Ramakrishna Mission has been added to Chapter 13 which deals with Swami Vivekananda's encounter with Christianity. Chapter 14 which deals with

Mahatma Gandhi's encounter with Christianity carries a long and critical postscript. Criticism of Mahatma Gandhi may sound startling. But I could not help saying what I have said. His role vis-a-vis Christianity has to be reassessed.

Finally, the book now carries a subtitle — AD 304 to 1996. This was suggested by Shri Harish Chandra, a keen reader and evaluator of VOICE OF INDIA publications.

It is hoped that readers will find this revised and enlarged edition as informative as the old one. The comments I received on the first edition were rewarding as well as encouraging. Koenraad Elst came to me in 1989 as soon as he read the book. His cryptic comment was, "Hindus have a very good case vis-a-vis Christianity and Islam, but at present it is either not presented at all or presented very badly. This book is a departure." It was not long before he became a scholar-writer of the VOICE OF INDIA family. I look forward to comments from new readers of this work as a whole, and from the old readers on my critical notes and the new chapters, particularly the one which advocates rejection of Jesus as junk.

II

History of Hindu-Christian encounters, as surveyed in this book, falls into five distinct phases. In all of them Christian missionaries stick to their basic dogma of One True God and the Only Saviour. But they keep on changing their methods and verbiage. To start with, spokesmen for Hinduism offer a stiff resistance to the Christian message as well as missionary methods. But due to a number of factors, Hindu resistance weakens in later stages and then disappears altogether so that Christianity forges ahead with a sense of triumph.

In the first-phase, which opens with the coming of the Portuguese pirates, Christianity presents itself in its true colours. Its language is as crude as in its homeland in Europe, and its methods as cruel. Hindus are helpless and suffer any number of atrocities. Fortunately for them, this phase does not last for long. The Portuguese lose power except in Goa and some other small territories. The other European powers that take over have no time to spare for Christianity except the French for a brief period in Pondicherry.

The second phase opens with the consolidation of the British conquest. The British do not allow Christian missions to use physical methods. But missionary language continues to be as crude as ever. Christianity enjoys a brief period of self-confidence. The phase ends with the rise of Hindu reform movements, particularly the Arya Samaj. Christianity suffers a serious set-back.

The third phase starts with the advent of Mahatma Gandhi and his slogan of *sarva-dharma-samabhāva*. Christianity is thrown on the defensive and forced to change its language. The foul-mouthed miscreants become sweet-tongued vipers. Now they are out to "share their spiritual riches" with Hindus, reminding us of the naked beggar promising to donate his wardrobe to wealthy persons. The phase ended with the Tambram Conference of the International Missionary Council in 1938 which decided to reformulate Christian theology in the Indian context.

The fourth phase which commenced with the coming of independence proved a boon for Christianity. The Christian right to convert Hindus was incorporated in the Constitution. Prime Minister Jawaharlal Nehru who dominated the scene for 17 long years promoted every anti-Hindu ideology and movement. The regimes that followed till the rise of P.V. Narasimha Rao raised the spectre of 'Hindu communalism' as the most frightening phenomenon. Christian missionaries could now denounce as a Hindu communalist and fascist, even as a Hindu Nazi, any one who raised the slightest objection to their methods. All sorts of 'secularists' came forward to join the chorus. New theologies of Fulfilment, Indigenisation, Liberation, and Dialogue were evolved and put into action. The missionary apparatus multiplied fast and manifold. Christianity had never had it so good in the whole of its history in India. It now stood recognized as 'an ancient

Indian religion' with every right to extend its fold. The only rift in the lute was K. M. Panikkar's book, the Niyogi Committee Report, and Om Prakash Tyagi's Bill on Freedom of Religion.

The fifth phase which is continuing now started with Hindu awakening brought about by conversion of some Harijans to Islam at Meenakshipuram, renewed Muslim aggression in many ways, and Pakistan-backed terrorism in Punjab and Kashmir. The Sangh Parivar which had turned cold towards Hindu causes over the years was startled by the rout of the Bharatiya Janata Party in the 1984 elections, and decided to renew its Hindu character. The Ramajanmabhumi Movement was the result. The Movement was aimed at arresting Islamic aggression. Christianity or its missions were hardly mentioned. Nevertheless, it was Christianity which showed the greatest concern at this new Hindu stir, and started crying 'wolf'. Its media power in the West raised a storm saying that Hindus were out to destroy the minorities in India and impose a Nazi regime. The storm is still raging and no one knows when it will subside, if at all.

III

Hindus from seventeenth century Pandits of Tamil Nadu to Mahatma Gandhi have wasted no end of breath to demolish the dogma of Christianity. But it has hardly made any difference to the arrogance of Christian theologians and missionaries. That is because dogma was never meant for discussion. It is an axiom of logic that that which has not been proved cannot and need not be disproved. Who has ever proved that the non-descript Jew who was crucified by a Roman governor of Judaea in 33 AD atoned for the sins of mankind for all time to come? Who has ever proved that those who accept that Jew as the only saviour will ascend to a heaven of everlasting bliss and those who do not will burn for ever in the blazing fire of hell? Nor can the proclamation or the promise or the threat be disproved. High-sounding theological blah blah notwithstanding the fact remains that the dogma is no more than a subterfuge for forging and wielding an organizational weapon for aggression against other people. It is high time for Hindus to dismiss the dogma of Christianity with the contempt it deserves, and pay attention to the Christian missionary apparatus planted in their midst.

The sole aim of this apparatus is to ruin Hindu society and culture, and take over the Hindu homeland. It goes on devising strategies for every situation, favourable and unfavourable. It trains and employs a large number of intellectual criminals ready to prostitute their talents in the service of their paymasters, and adept at dressing up dark designs in high-sounding language. The fact that every design is advertised as a theology in the Indian context, and every criminal euphemized as an Indian theologian should not hoodwink Hindus about the real intentions.

Hindus are committing a great mistake in regarding the encounter between Hinduism and Christianity as a dialogue between two religions. Christianity has never been a religion; it has always been a predatory imperialism par excellence. The encounter, therefore, should be viewed as a battle between two totally opposed and mutually exclusive ways of thought and behaviour. In the language of the Gita (Chapter 16), it is war between *daivī* (divine) and *āsurī* (demonic) *sampads* (propensities). In the larger context of history, it can also be described as war between the Vedic and the Biblical traditions.

This is not the place to go into the premises from which the two traditions proceed. I have presented them in some detail elsewhere.[1] Here I will indicate briefly the behaviour patterns they promote.

The Vedic tradition advises people to be busy with themselves, that is, their own moral and spiritual improvement. Several disciplines have been evolved for this purpose — *tapas* (austerity), *yoga* (meditation), *jñāna* (reflection), *bhakti*

---

1. Sita Ram Goel, *Defence of Hindu Society*, Third revised edition, Voice of India, New Delhi, 1994.

(devotion), etc. A seeker can take to whatever discipline suits his *adhāra* (stage of moral-spiritual preparation). There is no uniform prescription for every body, no coercion into a belief system, and no regimentation for aggression against others.

The Biblical tradition, on the other hand, teaches people to be busy with others. One is supposed to have become a superior human being as soon as one confesses the 'only true faith'. Thenceforward one stands qualified to 'save' others. The only training one needs thereafter is how to man a mission or military expedition, how to convert others by all available means including force and fraud, and how to kill or ruin those who refuse to come round.

The Vedic tradition has given to the world schools of Sanatana Dharma which have practised peace among their own followers as well as towards the followers of other paths. On the other hand, the Biblical tradition has spawned cults such as Christianity, Islam, Communism, and Nazism which have always produced violent conflicts as much within their own camps as with each other.

New Delhi,
15 June 1996 Sita Ram Goel

Preface to the First Edition

Christian historians, in India and abroad, have written many accounts of how Christian theologians, missionaries and warlords have looked at Hinduism[1] in different phases of Christian aggression against this ancient religion and culture. But there is no connected account of how Hindu thinkers, saints and sages have viewed Christianity and its exclusive claims. The present study is an attempt to fill that gap. It is far from being exhaustive. It seeks to cover only some of the high spots in a prolonged encounter starting with the Christian attack on Hindu temples in the Roman Empire, a few years before Constantine enthroned Christianity as the state religion of Rome.

The absence of such a study has given rise to misunderstanding as well as misrepresentation. An ever-increasing section of the Hindu intelligentsia has been led to believe that it is uncharacteristic of Hinduism to examine critically the claims advanced by another religion. This is a complete misunderstanding as this study goes to show in the context of Christianity. Meanwhile, Christian theologians have been presenting the leading spokesmen for Hinduism as if they were disciples of Jesus Christ rather than exponents of Sanatana Dharma. It is difficult to say whether the misrepresentation is deliberate or due to the theologians' penchant for seeing their own pet god presiding over every manifestation, in the realm of thought as well as of things. But all the same it is there.

Readers of the dialogue between Swami Devananda Saraswati and Fr. Bede Griffiths which has been summarised

1. The term "Hinduism" is used here, as throughout this study, in the sense in which Gandhiji used it, that is, to cover all schools of Sanatana Dharma — Buddhism, Jainism, Shaivism, Shaktism and Vaishnavism which includes the Santa-*mata* and Sikhism. Treating these segments of a single spiritual vision as separate religions is not only misleading but also mischievous.

in this study (pp. 386-98) can see for themselves how confidently Fr. Bede invokes the names of Sri Ramakrishna, Swami Vivekananda, Sri Aurobindo, Ramana Maharshi, Mahatma Gandhi and Ramalinga Swamigal and regards them as "Hindu in religion while being Christian in spirit." Dr. M. M. Thomas, a noted theologian, goes much further in his thesis, *The Acknowledged Christ of the Indian Renaissance,* first published in 1970 and republished in a second edition in 1976. It is supposed to be a rejoinder to Dr. Raymond Panikkar's *The Unknown Christ of Hinduism,* an earlier theological exercise published in 1964. But while the title of Dr. Panikkar's book had the merit of suggesting only a speculation, howsoever wild, the title of Dr. Thomas' book is a misrepresentation of the Hindu point of view, as he himself shows in course of presenting the views of Raja Ram Mohun Roy, Keshub Chander Sen, P. C. Mozoomdar, Sri Ramakrishna, Swami Vivekananda, Dr. Radhakrishnan and Mahatma Gandhi. None of these Hindu thinkers ever admitted that the Jesus of history was the Christ of Christian theology, that is, the only son of God and the sole saviour of mankind.

And that brings us to the crux of the encounter between Hinduism and Christianity. No Hindu thinker has had the least objection to Christians believing in and seeking salvation through Jesus. Nor do Hindus bother about the dogmas of the only sonship, the virgin birth, the atoning death, the resurrection and the rest, so long as Christians keep these to themselves. It is only when the Christian missionary apparatus tries doggedly to impose these dogmas on other people that Hindu thinkers are forced to register a protest and have a close look at the Jesus of history.

Christian missionaries should thank their stars that the historical and critical research undertaken by Western scholars regarding Jesus and New Testament stories, has not yet reached the Hindu intelligentsia,[2] partly due to the traditional

---

2. Since this Preface was written, an attempt to make this research available to the Hindu intelligentsia has been made in Sita Ram Goel, *Jesus Christ: An Artifice for Aggression,* Voice of India, New Delhi, 1994.

Hindu indifference towards the historicity of saints and sages and partly due to the Christian domination over education and mass media in this country. The Hindu intelligentsia at large is also not yet acquainted with the history of Christianity in Europe and its missions elsewhere. Western scholarship has already produced several hundred well documented studies which have made the historical Jesus of Christian theology evaporate into thin air and Christian history look like a tale of terror and wanton bloodshed. The Christian missionaries in India will run for cover whenever the findings of Western research become widely known to the Hindu intelligentsia, the same way as the churches have been doing in all Western countries since the middle of the eighteenth century. The missionaries know it very well that Christianity being in a very bad shape in the West is trying desperately to find a safe-house in the East.

We have also something to say about "dialogue" which has become the most famous as well as the most frequent word in current Christian parlance. The Second Vatican Council is supposed to have made a radical departure from the earlier Christian stand vis-a-vis other religions. "The Catholic Church," says a proclamation, *Nostra aetale,* dated October 28, 1965, "rejects nothing of what is true and holy in these religions [Hinduism and Buddhism]. She has a high regard for the manner of life and conduct, the precepts and doctrines which although differing in many ways from her own teaching, often reflect a ray of that truth which enlightens all men. Yet she proclaims and is duty bound to proclaim without fail, Christ who is the way, the truth and life (Jn. 14:6). In him, in whom God reconciled all things to himself (2 Cor. 5:18-19), men find the fullness of their religious life. The Church, therefore, urges her sons to enter with prudence and charity into discussion and collaboration with members of other religions. Let Christians, while witnessing their own faith and way of life, acknowledge, preserve and encourage the spiritual and moral truths found among non-Christians, also their social life and culture."[3] Before we offer our own comments on this proclamation, we like to quote a Christian missionary regarding how difficult the dialogue remains. "But if we accept," says J. Dilasa, Superior General, I.M.S., "the unique claim of Christ as the only Son of God who entered human history and radically changed it as the Lord of history, there is very little scope for inter-religious collaboration. As heralds of the one Gospel of salvation we have to proclaim it and others have to accept it. Similarly if we consider the unique mission of the Church to continue the work of Christ, I wonder how an inter-religious missionary activity is possible."[4]

It should be plain to any reader who is not over-awed by the pope and his ex-cathedra ordinances that apart from being patronising in its tone, the proclamation breathes an air of reserve and reluctance in conceding even the little it does. The most amazing part, however, is that it has taken the disciples of Jesus well-nigh two thousand years to find in Hinduism and Buddhism only "a ray of that truth which enlightens all men." It speaks volumes of the wisdom which the Church of Christ is supposed to have enshrined down the ages. The less said about that Church's new role in preserving and encouraging "the spiritual and moral truths found among non-Christians", the better. The non-Christian religions have preserved on their own their truths, their social life and their culture throughout these long centuries; they certainly do not stand in need of help from an apparatus which has tried its utmost to uproot them. The stark truth seems to be the other way around; it is the Church of Christ which is seeking desperately the help of non-Christian religions in order to save whatever little is left of its superstitions. That is the meaning of the "dialogue" for which

---

3. *Vatican Council II: The Conciliar and Post Conciliar Documents* edited by Austin Flannery, O.P., St. Paul Publications, Bombay, 1983, p. 668.

4. 'Problems of Evangelisation', in *Jeevandhara: A Journal of Christian Interpretation,* September 1988, pp. 330-31.

Christian theologians and missionaries are crying now-a-days. The "dialogue" does not seem to be a sincere attempt at reconciliation; on the contrary, it is only a strategy for survival on the part of Christianity.

The Church will sound sincere only when it stops saying that Jesus should be accepted by all as the one and only saviour of mankind and that Christianity holds a monopoly of the highest truth. That will also lead it to renounce its ridiculous exercises in theologies of fulfilment, inculturation and liberation, etc. The missionary apparatus which was created with the help of imperialist armies and which is now being sustained by means of massive money and media power of the West will have to be dismantled. Exclusive claims and missionary efforts stand or fall together.

As the following pages make it clear, the spokesmen for Hinduism have examined and rejected every exclusive claim of Christianity. If orthodox Christianity survives in this country, it is not because there is any merit in its dogmas but simply because it has established itself over the centuries as a powerful political and economic entity. It is high time for Christian theologians to come down to earth and recognize every person's right to seek truth and salvation in his or her own way. They should know that while they invoke the Universal Declaration of Human Rights and the Constitution of India in order to protect their aggressive apparatus, they are riding roughshod over the most fundamental human right, that is, to know God directly, without the aid of officious intermediaries most of whom are no better, if not worse, than those whom they choose to evangelize. Dr. Radhakrishnan put the matter straight when he told a missionary friend, "You Christians seem to us Hindus rather ordinary people making extraordinary claims." When the missionary explained that the claims were being made on behalf of Christ, he observed, "If your Christ has not succeeded in making you better men and women, have we any reason to suppose that he would do more for us, if we became Christians?" He reminded the missionary that Hinduism was "more modest and more logical" in teaching that "the divine immanence in every man and women makes it possible for all to seek the truth in their own ways." Finally, he pointed towards a living example of what religion means to the Hindus. "The fact of Gandhi," he said, "is a challenge to the exclusive claims of Christianity."[5]

Rakshabandhana Purnima
August 17, 1989, New Delhi.

Sita Ram Goel

---

5. Sarvepalli Gopal, *Radhakrishanan: A Biography,* OUP, 1989, p.195.

The Christian god is cruel, vindictive, capricious and unjust.

—Thomas Jefferson

It will be more consistent that we call it [Bible] the work of a demon than the word of God.

—Thomas Paine

What have been Christianity's fruits? — superstition, bigotry and persecution.

—James Madison

Missionaries are perfect nuisances and leave every place worse than they found it.

—Charles Dickens

1

Encounter on the Euphrates

Christian historians will have us believe that Hinduism first came in contact with Christianity in AD 52 when St. Thomas, an apostle of Jesus Christ, landed in Malabar. He is supposed to have travelled in South India and founded seven churches before he was "murdered" by the "malicious" Brahmanas. The old Christians in Kerala, who knew as well as introduced themselves as Syrian Christians till the other day, now take pride in calling themselves St. Thomas Christians. We have examined this story elsewhere[1] as also the motives for floating it. Here it should suffice to say that the more scrupulous Christian historians have found the story too fanciful to be taken seriously.

Coming to facts of history, the first encounter between Hinduism and Christianity took place not in India but in those parts of West Asia, North Africa and Southern Europe which comprised the Roman Empire at the dawn of the Christian era. There is evidence, archaeological as well as literary, that Hinduism had made its presence felt in Graeco-Roman religions and philosophies long before Jesus was born. The imprint of Samkhya, Yoga and Vedanta on Eleatic, Elusinian, Orphic, Pythagorean, Platonist, Stoic, Gnostic and Neo-Platonist philosophies is too manifest to be missed easily. It was widely believed in the ancient Western world that the Greeks had learnt their wisdom from the Brahmanas of India.

---

1. Sita Ram Goel, *Papacy: Its Doctrine and History*, Voice of India, 1986, pp. 55-58. The St. Thomas story has since been examined in great detail in *The Myth of Saint Thomas and the Mylapore Shiva Temple* by Ishwar Sharan, Voice of India, New Delhi, 1991, reprinted in a revised and enlarged second edition in 1995.

Evidence of Hindu colonies in some leading cities of the Roman Empire is also available. Hindu temples had come up wherever Hindu merchants and traders had established their colonies. Hindu saints, sages and savants could not have lagged behind.

Christianity did not fail to notice this Hindu presence as soon as it became a force in the Roman Empire. It was, from its very birth, wide awake towards all currents and cross-currents of thought and culture. We find St. Hippolytus attacking the Brahmanas as a source of heresy as early as the first quarter of the third country.[2] It was not long after that Hinduism faced a determined assault from Christianity as did other ancient religions of the Roman Empire.

Hindu temples were the most visible symbols of the Brahmana religion. They became targets of Christian attack like all other Pagan temples. "According to the Syrian writer Zenob," writes Dr. R. C. Majumdar, "there was an Indian colony in the canton of Taron on the upper Euphrates, to the west of Lake Van, as early as the second century B.C. The Indians had built there two temples containing images of gods about 18 and 22 feet high. When, about AD 304, St. Gregory came to destroy these images, he was strongly opposed by the Hindus. But he defeated them and smashed the images, thus anticipating the iconoclastic zeal of Mahmud of Ghazni."[3]

---

2. D. P. Singhal, *India and World Civilization,* Calcutta, 1972, Volume I, p. 85.

3. *The History and Culture of the Indian People,* Volume II, *The Age of Imperial Unity,* Fourth Edition, Bombay, 1968, pp. 633-634. It would have been more appropriate to mention Francis Xavier in this context. Islamic iconoclasm is not the only iconoclasm which Hinduism has known. Christian iconoclasm pioneered by Xavier was no less ferocious and predatory. It is true that due to geographical and historical factors, Christian iconoclasm came to this country much later, was confined to a much smaller area and spread over a much shorter time-span as compared to the large-scale and prolonged iconoclasm practised by Islam. But, it was no less criminal in its inspiration. Moreover, Islam did not invent iconoclasm. It had learnt it from the Bible and the Christian practice down the ages.

Historians of the Roman Empire have documented the large-scale destruction of Pagan temples by Christianity from the fourth century onwards.[4] It is more than likely that some of these were places of Hindu worship. The word "pagan" is a comprehensive term in Christian parlance and covers a large variety of religious and cultural expressions. Hindu historians will have to examine all archives, Pagan as well as Christian. Meanwhile, let Christian theologians tell us of the Christian virtues for which Gregory was canonised as a saint.

4. The evidence of Christian iconoclasm in many countries for many centuries lies scattered in many Christian and non-Christian accounts. During my travels in 1989, I searched several leading libraries in Switzerland, Germany, France, England and the USA for a consolidated study of the subject but failed to find any. A glimpse of what Christianity did to Pagan temples in the Roman Empire can, however, be had from Pierre Chuvin, *A Chronicle of the Last Pagans,* Harvard University Press, Cambridge, Massachussetts, USA, 1990.

2

Encounter in Malabar

It is not known whether the news of the Christian onslaught on Hinduism in the Roman Empire reached India. One wonders whether the merchants and monks who survived and returned home grasped the import of what was happening. If they gave to their countrymen an account of what they had witnessed in a distant land, the record has not survived or is not yet known. Nor do we know how the Hindus at home reacted, if at all. What we do know, however, is that Hinduism in India had not heard of Christianity when the two had their second encounter, this time inside the homeland of Hinduism.

The Hindus of Malabar were the first to see Christians arriving in their midst. They were mostly refugees from persecution in Syria and later on in Iran. Christians in Syria were persecuted by their own brethren in faith. They had become suspect in Iran from the fourth century onwards when Iran's old adversary, the Roman Empire, became a Christian state. They suffered repeated persecutions in both countries. As most of them were heretics in the eyes of Christian orthodoxy, they could not go west. So they fled towards India and China, which two countries were known for their religious tolerance throughout the ages. Later on, they were joined by refugees from Armenia flying from Christian heresy-hunters.

The record that has been preserved by the Christian refugees themselves tells us that they were received well by the Hindus of Malabar. Hindu Rajas gave them land and money grants for building houses and churches. Hindus in general made things so pleasant for them that they decided to stay permanently in Malabar. No Hindu, Raja or commoner, ever bothered about what the refugees believed or what god they worshipped. No one interfered with the hierarchs who came from Syria from time to time to visit their flock in India and collect the tithes. In due course, the refugees came to be known as Syrian Christians.

It is not known how the Syrian Christians viewed their Hindu neighbours. If they despised the Hindus as heathens, they kept it a closely guarded secret. Nor did they try to evangelize and convert the Hindus, the two practices which had been proclaimed by the Founding Fathers of the Church as inseparable parts of the Christian Creed and inalienable rights of Christians everywhere. On the contrary, they lost their separate identity and became a part of the local population, so much so that Christian travellers who came to these parts in the thirteenth and fourteenth centuries did not notice them as different from Hindus. They learnt the local language and took to Hindu modes in dress and food and the other externals of life. They intermarried with certain sections of Hindu society. Even inside their churches, their rituals acquired the character of Hindu *pūjā*.

Latter-day Christian theologians and historians would claim that Syrian Christianity had a tremendous impact on Hinduism. The notion of One God which some sixteenth-century missionaries "discovered" in Hinduism would be seen as a contribution of Christianity. Nineteenth-century Christian scholars would assert that Hindus had derived the concepts of *bhakti* (devotion) and *mukti* (salvation) from the Christian contact in South India which was held by Hindus as the original home of the medieval Bhakti Movement. Christ was seen disguised in Krishna who figured prominently in certain Vaishnava schools of *bhakti*. Hindu philosophies like the *advaita* of Shankara and the *vishiṣṭādvaita* of Ramanuja were also traced to Christian sources.

No scholar today takes these hair-brained Christian speculations seriously. The current fashion among scholars of medieval India is to see Islam as the source of the Bhakti

Movement. But that is a different story. It is also a different story that some Christian theologians are trying to use *advaita* and *vishiṣṭādvaita* as vehicles for implanting Christianity into the heart of Hinduism. What is pertinent in the present context is that the Syrian Christians were never known to their Hindu neighbours for spiritual or philosophical profundities. The only thing that was known about them was that they were hardworking and intelligent businessmen, some of whom had succeeded as prosperous spice merchants. They were also known for keeping slaves as well as trading in them.

The significant point to be noted about the Syrian Christians, however, is their sudden change of colour as soon as the Portuguese arrived on the scene. They immediately rallied round the Portuguese and against their Hindu neighbours, and when the Portuguese started pressurizing the Hindu Rajas for extra-territorial rights so that their co-religionists could be "protected", the Syrian Christians evinced great enthusiasm everywhere. They became loyal subjects of the king of Portugal and pious adherents of the Roman Catholic Church. Was it the demonstration of Portuguese power which demoralised the Syrian Christians and made them do what they did? Or was it the Christian doctrine which, though it lay dormant for a long time, surfaced at the first favourable opportunity? The matter has to be examined. Looking at the behaviour of Syrian Christians ever since, the second proposition seems to be nearer the truth.[1]

1. cf. K.M. Panikkar, *Malabar and the Portuguese,* Bombay, 1929.

3

Hallucinations of the Devil's Devotees

For a long time, the Syrian Christians provided the only contact which Hinduism had with Christianity. India lost touch with the Christian West for well-nigh seven centuries because Islamic empires in the Middle East and Central Asia, had raised a barrier between the two. Christians and Muslims were involved in mortal combat soon after the death of prophet Muhammad in AD 632. Christian travellers ran the risk of death if they tried to come east through Muslim dominated routes on land and sea. Hindu merchants, too, lost the incentive for going to Europe. Muslim merchants had monopolised all trade between the East and the West. Hindu sages and savants could hardly think of going abroad; they were having a very difficult time at home where Islam was heaping humiliations on them.

It goes to the credit of medieval Christianity that in spite of this total loss of physical contact, it kept alive the memory of the Brahmanas in its theology. Christian theologians never forgot to remember the Brahmanas whenever they thought of the Pagan Greeks, which was quite often. Only the status of the Brahmanas vis-a-vis the Greeks had suffered a decline. In Pagan times, the Brahmanas were known as teachers of the Greeks, but in Christian centuries they came to be known only as Pythagoreans who avoided animal food and believed in transmigration. That, however, did not make a difference to Christian perception of the Brahmana religion.

So, when the Church Fathers converted the Gods of the Greeks into devils, the Gods of the Brahmanas suffered a similar fate. "St. Augustine," writes Professor Partha Mitter, "sanctioned the idea that demons persuaded the ancients to false belief. Some of the most virulent attacks on pagan gods are to be found in St. Augustine's *De Civitate Dei*, where he argued that devils presented themselves to be adored, but they were no gods but wicked fiends and most foul, unclean and impotent spirits."[1] The Christian travellers who started trickling into India from the fourteenth century onwards, could not help seeing the hosts of hell in Hindu temples.

The first Christian traveller to India who has left a written account was a friar, Father Odoric of Podenone. He was in South India from AD 1316 to 1318. "He was the first traveller," proceeds Professor Mitter, "to leave a description of a monstrous idol in the form of half man and half ox. The monster at Quilon in South India gave responses from its mouth and demanded the blood of forty virgins to be given to it."[2] This description passed into a painting by Boucicau Master, the greatest illuminator of manuscripts in Paris in the first years of the fifteenth century. One of his illustrations in *Livres de marveilles*, a famous manuscript, is "on human sacrifice taking place in Quilon in front of an idol."[3] This painting "for the first time assigned horns and goat-head to an Indian god which had until now been the common features of the devil."[4]

But by far the best Christian commentator on Hindu Gods was the Italian traveller, Ludovico di Varthema, from Bologna. He was in South India between AD 1503 and 1508. According to his "description of the religion prevailing in the area", the Raja of Calicut "paid respect to a devil known as Deumo in these parts." He had an eye for detail, small and big, as is evident from his *Itineratio* published in AD 1510. The Raja of Calicut, he wrote, "keeps this Deumo in his chapel in his palace." The chapel had in its midst "a devil made of metal." This devil had "four horns and four teeth

1. Partha Mitter, *The Much Maligned Monsters*, Oxford, 1977, p. 9.
2. *Ibid.*, p. 11.
3. *Ibid.*
4. *Ibid.*, p. 14.

with a very large mouth, nose and most terrible eyes." Its hands were "made like those of a flesh-hook and the feet like those of a cock." Varthema saw many more devils in "pictures around the said chapel." On each side of the chapel, he found a Satan "seated in a seat, which seat is placed in a flame of fire, wherein are a great number of souls, of the length of half a finger and a finger of the hand." He concluded his account of the Raja's chapel by stating that the Satan "holds a soul in his mouth with the right hand and with the other seizes a soul by the waist."[5]

An illustrated edition of Varthema's *Itineratio* was published in Germany in AD 1515. The Deumo of Calicut came alive in a woodcut by an Augsburg artist. Varthema was translated in all major European languages and ran into numerous illustrated editions. It became the best travel guide for most European visitors to India during the two succeeding centuries. Professor Mitter has summarised the reports of these travellers so far as they refer to Hindu Gods. He has also reproduced pictorial samples of what these travellers "saw with their own eyes" in one Hindu temple after another. He prepares his readers before he proceeds with the travelogues. "It does not surprise us," he explains, "that these travellers believed in the essential truthfulness of their reports which were of course unquestionably accepted by their contemporaries. Yet as a comparison of actual Indian sculptures with their early descriptions reveals, the early travellers were far from being objective. That is not to say that there was a deliberate conspiracy, for that would have made things easy for us. It is simply that early travellers preferred to trust what they had been taught to expect instead of trusting their own eyes."[6]

Professor Mitter puts the blame on the Church Fathers who had taught that "all pagan gods were demons and devils."[7]

---

5. *Ibid.*, p. 17
6. *Ibid.*, p. 2.
7. *Ibid.*, p. 17. The medieval Christian image of Hindu Gods persists in our own times. Abbe Duboi, the famous French missionary, wrote a whole chapter on Hindu temples in his book, *Hindu Manners, Customs and*

But that does not explain why devils and demons occupied all the attention of the Church for many centuries to the exclusion of everything else even when no "pagan gods" were around any more. It has been calculated by scholars of the subject that the number of devils and demons known to the Church ran up to eight millions. We have to face the fact that Christianity has been and remains a cult of devil-worship. That is why its adherents see only devils and demons wherever they go. There is no other explanation for the hallucinations of Varthema and Company. The fact that the Devil is described as God in the Bible should make no difference.

Ceremonies. Coming to Hindu idols he says, "Hindu imagination is such that it cannot be excited except by what is monstrous and extravagant" (p. 607). The third and final edition of this book was published in 1897, nearly a hundred years ago. But it remains the best primer on Hinduism for the average Western traveller to India. Max Muller recommended it "as containing views of an eye-witness, a man singularly free from all prejudice" (p. vii). It has run through a dozen reprints in England. The Oxford University Press has printed its Fifth Indian impression as recently as 1985. Several other Indian publishers have produced it in different shapes and sizes because it is in constant demand. We have no idea in how many languages it has been translated and how many reprints it has run elsewhere. The total turnout over the years must have been considerable. For many modern Hindus, it is the only source of their knowledge about the religion of their ancestors.

4

Pirates in Priest's Clothing

The next encounter between Hinduism and Christianity commenced with the coming of Christian missionaries to Malabar after Vasco da Gama found his way to Calicut in AD 1498. It took a serious turn in AD 1542 when Francis Xavier, a rapacious pirate dressed up as a priest, arrived on the scene. The proceedings have been preserved by the Christian participants. They make the most painful reading in the history of Christianity in India. Francis Xavier had come with the firm resolve of "uprooting paganism" from the soil of India and planting Christianity in its place. His sayings and doings have been documented in his numerous biographies and cited by every historian of the Portuguese episode in the history of India.

Francis Xavier was convinced that Hindus could not be credited with the intelligence to know what was good for them. They were completely under the spell of the Brahmanas who, in turn, were in league with evil spirits. The first priority in India, therefore, was to free the poor Hindus from the stranglehold of the Brahmanas and destroy the places where evil spirits were worshipped. A bounty for the Church was bound to follow in the form of mass conversions.[1]

---

1. Francis Xavier was the pioneer of anti-Brahmanism which was adopted in due course as a major plank in the missionary propaganda by all Christian denominations. Lord Minto, Governor General of India from 1807 to 1812, submitted a Note to his superiors in London when the British Parliament was debating whether missionaries should be permitted in East India Company's domain under the Charter of 1813. He enclosed with his Note some "propaganda material used by the missionaries" and, referring

We shall let a Christian historian speak about what the Portuguese did in their Indian domain. "At least from 1540 onwards," writes Dr. T. R. de Souza "and in the island of Goa before that year, all the Hindu idols had been annihilated or had disappeared, all the temples had been destroyed and their sites and building materials were in most cases utilised to erect new Christian churches and chapels. Various viceregal and Church council decrees banished the Hindu priests from the Portuguese territories; the public practice of Hindu rites including marriage rites, was banned; the state took upon itself the task of bringing up the Hindu orphan children; the Hindus were denied certain employments, while the Christians were preferred; it was ensured that the Hindus would not harass those who became Christians, and on the contrary, the Hindus were obliged to assemble periodically in churches to listen to preaching or to the refutation of their religion."[2]

Coming to the performance of the missionaries, he continues: "A particularly grave abuse was practised in Goa in the form of 'mass baptism' and what went before it. The practice was begun by the Jesuits and was later initiated by the Franciscans also. The Jesuits staged an annual mass baptism on the Feast of the Conversion of St. Paul (25 January), and in order to secure as many neophytes as possible, a few days before the ceremony the Jesuits would go through the streets of the Hindu quarters in pairs, accompanied by their Negro slaves, whom they would urge to seize the Hindus. When the blacks caught up a fugitive, they would smear his lips with a piece of beef, making him an 'untouchable' among his people. Conversion to Christianity was then his only option."[3]

---

to one missionary tract in particular, wrote: "The remainder of this tract seems to aim principally at a general massacre of the Brahmanas" (M. D. David (ed.), *Western Colonialism in Asia and Christianity*, Bombay, 1988, p. 85). Anti-Brahmanism has become the dominant theme in the speeches and writings of Indian secularists of all sorts.

2. M.D. David (ed.), *op.cit.*, p. 17.

3. *Ibid.*, p. 19.

Finally, he comes to "Financing Church Growth" and concludes : "...the government transferred to the Church and religious orders the properties and other sources of revenue that had belonged to the Hindu temples that had been demolished or to the temple servants who had been converted or banished. Entire villages were taken over at times for being considered rebellious and handed over with all their revenues to the Jesuits. In the villages that had submitted themselves, at times *en masse,* to being converted, the religious orders promoted competition to build bigger and bigger churches and more chapels than their neighbouring villages. Such a competition, drawing funds and diverting labour, from other important welfare works of the village, was decisively bringing the village economy in Goa into bankruptcy."[4]

During the same period, Christianity was spreading its tentacles to Bengal. Its patrons were the same as in Goa; so also its means and methods. "The conversion of the Bengalis into Christianity," writes Dr. Sisir Kumar Das, "not only coincided with the activities of the Portuguese pirates in Bengal but the pirates took an active interest in it."[5] The Augustinians and Jesuits manned the mission with bases at Chittagong in East Bengal and Bandel and Hooghly in West Bengal. Mission stations were established at many places in the interior. "It was the boast of the Hooghly Portuguese," records Dr. P. Thomas, "that they made more Christians in a year by forcible conversions, of course, than all the missionaries in the East in ten."[6]

The Portuguese captured the young prince of Bhushna, an estate in Dhaka District. He was converted by an Augustinian friar, Father D'Rozario and named Dom Antonio de Rozario. The prince, in turn, converted 20,000 Hindus in and

4. *Ibid.*, pp. 24-35. For a detailed account of Christian doings in Goa, see A.K. Priolkar, *The Goa Inquisition,* Bombay, 1961, Voice of India reprint, New Delhi, 1991 and 1996.

5. Sisir Kumar Das, *The Shadow of the Cross,* New Delhi, 1974, p. 4.

6. P. Thomas, *Christians and Christianity in India and Pakistan,* London, 1954, p. 114.

around his estate. "The Jesuits came forward," continues Dr. Das, "to help the neophytes to minister to the needs of the converts and this created bitterness between Augustinians and Jesuits... In 1677, the Provincial at Goa deputed Father Anthony Magalheans, the Rector of the College at Agra, to visit and report on this problem. According to his report nearly 25,000, if not more, converts were there but they had hardly any knowledge of Christianity... He also observed that many of them became Christians to get money. The *Marsden Manuscripts* now preserved in the British Museum containing letters of Jesuit Fathers, give evidence that Portuguese missionaries gave money to perspective converts to allure them."[7]

The quality of the converts, though bewailed frequently by the missionaries, did not really perturb them. Frey Duarte Nunes, the prelâte of Goa, had foreseen the situation as early as 1522. According to him, "even if the first generation of converts was attracted by rice or by any other way and could hardly be expected to become good Christians, yet their children would become so with intensive indoctrination, and each successive generation would be more firmly rooted."[8]

It was a very difficult situation for Hinduism. But, by and large, Hindus chose to stay in the faith of their forefathers in spite of all trials and temptations. There was no mass movement towards the Church except the "mass baptisms" staged by the Jesuits. The mission was in a fix. The strategy of forced conversions recommended by Francis Xavier had failed.

Another Jesuit, Robert Di Nobili, came forward with a new strategy. When he came to the Madura Mission in 1606, he had found it a "desert" in terms of conversions. He had also seen that Hindus had retained their reverence for the Brahmanas in spite of missionary insinuations. So he decided that he would disguise himself as a Brahmana and preach the gospel by other means. The story is well-known — how he

7. Sisir Kumar Das, *op. cit.*, p. 5.

8. M. D. David (ed.), *op. cit.*, p. 8.

put on an ochre robe, wore the sacred thread, grew a tuft of hair on his head, took to vegetarian food, etc., in order to pass as a Brahmana. He also composed some books in Tamil and Sanskrit, particularly the one which he palmed off as the *Yajurveda*. When some Hindus suspected from the colour of his skin that he was a Christian, he lied with a straight face that he was a high-born Brahmana from Rome!

Some Christian historians credit Di Nobili with converting a hundred thousand Hindus. Others put the figure at a few hundred. But all agree that his converts melted away very fast soon after he was exposed by other missionaries who were either jealous of him or did not like his methods. Christian theologians hail him as the pioneer of Indigenisation in India and the founder of the first Christian Ashram. A truly ethical criterion would dismiss him as a desperate and despicable scoundrel.[9]

One wonders how Hinduism would have fared in South India if its encounter with Christianity under the Portuguese dispensation had continued uninterrupted. Hindus were helpless wherever Portuguese power prevailed and Hindus outside could not help as they themselves were groaning under the heel of Islamic imperialism after the defeat of the Vijayanagara Empire by a Muslim alliance in 1565 AD. The situation was saved by the Dutch in the second quarter of the seventeenth century. The Dutch destroyed the maritime monopoly of the Portuguese and drove them out of Malabar and southern Tamil Nadu. Christianity had to break its encounter with Hinduism except in the small Portuguese enclaves where it continued for two more centuries. But most of the heat applied on Hinduism had to be taken off because "the fear of retaliatory raids by the powerful Marathas in the neighbourhood acted as an effective check on the missionary zeal and coercion."[10]

---

9. The masquerade of Robert Di Nobili has been described in detail in Sita Ram Goel, *Catholic Ashrams: Sannyasins or Swindlers?*, Voice of India, New Delhi, 1995.

10. M.D. David (ed.), *op. cit.*, p. 19.

A plausible case has been made by Christian historians, namely, that the Portuguese were using Christianity as a cover for their predatory imperialism. But what about the Augustinians and the Dominicans and the Franciscans, all of whom belonged to the holy orders? And what about Francis Xavier and his Jesuits? It cannot be overlooked that the Catholic Church hails an arch criminal like Francis Xavier as the Patron Saint of the East. His carcass (or plaster cast) is still worshipped as a holy relic and the basilica where it is enshrined remains a place of Christian pilgrimage. It is shameless dishonesty to say that the Christian doctrine had nothing to do with the atrocities practised in Goa and Bengal and elsewhere under the Portuguese dispensation.

5

From Monologue to Dialogue

There is no known evidence of a dialogue between Hinduism and Christianity before the end of the seventeenth century, though by that time they had come into contact with one another on as many as four occasions. If individual Hindus and Christians ever exchanged any notes on the nature of God and soul and human destiny, the record was not kept or has not survived or is yet to surface.

The history of Hindus goes to show that they were fond of discussing spiritual and philosophical themes till very recent times. Hinduism would have gladly entered into a dialogue with Christianity if the latter had evinced an inclination in that direction. But for a long time, Christianity was in no mood to hold a dialogue with any type of Paganism. It was convinced that it held a monopoly of truth which others had to accept from it in all humility. What it preferred was a monologue, that is, it alone talked and the others were made to listen. It was ensured in advance that the monologue was not disturbed by arguments from the other side.

The Hindus in the far-off Roman Empire were too insignificant a minority to disturb the Christian monologue. The Syrian Christians in Malabar kept their counsels to themselves because the conditions were not conducive to a monologue. They came out in the open only when the Portuguese provided protection and saw to it that Hinduism kept mum. Christian travellers came to India not to see what India had to show but to secure concrete and visible proofs for what the Church Fathers had deduced about Paganism from the first premises of Christianity. They never felt the need to talk to

Hindus in order to find out what Hinduism really stood for.

The proper conditions for projecting a full and prolonged Christian monologue at Hinduism became ripe only when the Portuguese military machine arrived in Malabar. The missionaries did their best, but in spite of the fact that Hinduism had to observe silence, the monologue misfired. Instead of inspiring respect for Christianity and winning willing converts, it filled the Hindus with contempt for Christianity. The reports of Hindu reaction which reached the mission headquarters through its intelligence network were far from encouraging.

The school of Francis Xavier was all for augmenting the degree of force used in the advancement of the mission. The experience in Europe had proved that force could be quite effective and Xavier and his Jesuits were prisoners of that experience. Frantic appeals were made to the king of Portugal to see that the secular arm of the Church was used with the utmost rigour and determination. But the experiment failed partly because Portugal did not have the manpower to match the situation and partly because in AD 1580 Portugal became federated with the Spanish crown which had other priorities elsewhere.

The school of Robert Di Nobili believed that the heart of Hinduism could be reached by perfecting the fraud pioneered by Di Nobili. Of course, they did not use this word for their method. They preferred to call it *condescensio,* a Latin term coined by the Church Fathers and meaning "stooping down to conquer." They had drawn on the example set by St. Paul. The only problem which the missionaries faced was the colour of their skins. It was the colour of his skin which had betrayed Di Nobili. That difficulty had to be overcome by the use of a suitable lotion. Father Poenco of the Madura Mission made an appeal in his Annual letter for 1651. "Among my readers," he wrote, "there will be some who could procure for us some lotion of ointment which could change the colour of our skin so that just as we have changed our dress, language, food and customs, we may also change our complexion and become like those around us, with whom we live... It is not necessary that the colour should be very dark; the most suitable will be between black and red or tawny. It would not matter if it could not be removed when once applied; we would willingly remain all our lives the 'negroes' of Jesus Christ, for the greater glory of God."[1] But, unfortunately, no such lotion could be found and *condescensio* remained a pious aspiration until skin colour was eventually overcome with the induction of native missionaries. This also is an act of *condescensio* in the eyes of the white masters.

A modification of the monologue was also attempted on one occasion. An odd missionary had a lurking suspicion that Hinduism was being allowed to get away with the impression of remaining unconquered simply because its spokesmen had not been permitted to have their say. The fact, however, was that they had nothing or very little to say, which could be proved by bringing them to an open debate. Annals of the mission do record "one instance of a public debate in sixteenth century Goa, when Jesuits, aided by a convert, deputed with pandits, forty of whom proving obstinate, were banished."[2] The monologue was restored and never disturbed again in Portuguese possessions.

The chances of the monologue yielding place to a dialogue would have remained dim so long as the Catholic Church monopolised the mission and the Portuguese retained their stranglehold over South India. But conditions started changing towards the second half of the seventeenth century. Portuguese power suffered a steep decline and Protestant missionaries started coming to the trade settlements

---

1 'Roberto de Nobili and Adaption' by S. Rajamanickam, S.J. in *Indian Church History Review,* December 1967, p. 88.

2 Richard Fox Young, *Resistant Hinduism,* Vienna, 1981, pp. 20-21. This scholarly Christian publication concludes that simply because Hinduism resisted Christianity instead of accommodating it, Hindu tolerance towards other religions is a myth. The author sees nothing wrong with the wanton Christian onslaught of which he himself provides prolific proof. On the contrary, the onslaught is eulogised as "evangelism" and treated as a duty as well as a birthright of every Christian.

which the Dutch and the Danes had set up on the eastern side of South India with the permission of local Hindu Rajas.

Protestant missionaries were no less confident than their Catholic counterparts that Christianity possessed a monopoly of truth. Given a chance, they too would have thrust the "good news" down Hindu throats by force. But as there was no secular arm at their beck and call, they settled down to investigating why Hindus were resisting Christianity. Some of them learnt Tamil and Sanskrit and studied Hindu texts and thus had an opportunity to talk to Hindu Pandits who came to teach them. Some others travelled in the countryside to see first-hand how the simple Hindus lived and worshipped in the villages.

A Dutch missionary, Abraham Rogerius, functioning from Pulicat between AD 1630 and 1640, assembled in a book whatever he had learnt about Hindu beliefs. His book, *The Open Door to Secret Heathendom,* was published posthumously in 1651. It was full of the same old Christian prattle about demons and devils, but it contained one "great discovery" which took Christendom by surprise. "Rogerius came to the definite conclusion," writes Dr. S. Arasaratnam, "that the Hindus possessed the concept of a supreme divine being and paid homage to this being. This highest supreme being was worshipped in the form of one of the three major deities of Vishnu, Siva and Brahma. This led him to the general conclusion that the knowledge of God has always been present among men. We see here the germs of the idea that Hindus had discovered some eternal truths by means of natural light[3] that God had shed on all humanity. This light, he would assert, has remained dim and the vision blurred, and many have wandered away from this light. Rogerius ascribes the origin

3 Recently, Christian theologians have rephrased "natural light" to read "Cosmic Revelation" which they gallantly concede to the Hindus. Consistent with the logic of this changing language, Hindus have progressed from "pagans" to "natural men" to "cosmic men." There is reason for them to feel flattered by this continuous promotion. Father Bede Griffiths has written a whole book, *Cosmic Revelation,* in which he presents this thesis.

of this light among the Hindus to the revelation of Christ which had penetrated to different nations and peoples of the Indies. Something has remained of this light and he adduces in evidence the existence of Thomian Christians in Coromandel."[4]

The German Lutheran missionary, Bartholomaeus Ziegenbalg, who reached the Danish settlement at Tarankampadi (which name he soon corrupted to Tranquebar) in 1796, would find out how "The original light of nature by which Tamil Hindus had seen God in his true nature had been subsequently dimmed by the wily brahmans who had surrounded it in a cocoon of foolish beliefs, in a multiplicity of gods, other celestial beings and demons, and a system of abstract philosophies concerning man and the soul."[5] But before he could do that, he had to take the help of the Brahmanas themselves. That triggered the first recorded dialogue between Hinduism and Christianity.

---

4. S. Arasaratnam, 'Protestant Christianity and South Indian Hinduism 1630-1730: Some Confrontations in Society and Beliefs', *Indian Church History Review*, June 1981, pp. 17-18.

5. *Ibid.*, p. 22.

6

Encounter in Tamil Nadu

Ziegenbalg who was "the most aggressive evangelist of this period"[1] came from the Lutheran seminary at Halle in Germany. Ostensibly, the Lutheran mission to Tranquebar was patronised by Frederick IV, King of Denmark. But its real sponsor was the British Government who financed it through the Society for the Propagation of Christian Knowledge (SPCK), floated in 1798. This is obvious from *The Epistle Dedicatory* which J. Thomas Philipps attached to his English translation of Ziegenbalg's *Conferences* with Brahmanas.[2] The *Epistle* is addressed to the King of England. "The following *Conferences*," wrote Philipps, "being an essay to recommend to the *Heathens* in the *East Indies* that faith, of which Your Majesty is the *Glorious Defender*, I have humbly presumed to lay them at your Royal Feet, as a pledge of the indefatigable labours of the *Protestant Missionaries* sent thither by the King of Denmark. One of the *Missionaries* had the honour to be graciously received by Your Majesty here in *London* on his return to India. They have already acknowledged the charitable assistances they have received from Your Majesty's subjects both in *Europe* and in the *East-Indies*." The British invaders of India did not want to be known as patrons of Christianity till a more opportune time.

The places where Ziegenbalg had built his mission stations

1. S. Arasaratnam, *op.cit.*, p. 20

2. *Thirty-Four Conferences Between the Danish Missionaries and Malabarian Brahmans (or Heathen Priests) in the East Indies*, London, 1719. The Brahmanas referred to were really from Tamil Nadu. But Christian missionaries in that period were too full of Malabar to make the distinction.

were in the vicinity of great centres of Hindu learning such as Srirangam, Tanjore, Madura, Kanchi, Chidambram and Tirupathi. He travelled around, established contacts with the Brahmanas, and held as many as 54 conversations with them. He recorded the conversations in some detail and passed them on to Halle which published them from 1715 onwards. "In a notable debate," writes P. Thomas, "held under the auspices of the Dutch in Negapatnam, Ziegenbalg disputed with a Brahmin for five hours and far from converting the Brahmin, the missionary came away with an excess of admiration for the intellectual gifts of his adversary."[3] Sometimes, the Brahmanas visited Ziegenbalg and held discourse with him. Only thirty-four of these conversations were translated and published in English in 1719. The Preface to the English translation sums up the Brahmana's "Divine Law sent from Heaven" in the following eight Precepts:

> I. Thou shalt not kill any living creature whatsoever it be, having life in the same: For thou art a creature of mine and so is it: Thou art endued with soul and it is endued with the same. Thou shalt not therefore spill the blood of anything that is mine.
>
> II. Thou shalt make a covenant with all thy five senses. First, with thy eyes, that they behold not things that be evil. Secondly, with thy ears, that they hear not things that be evil. Thirdly, with thy tongue, that it speaks not things that be evil. Fourthly, with thy palate, that it takes nothing that be evil; as wine, or the flesh of living creatures. Fifthly, with thy hands, that they touch not things defiled.
>
> III. Thou shalt duly observe the times of devotion, thy washings, worshippings and prayers to the Lord thy God, with a pure and upright heart.
>
> IV. Thou shalt not tell false tales, or utter things untrue, by which thou mightest defraud thy brother in dealings, bargains or contracts; by this consenage to work thy own peculiar advantage.

3. P. Thomas, *op. cit.*, pp. 153-154.

V. Thou shalt be charitable to the poor and administer to his need, meat, drink, and money, as his necessity requires, and thine own ability enableth thee to give.

VI. Thou shalt not oppress, injure or do violence to the poor, using thy power unjustly to the ruin and overthrow of thy brother.

VII. Thou shalt celebrate certain festivals; yet not pampering thy body with excess of anything; but shalt observe certain seasons for fasting, and break off some hours by watching, that thou may'st be fitter for devotion and holiness.

VIII. Thou shalt not steal from thy brother anything, however little it be, of things committed to thy trust in thy profession or calling; but content thyself with that which he shall give thee as thine hire; considering that thou has not right to that which another man calleth his.[4]

Yet according to the same Preface, "there is not, perhaps, a more wicked race of men treading upon God's earth." "The Brahmanas", it continues, "are the greatest impostors in the world; their talent lies in inventing new fables every day, and making them pass for incomprehensible mysteries among the vulgar."[5] Whatever be the facts, Christian conclusions remain the same. That is because Christianity is compelled by its doctrine to be at war with other cultures, howsoever superior.

The next thing which Ziegenbalg did in 1712 was to send a large number of letters to a selection of Hindus — Brahmanas and non-Brahmanas — inviting answers to a number of questions. "The purpose of this correspondence," writes Dr. H. Grafe, "as stated by Ziegenbalg, is three-fold: 1. To make for increased publicity of the missionaries' work, 2. To reach people whom they are not able to meet personally, 3. To get better informed about Hinduism and particularly about Hindu objections to Christian Faith. In short: Publicity,

4. *Thirty-Four Conferences,* pp. v-viii.

5. *Ibid.*, pp. iii-iv.

evangelism and religious research, all these were in Ziegenbalg's mind."[6]

Ziegenbalg attached to these letters a printed booklet, *Abominable Heathenism,* which described Hinduism as a state of *ajñāna* (ignorance) and accused it of five sins—idolatory, fornication, fraud, quarrel, witchcraft and laziness.[7] It was "the very first product of the Tamil Press at Tranquebar 'inaugurating the modern era of Tamil book-printing'," as H.W. Gensichen puts it.[8]

The letters which Ziegenbalg received from Hindus in reply to his questions were translated by him into German and forwarded to Halle in two batches of 58 and 46. The theologian, A.H. Francke, who scrutinised them, flared up, "The missionaries were sent out to exterminate heathenism in India, not to spread heathen nonsense all over Europe." When Ziegenbalg received the reprimand, he wrote back, "We should be of the opinion that such materials quite certainly are suitable for communication to the public. Should you, however, find anything about which you have hesitations to communicate it to the public you have always the liberty *to change, to improve, or omit* the same in this as well as in other tracts."[9]

Finally, 99 letters were published, 55 in 1713 and 44 in 1717. Five letters were totally suppressed. No one knows how far the published ones were edited. The publication of the first batch, however, carried the following introduction: "On our part we could not decide in favour of withholding the Tamil correspondence from the public. True, it contains much which is partly foolish, partly detestable. Especially, it tells of fornication and impurity with which idol worship of our own past as well as Tamil worship are concerned. However, if we had omitted such things and communicated those

---

6. 'Hindu Apologetics at the Beginning of the Protestant Mission Era in India', by H. Grafe in *Indian Church History Review,* June, 1972, p. 48.

7. *Ibid.,* p. 64.

8. *Ibid.,* p. 58.

9. Francke and Ziegenbalg quoted in *Ibid.,* p. 46. Emphasis added.

good things only, which the heathens still recognise and possess by the *light of nature,* some might conceive of the false idea, that heathenism is not so bad and corrupt after all."[10]

We shall give only a summary of opinions which, according to these letters, Hindus had of Christianity.

The most common reason given by Hindus of why they despised Christianity was that most Christians led a very unclean life — slaughtering and eating cows and other animals, guzzling strong drinks, not washing after easing themselves, not brushing their teeth before or after meals, spitting around in their houses, mating with their wives in menses, etc. One correspondent was more forthright. The Christians, he said, "beat and kill one another, swear, fornicate, play, do not give any help to travellers and pilgrims and concern themselves only with eating and drinking, beautiful dresses and the decoration of their houses."[11] Ziegenbalg had himself observed that Christians were "so much debauched in their manners" and "so given to gluttony, drunkenness, lewdness, cursing, swearing, cheating, cozening" besides being "proud and insulting in their conduct" that many Indians, judging the religion by its effects upon its followers, "could not be inclined to embrace Christianity."[12]

Tamil Hindus were also telling Ziegenbalg that there was something seriously wrong with the doctrine which inculcated such beastly behaviour, particularly in the converts who were leading disciplined lives before they became Christians. Christian writers dismiss these Hindu observations as "superficial objections." But Mahatma Gandhi, as we shall see, noticed the same behaviour of converts and advised the Christians to demonstrate by their living rather than preaching that they had a better doctrine.

Hindus also pointed to the "hatred and persecution

10. *Ibid.*, p. 47. Emphasis added.

11. *Ibid.*, p. 55.

12. R.C. Majumdar (ed.), *The History and Culture of the Indian People,* Volume X: *British Paramountcy And Indian Renaissance,* Part II, 2nd edition, Bombay, 1981, p. 150.

between various Christian sects", leading to doubts as to which of them represented real Christianity. But more serious doubts were raised about Jesus, the god of the Christians. "To our reason," they said, "it does not appear very sensible that they believe in a God who was tortured and killed by his own people."[13] One correspondent asked, "Why did he at last have to hang on the cross like a thief? How is it possible that he being true God could die?"[14] Another correspondent put it more plainly: "Does it not seem the height of unreasonableness to suppose him to be the saviour of the world who was of mean parentage, had as mean an education, was persecuted by his countrymen, and at last was hanged by public Authority upon an infamous cross?"[15] Hindus found it hard to believe that Jesus was God and Son of God and Holy Ghost at the same time: "How is it possible that God who is only one nevertheless is threefold?"[16]

Hindus had no use for the Christian doctrine of original sin. They held that "the bad sins spring out of one's own wickedness, vice, evil will, haughtiness and corrupt desires of like nature,"[17] rather than inherited from Adam and Eve. They rejected outright the doctrine of free grace: "Nobody attains salvation for nothing, because God does not give his grace to those who are lazy and live like animals. There must be good works, sacrifice, worship, faith and love."[18] One correspondent observed, "I have never seen hitherto any of all you Christians taking any care of the saving of his own soul by doing Penance for his sins: whereas we Malabarians undergo many tedious and long Penances, denying ourselves all the pleasures of this Life... But I see no such thing practis'd among you Christians."[19] Another asked, "Will nobody else

13. Quoted in H. Grafe, *op. cit.*, p. 56.
14. *Ibid.*, p. 57.
15. Quoted in Richard Fox Young, *op. cit.*, p. 24.
16. Quoted in H. Grafe, *op. cit.*, p. 56.
17. Quoted in *Ibid.*, p. 63.
18. Quoted in *Ibid.*, p. 56.
19. Quoted in Richard Fox Young, *op. cit.*, p. 24.

be saved in the world except Christians?"[20]

The doctrine of ever-lasting punishment for "unbelievers" was found repugnant: "Seeing that we live in this world but a few years and our sinful Actions are, as to their Duration, transitory; why then should the Punishment be Eternal? The necessary proportion attending distributive Justice, is not observ'd here."[21] One correspondent asked, "If the evil ones are being condemned to hell, do they have to remain in hell or may hope for salvation afterwards?"[22] Another juxtaposed the Hindu doctrine of *mukti* for all creatures: "(It is) firmly believed, among us, that not only mankind but all Birds, and Beasts of the Fields, shall be Eternally Happy after many repeated Nativities or Regenerations, qualifying them for the Enjoyment of God."[23] The central Christian sacrament also came in for criticism: "When they administer the Sacrament, they say that the bread is the holy body and they drink the holy blood of Christ, which I am at a loss to grasp."[24]

That exhausted the list. There was nothing else in Christianity which Hindus could examine specifically, however verbose Ziegenbalg might have been about the merits of his creed.

Next, the Hindus turned to a defence of their own Sanatana Dharma. The first thing they said was that "we have a venerable Antiquity on our side" and that "we are an Ancient Nation, whose Religion is as old as the world itself."[25] There was an implied advice that Christianity which was born only yesterday should have some sense of humility.

Religion, it was pointed out, was not such a simple matter as the missionaries had assumed. It needed deep deliberation. "Every religion," said one correspondent, "claims to be the only true religion. There is even dispute among the

---

20. Quoted in H. Grafe, *op. cit.*, p. 57.
21. Quoted in Richard Fox Young, *op. cit.*, p. 24.
22. Quoted in H. Grafe, *op. cit.*, p. 57.
23. Quoted in Richard Fox Young, *op. cit.*, p. 24.
24. Quoted in H. Grafe, *op. cit.*, p. 55.
25. Quoted in Richard Fox Young, *op. cit.*, p. 23.

Tamilians whether Vishnu or Siva is the highest god... how can we accept a strange religion as long as we do not properly know the truth in our own."[26] In reply to Ziegenbalg's question, "why do the Tamilians not leave their false precepts and convert to the true precepts of Christianity?", another correspondent replied, "You have to prove the presupposition of the question."[27]

Ziegenbalg's most serious charge was that Hindus neglected One God and worshipped many others. One correspondent replied, "The One God is not being neglected even where a multitude of Gods is believed in because in them he alone is being worshipped, after they have obtained salvation through him."[28] Another observed, "We teach the people to worship one only, and not many Gods; and the Notion of a plurality of Gods comes hence, viz., because God is variously represented under different names; Yet he is still but One God as Gold is but one, as to its kind, tho' wrought into a Thousand different figures."[29] Yet another replied, "Siva is not more than one, but has many names, Vishnu is not more than one... and one is all in all, and through him alone we attain to salvation, but not through anybody else."[30]

Hindus pointed out repeatedly that different religions are suited to different temperaments so that different nations have different religions. Chiding Ziegenbalg for prescribing one religion for all, a correspondent said, "Everything you write and speak amounts to contempt and total rejection of our religion and our worship of God... God is manifold in his creatures and manifold in his creations. Hence he wants also to be worshipped in manifold way."[31] Another correspondent said the same thing more concretely: "For as Christ in Europe

26. Quoted in H. Grafe, *op. cit.*, p. 61.
27. Quoted in *Ibid.*, p. 64.
28. Quoted in *Ibid.*, p. 60.
29. Quoted in Richard Fox Young, *op. cit.*, p. 24.
30. Quoted in H. Grafe, *op. cit.*, p. 66.
31. Quoted in *Ibid.*, p. 65.

was made Man, so here our God Wischtnu[32] was born among us Malabarians, and as you hope for salvation through Christ, so we hope for salvation through Wischtnu, and to save you one way, and us another, is one of the Pastimes and Diversions of Almighty God."[33]

One of Ziegenbalg's questions was whether "Hindu worship exists in external rites only or whether there is something in one word to it which is done from the heart of hearts." One correspondent replied, "Yes, Love, Faith, and Faithfulness, or in one word Bhakti are much more important than rites, and all external works are useless and vain without love, faith and faithfulness towards the Lord."[34] Another explained, "Although the Supreme Being is present in all souls and there is faith and faithfulness in many men, whatever religion they adhere to, still this faith and faithfulness cannot be perceived and recognised in their hearts. It must find outward expression."[35] In other words, a good life alone proves that there is inner faith.

There is no evidence that Ziegenbalg ever pondered over what the Brahmanas had told him during his conversations with them or what his Hindu correspondents had conveyed to him. What we know is that he used the conversations as well as the correspondence for compiling two books — *Genealogy of Malabar Gods* completed in 1711 and *Malabar Heathendom* completed in 1713 — in which he repeated all that he had said in his earlier book, *Abominable Heathenism.* The dialogue with Hindus had gone completely over his Christian head.

In his Preface to *Malabar Heathendom*, he wrote: "Meanwhile, the clear exposure of this Indian heathenism may be regarded as a sign that God, at this time, intends to do some special thing for these heathens, and to visit them by granting them grace to be converted. He will thereby also try the

32. The missionary spelling of Vishnu.
33. Quoted in Richard Fox Young, *op. cit.*, p. 23.
34. Quoted by H. Grafe, *op. cit.*, p. 66.
35. Quoted in *Ibid.*, pp. 66-67.

Christian people in Europe to whom this is made known, if some will pity their condition, and think of means through which the Word of grace and all the means of salvation may be offered unto them effectually for their conversion." Again, whatever be the facts, the conclusions drawn by Christian missionaries remain the same!

The latter-day Christian historians, however, have understood what had really happened. "This encounter shows," comments Dr. H. Grafe, "that Hindus seriously examined the challenge to their religion that came from Christianity. They were drawn into a dialogue of asking and replying, of accusing and excusing, and of trying to understand... However, although some subjects treated show considerable depth in spiritual quest, on the whole one cannot escape the impression that politeness and cautiousness exerted some restraint and the whole exchange was regarded as a sort of vanguard battle at which not all ammunition was used up."[36] Dr. Arasaratnam observes, "It was now clear that Christian evangelism was going to be a hard, rigorous, intellectual grind and missionaries would come up against the custodians of Hindu tradition who would present the case for Hinduism."[37]

---

36. H. Grafe, *op. cit.*, pp. 68-69.
37. S. Arasaratnam, *op. cit.*, p. 33.

7

Encounter at Pondicherry

The following account of what the Christians did to Hindus in Pondicherry has been taken from the Diary maintained by Anand Ranga Pillai, scion of a Tamil merchant family from Madras. His family along with several others had migrated to Pondicherry at the invitation of the French who occupied that town as the headquarters of their possessions in India. These families had brought considerable prosperity to it. Pillai was appointed Chief Dubash towards the end of 1747, five years after M. Dupleix became the Governor of Pondicherry. He held the post till 1756, two years after Dupleix's departure. He had, however, kept an account of what he saw and heard since September 1736. His Diary which was written in Tamil continued till 1761 when he died.

The editor of the translation in English writes as follows regarding the treatment of Hindus in Pondicherry: "The religious policy pursued in the early part of the century at Pondicherry is remarkable. It appears to have been ordered that no temple should be repaired; Nainiyappau was ordered to be converted within six months under pain of losing his post as Chief Dubash; Hindu festivals were prohibited on Sundays and the principal Christian feasts; even when these regulations had caused the greater part of the town to be deserted, the Jesuits urged that a temple should be pulled down instead of conciliatory measures being employed. (Registre des deliberations du Conseil Souverin, i, pp. 125,140, 142, 153 etc. This valuable collection of documents is being printed by the 'Societe di 1'Histoire de 1'Inde Francaise' at Pondicherry.) It is difficult to avoid the conclusion that in this zealous proselytising policy lies one reason why Pondicherry was far inferior to Madras as a commercial centre; and perhaps the same cause also contributed to the absolute failure of Dupleix's efforts to induce the Madras merchants to settle under the French."[1]

The Vedapuri Iswaran Temple was the principal place of worship for the Hindus of Pondicherry. The Jesuit missionaries built the Church of St. Paul adjacent to it and obtained an order from the King of France that the Hindu temple should be destroyed. It could not be done due to strong resistance from the Hindus who constituted the most important native community in the town. Pillai gives an account of how the temple was desecrated repeatedly by the Jesuits and finally destroyed with active help from the French establishment, particularly Madame Dupleix.

The first incident at the Vedapuri Temple took place on March 17, 1746. "On Wednesday night at 11," writes Pillai, "two unknown persons entered the Iswaran temple carrying in a vessel of liquid filth, which they poured on the heads of the gods around the altar, and into the temple, through the drain of the shrine of Iswaran; and having broken the pot of dirt on the image of the god Nandi, they went away through a part of the building which had been demolished. Early this morning, when the Nambiyan and the servants of the temple, opening the main gate, entered, and saw the nuisance which had been committed, they at once reported the matter to their superiors, and to the Mahanattars; and bringing them to the spot, showed them what had been done."[2]

As the report of this sacrilege spread, Hindus, "from the Brahman to the pariah", held a public meeting. The Governor, Dupleix, when he heard of it, sent his chief peon to disperse the meeting. The peon "struck a Chetti on the cheek"

---

1. *The Private Diary of Anand Ranga Pillai* translated from Tamil by Rev. J. Frederick Price and K. Rangachari, Madras, 1904, Volume IV, p. 144, Footnote.

2. *Ibid.*, Volume I, p. 332. Filth was quite an appropriate weapon for the filth that Christianity has been all along.

and ordered the people to go away. The people, however, defied the order and protested, "You better kill us all."[3]

When this resistance was reported to the Governor, he sent for some Hindu leaders. He reprimanded them but promised to settle the matter in consulation with Pillai who was present. "No sooner," continues Pillai, "had the Mahanattars departed than from 100 to 200 Muhammadans of Mahe appeared before the Governor, for the purpose of shooting them [the Hindus]. As prior to the arrival of these, the Mahanattars had consented to a settlement, he directed the Muhammadans to guard the four gates, so that they could not go out. They obeyed this order. All this took place before 4 this afternoon. What will occur hereafter is not known."[4] He does not record what settlement, if any, was arrived at.

The next incident recorded by Pillai took place on December 31, 1746. "It was reported," he writes, "to-night at 7, that an earthen jar, filled with filth, was thrown from within the grounds of the Church of St. Paul, into the temple of Vedapuri Iswaran. It very nearly fell on the head of Sankara Aiyan, who was at the shrine of the god Pillaiyar, on his way round the temple, in the performance of religious duties. When the jar struck the ground, and broke to pieces, the stench emitted was unbearable."[5]

The outrage was reported to Pillai by ten men including some "heads of castes." He made a representation to the Governor who deputed some councillors to "inspect the place." But before the officials could start on their job, they were briefed privately by Madame Dupleix, the Governor's wife, who was in league with the priests of St. Paul. An inspection at the temple followed. "The gentlemen," continues Pillai, "then entered the temple, smelt the broken jar, pronounced that it had contained filth, and judging by the position

---

3. *Ibid.*, p. 333.

4. *Ibid.*, p. 334. Muhammadan hoodlums have always been available to whosoever wants to torment the Hindus in India or elsewhere.

5. *Ibid.*, Volume III, p. 220. The stench symbolized the stench which Christian missionaries spread wherever they are present.

of the scattered fragments, arrived at the decision that it must have been thrown from the church, and that there could be no mistake on that point."[6]

But before a report could be submitted to the Governor, a member of the team insisted that the "priests should be consulted." So the team went to the church and rang its bell. "On hearing the sound," records Pillai, "the senior priest, Father Coeurdoux, came out, and opening the door, asked the business that had brought them there. They then explained what had taken place. They remarked that, from the position of the pieces of the broken jar, and an examination of the ground about the temple and church, there could be no doubt that the direction from which the jar came was that of the latter. They also noticed that the stones at the base of the temple wall on the side of the church had all been pulled down. When those holding the investigation urged that this was not right, the priest exclaimed: 'It was not our doing. They, themselves, must have dug them out, with the view of lodging a complaint, and getting the wall, which is in a ruinous state, restored.'"[7]

Finally, a report was made to the Governor that "the complaint made was true, and that the priests of the Church of St. Paul were responsible." The Governor asked for a written report and exclaimed, "I will not only write to France regarding this affair, but will also take such action with respect to it, that the priests of the Church of St. Paul will ever remember it."[8] But he went to bed soon after and did not remember the matter when he rose next morning.

Pillai, however, brought it to his notice. The Governor told him that "with a view to making the people of the Church of St. Paul smart for what they had done, he would consult with the members of the Council and take measures

6. *Ibid.*, p. 221.

7. *Ibid.*, pp. 221-222. Father Coeurdoux's logic was unbeatable. It represented the way the missionary mind has always functioned.

8. *Ibid.*, p. 222.

9. *Ibid.*, p. 224.

accordingly."[9] Next, the Governor himself accompanied Pillai to the church in order to make further enquiries. The priests who used to be warm when meeting Pillai were now dead cold towards him, "the reason being that they thought it was I who had brought the matter of the filth being thrown into the Vedapuri Iswaran temple, on the previous night, to the notice of the Governor, and had him to send the Councillors, to inquire regarding it."[10]

The Governor agreed to meet the Mahanattars on January 5, 1747 and listen to their complaint about desecration of the temple. In the morning of that day, however, he asked Pillai to advise the Mahanattars not to raise the question of the temple when they met him. Pillai advised them accordingly and in private when they arrived. But "in spite of my advice they began to do so" and the Governor "rose up, addressed a few kind words to them and went into his wife's room."[11] That was the end of the matter so far as the second incident was concerned.

Pillai started functioning as the Chief Dubash when the earlier incumbent who was a native Christian and had held the post for 20 years, died on June 25, 1747. His formal appointment, however, was still in the future. The Jesuits became more and more hostile to him because they thought he was coming in the way of their demolition of the Hindu temple. The Governor had a low opinion of the Jesuits whom he regarded as "deceitful people." But he was under pressure from Christians in the town and advised Pillai to meet the Superior in the Church of St. Paul and try to improve his relations with them.

The Superior who was no other than that criminal, Father Coeurdoux, asked Pillai to become a Christian when he met him on September 20, 1747. "We all know," said Father Coeurdoux, "that you belong to a respectable family that has been held in esteem for generations... But if you had been a

10. *Ibid.*, p. 225.
11. *Ibid.*, p. 231.

Christian, many others would have become so too."[12] Pillai was surprised and protested that he had always been impartial between Hindus and Christians. But the priest persisted, "Say that you will, I am sure that all will become Christian if only you would set the example. We should be quite satisfied with you as Chief Dubash if you were a Christian. As you are not, we have had several times to urge M. Dupleix to appoint one. We have written to Europe, and we will write again. We shall do our utmost, we will speak in the Council, for we have got a letter from the King that the post must be reserved for Christians."[13] He also asked Pillai "to explain to the heads of castes the orders about the Vedapuri Iswaran temple", to which Pillai replied that he "would spare no pains."[14]

A man named Annapurna Ayyan came to Pillai on October 8 and reported, "Louis Prakasan came and told me that the Karikal priest [Coeurdoux] wished to see me. When I went to him, he told me I was a good man, always did as they wished, and there was a favour I must promise them. I asked what it was that I could do. He said he had heard that you [Pillai] would do whatever I asked, and I was therefore to ask you to get the Vedapuri Iswaran Temple pulled down. I told him it was impossible, that you would never listen to me, and that, had it been possible, Kanakaraya Mudali[15] would have got it done. The priest answered that he [Mudali] did not because he was a Christian and besides he was not so clever as you. He said you could persuade people with a thousand reasons, put your opponents to silence, and do as you pleased. If I explained the matter to you and got the temple removed, he promised they never would forget it so long as their church lasted. That is what he told me."[16] Pillai laughed and said that "they were always saying things like that." But

12. *Ibid.*, Volume IV, pp. 147-48.

13. *Ibid.*, pp. 149-50.

14. *Ibid.*, p. 151. The reference is to the order from the King of France that the temple be destroyed.

15. The earlier Chief Dubash.

16. *Ibid.*, pp. 164-65.

he suspected that Ayyan had "promised his [Pillai's] assistance to the priests."[17]

The Jesuits succeeded in destroying the temple in September 1748 when Pondicherry was besieged by the British and the bulk of the Hindu population had moved out of the town. "This morning," writes Pillai in his Diary for September 7, "tents were pitched round St. Paul's Church, and two hundred soldiers and a hundred sepoys were quartered there. The Governor, M. Paradis and others went thither and desired that a mortar might be mounted there. But they asked that the Iswaran temple should be pulled down. I think the Governor may have arranged (through Madame) for their help in certain Europe matters; so, as this is a time of war, there was much talk, a council was held, and the priests were told that the Iswaran temple would be demolished. The Governor then went home."[18]

Pillai was very unhappy when he heard the news. "The Governor," he wrote, "has dishonoured himself. Firstly, he has listened to his wife's words and allowed her to manage all affairs and give all orders... The priests of St. Paul's Church have been trying for the last fifty years to pull down the Vedapuri Iswaran temple; former Governors said that this was the country of the Tamils, that they would earn dishonour if they interfered with the temple, that the merchants would cease to come here, and that the town would decay; they even set aside the king's order to demolish the temple; and their glory shone like the sun. But the Governor listens to his wife and has ordered the temple to be destroyed, thereby adding shame to his dishonour."[19]

The temple was now doomed to destruction. "Yesterday," Pillai continued in his Diary of September 8, "200 soldiers, 60 or 70 troopers and sepoys were stationed at St. Paul's Church in view of the matter in hand. This morning, M. Gerbault (the Engineer), the priests with diggers,

17. *Ibid.*, p. 166.

18. *Ibid.*, Volume V, pp. 295-96.

19. *Ibid.*, p. 297.

masons, coolies and others, 200 in all, with spades, pick-axes and whatever is needed to demolish walls, began to pull down the southern wall of the Vedapuri Iswaran temple and the out-houses. At once the temple managers, Brahmans and mendicants came and told me."[20]

Pillai recollected how the Governor had been working to this end since his arrival. "Before M. Dupleix," he observed, "was made Governor, and when he was only a Councillor, all the Europeans and some Tamils used to say that if he became Governor, he would destroy the Iswaran temple. The saying has come to pass. Ever since his appointment, he has been seeking to do so, but he has had no opportunity. He tried to get Muttayya Pillai to do it in May or June 1743. But the latter would not consent, though the Governor threatened to cut his ears off and beat him publicly and even to hang him."[21]

He reflected on the situation that had been deliberately created by the Governor, taking advantage of the British invasion. "The Governor," he wrote, "allowed the Brahmans to depart, because ten or twenty of them might be bold enough to suffer death, and because he suspected them of being spies; but he ordered that those who went should not be readmitted, thus taking advantage of the war to get rid of the Brahmans, though other caste people might return. So all, both men and women, had departed. Besides, he has posted soldiers to frighten away even fifty or a hundred persons, should so many come to speak on behalf of the Brahmans. The four gates of the Fort have been closed by reason of the troubles; and he has ordered the destruction of the temple. What can we do? There are not even ten of the heads of castes to assemble and speak. We can do nothing, because he has taken advantage of this time of war to accomplish his long-standing object and demolish the temple."[22]

So Pillai advised the Brahmans that "they could do

20. *Ibid.*, pp. 229-300.
21. *Ibid.*, p. 300.
22. *Ibid.*, pp. 301-02.

nothing but remove the images and other things to the Kalahasti Iswaran temple." But they did not agree with him and said, "We will speak to the Governor about it, and tell him that if he insists, some of us will die and none will care to remain here."[23] He told them that the Governor had made up his mind, that he was not likely to listen to them, that the temple was already being demolished, and that the only thing that could be done was to save the images and other sacred articles. "I heard just now," he said to them, "that the southern wall and the out-houses had been pulled down, and that they were demolishing the Arthamantapam and Mahamantapam. Don't delay. Remember how blindly matters are being driven on. The St. Paul's priests will send the European soldiers, Coffrees, Topasses, and even their parish converts with clubs into the temple to carry away, break and damage all they can. If you complain, they will only beat you. So you will lose not only the temple, but also the articles, the images used in the festivals, the Pillaiyar and all the other images. Any one can do what he pleases here now, and there is no man to question him. Still worse is it in matters connected with our temples. By his wife's advice, M. Dupleix has accomplished what has been attempted in vain for the last fifty years. But now the time has come. I cannot describe the boundless joy of the St. Paul's priests, the Tamil and pariha converts, Madame Dupleix and M. Dupleix. In their delight, they will surely enter the temple, and will not depart, without breaking and trampling under foot the idols and destroying all they can. So go quickly and remove all the articles."[24]

More news came in quick succession. "Just then," proceeds Pillai, "news was brought that Father Coeurdoux, the Superior of St. Paul's Church, had kicked the inner shrine with his foot, and had ordered the Coffrees to remove the doors, and the Christians to break the Vahanams."[25] He now went to the Governor, hoping that the latter would himself

23. *Ibid.*, p. 302.
24. *Ibid.*, p. 306.
25. *Ibid.*, p. 307.

mention the subject. But the Governor did not, as if he was unware of what was being done. Some ten heads of castes also arrived and "salaamed the Governor." The Governor did not talk to them directly but asked Varlam, a native Christian, to find from them what they wanted. Varlam told him that "they sought his permission to remove the articles from the temple which was being destroyed." The Governor "gave them the permission but told the peons to beat and disperse the crowd."[26]

The Governor's permission, however, served no purpose. Pillai records:

"I heard that the priests of St. Paul's Church told the Coffrees, soldiers and pariahs to beat the heads of castes when they went to the temple to remove their articles. They were scarcely suffered to approach the temple, and when they were removing the Vahanams, shoulder-poles and temple documents, each man was beaten twenty or thirty times. It was with extreme difficulty that they rescued the idols used in the processions and the Pillaiyar.

"Then Father Coeurdoux of Karikal came with a great hammer, kicked the lingam, broke it with his hammer, and ordered the Coffrees and the Europeans to break the images of Vishnu and the other gods. Madame went and told the priest that he might break the idols as he pleased. He answered that she had accomplished what had been impossible for fifty years, that she must be one of those Mahatmas who established this religion [Christianity] in old days, and that he would publish her fame throughout the world. So saying he dismissed them.

"Then Varlam also kicked the great lingam nine or ten times with his sandals in the presence of Madame and priest, and spat on it, out of gladness, and hoping that the priest and Madame would regard him also as a Mahatma. Then he followed Madame. I can neither write nor describe what abominations were done in the temple. I know not what fruit

26. *Ibid.*, p. 308.

they will reap. All the Tamils think that the end of the world has come. The priests, the Tamil Christians, the Governor and his wife are more delighted than they have ever been before, but they have not yet considered what will befall them in future."[27]

Pillai learnt later on that "the temple had been levelled with the ground and that the whole people were troubled at heart." He reflected, "The wise men will say that the glory of an image is as short-lived as human happiness. The temple was destined to remain glorious till now, but now has fallen."[28]

---

27. *Ibid.*, pp. 310-311.

28. *Ibid.*, p. 312. I summarized Pillai's story in three paras in a letter to *The Statesman* when the Cathedral occupying the site of the Vedapuri Iswaran Temple was in the news in early 1995. The daily had been publishing aggressive letters from Christians, pleading innocence and accusing Hindus of inventing stories. But my letter was ignored. I also tried to get the story published in the *Organiser*, the mouthpiece of the Sangh Parivar. In this, too, I failed.

8

Encounter with Raja Ram Mohun Roy

The next significant dialogue between Hinduism and Christianity commenced more than a hundred years later, in 1820 to be exact. The venue was Calcutta. Raja Ram Mohun Roy was ranged on one side and the Serampore Missionaries on the other. By that time, British arms had subdued the whole of India except Ranjit Singh's Sikh state beyond the Satlaj. Calcutta had emerged not only as the premier city of the British empire in India but also as the storm centre of Christianity.

Bengal had known Christianity since the days of Portuguese pirates in the sixteenth and the seventeenth centuries. Small wonder that, in the Bengali mind, it was associated with savagery. Some missionaries who came with the Portuguese had, however, learnt the Bengali language and composed a few tracts, attacking Hinduism and selling Christianity. Dom Antonio had written even a *Brāhman-Roman Catholic Sambād* "containing imaginary dialogues between a Brahmin and a Roman Catholic Christian."[1] Some Protestant missions had also worked in Calcutta and Serampore from AD 1758 to 1791. But Christianity had failed to have any impact in Bengal till the foundation of the Baptist Mission at Serampore in 1800 under the leadership of Williams Carey (1761-1834).

Carey, a cobbler by profession, had published a book, *An Enquiry into the Obligations of Christians to use means for the Conversion of the Heathens,* in 1792 while he was still in England. He had also organised The Particular Baptist Society for Propagating the Gospel Among the Heathens. He was

1. Sisir Kumar Das, *op.cit.,* p. 6.

noticed by a prosperous doctor who was coming to Calcutta in 1793 and brought along for preaching Christianity. Carey worked at several places in Bengal for seven years without winning a single convert; his only achievement was a Bengali translation of the Bible.

Another group of missionaries including Joshua Marshman and William Ward arrived in Calcutta in 1799. The East India Company's government was still maintaining the pretence of non-interference in the religion of the natives. So the missionaries were diverted to Serampore which was a Danish settlement like Tranquebar. They were joined there by Carey and together they founded the Baptist Mission on January 10, 1800. The same year they made their first convert, a Bengali Hindu named Krishna Chandra Pal. In 1801 Carey was appointed a teacher in the Fort William College at Calcutta where he polished his Bengali and Sanskrit in the company of Hindu Pandits.

The Serampore Missionaries did not make any headway in securing converts but they used their time profitably in collecting materials "derogatory" to Hinduism. This "evidence" was supplied by them to William Wilberforce and party who were agitating in England for opening the Indian field to Christian missionaries. There were some Englishmen in India as well as in England who were sincere admirers of Hindu culture and convinced that Christianity had nothing to teach to the Hindus. They presented their case forcefully in the British Parliament when the Charter of the East India Company came up for renewal in 1813. "A number of people," writes Dr. R.C. Majumdar, "including Wilberforce, sought to refute these arguments by painting in black colours the horrible customs of the Hindus such as *sati*, infanticide, throwing the children into the Ganga, religious suicides, and above all, idolatry. Vivid descriptions were given of the massacare of the innocents resulting from the car procession of Lord Jagannath at Puri, and the Baptists put down the number of annual victims at not less than 120,000. 'When challenged they had to admit that they did not actually count the dead bodies but arrived at the figure by an ingenious calculation.'"[2]

Wilberforce won the day. Missionaries were given full freedom to enter India and propagate their criminal creed. The main reason for his victory was the collapse of Maratha power which had so far prevented the British government from patronising Christianity openly. "The consequence," continues Dr. Majumdar, "was a heavy influx of missionaries into India from England and America. They first directed their attention to the East India Company and asked them to give up such practices as might be construed as indirect sympathy or support for heathen practices. In particular, they took umbrage at the management of temples by the Company's Government, a task which they had taken over from their Hindu predecessors and was described by the missionaries as 'the office of dry nurse of Vishnu'."[3] Many white officials of the Company also started supporting the missionaries and interfering with religious institutions and practices of the native people.

Meanwhile, the triumph of British arms had swelled the head of the ruling race and turned it against the vanquished. Charles Grant (1746-1823), some time Chairman of the East India Company, had written in AD 1697 that "we cannot avoid recognising in the people of Indostan a race of man lamentably degenerate and base... governed by malevolent and licentious passions... and sunk in misery by their vices."[4] Claudius Buchanan, a chaplain attached to the East India Company, counted himself among those who had known the Hindus for a long time. He had concluded, "Those, who have had the best opportunities of knowing them, and who have known them for the longest time, concur in declaring that neither truth, nor honesty, honour, gratitude, nor charity, is

---

2. *The History and Culture of the Indian people*, Volume X: *British Paramountcy And Indian Renaissance*, Part II, 2nd Edition, Bombay, 1981, pp. 152-153.

3. *Ibid.*, p. 153.

4. Paul Johnson, *A History of Christianity*, Penguin Books, London, 1978, p. 442.

to be found pure in the breast of a Hindoo. How can it be otherwise? The Hindoo children have no moral instruction. If the inhabitants of the British isles had no moral instruction, would they be moral? The Hindoos have no moral books. What branch of their mythology has not more of falsehood and vice in it, than of truth and virtue? They have no moral gods. The robber and the prostitute lift up their hands with the infant and the priest, before an horrible idol of clay painted red, deformed and disgusting as the vices which are practised before it."[5]

Buchanan was convinced that God had given the Company dominion over India for the specific purpose of India's christianization. "No Christian nation," he wrote, "ever possessed such an extensive field for the propagation of the Christian faith, as that afforded to us by our influence over the hundred million natives of Hindoostan. No other nation ever possessed such facilities for the extension of the faith as we have in the government of a passive people, who yield submissively to our mild sway, reverence our principles, and acknowledge our dominion to be a blessing. Why should it be thought incredible that Providence hath been pleased, in a course of years to subjugate this Eastern empire to the most civilised nation in the world, for this very purpose?"[6] His conviction was fully shared by William Wilberfore who proclaimed in the British Parliament in June 1813, "Our religion is sublime, pure and beneficent. Theirs is mean, licentious, and cruel. Of our civil principles and condition, the common right of all ranks and classes to be governed, and punished by equal laws, is the fundamental principle. Equality, in short, is the vital essence and the very glory of our English laws. Of theirs, the essential and universal pervading general character is inequality, despotism in the higher classes,

5. Claudius Buchanan, ***Memories of the Expediency of an Ecclesiastical Establishment for British India: Both as the means of Perpetuating the Christian Religion Among Our Countrymen; And as a Foundation for the Ultimate Civilization of the Natives,*** London, 1805, Part II, para 6.

6. *Ibid.*, para 15.

degradation and oppression in the lower."[7]

Lord Hastings wrote in his diary on October 2, 1813, the day he arrived in India as Governor General, that, "The Hindoo appears a being nearly limited to mere animal functions... with no higher intellect than a dog or an elephant or a monkey, might be supposed capable of attaining." John Stuart Mill, the British historian, did not lag behind and wrote in 1819 that "In truth, the Hindu, like the eunuch, excels in the qualities of a slave."[8] Now the missionaries added their own invectives derived from "divine wrath". Hindu society was soon faced with a filthy smear campanion.

It has to be remembered that most of the missionaries came from the lowest strata of Western society. Their motive in joining the mission was not entirely a love for Jesus. Dr. Dick Kooiman has studied the social background of some nineteenth century missionaries. He says that their "spiritual motives did not exclude the possibility of missionary employment bringing substantial improvement in their social and economic position, whether anticipated or not."[9] Most of them had no formal education. They were trained in theological seminaries where they crammed the set doctrines. At the same time, they became experts in the use of foul language which abounds in the Bible *vis-a-vis* non-believers. Like their paymasters at home and in India, most of them were plain scoundrels in the service of an Evil Spirit which inspired their creed from A to Z. It was not surprising that their manners and parlance remained beastly and brutal. They "occupied a rather humble position,"[10] in the British social order in India. But all the same, they shared the arrogance of the ruling race and inspired awe among the natives.

Hindu society experienced a deep resentment when

---

7. Quoted in Hansard, XXVI, June 1813, pp. 831-32.

8. Quoted in R.C. Majumdar, *op.cit.*, p. 338.

9. Dick Kooiman, 'Social and Economic Backgrounds of Nineteenth Century London Missionaries in Southern Travencore', ***Indian Church History Review,*** December 1985, p.117.

10. *Ibid.*, p. 112.

these hoodlums of Jesus Christ were let loose upon it, but there was nothing that could be done to stop them immediately. The coercive apparatus of the Raj was on the side of the miscreants. Raja Ram Mohun Roy contemplated the scene with a cool head. He was a scholar and a social reformer who had so far shown admiration for the British Raj as well as Jesus. He had met and conversed with some leading missionaries and mastered the Christian scriptures after studying Greek and Hebrew. For a long time, the missionaries had thought he was their man and were waiting for him to embrace the "only true faith". On the other hand, he had aroused hostility in Hindū society by openly speaking and writing against its traditional religion and social customs. No one suspected that the missionaries had pained and disgusted him deeply.

One wonders whether the Raja related the crude missionary methods directly to Christian dogmas such as the divinity of Jesus, his miracles, his atoning death and his resurrection. Perhaps his perceptions were derived from his rigorous monotheism which he had expounded in his Persian monograph, *Tuhfāt-ul-Muhawwidīn*. What is known for sure is that he presented the founder of Christianity only as a moral preacher in his book, *The Precepts of Jesus,* published in 1820. It was a compilation from the four gospels. "Rammohan had left out," writes Dr. Sisir Kumar Das, "all passages in these gospels which describe either any miracle or refer to any prophecy or to the doctrines of atonement, Logos or the divinity of Christ... Rammohan is almost ruthless in his rejection of materials from the fourth gospel which is... the most important interpretation of Christ's teaching and the meaning of his life and death on the cross."[11] The fourth gospel is the most suspect of all the New Testament books. Certainly its author is unknown. Yet it remains perhaps the most important book for Christian dogma.

The missionaries were taken aback. The book was

11. Sisir Kumar Das, *op.cit.*, p. 25.

reviewed in the missionary magazine, *Friend of India,*[12] by Deocar Schmit. Joshua Marshman, the Serampore Missionary who edited the paper, introduced Ram Mohun as "an intelligent heathen whose mind is as yet completely opposed to the grand design of the Saviour's becoming incarnate." The reviewer himself reprimanded the Raja for "separating the moral doctrines of the New Testament from the mysteries and historical matters contained therein." Ram Mohun was now labelled as "an injurer of the cause of truth."[13] A dialogue was round the corner if the Raja chose to defend his position.

He did, and published immediately *An Appeal to the Christian Public in Defence of the Precepts of Jesus.* Marshman was now angry and made "a fiery criticism."[14] Ram Mohun followed up in 1821 with a *Second Appeal* in which he came out with criticism of the divinity of Jesus and the doctrine of Trinity. Marshman defended both and became more angry. Ram Mohun wrote his *Final Appeal* in 1823 "with a formidable array of Hebrew and Greek quotations."[15] Before we take up his demolition of the central Christian dogmas, it would be worthwhile to mention his work on another front.

He had started publishing in 1821 a bilingual periodical, *The Brahmanical Magazine,* in Bengali and English. In the very first issue he had launched a spirited attack on missionary methods. "During the last twenty years," he wrote, "a body of English gentlemen, who are called missionaries, have been publicly endeavouring, in several ways, to convert

---

12. Predecessor of *The Statesman*, Calcutta. The newspaper has maintained its tradition of Hindu-bating. It is now owned by the Tatas, a Parsi industrial house, and edited by C.R. Irani, a Parsi pen-pusher. But neither the owners nor their hireling seem to remember that but for the protection provided by Hindus to their forefathers, they would not have been here at all. Irani's love for Islam is intriguing indeed. Had he read any history, he would have known what Islam did to his overbrimming forefathers and their religion in Iran, and what a miscarriage he happens to be.

13. Sisir Kumar Das, *op. cit.*, p. 26.

14. *Ibid.*, p. 27.

15. *Ibid.*, p. 28.

Hindus and Mussalmans of this country into Christianity. The first way is that of publishing and distributing among the natives various books, large and small, reviling both religions and abusing and ridiculing the gods and saints of the former: the second way is that of standing in front of the doors of the natives or in the public roads to preach the excellency of their own religion and the debasedness of that of others: the third way is that if any natives of low origin become Christians from the desire of gain or from any other motives, these gentlemen employ and maintain them as a necessary encouragement to others to follow their example... Were the missionaries likewise to preach the Gospel and distribute books in countries not conquered by the English, such as Turkey, Persia, etc., which are much nearer England, they would be esteemed a body of men truly zealous in propagating religion and in following the example of the founders of Christianity. In Bengal, where the English are the sole rulers, and where the mere name of Englishman is sufficient to frighten people, an encroachment upon the rights of her poor, timid and humble inhabitants and upon their religion cannot be viewed in the eyes of God or the public as a justifiable act. For wise and good men always feel disinclined to hurt those that are of much less strength than themselves, and if such weak creatures be dependent on them and subject to their authority, they can never attempt, even in thought, to mortify their feelings."[16]

In the same issue, he "hinted at the indirect support of the Government in the missionary activities."[17] He objected to the language used in the *Friend of India* for Hindus and Hinduism. He called upon the missionaries to have a fair debate. "To abuse and insult," he said, "is inconsistent with reason and justice. If by force of argument they can prove the truth of their own religion and the falsity of that of Hindus, many would of course, embrace their doctrines, and in case

16. Quoted in R.C. Majumdar, *op. cit.*, pp. 15-16.
17. Sisir Kumár Das, *op. cit.*, p. 33.

they fail to prove this, they should not undergo such useless trouble to tease Hindus any longer by their attempts at conversion."[18] He continued, "They should not abstain from a debate considering the humble way of living of Brahmin scholars because Truth and Virtue do not necessarily belong to wealth and Power and Distinctions of Big Mansions."[19]

The Raja not only knew the Christian scriptures and theology at least as well if not better as any missionary, he was also aware that Christianity was divided into many sects, each at war with all others. He was well aware that the language which Christian sects hurled at each other was not much better if not worse than that which Christian missionaries were hurling at Hinduism. But his greatest asset was his knowledge of the humanist and rationalist critique of Christianity which had come to the fore in the modern West. That came to his help when he presented his case progressively in his three appeals.

"In the nineteenth Century," writes Richard Fox Young, "Christianity's advocates in India were sometimes required to answer arguments drawn from non-orthodox Western scholars. Rammohan Roy, for instance, studied the literature of Unitarians and freethinkers who documented the rise of Trinitarian theology in order to prove its allegedly unbibilical origin. The findings buttressed Roy's critique of 'Christian polytheism'. Evangelical missionaries (e.g. John Marshman) were greatly discomfited being out of contact with developments in contemporary biblical criticism."[20]

Marshman had called Ram Mohun a heathen at the very start of the dialogue. Ram Mohun replied, "The editor perhaps may consider himself justified by numerous precedents among the several partisans of different Christian sects in applying the name of heathen to one who takes the Precepts of Jesus as his principal guide in matters of religious and civic duties; as Roman Catholics bestow the appellation of heretics

18. Quoted in Richard Fox Young, *op.cit.,* p. 59.
19. Quoted in Sisir Kumar Das, *op. cit.*, p. 34.
20. Richard Fox Young, *op. cit.*, p. 64.

or infidels on all classes of Protestants; and the Protestants do not spare the title idolater to Roman Catholics; Trinitarians deny the name Christian to Unitarians, while the latter retort by stigmatising the worshippers of the son of man as Pagans who adore a created and dependent being."[21]

Schmit had felt offended by the Raja's "attempts at separating the moral doctrines of the New Testament from the mysteries and historical matters contained therein." Ram Mohun referred the missionary to New Testament passages to prove that "the aim and object of all commandments of God is to teach us our duty towards our fellow-creatures." He pointed his finger at the fourth gospel as the villain of the piece in placing dogmas above moral precepts. "It is from this source," he said, "that the most difficult to be comprehended of the dogmas of the Christian religion have been principally drawn, and on the foundation of passages of that writer, the interpretation of which is still a matter of keen discussion amongst the most learned and most pious scholars in Christendom, is erected the mysterious doctrine of three Gods in one Godhead."[22]

The Raja hit hard at the doctrine of Trinity. He asked his adversary in the dialogue "whether it is consistent with any rational idea of the nature of Deity that God should be appointed by God to act the part of a mediator by laying aside his glory and taking upon himself the form of a servant", and "whether it is not most foreign to the nature of the immutable God that circumstances could produce such a change in the condition of the Deity as that he should not only have been divested of his glory for more than thirty years but even subjected to servitude."[23] He raised a very inconvenient question: How was the doctrine of Trinity different from Hindu polytheism?

Two Serampore Missionaries, William Yates and William

21. Quoted in Sisir Kumar Das, *op. cit.*, pp. 26-27.
22. Quoted in *Ibid.*, p. 27.
23. Quoted in *Ibid.*, p. 29.

Adam, were taking the help of Ram Mohun in translating the New Testament into Sanskrit. Ram Mohun suggested a certain translation of a Greek term which was first accepted and then turned down because it was damaging to the doctrine of Trinity. Serious doubts, however, arose in the mind of William Adam. He disowned Trinitarianism and joined Ram Mohun in the Unitarian Committee which the latter had formed in 1822. "The Serampore Missionaries flew into a rage and described him as 'the second fallen Adam'."[24]

Ram Mohun replied by writing a satire in Bengali, *Pādarī Śisya Sambād*, published in 1823, in order to ridicule the doctrine of Trinity. It was an imaginary dialogue between a European missionary and his three Chinese students. After having taught the dogma, the missionary asked his students whether God was one or many. "The first disciple replied that there were three Gods, the second that there were two and the third that there was no God. The teacher rebuked them and demanded an explanation of their answers. The first one said, 'You said that there are God the Father, God the Son and God the Holy Ghost. According to my counting that is one plus one plus one, making three.' The second one said, 'You told us that there were three Gods and that one of them died long ago in a village in a Western country. So I concluded that there are two Gods, now living.' The third one said, 'You have said again and again that God was one and that there is no other God and Christ is the real God. But about 1800 years have passed since the Jews, living near the Arabian Sea, crucified him. What else, do you think I can say, Sir, except that there is no God.'"[25]

He handled the divinity of Jesus in the same manner. "I ask," he wrote, "whether it is consistent with the human notion of justice to release millions of men each guilty of sins unto death, after inflicting death upon another person (whether God or man) who never participated in their sins,

24. *Ibid.*, pp. 28-29.
25. Quoted in *Ibid.*, pp. 30-31.

even though that person had voluntarily proposed to embrace death, or whether it is not a great violation of justice according to the human notion of it, to put an innocent person to painful death for the transgressions of others."[26] He asked a straight question, "If Jesus actually atoned for sin, and delivered men from its consequences, how can those men and women, who believe in his atonement, be still, equally with others, liable to the evil effects of the sins already remitted by the vicarious sacrifice of Jesus?" In place of substitutionary atonement, he recommended the Hindu view that "repentance alone is the sure and early remedy for human failure."[27]

Finally, he came to the miracles of Jesus. The missionaries maintained that those miracles could not be questioned because it was written in the Bible which was a divine book and that they were witnessed by many people. Ram Mohun observed, "If all assertations were to be indiscriminately admitted as facts, merely because they have been testified by numbers, how can we dispute the truth of those miracles which are said to have been performed by persons esteemed holy amongst natives of this country?... Have they not accounts and records handed down to them, relating to the wonderful miracles stated to have been performed by their saints, such as Agastya, Vasistha, and Gotam, and their gods incarnate, such as Rama, Krishna and Narsimgh, in the presence of their contemporary friends and enemies, the wise and ignorant, the select and the multitude?"[28]

The Raja had gone too far. White Christians outside the missionary circle now moved into the dialogue in their own way. Here was a mere Hindu, a member of an enslaved society, comparing the Bible with Hindu books and equating the incarnation of Jesus with Hindu avatars! Ram Mohun received abusive letters from Englishmen who had been his friends.

26. Quoted by Richard Fox Young, *op. cit.*, p. 116n.
27. Quoted in *Ibid.*, p.117n.
28. Quoted in *ibid.*, pp. 111-12.

One of them made a public attack on him. "It was arrogance," he said, "on the part of a Hindu to say that there could be any common basis for both Hinduism and Christianity." He invited his countrymen to put the Hindu in his proper place. "Are you so degraded by Asiatic effeminacy," he asked his countrymen, "as to behold with indifference your holy and immaculate religion thus degraded by having it planted on an equality with Hinduism, with rank idolatry, with disgraceful ignorance and shameful superstition?" At the same time, he denounced the Hindus as ungrateful for not remembering that the Christians had given them civil liberty and education. The Raja thanked the British administration for civil liberty. He also pointed out that "all ancient prophets and patriarchs venerated by Christians nay even Jesus Christ himself...were Asiatics." But he refused to accept that he owed his education to Christianity. For that, he said, he "was indebted to *our ancestors* for the first dawn of knowledge."[29]

"The religious debate," observes Dr. Sisir Kumar Das, "took a new turn. The issue of racial superiority slowly clouded the whole atmosphere. The area of controversy was enlarged. The Indian intellectual slowly realized that Christianity was linked with European civilization — it was linked up with the power that ruled India."[30] The dialogue had reached a point where the Raja had to exercise restraint.

He had demolished the most important Christian dogmas. But all along, he had kept Jesus on a high pedestal. Perhaps he was convinced that Jesus was a great moral teacher. Perhaps he was using Jesus only to beat the missionaries with their own stick. In any case, the Brahmo Samaj he founded had to pay a high price for his praise of Jesus. Keshub Chunder Sen who took over the Brahmo Samaj at a later stage, became infatuated with Jesus, so much so that he got alienated more or less completely from the Hindu society at

29. Quoted in Sisir Kumar Das, *op.cit.*, p. 37. Dr. Das surmises that Rabindranath's famous song, *prathama prabhāta udaya taba gagane,* is a verbatim rendering of Ram Mohun Roy's tribute to his ancestors.

30. *Ibid.*

large. Keshub's disciples tried to get Jesus endorsed by Sri Ramakrishna who knew nothing about the mischievous myth. And that, in due course, led to Ramakrishna Mission's antics of denying its Hindu ancestry.[31]

---

31. See Ram Swarup, *Ramakrishna Mission in Search of a New Identity*, Voice of India, New Delhi, 1986.

9

Encounter in Maharashtra

Another dialogue between Hinduism and Christianity was held soon after the one in Calcutta. This time the venue was Bombay, the second most important city founded by the British and another storm centre of missionary activity against Hinduism. John Wilson, after whom the Wilson College in Bombay is named, was an important Presbyterian missionary from Scotland. He "debated for six successive evenings with a pandit named Morabhatta Dandekara" in February, 1831. "John Wilson's knowledge of Hindu literature," we are told, "was first-rate, but he did not hesitate to subject what he read to withering ridicule from his perspective as a Christian. Inconsistencies in the Puranas were among his special targets." He held debates with Zoroastrians and Muslims also. But "Hindus proved to be his dogged opponents."[1]

Wilson invited the Brahmanas for a debate on May 31, 1830, but he himself failed to turn up. A native convert, Ram Chandra, had to serve as his substitute. Ram Chandra informed the Brahmanas that Jesus was the second person of the Trinity who took "a human birth, and died for the world." A Brahmana asked Ram Chandra not to "use that expression" and said that "God does not die." Next the Brahmana speculated that "Jesus Christ was some philosopher (*sadhoo*) among you" but wondered why so much fuss was being made about him when "we have a thousand philosophers and saints like Jesus Christ." Ram Chandra asked if Rama or Krishna or any other Hindu god "gave his life for you." The Brahmana replied, "Why should they give their lives when

1. Richard Fox Young, *op. cit.*, p. 25.

they could save us in many other ways?" Ram Chandra asked a few more questions about Rama and concluded that Rama had lived for himself and not for others.[2]

The proceedings of the debate that finally took place between Dandekara and Wilson in February 1831, have not been preserved. Wilson wrote a book, *An Exposure of the Hindu Religion,* in 1832. It was a reply to Dandekara's Marathi book, *Śrīhindudharmasthāpanā*, published earlier. The original in Marathi has been lost, but Wilson "prefixed" to his reply an English translation of it. We do not have Wilson's book before us. What we have are extracts from it regarding Dandekara's view of several Christian doctrines.

Dandekara defends the deeds of Hindu gods which the missionaries considered immoral. He says that those deeds are virtuous which "have as much power as image worship itself to create in some pure and holy dispositions." In any case, "These deeds, when narrowly conceived, are even far better than those virtuous actions of Christ's that you mention."[3] Next, he takes up the Christian doctrine of Trinity. He finds it difficult to understand how "Those who hold these doctrines" of three divinities "maintain that the Unity of God is undestroyed." But the more important point he makes is that if "these three divinities occasion no bewilderment of mind" to the Christians "how can the worship of Rama, Krishna and other gods, occasion... bewilderment to us?"[4]

Coming to the atoning death of Jesus, Dandekara sees no merit in a God who "sent his son into the world... for the salvation of men" and then "brought him into a state so reproachful and so appalling." He wonders why this God started by creating sin and then "unheard of suffering" for the redemption of that sin. He asks, "Had he no other way of saving the world? Why, pray, should he put himself to so much ado?" He says that Rama, Krishna and other incarnations have for their "appropriate object the salvation of the world." But

2. *Ibid.*, p. 25-26.
3. *Ibid.*, p. 26.
4. *Ibid.*, p. 27.

they "sported themselves at pleasure, and by these very sports accomplished the salvation of those who took refuge in their mercy." They gave salvation "without suffering pain at all to be compared with that of Christ and without submitting to a reproachful death like him." He asks the Christians "whether these actions of Rama, Krishna and the rest, or those of your Jesus Christ are better."[5]

Dandekara sees no sense in Christian sacraments such as taking "a piece of bread, and muttering a few words to eat it up," drinking wine and pouring "water on the head." These, he says, are "all material things" from which no "merit and holiness" can result. They cannot entitle a man "to a state of nearness to God and emancipation from matter." Compared to the bread and wine and water in a pot, the water of the Ganga "sanctified by the touch of Krishna's feet or from the contemplation of his image" is far more pure. Yet the Christians say that the water of the Ganga creates "an increase of ignorance." Dandekara concludes that Christians doctrines being hollow and Christian sacraments meaningless, the Hindu who favours them and finds Hinduism objectionable, does so as a result of sin committed in his former birth. The Hindu who converts to Christianity is like the man who suspects his own mother of adultery, "when he himself was conceived in her womb."[6]

Another Hindu whom Wilson tried to refute in *A Second Exposure of Hindu Religion,* published in 1834, was Narayan Rao, a teacher of English in a college at Satara. Rao wrote a Marathi book *Svadeshadharmābhimānī*, expounding Vedanta and examining the Bible. We have with us neither Rao's book nor Wilson's refutation of it. What we have are extracts in an English translation from Rao's criticism of the Old and the New Testaments.

Rao finds the God of the Old Testament frail as he had to take rest for a day after being busy with creation for six days.

5. *Ibid.*, pp. 27-28.
6. *Ibid.*, p. 28.

He seems to have "a figure like man" because the first man he created by breathing into an "image of clay" was "after his own image." He cannot be credited with omniscience because he forgot to create a female companion when he created Adam. He had to put Adam to sleep and steal one of Adam's bones for making Eve. As he did not seek Adam's permission, he "was guilly of theft." He is also unjust and vindictive. He cannot be credited with omnipotence either as he could not stop the Devil from telling to Adam and Eve the truth about the Tree of Knowledge. Moreover, the Devil is more truthful because he revealed to Adam and Eve what God had concealed from them. The God of the Old Testament, on the other hand, proved himself to be unjust and vindictive by cursing Adam and Eve for no fault of their's.[7]

Coming to the New Testament, Rao finds no improvement in the character of its God. He consorted secretly with the wife of Joseph "who was an upright man." It was only when Joseph found Mary pregnant and "thought of dimissing her privately" without raising a public scandal that God told the truth to him in a dream. A better course for him would have been that since he desired Mary, he should have secured her divorce from Joseph. One wonders whether the Christians are praising or denouncing God by presenting him in this manner. God should certainly feel irritated with the Christian scripture.

Nor is the birth of Jesus a commendable event. As soon as Jesus is born, "a great number of infants are unreasonably put to death" by Herod. Jesus did not act like God at all. Instead of facing Herod and preventing the death of the infants, he ran away to Egypt. He "did nothing whatever for the establishment of religion" as long as Herod lived. He came out of hiding only when Herod was dead. "It hence appears that Herod was more powerful than Jesus. It is impossible, therefore, that he, who by his flight, became murderer of children, and was so despicable in power, can be either the Son of

7. *Ibid.*, p. 29.

God, or bear any relation to God whatever."[8]

Rao finds the Christian scripture equally despicable for saying that all those who have not accepted Christ as the only saviour will go to hell. Yet Christian teachers "are sent to Hindustan eighteen hundred years after Christ." The consequence of this delay has been that "innumerable millions of people have gone, and will continue to go, into hell." That only proves that the Christian scripture is false. If there had been any truth in it "Christian teachers... should have been sent forth into all the world at the time of Christ." Finally, Rao draws the "unavoidable conclusion" from these contradictions in the Christian scripture. He says that "the Christian religion is false" and "the Padres, taking advantage of the sovereignty of the people of their caste, have come to this country for the express purpose of practising deceit, and leading the people to apostasy."[9]

Dr. Richard Fox Young to whose book we owe the extracts from Narayan Rao's examination of the two Testaments, sees only "literalistic exegesis" in Narayan Rao's conclusions. He sees nothing wrong in the Christian exegesis which he himself admits to be equally literalistic. On the contrary, he justifies missionary retailing of miracles in terms of Hindu credulity! The implication is that the missionaries would have been philosophical in their approach if they had found a philosophically inclined audience among the Hindus. There is no evidence that Christianity has had any philosophical equipment at any time. Christians insist on a literal acceptance of their own scripture because they themselves believe that this scripture is divinely inspired. And they believe just the opposite about Hindu Shastras. Narayan Rao was only meeting them on their own level. Wilson's mention of his work on Vedanta proves that unlike the Christian missionaries he was quite capable of philosophical discourse also.

---

8. *Ibid.*, pp. 29-30.
9. *Ibid.*, p. 30.

10

Encounter with Sanskrit Pandits

Yet another dialogue between Hinduism and Christianity was held from 1839 to 1845. It is particularly interesting because it took place through the medium of Sanskrit. John Muir (1810-1882) published the first draft of his *Matapar̄ikshā* in 1839 and the final in 1840. It drew three rejoinders from Hindu Pandits. Somanātha, whose real name was Subaji Bapu, published his *Matatapar̄ikshāsikshā* in 1839. Harachandra Tarkapañchānana came out with his *Matapar̄ikshottara* in 1840. Nīlakaṇṭha Goreh reacted somewhat late and published his *Shāstratattvavinirṇaya* at the end of 1844.

John Muir had come to Calcutta in 1828 as a civil servant of the East India Company. He was, for some time, a student of William Carey at the Fort William College. From 1840 to 1853, he occupied several senior positions in the administration of North Western Provinces (later on the United Provinces and now Uttar Pradesh). In 1844-1845 he "supervised the reorganisation" of the Benares Sanskrit College founded by Jonathan Duncan in the late eighteenth century. By that time he had acquired a working knowledge of Sanskrit and collected what he considered an arsenal against Hinduism. All through his service career, he was a Christian missionary except in name.

The atmosphere in North Western Provinces (NWP) at that time was particularly favourable for his mission because the majority of Englishmen in the administration were inclined the same way. "Historians have long recognised," writes Dr. Young, "that committed Christians took an active role in the British administration in NWP and that many of them engaged, privately or publicly, in religious and social causes... The ideals that drew these administrators (for the most part Hailesbury graduates from the 1820s and 1830s) together were evangelical, expansionist, and reformist. Under the leadership of James Thomason, Lieutenant Governor of NWP (1843-1853), these Christian administrators coalesced even more tightly."[1] It may be added that by "social reform" they meant interference with Hindu religious and social traditions. Whatever Hindu practice did not conform to the Christian standard of correctness was a "social evil" for them.

James Thomason was a follower of Charles Simeon, a Cambridge clergyman and leader of the Clapham Sect, the missionary brigade of the Church of England organised earlier by William Wilberforce. Simeon exercised great influence on Charles Grant, member of the Board of Directors of the East India Company. He secured through Grant the appointment of many administrators in India. They were and remained "his own curates." Thomason was one of them. "Administrators," continues Dr. Young, "who looked to Thomason for leadership in matters of government and religion, linked themselves with missionaries, especially Evangelicals, wherever they served. Pockets of Evangelicals, consequently, existed in most provincial centres wherever Muir served."[2]

At the time Muir started using his official prestige and power for spreading Christianity, a section of the missionaries, led by William Carey were experimenting with what came to be known as Church Sanskrit. Carey was convinced that Hindus believed what they believed because it was written in Sanskrit, a language which they regarded as sacred. He wanted to train a group of "Christian Pandits" who would probe "these mysterious sacred nothings" and expose them as worthless. He could not help being deeply impressed by the structure and diction of Sanskrit, but he was distressed

1. Richard Fox Young, *op. cit.*, p. 51
2. *Ibid.*, p. 52

that this "golden casket exquisitely wrought" had remained "filled with nothing but pebbles and trash."[3] He was out to fill it with "riches—beyond all price", that is, the doctrines of Christianity. That was what he meant by Church Sanskrit. He was joined in this enterprise by several other Sanskritists, notably William Hodge and H. H. Wilson. Helped by Hindu Pandits, they translated Christian terminology and the New Testament into Sanskrit and wrote some other Christian tracts in this language. The enterprise continued till long after Carey was dead. "Such, indeed, is the exuberance and flexibility of this language and its power of compounding words," M. Monier-Williams would write in 1861, "that when it has been, so to speak, baptised and thoroughly penetrated with the spirit of Christianity, it will probably be found, next to Hebrew and Greek, the most expressive vehicle of Christian truth."[4]

These learned men believed sincerely that Hindus honoured certain doctrines simply because they were expressed in Sanskrit. It never occurred to any of them that Hindus honoured those doctrines no less when they were stated in other languages. Long before Carey and his tribe appeared on the Indian scene, the Alvars, the Nayanars, the Siddhas, the Sants and the Bhaktas had produced a prolific literature in all Indian vernaculars, expounding the same spiritual truths as the earlier spiritual seekers had done in Sanskrit. All this vernacular literature was held by Hindus in equal reverence. The missionary conviction that Hindus will buy the abomination that is Christianity if it is wrapped up in Hindu forms, persists in our own days. The missionary mind has so far failed to grasp the simple truth that what Hindus find fundamentally objectionable in Christianity is its doctrine. The objection will not disappear because that doctrine is stated in Sanskrit or dressed in an ochre robe.[5]

---

3. *Ibid.*, p. 34.
4. *Ibid.*, p. 48.
5. Fr. Bede Griffiths and Henri le Saux have been the main exponents of this Christian self-deception in recent years. See *Catholic Ashrams: Sannyasins or Swindlers?*, Voice of India, New Delhi, 1994.

Turning back to Muir, he started "urging missionaries to learn Sanskrit in order to 'combat... hydra-headed paganism'."[6] As no other missionary came forward with Christian lore composed in Sanskrit, he himself took the lead by publishing his *Mataparīkshā* in 379 *anuṣṭubha* verses in the form of a dialogue between a teacher and his disciple. It was published by Bishop's College, Calcutta, in 1839. Next year it was expanded to 1032 *ślokas,* quoting many Sanskrit sources. Muir was out to impress Hindu Pandits with his mastery of Sanskrit literature. The mastery came easy to him, as to many other Christian scholars and missionaries, because he could employ poor Hindu Pandits to find for him the references he fancied.

Muir said nothing in his *Mataparīkshā* that had not been stated earlier by other missionaries. He laid down three criteria for characterising a true scripture: the founder's power to work miracles, source in the one True God, and universality, that is, equal validity for every race. He faced no trouble in "proving" that the Christian scripture alone was true in terms of these criteria, while Hindu Shastras were false. He asserted that miracles mentioned in Hindu Shastras were "merely ornamental in that religion instead of being at its very centre as in Christianity."[7] This way of arguing is pompously called Evidential Apologetics in Christian theology. At one point, however, Muir was deliberately dishonest. He criticised the cosmography of the Puranas as erroneous. Surely he must have known what Galileo and Copernicus had done to the cosmography of the Bible and how they had suffered persecution at the hands of the Church.

Somanātha

The challenge thrown by Muir was accepted immediately by a Maharashtrian scholar, Subaji Bapu, who published his *Mataparīkshāsikshā* soon after Muir's shorter treatise became

6. Quoted in Richard Fox Young, *op. cit.,* p.64.
7. Quoted in *Ibid.,* p. 72.

known in 1839. Subaji published his work under a pseudonym, Somanātha.[8] He was working in Central India with an English civil servant and Orientalist, Lancelot Wilkinson, as an interpreter of Jyotisha (Hindu astronomy and astrology) and thought it prudent not to use his real name. Association with an Englishman had earned him some bad name among his own people. But work with Wilkinson had proved advantageous to him in one way. He had acquired knowledge of Christianity and come to know that "on rational grounds, Christianity, too was defective in physical sciences."[9]

Matapariksbāsiksbā was a short treatise of 107 verses divided in three chapters. It was also in the form of a dialogue between a teacher and a disciple. Subaji started by dismissing the miracles of Jesus as nothing special. Books belonging to all *mārgas* mention miracles. If the miracles of Jesus are true, so also those of the others, and vice versa: "But if some believe that Christ alone was the greatest by virtue of his power, then why was he killed by weak men?"[10] Nor can Jesus be held as the only saviour: "If (Christ) destroyed mankind's sins by the sacrifice of his own body, then can that not be done... by those who, like him, are virtuous?"[11]

Next, he showed that what Muir regarded as universality was, in fact, uniformity and unsuited to all because human nature varied from race to race: "Since God made men with particular natures, those belonging to a specific race must follow a particular scripture uttered by God. If only one scripture is agreeable to God, why did he... not make mankind singlenatured? For this very reason, that he made spatial, temporal and other differences, it would be perfectly certain that differences between scriptures would also he quite pleasing to him." It is, therefore, the same One God who gave different scriptures to different people: "Worship him, the universal

8. It is not known from what place he published his work. It is not mentioned in the only copy now available in the India Office Library.

9. *Ibid.*, p. 92.

10. Quoted in *Ibid.*, p. 110.

11. Quoted in *Ibid.*, p. 115.

atman, true God who is honoured as Buddha in the Buddhist *darshana*, Jina in the Jain scripture, known by the name Christ in the Christian religion, as Allah in the Mohammedan religion and by the name Arka, Pramathesha, Shakti, Girisha, Srisha and so forth in the threefold Veda, various Tantras and Puranas."[12]

In one respect, however, Subaji found Christianity quite sinful. The followers of this religion injure and slaughter animals: "The worst sin is injuring bulls, helpers in ploughing, and cows, who regularly give milk."[13] He weakened his argument by giving economic grounds for protection of animals. The Hindu doctrine of *ahiṁsā* goes much deeper. Perhaps he thought that economic justification was better suited to minds for whom life by itself held no sanctity.

Finally, he appealed to the missionaries to stop their campaign against other religions: "You should never revile people who are satisfied with their own religion... Listen you disciples of Christ! I, solicitous of your own welfare, tell you this truthfully... Diminution of Hari's religion, anger, cruelty, subversion of authority and dissensions among the populace would result from reviling the religion of others. Increase of God's religion, contentment, gentleness, harmony between the ranks would result from praising all religions. For each person his own religion is best; the same religion would be perilous for another person."[14]

Harachandra Tarkapañchānana

The *Matapariīkshottara* of Harachandra was published in Calcutta but before Muir brought out the second and bulkier edition of his *Matapariīkshā*. Harachandra was a poor Bengali Brahmana about whom nothing is known except the authorship of this book. The book itself was a short treatise of only 137 Sanskrit verses in Bengali script with a two-page Preface in English. He was, however, prepared to write more if Muir

12. Quoted in *Ibid.*, p. 92.
13. Quoted in *Ibid.*, p. 120.
14. Quoted in *Ibid.*, p. 145.

agreed to "bear the cost of printing and remunerated him for his labours."[15]

Harachandra started by taking note of the missionary epidemic. He said that there was no escape from the missionaries "either in the market-place or on the roads, with their constant refrain, 'convert to our religion and be happy for ever.'" He rebuked rather strongly the Hindu converts: "Only that man... who is deluded, who is desirous of acquiring profits, who has neither deliberated upon his own religion, nor looked at the defects in Christianity, would become a Christian."[16] They should have known that compared to Christianity Hinduism was a very ancient religion and had prevailed through the ages because of its innate strength: "If there is to be faith in a book, let it be in the Veda, since it has prevailed on earth from the time of creation onward."[17]

Harachandra was familiar with the debunking of Christianity at the hands of Western scholars: "Since many fearless, intelligent men such as Hume, Tom Paine, the great Voltaire, Palmer and Gibbon, confuted these priests, the priestly classes, answerless, called them infidels."[18] Pointing to the rise of successive Christian sects, he asked, "How could that religion, the religious customs of which would constantly change, deserve respect from intelligent men endowed with reasoning?" He added sarcastically, "As the world-creator was powerless at the time of creation to establish religious customs, he (taking) the form of Christ established them afterwards: when Christ died, the world-creator (assuming) the form of Pope and others established them." Being devoid of substance, Christianity has always depended upon force and fraud: "Formerly there was a certain king there, named Constantine. This deluded king stupidly converted to Christianity and strove to propagate this worthless religion by fraud, distributing wealth, craft and force. He made citizens

15. Quoted in *Ibid.*, p. 93.
16. Quoted in *Ibid.*
17. Quoted in *Ibid.*, p. 99.
18. Quoted in *Ibid.*, p. 96.

everywhere in his realm convert to that religion. From that time until now, its propagation comes by nothing other than royal decree. Men don't convert to it by their own will."[19]

Harachandra demonstrated what could be done to Jesus if Hindus resorted to missionary methods of polemics. He knew how historico-critical studies in Europe had reduced Jesus to a pathetic figure. The story of his virgin birth had been subjected to searching questions. In the gospel of Luke, the Pharisee contemporaries of Jesus had told him to his face that he was a "bastard", a "wine-bibler" and a "glutton" Harachandra had "read the New Testament — between the lines."[20]

Finally, Harachandra presented the ten tenets of Sanatana Dharma — constancy (*dhriti*), forgiveness (*kshamā*), self-control (*dama*), non-stealing (*asteya*), purity (*śaucha*), restraint of senses (*indriyanigraha*), devout thought (*dhī*), knowledge (*vidyā*), truth (*satyam*) and absence of anger (*akrodha*). He invited the Christians to practise these *dharmas*. They will be born as Hindus in their next life.[21] What he was saying was that Christians will then make a start on the path of *moksha* (freedom from the bondage of birth, disease, old age and death). This was his way of putting Christianity in its proper place in the scale of spiritual evolution. He was anticipating Mahatma Gandhi who will say, "For me there can be no deliverance from this earthly life except in India... anyone who seeks such deliverance... must go to the sacred soil of India."[22]

The *Mataparīkshottara* "caused a sensation in Calcutta."[23] Christians, white and native, were up in arms against Harachandra. Krishna Mohan Banerjea, a Hindu convert, wrote a tract in Bengali in order to refute Harachandra's "insinuations" against converts and explain away the differences

19. Quoted in *Ibid.*, p. 97.
20. *Ibid.*, p. 99.
21. *Ibid.*, p. 150.
22. Quoted in *Ibid.*, p. 152n.
23. *Ibid.*, p. 100.

among various Christian sects. On the other hand, Harachandra was hailed as "defender of the faith" in awakened Hindu circles. Christian scholars find it difficult to forgive him even today. Dr. Young calls him "tactless and pugilistic."[24] It is a classical case of seeing the mote in the other man's eye while missing the beam in one's own.

Nīlakaṇṭha Goreh

The third Hindu who reacted to Muir's *Matapari̅kshā* was Nīlakaṇṭha Goreh, a Maharashtrian Brahamana resident in Varanasi. He had been "outraged by bazaar preaching in his sacred city" and wanted "to silence the missionaries." He said he would "compel them either to leave the country or confine themselves to the instruction of Christians."[25] He had been holding a dialogue with William Smith of the Church Missionary Society (CMS) when he was given a copy of *Matapari̅kshā* in April 1844. It was the second and enlarged edition which Muir had completed in 1840. Muir had tried to dispute Harachandra's argument about the antiquity of the Vedas by borrowing H. T. Colebrook's historico-criticism of the Vedic literature.

Before he wrote his *Shāstratattvavinirṇaya* in reply to Muir, Goreh had sent to Smith a small treatise in Hindi which he had circulated in Varanasi "in order to stem the tide of conversions." He had raised in it six "Doubts concerning Christianity."[26]

First, he had wondered that if "none can be saved except those who believed in Christ", why had God delayed the message for so long and "created many nations and innumerable generations for hell?"

Second, he had asked, "Is it justice that the innocent should suffer for the guilty and the guilty escape?" Only an unjust God could devise this scheme of atonement. If God is just, "repentance and amendment" are what he should demand.

24. *Ibid.*, p. 93.
25. *Ibid.*, p. 103.
26. *Ibid.*, p. 104.

Third, the miracles ascribed to Jesus are tales "not worthy of credit" by wise men. One hears such tales everywhere. Moreover, Christians refuse to believe the "wonderful works, which wise men amongst us have related." Why should Hindus "believe in yours?"

Fourth, why do Christians ascribe justice and mercy to a God who created "disordely" and "unfortunate" souls though it was in his power to create only good souls because he created them out of nothing?

Fifth, Christianity condemns image-worship as if the worshipper regards the image as the creator of the world. This is a misconception. Hindus "set apart one thing in particular, in order, by meditating upon it, to remember God." This is quite in keeping with the Hindu perception that "God's essence is in everything."

Sixth, Christians reject transmigration and believe that there is only one birth. This is convenient only for those "who after death attain salvation." But it is very unjust to those who "die in their sins and are never to obtain birth again." Sending these souls to ever-lasting punishment, "is not only useless, but it would prove God guilty of enmity, cruelty and injustice."[27]

Goreh's *Shāstratattvavinirṇaya*, published at the end of 1844, consisted of 786 *anuṣṭubh* verses divided into six chapters. It has survived in one complete and two fragmentary manuscripts. A critical edition prepared by S. L. Katre was published in 1951 by the Scindia Oriental Institute of Ujjain.

Goreh starts where Muir had started — the miracles of Jesus. How can people at present know that the powers ascribed to Jesus really existed in him? Christians claim that those powers were witnessed by contemporary people who were adversaries of Jesus. They also claim that their scriptures have a divine source and cannot lie. But these are not rational proofs. Miracles and contemporary witnesses can be invented once you have decided to claim divine origin for

27. Quoted in *Ibid.*, pp. 104-105

some books. Conversely, when Christians say that those miracles really happened because they are mentioned in divinely inspired books, they are only proving what they have already assumed. If Jesus was God incarnate and cured blind people in the past, "why are blind people who firmly believe in him, not now also possessed of eyesight?" Has God ceased to be compassionate as before? Moreover, Christians say that Jesus performed miracles "for the sake of confidence in (his) divinity." Why has he stopped doing the same today? "Are not people anxious to have confidence now as well?" The entire argument based on miracles is bogus. Christians are simply saying, "Believe it because we say so."

The Christian doctrine that God created everything including human souls out of nothing, involves God in serious difficulties. "If God was going to create people intending only to send them to heaven, he would neither have frivolously made them human beings in the meantime nor have given them a place to sin." But if he created them so that they may commit sins, he and not human beings are responsible for those sins. If he sends sinners to hell, he is unjust. "The one who brings thieves into existence" is himself a thief. Moreover, what is the sense in bringing into existence human beings who die in childhood or are retarded since their birth? It is funny that the same God who creates sinners comes out next to give them salvation. Hindus have a better doctrine. They explain human nature in terms of deeds done in past births. Sounder still is Vedanta which says that sin and suffering and salvation are illusions from the viewpoint of Brahma.

The Christian doctrine of ever-lasting punishment for human beings whom God himself created sinful, turns God into a criminal. Why should souls suffer in an eternal hell for no fault of theirs? According to Hindu perceptions, sinful souls suffer in hell for a limited period. "Thus, experiencing pleasure and pain in numerous existences, they also gradually attain mukti."[28]

The Christian doctrine of original sin makes no sense at all. Why should all human beings at all times inherit the sin

---

28. Quoted in *Ibid.*, pp. 113-14.

of Adam and Eve? Biologically also, the doctrine is absurd. "The child's body indeed but not his intellect is derived from his father." This can be easily verified. "The son even of a very wicked-minded man is seen to be the crest-jewel of virtuous people." A child cannot be blamed because he has been begotten by a corrupt father. "Surely, birth depends on God, not on man."[29]

Coming to Jesus, it is preposterous to believe that he saved mankind by himself suffering the punishment for the sins of mankind. It is impossible for anyone to escape the consequences of one's sins even if someone else comes forward to suffer as a substitute. It is also unjust to make someone else suffer for one's own sins. Moreover, if sins get washed simply by believing in Jesus, "men who delight in sins would commit them at whim." But if, on the other hand, belief in Jesus has to be accompanied by repentance, belief becomes redundant because it is repentance which serves the purpose. That is what Hinduism teaches. Repentance is the real cure for sins.[30]

We see everywhere that persons who sincerely believe in Jesus continue to suffer in this world. How do we know that they will not continue to suffer in the next world as well? Christianity says that God inflicts suffering in order to test men's faith. Why, then, are human beings who die at birth brought into existence? They are not given a chance to pass the test. Where do these human beings go? To heaven, or to hell? In any case, "creating them is purposeless." Moreover, "There is no equally just punishment for both major and minor sins."[31]

Christian salvation also is a very poor concept. It "is a state of being called heaven where there are celestial pleasures." There is no place for "inward peace of good people" which comes from "world-renunciation, meditation and equanimity." Celestial pleasures also arise from sense-objects.

29. Quoted in *Ibid.*, pp. 114-115.
30. Quoted in *Ibid.*, pp. 115-16.
31. Quoted in *Ibid.*, pp. 116-17.

Hankering for such pleasures cannot he extinguished by enjoying them. On the contrary, the hankering grows. The Christian heaven is, therefore, a place of perpetual dissatisfaction. Hinduism says that "merit and demerit are produced because of ego-centric activities." It is only when such activities cease that the wheel of pleasure and pain stops turning. The *ātman* is completely purified by the destruction of Karma and exists in its own essential nature.[32]

Christianity has not spared any thought for animals, birds and God's other creatures. If God has created them only to suffer as they do under man's dispensation, he is very obnoxious. Human hearts melt on seeing the suffering of animals. "Does not God's, too, who is compassionate?" Why has Christianity failed to see that animals and birds and other creatures are so much like human beings in many respects? They know hunger and thirst, sleep and sex, fear and hope. Birds build houses and rear families. What is more, they do not need a scripture to tell them what is good and what is bad for them. They know it by instinct. Does not God who created them want them to have the happiness of knowing him? Do they continue to exist after death? Christianity has no answers for these questions. Hinduism, on the other hand, envisages that "creatures become animals by reason of sins in previous existences" and that "having experienced the fruit of their deeds, they are released" from their animal status.[33]

Compared to Christianity, Hinduism is a very comprehensive philosophy. Only "those who are dull-witted, their understanding vitiated by argumentation, have no aptitude for truth explained in the Upanishads." But God is compassionate and solicitous of salvation for everyone. He has, therefore, provided these dull-witted people with other scriptures suited to their understanding. "Men have an endless number of aptitudes, high and low, in nature" on account of their "good and bad *karman*." They worship Govinda in various ways and come to Vedanta in due course. "Bhagwan, an

32. Quoted in *Ibid.*, pp. 117-118.
33. Quoted in *Ibid.*, pp. 123-24.

ocean of compassion, made various kinds of *margas* by which everyone may attain salvation." To each according to his aptitude. Missionaries insist that there is only one *mārga*. They have missed the point from which Hinduism makes its start.[34]

"Images are never worshipped with the mind on either clay or wood — only with the mind on God, who is all-pervasive." What is wrong with that? "God is spotless like the sky." He accepts whatever worship is offered to him, in whatever way. Those who know the purpose of pilgrimages and image-worship "know that, although these things are said to cause merit, surely this, too, aims at commending knowledge of God, patience of mind, purification of consciousness, etc." The sun and the other symbols we worship, indicate God. The worshipper's imagination is fixed "squarely on God."[35]

Muir says that the differences in language render the Vedas defective. "Now on account of the difference in subject-matter, the language of Mantras, Brahmanas and the Upanishads is somewhat mutually distinct... The language in the Mahabharata is seen to be clearer than the Veda; language of that sort, somewhat different than the Puranas, is also found in the Smritis." That does not make them contradict each other. Language is adopted to the theme and also to the level of understanding. Nor do the variations in language make the Vedas less ancient.[36]

Lastly, the Puranas are not books of geography. The subject-matter of the Puranas is the glorification of God. They describe the Cosmos in various ways. If one is looking for science, one should go to the Siddhantas. Moreover, it is not for Christians to find fault with the astronomy of the Puranas. "In your religion there is also a conflict between religion and science. In science it is acknowledged that the earth moves, but in (your) scripture the sun moves."[37]

---

34. Quoted in *Ibid.*, pp. 123-124.
35. Quoted in *Ibid.*, p. 127.
36. Quoted in *Ibid.*, pp. 131-32.
37. Quoted in *Ibid.*, pp. 133-134.

Summing Up

"Perhaps the most remarkable feature," concludes Dr. Young, "of Hindu apologetics within the *Mataparīksha* Context is not so much what it contained but what it lacked. A most curious absence is Jesus Christ, the figure in the very centre of Christianity. This lack of interest is especially surprising in view of the awe in which he was held even during the time of the *Mataparīksha* Controversy by Hindus such as Rammohun Roy and Keshab Chandra Sen in Calcutta and the reverential fascination of contemporary Hindus. To Somanatha, Harachandra and Nilakantha, Jesus was mostly a *deus ex machina* introduced by Christians to extricate their creator God from the dilemma he had brought upon himself by his *ex nihilo* creative act. They were not interested in his beatitudes... neither did they adopt him as an *avatara... or* identify his name with Krishna."[38] He is right when he identifies the role which, according to Hinduism, Jesus plays in Christian theology. Jesus is, in fact, no more than a *deus ex machina.* But, like most Christians, he is sadly mistaken when he says that contemporary Hindus had a fascination for the figure of Jesus. We shall see when we come to contemporary Hindu views of what they think of this myth.

Impact of *Matapar̄ikshā* Controversy on Muir

Muir revised his *Mataparīkshā* once more between 1852 and 1854 when he returned to Scotland. Then he gave up writing in Sanskrit and took to publishing Original Sanskrit Texts. "The materials in these still standard books never betray the author's original purpose in amassing them: to demonstrate that Christianity is rationally superior to Hinduism."[39] Sanskrit studies had a beneficial effect on Muir and he no more regarded the language as a "golden casket full of pebbles and trash." The contents of Sanskrit texts now so fascinated him that he endowed a Chair of Sanskrit Language,

38. *Ibid.*, p. 137.
39. *Ibid.*, p. 166.

Literature, Philosophy and Comparative Philology at the University of Edinburgh in 1862.

Muir also moved away from Evangelism and towards the Broad Church movement which thought that "Christian doctrine was sorely out of alignment with modern science." He now believed that "the Bible could not be exempted from the rigorous philological and historical analysis to which he had subjected the Vedas." In 1861, Muir published his *Brief Examination of Prevalent Opinions on the Inspiration of the Old and New Testaments*. He found that both had mutual discrepancies besides several other shortcomings. The introduction to this book was written by H. B. Wilson who said that it "clearly reveals the impact of the *Matapariksha* Controversy upon Muir's belief in the Bible." Muir himself wrote, "We may be assured that as Christianity comes into actual close contact with Orientals of acute intellects...it will be met with a style of controversy which will come upon some among us with surprise. Many things will be disputed which we have been accustomed to take for granted, and proofs will be demanded, which those who have been brought up in the external evidence school of the last century, may not be prepared to supply."[40]

Muir continued to believe for some time that Christianity had an immeasurably superior message in the sphere of morality. But after a few years he gave up that belief also "admitting that Christian virtues are neither superior to others nor *sui generis*." In 1879, he published *Metrical Translations from Sanskrit Writers* in which "didactic passages from Indian literature were juxtaposed with others from Biblical and classical Greek authorities." He concluded, "These sentiments and observations are the natural expression of the feelings and experiences of Universal humanity; and the higher and nobler portion of them cannot he regarded as peculiarly Christian."[41]

40. Quoted in *Ibid.*, pp. 167-68.
41. Quoted in *Ibid.*, pp., 168-69.

11

Encounter with Maharshi Dayananda

Compared to the intervals between the encounters narrated so far, the next encounter between Hinduism and Christianity took a much longer time in coming. John Muir had published the third and final edition of his *Mataparīkshā* in 1854. Before Hindu Pandits could take notice of any new points raised in it, the Great Rebellion broke out in 1857. Christianity was no longer a subject of public debate. It became one of the issues in the war that ensued.

After the Rebellion was suppressed, some military brass and civil administrators among the triumphant British were openly advocating the use of the sword in the service of the gospel. British military success had convinced many missionaries that God was also looking forward to a triumph of the "only true faith". Missionary language became more crude and missionary methods more criminal. Spokesmen for Hinduism, on the other hand, had to lie low. Even a mild criticism of the imperial creed was likely to be interpreted as attack on the imperial establishment. It was not easy to bridge the gulf which the war had created between the spokesmen for Hinduism and the standard-bearers of Christianity.

Hindu society was rescued from this slough of despondence by Maharshi Dayananda (1824-1883). Sir Syed Ahmad Khan rendered the same service to Muslim society. But there was a world of difference between the two in terms of approach. Sir Syed advocated servility to the British rulers and slurring over of differences between Christianity and Islam. Maharshi Dayananda, on the other hand, laid stress on *svadeshī* and *svarājya* and forcefully identified Christianity as a crude cult suited to savage societies.

Dayananda was deeply pained by the humiliations suffered by his people which were caused by the military government's repression and debased Christian harangues against Hinduism. His first priority was to restore his people's pride in their country and their cultural heritage. Centuries of foreign invasions had sunk Hindu society into poverty, sloth and defeatism. He mounted a frontal attack on some Hindu sects and systems of thought which he held responsible for this state of affairs. Hindu orthodoxy reacted by branding him as a hireling of Christian missionaries. There were certain strains in his thought which sounded like those of the alien creed. The missionaries themselves watched him for some time, for it appeared as if he was making things easy for them.

It was a matter of principle with Maharshi Dayanand not to speak on a subject which he had not studied and understood in advance. So he listened patiently to the Christian missionaries whenever and wherever they met him. There were seven such meetings between 1866 and 1873. He met J. Robson at Ajmer in 1866. During his stay in U.P. he had talks with J. T. Scott who presented to him the Christian position on various themes as well as a copy of the New Testament. In 1870, he met Dr. Rudolf Hoernle at Varanasi. On his way to Calcutta in 1872, he met the well-known Hindu convert Lal Behari De at Mughal Sarai and exchanged notes with him on the nature of sin and salvation. He discussed the nature of God with some English and native clergymen while he was staying at Bhagalpur in the course of the same journey.

By the time he reached Calcutta, the Brahmo Samaj had split into two. A minority consisting of those who wanted to retain their. Hindu identity had remained with the Adi Brahmo Samaj led by Debendra Nath Tagore and Rajnarayan Bose. The majority had walked away with Keshub Chunder Sen who had formed his Church of the New Dispensation (*Nababidhāna*) and started dreaming of becoming the prophet of a new world religion. Dayananda saw with his own eyes how infatuation with Christ had reduced Keshub Chunder to a sanctimonious humbug and turned him into a rootless cosmopolitan. He also witnessed how Debendra Nath Tagore was finding it difficult to retrieve the ground lost when the Adi Brahmo Samaj had repudiated the fundamental tenets of Hinduism — the authority of the Vedas, *Varṇāshrama-dharma,* the doctrine of rebirth, etc. The only consolation he found in Calcutta was a lecture, *The Superiority of Hinduism,* which Rajnarayan Bose had delivered earlier and a copy of which was presented to him.

Dayananda wrote a critique of Brahmoism soon after he returned from Calcutta. It was incorporated in Chapter XI of his *Satyārthaprakāsha* which was first published from Varanasi in the beginning of 1875. The Brahmos, he wrote, have very little love of their own country left in them. Far from taking pride in their country and their ancestors, they find fault with both. They praise Christians and Englishmen in their public speeches while they do not even mention the *rishis* of old. They proclaim that since creation and till today, no wise man has been born outside the British fold. The people of Aryavarta have always been idiotic, according to them. They believe that Hindus have never made any progress. Far from honouring the Vedas, they never hesitate in denouncing those venerable Shastras. The book which describes the tenets of Brahmoism has place for Moses, Jesus and Muhammad who are praised as great saints, but it has no place for any ancient *rishi,* howsoever great. They denounce Hindu society for its division in castes, but they never notice the racial consciousness which runs deep in European society. They claim that their search is only for truth, whether it is found in the Bible or the Quran, but they manage to miss the truth which is in their own Vedic heritage. They are running after Jesus without knowing what their own *rishis* have bequeathed to them. They discard the sacred thread as if it were heavier than the foreign liveries they love to wear. In the process, they have become beggars in their own home and can do no good either to themselves or to those among whom they live.[1]

The critique of Christianity which Dayananda had written at the same time and which formed Chapter XIII of the *Satyārthaprakāsha* was left out of the first edition by the publisher in Varanasi. He was a deputy collector in the British administration and thought it prudent not to annoy the missionaries. He dropped Chapter XIV also because it was a critique of Islam and he had many friends among the Muslim gentry of United Provinces. Dayananda himself became heavily preoccupied from 1876 onwards, first in the Punjab and then in Rajasthan. The Arya Samaj he had founded in 1875 was being placed on a firm footing. He had also several other major books in hand. It was only in 1882 that he undertook a revision of the *Satyārthaprakāsha* for its second edition. The copy which was sent to the press in instalments included the chapters on Christianity and Islam. He did not live to see the second edition which was published an year after his death in 1883. But by now the public at large had come to know his position vis-a-vis Christianity. His two dozen disputations with leading Christian missionaries, mostly in the Punjab, had left nobody in doubt that he had only contempt for the imported and criminal creed.

Dayananda did not know the English language, though he had tried to learn it at one time. He had to depend on Sanskrit and Hindi translations of the Bible done by some leading missionaries. Nor was he acquainted with the critique of Christianity which had, by his time, snowballed in the West. But his handling of the two Testaments shows that these were no disadvantages for him. His sense of logical consistency was quite strong. So was his humane and universal ethics derived from Vedic exegesis.

In his examination of the Old Testament, Dayananda concentrated his attention on the character of Jehovah. He found that Jehovah was not only blood-thirsty, vindictive and unjust

1. Translated and summarised from *Satyārthaprakāsha*, Delhi, 1975, pp. 330-335

but also extremely whimsical. Jehovah alone, said Dayananda, could choose a monster like Moses as his prophet and reveal a barbarous book like the Pentateuch. Dayanand summed up the character of Jehovah in a Sanskrit *śloka* which deserves to be quoted verbatim: *kshaṇe rushtaḥ kshaṇe tushṭaḥ, rushṭatushṭaḥ kshaṇe kshaṇe; avyavāsthitachittasya prasādo'pi bhayaṅkaraḥ* (He is displeased in this moment and pleased in the next. He takes no time in travelling from dissatisfaction to satisfaction. His mind is deranged. Even a favour from such a being is to be feared). Only a savage society, said Dayananda, can project and worship such a being. He is no better than a tribal leader who sides with his own gang even if it is unjust and cruel and who reserves his wrath for every other people even if they are just and compassionate. Such a being should not be sold as the father of all mankind. Nor can he be entrusted with presiding over the world.

Coming to Jesus, Dayananda found him wanting even as a man, not to speak of as the son of God. One of the ten commandments required him to serve his parents. But instead of doing so himself, he made others leave their parents in the lurch. It was quite fit that he called himself and his disciples the "fishers of men". They did ensnare ignorant people in the net of a creed they had invented to serve their own purpose. Their poor victims also left their homes. Jesus claimed that he had come with a sword and that his mission was to separate the son from the father, the daughter from the mother, the brother from the brother, and so on. The missionaries today are only following the example set by Jesus himself. They too entice ignorant people and separate them from their near and dear ones. The fraud, said Dayananda, should be exposed and the innocent people saved.

Coming to the miracles of Jesus, Dayanand said that the missionaries should be sent to share the company of sorcerers if they really believe in those miracles. The least they could do is to stop decrying the far more wonderful miracles mentioned in other people's books. Those who denounce other people's faith as false and sell their own falsehoods as truths, deserve to he described as dolts.

The apostles of Jesus, said Dayananda, were no better. One of them sold his teacher for thirty pieces of silver, others ran away when the teacher was caught and hanged. Yet we are told that these apostles will sit with Jesus on the day of judgment! Who could expect justice from judges of this kind? The missionaries are revealing the Christian standard of justice when they say that those alone who believe in Jesus will be saved and the rest sent to hell to rot there for ever. We see the same standard of justice in the Christian administration of this country. If a white man kills a black native, the murderer goes free! Moreover, is it not a mockery of justice that those who died soon after creation will have to wait to be judged in their graves for a long time while those who die close to the day of judgment will be judged very soon? All this proves that Christianity is the product of a primitive mind which lacks all sense of justice and fair play.

Jesus had said that the pieces of bread he was distributing were his body and the wine with which he was filling his disciples' cups was his blood. Can a civilized man speak this language? No one except an uncouth savage would command his disciple's to eat his flesh and drink his blood. Yet Christians applaud the practice as the Lord's Supper! Jesus was no lord. He was only a trickster. Had he had any spiritual powers, he would have saved himself from a shameful death. Nor was he a man of honour. Had he been one, he would have fought back and died a hero's death. Yet we are told that Jesus was the Only Son of God and that nobody can reach God except by his recommendation. God is thus reduced to the status of a servant of Jesus. The only conclusion we can draw from such statements of Jesus is that he was an impostor. He can be honoured only in a savage society. Hindus have a saying that even a castor plant can pass as a tree in a land devoid of real trees. Jesus can pass as God only among people who have never known what constitutes Godhood.

Dayananda was thus fully equipped when he met the missionaries in a public debate at Moradabad in 1876. "When the missionaries said that Christ was the only Saviour, the Swami retorted that Krishna and Shankaracharya were men of better calibre and that belief in salvation through the intercession of a man was worse than idolatry."[2] In March 1877, there was a three-cornered contest at Chandpur Mela between Dayananda on one side and Muslim *maulanas* and Christian missionaries on the other. The theme was creation and salvation. Dayananda demonstrated how the literalistic methods which the missionaries employed in attacking Hindu Shastras and saints, could be used more effectively in dealing with the Bible and Jesus.

He had to rush to the Punjab in the same month as a wave of conversions in that province had made the missionaries feel triumphant and alarmed Hindu society. He met a missionary at his first stop in Ludhiana and silenced him immediately when he criticised Sri Krishna. A poor Brahmana had found employment in the missionary establishment and started feeling inclined towards Christianity. Dayananda demonstrated to him the errors of the alien creed and the merits of his own ancestral faith. The Brahmana was saved, though the missionaries sacked him.

During his prolonged tour of the Punjab, Dayananda faced the missionaries in no less than twenty public debates in different towns. Luminaries like E. M. Wherry, W. Hooper, W. C. Forman and Robert Clark were pitted against him, but he silenced them all. His performance in public debates not only stopped further conversions but also gave birth to a new movement — *shuddhi* (purification) of those who had been enticed away from Hindu society at one time or the other. It sent a wave of consternation through the missionary circles and restored Hindu confidence. In days to come, the missionaries became more and more reluctant to meet Dayananda in open forums.

---

2. J.T.F. Jordens, 'Dayananda Sarasvati and Christianity', *Indian Church History Review*, June 1981, p. 37.

Dayananda's work was continued after his death by the scholars of the Arya Samaj. They challenged the missionaries again and again to show the worth of Christianity as compared to the *Vaidika Dharma*. That is a long story which needs to be told in greater detail, and we reserve it for some other time. For the present, we would like to draw attention to a significant fact. Compared to the South, the progress of Christianity has been very, very slow in the North. The credit for reversing the trend in the North goes overwhelmingly to the lead given by Maharshi Dayananda and the Arya Samaj he founded.

12

Second Encounter in Tamil Nadu

While a heated dialogue between Hinduism and Christianity was going on in the North, with Maharshi Dayananda in the forefront, another dialogue was taking shape in South India. Its centre was in the Cauvery Delta, particularly the District of Tiruchirapally, which had witnessed the first Hindu-Christian dialogue nearly 175 years earlier. This stronghold of Hindu learning had invited concentrated missionary attention since the days of the Portuguese pirates. One foreign mission after another had descended on the scene and mounted assaults on Hinduism in various forms. The flow of Christian finance and manpower from abroad was unceasing and in ever-increasing quantities, as it remains today.

We have seen already how the British sponsored Royal Danish Mission (RDM) had set up a station at Tranquebar in 1706 under the leadership of Ziegenbalg. The same mission set up another station at Tanjore in 1732. In the same year, the Society for Promotion of Christian Knowledge (SPCK) started operating from Tiruchirapally and Tanjore and the Society for Propagation of the Gospel (SPG) from Tiruchirapally. The region remained disturbed during the next fifty years due to English and French intrusions and internecine wars among native powers. But as soon as conditions became favourable for missionary work, the SPCK set up a second centre at Negapatinam in 1785. It was followed by the London Missionary Society (LMS) which started working from Kumbakonam in 1805. In 1825 the SPG set up a second station at Tanjore and the Church Missionary Society

(CMS) began work from Mayavaram. In 1833, the SPG set up its third and fourth stations at Tranquebar and Negapatinam. Meanwhile, the Methodists had arrived at Negapatinam in 1820 and Melanattam in 1830. They extended their activities to Mannargudi in 1835, Tiruchirapally in 1847, Tiruvarur in 1859, Karur in 1861 and Dharapuram in 1881. In due course, they were to become the dominant mission in this area. But other missions were not slack. In every case, the headquarters was only the starting point for reaching out into the interior. By the beginning of the ninth decade of the nineteenth century, the whole region had become honeycombed with mission stations.

The message which the missionaries carried everywhere was very simple. "That all might understand," reported Dr. Elijah Hoole in 1824, "I spoke plain and loud, and set forth the value of the soul and the importance of its salvation, and that my business was to raise concern for its welfare in all to whom I had access; that by sin we are exposed to death and hell, but that the one true God who had made us, not willing that any should perish, had found a ransom, at the same time giving us true Vedam, teaching us how to obtain and keep the blessings purchased for us by Jesus Christ; that the truths of the Bible were the object of faith, and the precepts of it the rule of practice."[1]

The missionary view of Hinduism had remained stable since the days of Ziegenbalg. According to a missionary report of 1821, "an immense population lies enslaved in the grossest darkness." Hindu temple worship was "calculated to corrupt the heart, to sensualize the mind and to lead to every description of vice." James Mowat, a Methodist missionary wrote in a letter to his headquarters at London, "I never had so plain demonstration of depravity heathenism binds upon its votaries in the shape of religion. The principal pagoda abounds with the most obscene and polluting representations,

1. Quoted by S. Manickam, 'Hindu Reaction to Missionary Activities in the Negapatam and Trichinopoly District of the Methodists, 1870-1924', *Indian Church History Review*, December 1981, p. 84.

and decidedly proves, if proof be necessary, how greatly this people need the hallowing light of Christianity." Naturally, the Hindus invited "tenderest pity" from the missionaries who used "all their means to rescue them from impending destruction."[2]

The missionaries were fully equipped to undertake the task. "They visited Choultries, market places and bathing tanks, preached in the city streets, under the shadow of idol-cars, under the canopy of country-trees, in the open square of the villages and other places where they could meet a good number of people. In the villages situated in the immediate neighbourhood of each mission station, the Gospel was preached very often, while places more remote were visited less frequently. These visits were generally undertaken by missionaries accompanied by a staff of native preachers. A tent would be pitched at a suitable centre and the whole neighbourhood would be visited. The singing of Christian lyrics and hymns accompanied by musical instruments soon attracted a congregation."[3]

A more effective weapon in the hands of the missionaries was their network of educational institutions. The South Indian Missionary Conference held in 1858 had left nobody in doubt as to what the missionary schools and colleges were trying to achieve. "The object of all missionary labour," proclaimed the Conference report, "is, or should be not primarily the civilization but the evangelisation of the heathen. Schools may be regarded as converting agencies, and their value estimated by the number who are led by the instruction they receive to renounce idolatry and make an open profession of Christianity; or the principal object aimed at may be the raising up of Native helpers in the Missionary work. Each of these is a legitimate object of Missionary labour and the value of any system of education as a Missionary Agency, must be tested by its adaptedness to accomplish one or more

2. *Ibid.*, p. 82.
3. *Ibid.*, p. 83.

of these objects."[4] The Bible was compulsory reading in all missionary schools and colleges. A Christian atmosphere was created all around by daily public worship, conversations and essay competitions on theological themes, textbooks which praised Christianity and denounced Hinduism, and employment of as many Christian teachers as possible.

Missionary education was showing results in Hindu homes. "The nation regrets," wrote *The Hindu Reformer and Politician* of Madras, "that money and trouble are spent on young men who return to their household with contempt for the practices and beliefs of their relations and ancestors, and the young men regret that their homes and community are attached to what seems to them to be foolishness and superstition."[5] Only a few Hindus who attended missionary schools and colleges came out unscathed. Among these few there could be found some spirited ones whose self-respect had been hurt by the missionary campaign against everything they cherished most and who harboured in their hearts nothing but contempt for Christianity. But they were helpless because the missionaries had a monopoly of educational institutions.

Hindus did try to meet the challenge with whatever means they could mobilise, but there was no question of matching missionary resources. Their ancient and catholic culture inhibited them from descending to the level of the missionaries, either in language or in demonstrativeness. The missionaries were aware of these tolerant and civilized inhibitions and were able to exploit them until the Theosophist leaders, Madame Blavatsky and Colonel Olcott, arrived on the scene in 1878. They knew Christianity A to Z and had witnessed its rapid decline in the West due to the humanist and rationalist examination of Christian scriptures, Christian institutions and Christian history. Their sympathies were entirely with Hinduism which they honoured as the most ancient and

4. Quoted in *Ibid.*, p. 91.
5. Quoted in *Ibid.*, p. 95.

profound religion known to man. From their headquarters at Adyar, Madras, they started publishing magazines which described the missionaries as "thickskulled, bigoted bloodhounds" and Christianity as "the purest idiotic trash." The Bible for them was "senseless gossip", "the most disgusting filth", and the "obscenest book ever touched by human hands." The captions and conclusions were backed by evidence from Christian sources. The writings of Bradlaugh, the anti-Christian British labour leader, also became known to the Hindus around this time.

The cumulative result of all these developments was the formation of the Hindus Tract Society in 1887. It had its headquarters in Madras. "We have painfully witnessed," said the founders of the Society, "the injustice done to our religion by foreign and native Christian missionaries. Baseless charges were trumped up against it; and relying on the poverty of the masses and the ignorance that generally prevails among them regarding their own religion and their own traditions, those apostles of foreign creeds have, by means fair or foul, attempted and even succeeded to some extent in leading our poor brethren astray. This aroused in us the instinct of self-preservation, and made us see the need of some organisation like the present one; and since the Christian propaganda could only thrive by destroying the better religion bequeathed to us by our ancestors, we were obliged to use against the missionaries their own weapons."[6] The Society soon engaged itself in publishing tracts, sending out Hindu preachers and arranging open air lectures.

We do not have any of the tracts before us, but a quotation from one of them published in 1888 shows the trend. "How many hundreds of thousands," it said, "have these padres turned to Christianity and keep on turning! How many hundreds of children have they swallowed up! On how many more they have cast their nets! How much evil is yet to come upon us by their means! If we sleep as heretofore, in a short

6. Quoted in *Ibid.*, p. 88.

time they will turn all to Christianity without exceptions, and our temples will he changed into churches... When Christianity has laid waste the land, will a blade of Hinduism grow there? When the flood rushes up over our heads it will be too late. It is because of our carelessness that these strangers insult our gods in the open streets during our festivals."[7] The names of the tracts which followed in 1889 are interesting — "Jesus only a man", "Are we also sinners?", "Is Jesus Christ God ?", "Supporting idol-worship and refuting Christianity", "Why should missionaries despise other religions without examining their own?", "History of Christianity", "Women's position according to the Bible", "The evil disguises and inconsistencies of the Salvation Army", "Jehovah's character according to the Bible".

The Hindu Tract Society was followed by the Advaita Sabha of Kumbakonam formed in 1895 and the Shaiva Siddhanta Sabha of South India formed in 1896. They met the missionary challenge in their own ways. More and more skeletons were brought out of Christianity's cupboard. The missionaries found it hard to hide them. They were being given a taste of their own medicine. Rev. Woodward had observed triumphantly in 1887 that "Christianity and Hinduism are in deadly conflict" and that "Hinduism is being put on its mettle."[8] By the end of the decade, his brethren in the various missions were moaning that Hinduism was shedding its traditional tolerance and showing hostility towards a sister religion!

---

7. Quoted in *Ibid.*, p. 89.
8. Quoted in *Ibid.*, p. 87.

13

Encounter with Swami Vivekananda

The spokesman for Hinduism in the next dialogue between Hinduism and Christianity was Swami Vivekananda (1863-1902). A significant feature of this dialogue was that, for the most part, it was held in the homelands of Christianity. Vivekananda not only carried the message of Hinduism to the USA and Europe during his two trips from 1893 to 1897 and from 1899 to 1900, he also turned the tide against Christianity in India so far as educated, upper class Hindus were concerned. Henceforward, Christian missionaries would reap a harvest either in the tribal belts or during famines when charitable organisations abroad and a patronising government at home placed funds for relief at their disposal and Hindu orphans fell into their hands in large numbers.

Vivekananda himself symbolised an irony of that system of education which had been deliberately designed to demolish Hinduism and promote Christianity. He was himself a product of that very education, but he turned against Christianity and in defence of Hinduism the knowledge and intellectual discipline which he had acquired as a student in a missionary college.

The renewal of East India Company's Charter in 1813 had opened the Company's dominions to Christian missionaries. It had also advised "introduction of useful knowledge and religious and moral improvement." A controversy had been going on ever since regarding the system of education suitable for India. The Orientalists among the British rulers advocated retention of the traditional Indian system. They were afraid that imparting of Western knowledge to natives would encourage them to claim equality with white men and demand democratisation of the administration. The Anglicists, on the other hand, were convinced that knowledge of Western literature, philosophy and science would wean Hindus away from their "ancestral superstitions" and draw them closer to the religion and culture of the ruling race.

Christian missionaries were, by and large, with the Anglicists. One of them had written in 1822 that, through Western education, Hindus "now engaged in the degrading and polluting worship of idols shall be brought to the knowledge of true God and Jesus Christ whom He has sent."[1] Missionaries felt immensely strengthened when Alexander Duff, an ardent advocate of Western education, reached Calcutta in 1830.

Alexander Duff was convinced that "of all the systems of false religion ever fabricated by the perverse ingenuity of fallen men, Hinduism is surely the most stupendous"[2] and that India was "the chief seat of Satan's earthly dominion."[3] He studied for some time the effect which Western education was having on Hindu young men attending the Hindu College and similar institutions which had come up in Calcutta and elsewhere in Bengal since more than a decade before his arrival. He came to the definite conclusion that Western education would make the Hindus "perfect unbelievers in their own system" and "perfect believers in Christianity." In an address delivered in 1835 to a General Church Assembly he proclaimed that knowledge of Western literature and science would "demolish the huge and hideous fabric of Hinduism" brick by brick till "the whole will be found to have crumbled into fragments."[4]

A Committee of Public Instruction had been set up by the

---

1. Quoted in R.C. Majumdar (ed.), *The History and Culture of the Indian People,* Volume X: *British Paramountcy And Indian Renaissance,* Part II, 2nd edition, Bombay, 1981, p. 36.

2. Quoted in *Ibid.*, p. 155.

3. Quoted in Sisir Kumar Das, *op. cit.*, p. 50.

4. Quoted in *Indian Church History Review,* December 1988, p. 90.

Government for recommending a suitable system of education. Alexander Duff had been made a member of the Committee in 1834. Next year, T. B. Macaulay, a member of the Governor General's Council, was appointed to preside over the Committee. He wrote a Minute on February 2, 1835, advocating Western education. There was a tie between the Anglicists and the Orientalists when the Minute came before the Committee on March 7. Macaulay used his casting vote and forced a decision. The Western system of education was adopted. In a letter written to his father in 1836, Macaulay predicated, "It is my firm belief that if our plans of education are followed up, there will not be a single idolator among the respectable classes of Bengal thirty years hence."[5]

The missionaries were trying hard to turn the dream into a reality. "And in what country," Louis Rousslet, a French traveller to India, wrote in 1876, "could such a spectacle be witnessed as that which met my eyes that day in this square of Benares? There, at ten paces from all that the Hindoo holds to be most sacred in religion, between the Source of wisdom and the idol of Siva, a Protestant missionary had taken his stand beneath a tree. Mounted on a chair, he was preaching in the Hindostani language, on the Christian religion and the errors of paganism. I heard his shrill voice, issuing from the depths of a formidable shirt-collar, eject these words at the crowd, which respectfully and attentively surrounded him— You are idolaters; that block of stone which you worship has been taken from a quarry, it is no better than the stone of my house. The reproaches called forth no murmur; the missionary was listened to immovably, but his dissertation was attended to, for every now and then one of the audience would put a question, to which the brave apostle replied as best as he could. Perhaps we should be disposed to admire the courage of the missionary if the well-known toleration of the Hindoos did not defraud him of all his merit; and it is this tolerance that most disheartens the missionary one of whom

5. Quoted in *Indian Church History Review,* December 1973, p. 187.

said to me — our labours are in vain; you can never convert a man who has sufficient conviction in his own religion to listen, without moving a muscle, to all the attacks you can make against it."[6]

The fond hope that Hinduism will die out before long was expressed by Richard Temple before a Christian audience in England in 1883. "India is like a mighty bastion," he wrote, "which is being battered by heavy artillery. We have given blow after blow, and thud after thud, and the effect is not at first very remarkable; but at last with a crash the mighty structure will come toppling down, and it is our hope that some day the heathen religions of India will in like manner succumb."[7] At the same time, he felt sure that Christianity had a very bright future in India. "But we are not chasing a shadow," he continued, "we are not rolling a Sisyphean stone, we are not ascending an inaccessible hill; or, if we are going up hill, it is that sort of ascent which soon leads to a summit, from which we shall survey the promised land. And when we reach the top what prospect shall we see ? We shall see churches in India raising up their spires towards heaven, Christian villages extending over whole tracts of country, churches crowded with dusky congregations and dusky communicants at the altar tables. We shall hear the native girls singing hymns in the vernacular, and see boys trooping to school or studying for the universities under missionary auspices. Those things, and many others, I have seen, and would to God I could fix them on the minds of my audience as they are fixed upon my own."[8] Vivekananda shattered the hope and the dream in the next decade.

Narendranath Datta, who was to become Swami Vivekananda, was born in 1863, the year when Alexander Duff left India well satisfied that Hinduism was on its way out

---

6. Louis Rousslet, *India and its Native Princes,* published in 1876, cited by Marie Louis Burke, *Swami Vivekananda in America,* Calcutta, 1958, p. 145.

7. Richard Temple, *Oriental Experience,* London, 1883, p. 142.

8. *Ibid.*, pp. 142, 143.

and Christianity on its way in, at least in Bengal. Macaulay's prediction appeared to be coming true as there had been a spate of conversions to Christianity. In 1832 Alexander Duff had converted Krishnamohan Banerji, a student of the Hindu College. Banerji, in turn, converted fifty-nine young men in the next few years. He became a minister of the Christ Church and was "instrumental in converting several hundred Hindus in Krishnanagar in 1839."[9] The other important converts made by Duff were K. C. Banerji and M. L. Basak in 1839 and Lal Behari De and Madhusudan Dutta in 1843.

Leaders of the Brahmo Samaj were perturbed and tried to arrest the trend. A meeting held in Calcutta in May 1845 and attended by a thousand Hindus, gave a call that Hindus should not send their boys to missionary schools and colleges. Some funds were collected for promoting Hindu educational and humanitarian institutions. But their efforts did not make much headway. The missionaries commanded much larger resources and official patronage. There was a craze for Western education which was thought best when imparted in missionary institutions. Moreover, the coming of Keshub Chunder Sen to the top in the Brahmo Samaj gave a further blow to Hinduism. He was infatuated with Jesus and the Bible and made hysterical outbursts in praise of both.

The only resolute defender of Hinduism in this intellectually hostile atmosphere was Bankim Chandra Chatterji. He was well-versed in Western literature and philosophy and his knowledge of Hindu Shastras and history was deep as well as discerning. He had come to the definite conclusion that Hindus had nothing to learn from Christianity. For him, Jesus was "an incomplete man", the Christian God "a despot" and the Christian doctrine of everlasting punishment "devilish". He repudiated the missionary accusation that Hinduism was responsible for corruptions that had crept into Hindu society in the course of history. "If the principles of Christianity," he wrote, "are not responsible for the slaughter of the crusades,

9. Sisir Kumar Das, *op.cit.*, 52.

the butcheries of Alva, the massacre of St. Bartholomew or the flames of the Inquisition... If the principles of Christianity are not responsible for the civil disabilities of Roman Catholics and Jews which till recently disgraced the English Statute Book, I do not understand how the principles of Hinduism are to be held responsible for the civil disabilities of the sudras under the Brahmanic regime. The critics of Hinduism have one measure for their own religion and another for Hinduism."[10] For him, Sri Krishna was the highest ideal, both human and divine. His novels and essays were creating a consciousness of pride in the Hindu heritage in that large section of Hindu society which had not yet passed under the spell of Jesus.

Narendranath was a student in Alexander Duff's General Assembly's Institution which later on became the Scottish Church College. He had made a wide study of Western literature, history and philosophy, had joined the Brahmo Samaj and come to share Keshub Chunder Sen's admiration for Jesus. But a turning point came in his life when he met Sri Ramakrishna Paramahamsa in November 1880. For the first time, he was face to face with a powerful expression of Hindu spirituality and that, too, in a simple man who had not been even to a primary school. His travels all over India after Sri Ramakrishna's death gave him further glimpses of how Hindu spirituality had percolated effortlessly to the lowest levels of Hindu society. He was thus in a position to process Christianity from the vantage point of a new vision. In the end, he frustrated Alexanders Duff's hope and falsified Macaulay's and Temple's prediction.

Sri Ramakrishna had never heard of Jesus till Jesus was thrust under his nose by those disciples who had come to him from the fold of Keshub Chunder Sen. Mahendra Nath Gupta, whose record of the talks of Sri Ramakrishna was to become famous as *The Gospel of Sri Ramakrishna* had an infantile fascination for Jesus and never missed an opportunity to

---

10. Quoted in Sisir Kumar Das, *op. cit.*, pp. 117-118.

compare the sayings and doings of Jesus with those of the Paramahamsa. But to the last, Jesus remained for Sri Ramakrishna only a figure which people belonging to a foreign religion worshipped as God. He did not have even a remote knowledge of the dogmas of Christianity. The only dogma, that of the original sin, which was presented to him by some disciples, he repudiated with repugnance. "Once someone gave me," he said on October 27, 1882, "a book of the Christians. I asked him to read it to me. It talked about nothing but sin." Turning to Keshub Chunder Sen, who was present, he continued, "Sin is the only thing one hears at your Brahmo Samaj too... He who says day and night, 'I am a sinner, I am a sinner', verily becomes a sinner... Why should one only talk about sin and hell, and such things?"[11] Thus he knocked the bottom out of Christianity. Without sin, there was no need for the atoning death of a historical saviour.

Vivekananda carried forward the same idea. "The greatest error," he said, "is to call a man a weak and miserable sinner. Every time a person thinks in this mistaken manner, he rivets one more link in the chain of *avidyā* that binds him, adds one more layer to the 'self-hypnotism' that lies heavy over his mind."[12] He compared the Hindu and Christian concepts of the soul. "One of the chief distinctions," he said, "between the Vedic and the Christian religion is that the Christian religion teaches that each human soul had its beginning at its birth into this world, whereas the Vedic religion asserts that the spirit of man is an emanation of the Eternal Being and has no more a beginning than God Himself."[13] He hailed humans as Children of Immortal Bliss —*amritasya putrāḥ* — in the language of the Upanishads. "Ye are the children of God," he proclaimed while addressing the Parliament of Religions, "the sharers of immortal bliss, holy and

11. *The Gospel of Sri Ramakrishna,* Volume 1, Madras, 1985, p. 138.

12. Quoted by M.M. Thomas, *The Acknowledged Christ of Indian Renaissance,* Second Edition, Madras 1976, p. 125.

13. *The Complete Works of Swami Vivekananda,* Calcutta, 1985, Volume VI, p. 85.

perfect beings. Ye divinities on earth — sinners! It is a sin to call man so; it is a standing libel on human nature. Come up, lions! and shake off the delusion that you are sheep; you are souls immortal, spirits free, blest and eternal."[14]

Vivekananda repudiated the idea of vicarious saving also. He proclaimed the Hindu doctrine that everyone has to work out his own salvation. "The Christians believe," he said, "that Jesus Christ died to save man. With you it is belief in a doctrine, and this belief constitutes your salvation. With us doctrine has nothing whatever to do with salvation. Each one may believe in whatever doctrine he likes; or in no doctrine. What difference does it make to you whether Jesus Christ lived at a certain time or not? What has it to do with you that Moses saw God in the burning bush? The fact that Moses saw God in the burning bush does not constitute your seeing him, does it?... Records of great spiritual men in the past do us no good whatever except that they urge us onward to do the same, to experience religion ourselves. Whatever Christ or Moses or anybody else did, does not help us in the least, except to urge us on."[15]

He was aware that the historicity of Christ had become highly controversial among scholars of the subject. "There is a great dispute," he wrote, "as to whether there ever was born a man with the name of Jesus. Of the four books comprising the New Testament, the Book of St. John has been rejected by some as spurious. As to the remaining three, the verdict is that they have been copied from ancient books; and that, too, long after the date ascribed to Jesus Christ. Moreover, about the time that Jesus is believed to have been born, among the Jews themselves there were born two historians, Josephus and Philo. They have mentioned even petty sects among the Jews but not made the least reference to Jesus or the Christians or that the Roman judge sentenced him to death on the cross. Josephus' book had a single line about it, which has

14. *Ibid.*, Volume I, p. 11.

15. *Ibid.*, Volume VI, pp. 98-99.

now been proved to be an interpolation. The Romans used to rule over the Jews at that time, and the Greeks taught them all arts and sciences. They have all written a good many things about the Jews but made no mention of either Jesus or the Christians." He also knew that doubts had been raised whether Jesus had himself said what was attributed to him in the gospels. "Another difficulty," he continued, "is that the sayings, precepts, or doctrines which the New Testament preaches were already in existence among the Jews before the Christian era, having come from different quarters, and were being preached by Rabbis like Hillel and others."[16]

The miracles of Christ also failed to impress Vivekananda. In fact, they repelled him strongly. "What were the great powers of Christ," he asked, "in miracles and healing, in one of his characters? They were low, vulgar things because he was among vulgar beings... Any fool could do those things. Fools heal others, devils can heal others. I have seen horrible demoniacal men do wonderful miracles. They seem to manufacture fruits out of the earth. I have known fools and diabolical men tell the past, present and future. I have seen fools heal at a glance, by the will, the most horrible diseases. These are powers, truly, but often demoniacal powers."[17]

And he was not at all interested in the historical Jesus. "One gets sick at heart," he said, "at the different accounts of the life of the Christ that Western people give. One would make him a great politician; another, perhaps, would make of him a great military general, another a great patriotic Jew; and so on."[18] What interested him was Jesus the spiritual teacher. He saw several points of strength in the life and teachings of Jesus, particularly the purity of heart and renunciation of worldly pursuits. "If you want to be Christian," he said, "it is not necessary to know whether Christ was born in Jerusalem or Bethlehem or just the exact date on which he pronounced the Sermon on the Mount; you only require to

---

16. *Ibid.*, Volume VII, pp. 370-71.
17. *Ibid.*, Volume IV, pp. 32-33.
18. *Ibid.*, p. 145.

feel the Sermon on the Mount. It is not necessary to read 2000 words on when it was delivered. All that is for the enjoyment of the learned. Let them have it; say amen to that . Let us *eat* the mango."[19]

Christians were welcome to seek salvation through Christ. According to Hinduism, everyone has the right to choose his own *ishṭadeva.* "It is absolutely necessary," he said, "to worship God as man, and blessed are those races which have such a 'God-man' in Christ; therefore, cling close to Christ; never give up Christ. That is the natural way to see God in man. All our ideas of God are concentrated there." Christians go wrong only when they insist that Christ is the only saviour. "The great limitation Christians have," he continued, "is that they do not heed other manifestations of God besides Christ. He was a manifestation of God; so was Buddha, so were some others, and there will be hundreds of others. Do not limit God anywhere."[20] Delivering a lecture on 'Christ, the Messenger', he quoted Sri Krishna, "Wherever thou findest a great soul of immense power and purity struggling to raise humanity, know that he is born of My splendour, that I am working there through him." And he advised the Christians, "Let us, therefore, find God not only in Jesus of Nazareth but in all the great ones that have preceded him, in all that came after him, and all that are yet to come. Our worship is unbounded. They are all manifestations of the same infinite God."[21]

Yet it was Christ that Vivekanand found missing from Christianity. He wondered which Church, if any, represented Christ. All churches were equally intolerant, each threatening to kill those who did not believe as it did.[22] The person of Christ rather than his teaching had become more important for Christianity. He had been turned into the "only begotten

---

19. *Ibid.*, Volume IV, pp. 25-26.
20. *Ibid.*, p. 31.
21. *Ibid.*, p. 152.
22. *Ibid.*, pp. 151-52.

son of God."[23] Christian baptism remained external and did not touch the inner man. It aimed at instilling some mental beliefs and not at transforming human behaviour. Most men remained the same after baptism as they were before it. What was worse, the mere sprinkling of water over them and muttering of formulas by a priest made them believe that they were better than other people. He quoted the Kenopanishad in this context: "Ever steeped in the darkness of ignorance, yet considering themselves wise and learned, the fools go round and round, staggering to and fro like the blind led by the blind."[24] The Eucharist was nothing more than the survival of a savage custom. "They sometimes killed their great chiefs," said Vivekananda, "and ate their flesh in order to obtain in themselves the qualities which made their leaders great." Human sacrifice was a Jewish idea which was borrowed by Christianity "in the form of atonement." This seeking for a "scapegoat" had made Christianity "develop a spirit of persecution and bloodshed."[25]

Christian missionaries were attacking the Puranas for containing passages which they considered somewhat obscene. Vivekananda had studied the Bible and knew that it contained a lot which was downright pornography. But he had his own method of exposing the Bible. "The Chinese," he wrote, "are the disciples of Confucius, are the disciples of Buddha, and their morality is quite strict and refined. Obscene language, obscene books, pictures, any conduct the least obscene — and the offender is punished then and there. The Christian missionaries translated the Bible into Chinese tongue. Now in the Bible there are some passages so obscene as to put to shame some of the Puranas of the Hindus. Reading those indecorous passages, the Chinamen were so exasperated against Christianity that they made a point of never allowing the Bible to be circulated in their country... The simple-minded Chinese were disgusted, and raised a cry, saying: Oh,

23. *Ibid.*, pp. 150-151.
24. *Ibid.*, Volume VIII, pp. 114-115.
25. *Ibid.*, Volume VII, pp. 71-71.

horror! This religion has come to us to ruin our young boys, by giving them this Bible to read... This is why the Chinese are very indignant with Christianity. Otherwise the Chinese are very tolerant towards other religions. I hear that the missionaries have printed an edition, leaving out the objectionable parts; but this step has made the Chinese more suspicious than before."[26]

The history of Christianity in Europe and elsewhere had simply horrified Vivekananda, as it does any person with any moral sensibility. Besides being blood-soaked, Christianity has been inimical to all free enquiry. "The ancient Greeks," wrote Vivekananda, "who were the first teachers of European civilisation attained the zenith of their culture long before the Christians. Ever since they became Christians, all their learning and culture was extinguished."[27] When he was passing by Egypt on his way to Europe, a missionary mentioned to him the miracles which, according to the Bible, Moses had performed in that country. But Vivekananda had read history. He knew the record of Christianity in Egypt. "Here was the city of Alexandria," he said, "famous all over the world for its university, its library, and its literati — that Alexandria which, falling into the hands of illiterate, bigoted and vulgar Christians suffered destruction, with its library burnt to ashes and learning stamped out. Finally, the Christians killed the lady savant, Hypatia, subjected her dead body to all sorts of abominable insult, and dragged it through the streets, till every bit of flesh was removed from her bones."[28]

Christianity had spread with the help of the sword since the days of Constantine and tried to suppress science and philosophy. "What support," asked Vivekananda, "has Christianity ever lent to the spread of civilisation, either spiritual or secular? What reward did the Christian religion offer to the European Pandit who sought to prove for the first time that

---

26. *Ibid.*, Volume V, p. 503.

27. *Ibid.*, Volume VII, pp. 361-361.

28. *Ibid.*, p. 347. He was referring to the doings of a mob of Christian monks led by St. Cyril in 391 AD.

the Earth is a revolving planet? What scientist has ever been hailed with approval and enthusiasm by the Christian Church?" Coming to modern times, Vivekananda found Christianity very vindictive: "The great thinkers of Europe — Voltaire, Darwin, Buchner, Flammarion, Victor Hugo and a host of others like him — are in the present time denounced by Christianity and are victims of vituperative tongues of its orthodox community."[29]

Christian missionaries in India were crediting to Christianity the rise and progress of modern Europe. This was a great falsehood. "Whatever heights of progress Europe has attained," continued Vivekananda, "every one of them has been gained by its revolt against Christianity — by its rising against the Gospel. If Christianity had its old paramount sway in Europe today, it would have lighted the fire of the Inquisition against such modern scientists as Pasteur and Koch, and burnt Darwin and others of his school at the stake. In modern Europe Christianity and civilization are two different things. Civilization has now girded up her loins to destroy her old enemy, Christianity, to overthrow the clergy and to wring educational and charitable institutions from their hands. But for the ignorance-ridden rustic masses, Christianity would never have been able for a moment to support its present despised existence, and would have been pulled out by its roots; for the urban poor are, even now, enemies of the Christian Church!"[30]

Christian missionaries were citing the prosperity of the modern West as an example of the superiority of Christianity. Much of that prosperity, however, was derived from the plunder of other peoples. "We who have come from the East," he said in an interview to a U.S. newspaper on September 29, 1893, "have sat here day after day and have been told to accept Christianity because Christian nations are

29. *Ibid.*, Volume V, p. 532. "The European Pandit" refers to Galileo on whom Mother Teresa frowns in our own times.

30. *Ibid.*, p. 533. The reference is to the working class movement in Europe.

the most prosperous. We look about us and see England, the most prosperous Christian nation in the world, with her foot on the neck of 250,000,000 Asiatics. We look back into history and see that the prosperity of Christian Europe began with Spain. Spain's prosperity began with the invasion of Mexico. Christianity wins its prosperity by cutting the throats of its fellow men. At such a price the Hindu will not have prosperity. I have sat here and heard the height of intolerance. I have heard the creed of Moslems applauded, when the Moslem sword is carrying destruction into India. Blood and sword are not for the Hindu, whose religion is based on the laws of love."[31] The newspaper described it as a "savage attack on Christian nations." Vivekananda had a lot to say on Western colonialism and the massacre of natives in America, Australia, New Zealand and elsewhere. But that is not the subject at present.

What really amazed him was the utter lack of logic in Christian propaganda. "On metaphysical lines," he wrote on his return to India in 1897, "no nation on earth can hold a candle to the Hindus; and curiously all the fellows that come over here from Christian lands have that one antiquated foolishness of an argument that because the Christians are powerful and rich and Hindus are not, so Christianity must be better than Hinduism. To which the Hindus very aptly retort that, that is the very reason why Hinduism is a religion and Christianity is not; because in this beastly world, it is blackguardism and that alone which *prospers*, virtue always suffers."[32]

Hindus have nothing to gain from Christianity as it is only a system of superstitions. Hindus should not get frightened when the missionaries threaten them with hell; in fact, hell is better than the company of a Christian missionary. "There came a Christian to me once," recalled Vivekananda, "and

31. *Ibid.*, Volume III, p. 474. The reference to Moslems found in *The Chicago Daily Tribune* has been omitted in this edition of *The Collected Works*. That is how the Ramakrishna Mission has "honoured" its founder!

32. *Ibid.*, Volume VI, pp. 390-91.

said, 'You are a terrible sinner.' I said, 'Yes, I am. Go on.' He was a Christian missionary. That man would not give me any rest. When I see him I fly. He said, 'I have very good things for you. You are a sinner and you will go to hell.' I said, 'Very good, what else?' I asked him, 'Where are you going?' 'I am going to heaven,' he answered. I said, 'I will go to hell.' That day he gave me up." If Christ could help people become good, why has he failed in the Christian countries where he has been worshipped for so long? "Here comes a Christian man," continued Vivekananda, "and he says, 'You are all doomed; but if you believe in this doctrine, Christ will help you out.' If this were true — but of course it is nothing but superstition — there would be no wickedness in Christian countries. Let us believe in it — belief costs nothing — but why is there no result? If I ask, 'Why is it that there are so many wicked people?' They say, 'We have to work more.' Trust in God but keep your power dry!"[33]

Criticism of Christianity, however, was not the primary task which Vivekananda had set for himself. He was first and foremost an exponent of Hinduism. He had to speak out about Christianity because the missionaries forced it upon him by their unceasing sallies against Hinduism. This is not the occasion even for a summary of his voluminous writings and speeches on various aspects of the subject he loved above all. We shall only touch a few points which he upheld against missionary attack.

The missionaries were highly critical of the Vedas which Hindus have always held in the highest esteem. Vivekananda upheld the Vedas as depositories of divine wisdom. For him, scriptures like the Bible and the Quran were *paurusheya*, that is, revelations accessible only to particular persons whose experience could not be verified by other people. The Vedas, on the other hand, were *apaurusheya*, that is, statements of spiritual truths which any seeker could verify by spiritual practice. "Although we find," he said, "many names, and

33. *Ibid.*, Volume VI, p. 132.

many speakers, and many teachers in the Upanishads, not one of them stands as an authority of the Upanishads, not one verse is based upon the life of any one of them. These are simple figures like shadows moving in the background, unfelt, unseen, unrealised, but the real force is in the marvellous, the brilliant, the effulgent texts of the Upanishads, perfectly impersonal. If twenty Yajnavalkyas came and lived and died, it does not matter; the texts are there. And yet it is against no personality: it is broad and expansive enough to embrace all the personalities that the world has yet produced, and all that are yet to come. It has nothing to say against the worship of persons, or Avataras, or sages. On the other hand, it is always upholding it. At the same time, it is perfectly impersonal."[34] Rather than processing the Vedas in terms of the Bible, as the Brahmos had started doing, the Bible should be weighed on the Vedic scale and prove its worth. "So far as the Bible," he observed, "and the scriptures of other nations agree with the Vedas, they are perfectly good, but when they do not agree, they are no more to be accepted."[35] On another occasion he said, "It is in the Vedas that we have to study our religion. With the exception of the Vedas every book must change. The authority of the Vedas is for all time to come; the authority of every one of our other books is for the time being. For instance, one Smriti is powerful for one age, another for another age."[36]

Brahmanas were the next target of missionary attack. Vivekananda stood by these custodians of Hinduism. "The ideal man of our ancestors," he said, "was the Brahmin. In all our books stands out prominently this ideal of the Brahmin. In Europe there is my Lord the Cardinal, who is struggling hard and spending thousands of pounds to prove the nobility of his ancestors and he will not be satisfied until he has traced his ancestry to some dreadful tyrant who lived on a hill and watched the people passing by, and whenever he had the

34. *Ibid.*, Volume III, p. 32.
35. *Ibid.*, p. 333.
36. *Ibid.*, Volume V, p. 125.

opportunity, sprang out and robbed them... In India, on the other hand, the greatest princes seek to trace their descent to some ancient sage who dressed in a bit of loin cloth, lived in a forest, eating roots and studying the Vedas... You are of the high caste when you can trace your ancestry to a Rishi, and not otherwise... Our ideal is the Brahmin of spiritual culture and renunciation."[37]

Another practice of Hinduism which the missionaries never missed pillorying was idolatry. "It has become a trite saying," said Vivekananda, "that idolatry is wrong and every man swallows it without questioning. I once thought so, and to pay the penalty of that I had to learn my lesson sitting at the feet of a man who realised everything through idols. I allude to Ramakrishna Paramahamsa. If such Ramakrishna Paramhamsas are produced by idol-worship, what will you have — the reformer's creed or any number of idols? I want an answer. Take a thousand idols more if you can produce Ramakrishna Paramahamsas through idol-worship, and may God speed you! Produce such noble natures by any means you can. Yet idolatry is condemned! Why? Nobody knows. Because some hundreds of years ago some man of Jewish blood happened to condemn it? That is, he happened to condemn everybody else's idols except his own. If God is represented in any beautiful form or any symbolic form, said the Jew, it is awfully bad; it is sin. But if He is represented in the form of a chest, with two angels sitting on each side, and a cloud hanging over it, it is the holy of holies. If God comes in the form of a dove, it is holy. But if He comes in the form of a cow, it is heathen superstition; condemn it! That is how the world goes. That is why the poet says, 'What fools we mortals be!'... Boys, moustached babies, who never went out of Madras, standing up and wanting to dictate laws to three hundred millions of people who have thousands of traditions at their back!"[38]

---

37. *Ibid.*, Volume III, pp. 196-197.

38. *Ibid.*, p. 218. "The reformer's creed" refers to the Brahmo Samaj and allied movements which had swallowed Christians polemics against Hinduism and tried to "purge" Hinduism of its "evils".

Lastly, he defended the caste system, the *bete noire* of all missionaries and reformers inspired by them. "Caste is a very good thing," he said. "Caste is the plan we want to follow... There is no country in the world without caste. In India, from caste we reach the point where there is no caste. Caste is based throughout on that principle. The plan in India is to make everybody a Brahmin, the Brahmin being the ideal of humanity. If you read the history of India you will find that attempts have always been made to raise the lower classes. Many are the classes that have been raised. Many more will follow till the whole will become Brahmin. That is the plan. We have to raise them without bringing down anybody... Indian caste is better than the caste which prevails in Europe or America. I do not say it is absolutely good. Where would you be if there were no caste? Where would be your learning and other things, if there were no caste? There would be nothing left for Europeans to study if caste had never existed. The Mohammedans would have smashed everything to pieces."[39] Caste was never a stationary institution. "Caste is continually changing," said Vivekananda, "rituals are continually changing. It is the substance, the principle that does not change... Caste should not go; but should only he readjusted occasionally. Within the old structure is to be found life enough for the building of two hundred thousand new ones. It is sheer nonsense to desire the abolition of caste. The new method is — evolution of the old."[40]

The great strength of Hinduism is that it does not lay down one dogma for everybody as is the case with Christianity and Islam. "The fault with all religions like Christianity," said Vivekananda, "is that they have one set of rules for all. But Hindu religion is suited to all grades of religious aspiration and progress. It contains all the ideas in their perfect form."[41] A universality which does not preserve individuality is false. "Individuality in universality," he continued, "is the

39. *Ibid.*, Volume V, p. 214.
40. *Ibid.*, p. 215.
41. *Ibid.*, Volume VI, p. 120.

plan of creation... Man is individual and at the same time universal. It is while raising the individual that we realise even our national and universal nature."[42] It is because of this spirit of universality that Hinduism has never been a persecuting religion: "You know that the Hindu religion never persecutes. It is the land where all sects may live in peace and unity. The Mohammedans brought murder and slaughter in their train, but until their arrival peace prevailed."[43]

The hour had come for Hinduism to carry its message abroad once more: "India was once a great missionary power. Hundreds of years before England was converted to Christianity, Buddha sent out missionaries to convert the world of Asia to his doctrine."[44] Vivekananda had himself given the lead. "I have planted the seed," he wrote from America to the Raja of Khetri, "in this country; it is already a plant, and I expect it to be a tree very soon. The more the Christian priests oppose me, the more I am determined to leave a permanent mark on their country."[45]

It was natural that Christian missionaries should notice Vivekananda the moment he spoke at the Parliament of Religions. They had never heard of the man before. They went into action in both the U.S.A. and India and were joined by some Brahmos of Keshub's school. "They joined," reported Vivekananda in a speech at Madras soon after his return, "the other opposition — the Christian missionaries. There is not one black lie imaginable that these latter did not invent against me. They blackened my character from city to city, poor and friendless though I was in a foreign country. They tried to oust me from every house and make every man who became my friend my enemy. They tried to starve me out." At the same time he hit out at the Brahmo leaders who saw salvation of India through Christianity. "I am sorry to say," added Vivekananda, "that one of my own countrymen took

42. *Ibid.*, p. 121.
43. *Ibid.*, Volume V, p. 190.
44. *Ibid.*, p. 191.
45. *Ibid.*, p. 91.

part against me in this. He is the leader of a reform party in India. This gentleman is declaring every day, 'Christ has come to India.' Is this the way Christ is to come to India?... Is that the lesson that he had learnt after sitting twenty years at the feet of Christ? Our great reformers declare that Christianity and Christian power are going to uplift the Indian people. Is that the way to do it? Surely, if that gentleman is an illustration, it does not look very hopeful."[46]

J. Murrary Mitchell who was working as a missionary in India at that time reacted adversely to reports about Vivekananda's popularity in the U.S.A. "We fear men from the East," he wrote, "mistook politeness with which they were received as guests for sympathy with their opinions. Very singular at all events, have been the accounts that have been transmitted to Asia regarding the effect of their exposition of the Oriental creeds. They had carried the war into the enemy's country, and were everywhere victorious." He selected P. C. Mozumdar as the real representative of "advanced and intelligent Hindus" at the Parliament of Religions. Mozumdar had said, "Representatives of all religions, may all your religions merge in the Fatherhood of God and the brotherhood of man, so that Christ's prophecy may be fulfilled and mankind become one Kingdom under God as our Father." Mr. Mitchell regretted that Mozumdar did not draw the applause he deserved because of his admiration for Christianity. "But Mr. Protap Chunder Mozumdar," he said, "seems to have made much less impression than a young man who has assumed the honorofic title of Swami — a step which Mr. [Keshub Chunder] Sen never ventured to take. Mr. Mozumdar appeared in plain Western dress, the Swami stood arrayed in all the colours of the rainbow. The ladies clustered around him in admiration."

What had hurt Mr. Mitchell the most was Vivekananda's denunciation of the doctrine of sin. "We need not dwell," he

46. *Ibid.*, Volume III, pp. 210-211. The gentleman was P. C. Mozumdar, a Brahmo leader who had also gone to the Parliament of Religions in Chicago, U.S.A.

mourned, "on the Swami's teaching. Let one specimen suffice." He quoted verbatim what Vivekananda had said when he hailed people at the Parliament as "sharers of bliss" and "divinities on earth." Vivekananda had hit Christianity in its solar plexus. How could Christianity thrive without selling sin? "We are truly sorry for the man," concluded Mr. Mitchell, "who can thus trifle with his hearers with deeply solemn questions."[47]

Vivekananda was rather mild in his criticism of missionaries when he spoke in the Parliament of Religions on September 29, 1893. "You Christians, who are so fond of sending out missionaries to save the soul of the heathen — why do you not try to save their bodies from starvation?... You erect Churches all through India but the crying evil in the East is not religion — they have religion enough — but it is bread that the suffering millions of burning India cry out for with parched throats... It is an insult to a starving people to offer them religion; it is an insult to a starving man to teach him metaphysics." He knew that missionaries were not preaching purely out of religious zeal, they had chosen the mission as a career and were paid for it. "In India," he said, "a priest who preached for money would lose caste and be spat upon by the people."[48]

He spoke in the same vein when he addressed the Parliament of Religions on October 11, 1893. "Christian missionaries," he said, "come to offer life but only on condition that the Hindus became Christians, abandoning the faith of their fathers and forefathers. Is it right?... If you wish to illustrate the meaning of 'brotherhood', treat Hindus more kindly even though he be a Hindu and is faithful to his religion. Send missionaries to teach them how better to earn a piece of bread, and not teach them metaphysical nonsense."[49]

But when he noticed that even his mild comments on

47. Sisir Kumakr Das, *op.cit.*, p. 141.

48. *The Complete Works*, Volume I, p. 20.

49. Quoted in Swami Jyotirmayananda, *Vivekananda, His Gospel of Man-Making*, Second edition, Madras 1988, p. 474.

missionary activities were received with great resentment in Christian circles, his tone became sharp. *The Detroit Free Press* dated February 21, 1894 reported a lecture which he had delivered on 'Hindus and Christians'. Coming to Christian missionaries he said, "*You train and educate and pay men to do what? To come over to my country to curse and abuse all my forefathers, my religion, and everything.* They walk near a temple and say, 'You idolators, you will go to hell.' But they dare not do that to the Mohammedans of India; the sword would be out. But the Hindu is too mild... And then you who train men to abuse and criticise, if I just touch you with the least bit of criticism, with the kindest purpose, you shrink and cry: 'Don't touch us; we are Americans. We criticise all the people in the world, curse them and abuse them, say anything, but do not touch us, we are sensitive plants?'... And whenever your ministers criticise us let them remember this: *If all India stands up and takes all the mud that is at the bottom of the Indian ocean and throws it up against the Western countries, it will not be doing an infinitesimal part of that which you are doing to us.* And what for? Did we ever send one missionary to convert anybody in the world? We say to you: 'Welcome to your religion, but allow me to have mine?'... With all your brags and boastings, where has Christianity succeeded without the sword? Show me one place in the whole world. One I say, throughout the history of the Christian religion — one; I do not want two. I know how your forefathers were converted. They had to be converted or killed; that was all. What can you do better than Mohammedanism, with all your bragging?"[50]

As he heard the malicious propaganda against Hinduism which missionaries were mounting in America and saw "their methods of raising money", he hit them hard. "What is meant," he asked, "by those pictures in the school-books for children where the Hindu mother is painted as throwing her children to the crocodiles in the Ganga? The mother is black

50. *Ibid.*, p. 486. Emphasis added.

but the baby is painted white to arouse more sympathy, and get more money. What is meant by those pictures which paint a man burning his wife at a stake with his own hands, so that she becomes a ghost and torments the husband's enemy? What is meant by the pictures of huge cars crushing over human beings? The other day a book was published for children in this country, where one of these gentlemen tells a narrative of his visit to Calcutta. He says he saw a car running over fanatics in the streets of Calcutta. I have heard one gentleman preach in Memphis that in every village of India there is a pond full of the bones of little children. *What have the Hindus done to these disciples of Christ that every Christian child is taught to call the Hindus vile, and 'wretches' and the most horrible devils on earth?* Part of the Sunday School education for children here consists in teaching them to hate everybody who is not a Christian, and the Hindu especially, so that from their very childhood they may subscribe their pennies to the missions."[51]

Vivekananda warned the missionaries about the effect which their propaganda was having on the moral and mental health of people who listened to them. "If not for the sake of truth," he said, "for the sake of the morality of their own children, the Christian missionaries ought not to allow such things going on. Is it any wonder that such children grow up to be ruthless and cruel men and women?... A servant-girl in the employ of a friend of mine had to be sent to a lunatic asylum as a result of her attending what they call here a revivalist-preaching. The dose of hell-fire and brimstone was too much for her."[52]

He saw how various missions were competing for collecting money and pouring calumny on each other. "Those to whom religion is a trade," he observed, "are forced to become narrow and mischievous by their introduction into religion

---

51. *Ibid.*, Volume IV, pp. 344-345. Emphasis added. Mother Teresa paints the same negative picture of India to her Western audiences. Only her language is less picturesque due to changed circumstances.

52. *Ibid.*, p. 345.

of the competitive, fighting and selfish methods of the world."[53] Having witnessed their ways, many educated Americans were losing respect for the missionaries. On the other hand, they were eager to listen to exponents of other cultures. "I have more friends," he wrote in a letter to India in 1895, "than enemies, and only a small number of the educated care about the missionaries. Again, the very fact of the missionaries being against anything makes the educated like it. They are less of a power here now, and are becoming less so every day."[54]

While Vivekananda caused a stir among the intellectual elite of America as was obvious from reports in the American press, the missionary circles were infuriated. "The Christian missionaries," wrote *The Indian Mirror* on June 23, 1897, "rage and fume over the success of Swami Vivekananda's mission in America. In its impotent fury, the *Missionary Review of the World* says that 'Swami Vivekananda is simply a specimen of the elation and inflation of a weak man over the adulation of some silly people. If America ever gives up Christ, it will be for the devil, not Buddha or Brahma or Confucius. It will be lapse into utter apostasy, unbelief and infidelity.' The writer, when penning these lines, was evidently under a fit of insanity brought on by the unlooked for spectacle of a Hindu preacher making disciples among American members of the Christian Church."[55]

The Christian Literature Society which had its headquarters in London and a branch in Madras published a book, *Swami Vivekananda and his Guru with letters from prominent Americans on the alleged programme of Vedantism in United States,* in 1897. The book was reviewed by *The Indian Mirror* which wrote, "The object of the first part of this book is to show that, on account of his *Shudra* birth and for his want of knowledge as well as on the part of his Guru, Vivekananda is not qualified for teaching the Vedanta; that

53. *Ibid.*, Volume V, p. 60.
54. *Ibid.*, p. 86.
55. Quoted in Swami Jyotirmayananda, *op. cit.*, p. 568.

he, in consequence of his doings, is not entitled to be called a 'Swami'; that Schopenhuer, the admirer of the Upanishads, was a bad man, and that Professor Max Muller (in connection with his opinion of Vedantic books) is a 'man having two voices'."

Rev. Dr. W. W. White, Secretary to the College Young Men's Christian Association of Calcutta, had written to "a number of ladies and gentlemen of America, mostly belonging to missions and educational institutions" in order to find out if there was any "likelihood of America abandoning Christianity and adopting... Hinduism... in its stead." The replies he had received were reproduced in the second part of the above-mentioned book. "Some of the writers say," continued *The Indian Mirror,* "that the Swami made no impression on the people, while some others asserted that the Swami may have made a few converts, but such converts were vaccilators and seekers of novelty. All of them consoled the enquirers with the assurance that Christianity had made a firm footing in America and there was no fear of its being supplanted by any other religion."[56]

Vivekananda had said again and again that he was not out to make any converts to Hinduism and that what he aimed at was the deepening and purification of Christianity which had been vulgarised by theologians and debased by missionaries. But the missionaries had their fears and wanted to be reassured that their citadel was not in danger of imminent collapse.

There was a corollary to Vivekananda's defence of Hinduism and critique of Christianity, particularly of the Christian missions. He called upon Hindu society to open its doors and take back its members who had been alienated from it by foreign invaders. Christian as well as Islamic missionaries were taking advantage of Hindu orthodoxy which was reluctant to receive those who had been forced or lured away from the Hindu fold but who were now ready to return to the faith

56. Quoted in *Ibid.*, pp. 591-592.

of their forefathers. Vivekananda viewed this orthodoxy as nothing but a blind prejudice induced by the Hindus' deep distrust of imported creeds. The distrust he regarded as well-founded but the prejudice against victims of force or fraud as unjustified. His thoughts on the subject were expressed in an interview he gave to the representative of the *Prabuddha Bharata*, a monthly magazine started by his disciples in Madras. The interview, published in the April 1899 issue of the monthly, deserves to be reproduced at some length:

> "I want to see you, Swami," I began, "on this matter of receiving back into Hinduism those who have been perverted from it. Is it your opinion that they should be received?"
>
> "Certainly," said the Swami, "they can and ought to be taken." He sat gravely for a moment, thinking, and then resumed. "Besides," he said, "we shall otherwise decrease in numbers. When the Mohammedans first came, we are said — I think on the authority of Ferishta, oldest Mohammedan historian — to have been six hundred millions of Hindus. Now we are about two hundred millions. *And then every man going out of the Hindu pale is not only a man less, but an enemy the more.*
>
> "Again, the vast majority of Hindu perverts to Islam and Christianity are perverts by the sword, or the descendants of these. It would be obviously unfair to subject these to disabilities of any kind. *As to the case of born aliens, did you say? Why, born aliens have been converted in the past by crowds, and the process is still going on.*
>
> "In my own opinion, this statement not only applies to aboriginal tribes, to outlying nations, and to almost all our conquerors before the Mohammedan conquest, but also to all those castes who find a special origin in the Puranas. I hold that they have been aliens thus adopted.[57]
>
> "Ceremonies of expiation are no doubt suitable in the

---

57. The Puranas mention a number of castes which arose after the descendants of *Pārasıkas* (Persians), *Yavanas* (Greeks), *Śakas* (Scythians), *Kushāṇas* and *Hunas*, etc., were integrated into Hindu society.

case of willing converts returning to their Mother-Church, as it were; but on those who were alienated by conquest — as in Kashmir and Nepal — or on strangers wishing to join us, no penance should be imposed."

"But of what caste would these people be, Swamiji?" I ventured to ask. "They must have some, or they can never be assimilated into the great body of Hindus. Where shall we look for their rightful place?"

"Returning converts," said the Swami quietly, "will gain their own castes, of course. And new people will make theirs. You will remember," he added, "that this has already been done in the case of Vaishnavism. Converts from different castes and aliens were all able to combine under that flag and form a caste by themselves, — and a very respectful one too. From Ramanuja down to Chaitanya of Bengal, all great Vaishnava teachers have done the same."

"And where should these new people expect to marry?" I asked.

"Amongst themselves as they do now," said the Swami quietly.

"Then as to names," I enquired, "I suppose aliens and perverts who have adopted non-Hindu names should be named newly. Would you give them caste-names, or what?"

"Certainly," said the Swami, thoughtfully, "there is a great deal in a name" and on this question he would say no more.

"But my next enquiry drew blood. 'Would you leave these new-comers, Swamiji, to choose their own forms of religious belief out of many visaged Hinduism, or would chalk out a religion for them?'

"Can you ask that?" he said. "They will choose for themselves. For unless a man chooses for himself, the very spirit of Hinduism is destroyed. The essence of our Faith consists simply in this freedom of the *Ishta*."[58]

---

58. Quoted in Ibid., pp. 587-88.

Vivekananda paid a second visit to the West from June 1899 to December 1900. During his stay in California in February-May 1900, he received a gift of 160 acres from one of his American admirers. The society which he had founded during his first visit for the propagation of Vedanta, had now a home in America. It was named the Shanti Ashram. This is not the place to tell the story of how the precedent set by Vivekananda was followed in years to come by many other Hindu missionaries. It should suffice to say that today no country in the West is without Hindu presence in some form or the other. Seekers in the West have become increasingly aware of the major schools of Sanatana Dharma — Yoga and Vedanta, Buddhism and Jainism, Shaivism and Vaishnavism, Shaktism and Tantra.

The impact of Vivekananda in his own country was far more momentous. He had taken over from where Bankim Chandra had left. Among the writers and thinkers of modern India, Bankim Chandra had fascinated him the most. During his lecture tour in East Bengal in 1901 he is reported to have advised Bengal's young men to "read Bankim, and Bankim, and Bankim again." Small wonder that Bankim's *Ānandamaṭha* inspired revolutionary organisations fighting for India's freedom and his *Vande Mātaram* became the national song par excellence when the awakening brought about by Vivekananda burst forth in a political movement soon after his death in 1902.

This was the Swadeshi Movement led by Sri Aurobindo. It was renascent India's first experiment in mass mobilization. Powerful *mantras* such as *svadeshī* and *svarājya*, first invoked by Maharshi Dayananda, came to the fore and fired the people's imagination. The struggle against Western imperialism in all its forms including Christianity became linked with the earlier struggle against Islamic imperialism. Maharana Pratap, Shivaji, Guru Govind Singh and Banda Bairagi resumed their full stature as national heroes after having suffered an eclipse in the national memory.

Sri Krishna gave a message to Sri Aurobindo while the

latter was incarcerated in the Alipore Jail. The Great Teacher of the Gita said, "Something has been shown to you in this year of seclusion, something about which you had your doubts and it is the truth of the Hindu religion. It is this religion that I am raising up before the world, it is this that I have perfected and developed through the Rishis, saints and Avatars, and is now going forth to do my work among the nations. I am raising up this nation to send forth my word. This is the Sanatan Dharma, this is the eternal religion which you did not really know before, but which I have now revealed to you... When you go forth, speak to your nation always this word, that it is for the Sanatan Dharma that they arise. It is for the world and not for themselves they arise. I am giving them freedom for the service of the world. When therefore it is said that India shall rise, it is the Sanatan Dharma that shall rise. When it is said that India shall be great, it is the Sanatan Dharma that shall be great. When it is said that India shall expand and extend herself, it is the Sanatan Dharma that shall expand and extend itself over the world. It is for the Dharma and by the Dharma that India exists. To magnify the religion means to magnify the country."[59]

The speech which Sri Aurobindo delivered at Uttarpara in 1909, soon after his acquittal in the Alipore Conspiracy Case, ended with the following words: "I say no longer that nationalism is a creed, a religion, a faith; I say that it is Sanatan Dharma which for us is nationalism. This Hindu nation was born with the Sanatan Dharma, with it it moves, and with it it grows. When the Sanatan Dharma declines, then the nation declines, and if the Sanatan Dharma were capable of perishing, with the Sanatan Dharma it would perish. The Sanatan Dharma, that is nationalism."[60]

The Brahmo Samaj which had been fascinated by Christianity could not remain unaffected. Rabindranath Tagore wrote his novel, *Gora*, in 1910. The following dialogue between

---

59. Keshavmurthi, *Sri Aurobindo : The Hope of Man*, Pondicherry, 1969, pp. 165-166.

60. *Ibid.*, pp. 167-68.

Suchitra, the heroine, and *Gora*, the hero, showed the new trend that had started emerging in Brahmoism:

> She put aside her shyness and said with simple modesty, "I have never before thought about my country so greatly and so truly. But one question I will ask: What is the relation between country and religion? Does not religion transcend country?"
>
> He replied, "That which transcends country, which is greater than country, can only reveal itself through one's country. God has manifested his one eternal nature in just such a variety of forms... I can assure you that through the open sky of India you will be able to see the sun — therefore there is no need to cross the ocean and sit at the window of a Christian church."
>
> "You mean to say that for India there is a special path leading to God? What is this speciality?" asked Suchitra.
>
> "The speciality is this," replied Gora, "it is recognised that the Supreme Being who is without definition is manifest within limits — the endless current of minute and protracted, subtle and gross, is of Him. He is at one and the same time with endless attributes and without attributes; of infinite forms and formless. In other countries they have tried to confine God with some one definition. In India no doubt there have also been attempts to realise God in one or other of his special aspects, but these have never been looked upon as final, nor any of them conceived to be the only one. No Indian devotee has ever failed to acknowledge that God in His infinity transcends the particular aspect which may be true for the worshipper personally."[61]

Later on in this novel Rabindranath rejects Christianity in more clear terms:

> Suchitra had been listening with her head bowed, but now she lifted her eyes and asked, "Then what do you tell

61. Rabindranath Tagore, *Gora*, translated into English, Calcutta, 1961 impression, p. 103.

me to do?"

"I have nothing more to say," answered Gora, "only this much I would add. You must understand that the Hindu religion takes in its lap, like a mother, people of different ideas and opinions, in other words, the Hindu religion looks upon man as man and does not count him as belonging to a particular party. It honours not only the wise but the foolish also and it shows respect not merely to one form of wisdom but to wisdom in all its aspects. *Christians do not want to acknowledge diversity; they say that on one side is Christian religion and on the other eternal destruction, and between these two there is no middle path. And because we have studied under these Christians we have become ashamed of the variety that is there in Hinduism.* We fail to see that through this diversity Hinduism is coming to realise the oneness of all. Unless we can free ourselves from this whirlpool of Christian teaching we shall not become fit for the glorious truths of Hindu religion."[62]

A new spirit was abroad. The English educated intelligentsia which had turned away from Hinduism, particularly in Bengal, was acquiring respect for it at a deeper level. The missionary machine had to change gear and turn towards the tribal areas.

It is an altogether different story that the Ramakrishna Mission which Swami Vivekananda had founded for the defence and spread of Hinduism, was taken over by the disciples of Keshub Chunder Sen. It was not long before an authoritative biography of Sri Ramakrishna depicted him not as a giant Hindu saint but as a unique *sādhaka* who had met and absorbed into himself both Jesus and Muhammad! The next inevitable step was to present Sri Ramakrishna as a synthesiser of Hinduism, Islam, and Christianity. Finally, the Mission was hailing Sri Ramakrishna as the founder of a new religion — Ramakrishnaism — which was "far

62. *Ibid.*, p. 296. Emphasis added.

superior" to Hinduism. Sri Ramakrishna, according to the Mission mystique, was the "first saint" (or prophet, if you please) in human history who had "demonstrated practically" that Hinduism and Christianity and Islam were only different paths for reaching the same spiritual goal!

It is useless to tell the salesmen of Ramakrishnaism that this country has known thousands of saints like Sri Ramakrishna, that he would have remained unknown like most of them if Vivekananda had not made him famous, and that Vivekananda who was his dearest disciple had viewed Islam and Christianity not as religions but as doctrines of the sword. The Mission has become a world-wide network, and a wealthy institution patronized by the high and the mighty, not only in India but also abroad. And the Mission knows that Hindus can always be taken for granted. The Mission is neither the first nor the last to fatten with the help of Hindu society and then render service to the enemies of that society. The story will be repeated till Hindu society learns how to deal with turn-coats and traitors.

14

Encounter with Mahatma Gandhi

The next dialogue between Hinduism and Christianity was the longest in duration and the richest in content. The spokesman for Hinduism was Mahatma Gandhi. Christianity was represented by many men and women from India and abroad. Some of them occupied high positions in the world-wide Christian mission.

The dialogue started in 1893 when Mohandas Karamchand Gandhi reached South Africa as a barrister and discovered that the Christians who befriended him were looking forward to his conversion. It ended on December 24, 1947 when Mahatma Gandhi, the father figure in independent India, offered Christmas greetings to Christians in India and abroad, wishing them well and hoping that they "will pursue the path of sacrifice and martyrdom shown by Jesus Christ." At the same time he asked his Christian countrymen to shed fears about their future in independent India.

Gandhiji was brought up in an atmosphere of religious tolerance. He had accompanied his mother and father to the Vaishnava Haveli and the temples of Shiva and Rama. Everywhere they worshipped with equal reverence. Jain monks "would pay frequent visits to my father" and talk with him "on subjects religious and mundane." So did Muslim and Parsi friends of his father who "listened to them with respect, and often with interest."[1]

Small wonder that when he saw the behaviour of Christian missionaries for the first time, he "developed a sort of dislike"

1. *The Collected Works of Mahatma Gandhi*, Volume 39, New Delhi, 1970, p. 32.

for Christianity. He was a school student at Rajkot. "In those days," he writes, "Christian missionaries used to stand in a corner near the high school and hold forth, pouring abuse on Hindus and their gods. I could not endure this. I must have stood there to hear them once only, but that was enough to dissuade me from repeating the experience." His dislike of Christianity deepened when he heard about the doings of a "well-known Hindu" convert. "It was the talk of the town," he continues, "that, when he was baptised, he had to eat beef and drink liquor, that he also had to change his clothes and that thenceforward he began to go about in European costume including a hat. These things got on my nerves. Surely, thought I, a religion that compelled one to eat beef and drink liquor and change one's own clothes did not deserve the name. I also heard the news that the new convert had already begun abusing the religion of his ancestors, their customs and their country. All these things created in me a dislike for Christianity."[2]

By the time Gandhiji read the Bible for the first time, he had developed an eager and reflective interest in religion. Towards the end of his second year in England, he read Sir Edwin Arnold's *The Song Celestial* and *The Light of Asia*. The first work is the famous English translation of the Gita. The second narrates the life of the Buddha. The Gita "struck me as one of priceless worth." As regards the life of the Buddha, "once I had begun it I could not leave off." Around the same time, he read Madame Blavatsky's *The Key to Theosophy* which "disabused me of the notion fostered by missionaries that Hinduism was rife with superstition." So he welcomed a copy of the Bible sold to him by a Christian friend who was a vegetarian and who did not drink. "I began reading it," writes Gandhiji, "but I could not possibly read through the Old Testament. I read the book of Genesis, and the chapters that followed invariably sent me to sleep. But just for the sake of being able to say that I had read it, I plodded through the

2. *Ibid.*, p. 33.

other books with much difficulty and without the least interest or understanding. I disliked reading the book of Numbers."[3]

The New Testament, however, "produced a different impression, especially the Sermon on the Mount which went straight to my heart." This first impression proved to be his last also. In years to come, he continued to identify "true Christianity" with the Sermon on the Mount and exclude everything else in Christian theology to the chagrin of Christian missionaries who could neither disown the Sermon nor stop at it. "My young mind," continues Gandhiji, "tried to unify the teaching of the *Gita, The Light of Asia* and the Sermon on the Mount. That renunciation was the highest form of religion appealed to me greatly."[4]

Gandhiji came in contact with some believing Christians during his stay in South Africa and had an opportunity to reflect on Christian theology. Mr. A. W. Baker, the attorney of Gandhiji's client in Pretoria "was a staunch lay preacher" and "one of the Directors of the South Africa General Mission." He showed interest in the religion of Gandhiji who confessed that though he was a Hindu, he did not "know much of Hinduism" and "knew less of other religions." Mr. Baker invited Gandhiji to the daily meetings of his missionary co-workers and promised to give him "some religious books to read."[5] Gandhiji was somewhat intrigued and asked himself, "What... can be the meaning of Mr. Baker's interest in me? What shall I gain from his religious co-workers? How far should I undertake the study of Christianity? How was I to obtain literature about Hinduism? And how was I to understand Christianity in its proper perspective without thoroughly knowing my own religion?" He came to the conclusion that "I should make a dispassionate study of all that came to me, and deal with Baker's group as God might guide me" and that "I should not think of embracing another religion before I

3. *Ibid.*, p. 61.
4. *Ibid.*
5. *Ibid.* p. 100.

had fully understood my own."[6]

He started attending the meetings where the "prayers did not last for more than five minutes." He was introduced to Mr. Baker's "co-workers" one of whom was Mr. Coates who "loaded me with books, as it were." The books were a mix of the stale and the stimulating. At the end, "the arguments in proof of Jesus being the only incarnation of God and the Mediator between God and man left me unmoved." But Mr. Coates "was not the man to accept defeat." One day, "He saw, round my neck, the Vaishnava necklace of Tulasi-beads" and said, "come, let me break the necklace." Gandhiji told him, "No, you will not. It is a sacred gift from my mother."[7] Mr. Coates "could not appreciate my argument, as he had no regard for my religion." He was convinced that "salvation was impossible for me unless I accepted Christianity which represented the truth, and that my sins would not be washed away except by intercession of Jesus, and that all good works were useless."[8]

Another Christian group which Gandhiji met at this time was that of the Plymouth Brethren who proclaimed that "as we believe in the atonement of Jesus, our own sins do not bind us."[9] One of the Brothers "proved as good as his word." He "committed transgressions" and remained "undisturbed by the thought of them." Gandhiji was relieved to know that "all Christians did not believe in such a theory of atonement" and assured Mr. Coates that "the distorted belief of a Plymouth Brother could not prejudice me against Christianity."[10]

By now Mr. Baker "was getting anxious about my future."[11] He took Gandhiji to the Wellington Convention of Protestant Christians. Gandhiji's colour created some problems for him in the hotel and the dining room but Mr. Baker "stood

6. *Ibid.*, p. 101.
7. *Ibid.*, p. 102.
8. *Ibid.*, p. 103.
9. *Ibid.*
10. *Ibid.*, p. 104. This was, however, the most logical and legitimate interpretation of the Christian doctrine.
11. *Ibid.*, p. 111.

by the guests of a hotel." The Convention lasted for three days and Gandhiji "appreciated the devoutness of those who attended it." But he "saw no reason for changing my belief in my religion." He found it impossible "to believe that I could go to heaven or attain salvation only by becoming a Christian." He made a frank confession of his doubts to his Christian friends who "were shocked."[12]

The Convention helped Gandhiji to make up his mind about Christianity. He adhered to these views for the rest of his life. "My difficulties," he writes, "lay deeper. It was more than I could believe that Jesus was the only incarnate son of God, and that only he who believed in him would have everlasting life. If God could have sons, all of us were his sons. If Jesus was like God or God Himself, then all men were like God and could be God Himself. My reason was not ready to believe literally that Jesus by his death and by his blood redeemed the sins of the world. Metaphorically there might be some truth in it. Again, according to Christianity only human beings had souls, and not other living beings, for whom death meant complete extinction, while I held a contrary view. I could accept Jesus as a martyr, as an embodiment of sacrifice and a divine teacher, but not as the most perfect man ever born. His death on the cross was a great example to the world, but that there was anything like a mysterious or miraculous virtue in it my heart could not accept. The pious lives of Christians did not give me anything that the lives of men of other faiths had failed to give. I had seen in other lives just the same reformation that I had heard of among the Christians. Philosophically there was nothing extraordinary in Christian principles. From the point of view of sacrifice, it seemed that the Hindus greatly surpassed Christians. It was impossible for me to regard Christianity as a perfect religion or the greatest of all religions."[13]

At the same time, Gandhiji felt greatly dissatisfied with

12. *Ibid.*, p. 112.
13. *Ibid.*, pp. 112-13.

Hinduism as he saw it. He could not understand how "untouchability could be a part of Hinduism." As not only his Christian but also Muslim friends were trying to convert him, he wanted to know more about Hinduism. He presented his problem to Raychandbhai, his mentor in India, and "corresponded with other religious authorities in India."[14] Raychandbhai assured him that "no other religion has the subtle and profound thought of Hinduism, its vision of the soul, or its charity." Thus Gandhiji "took a path which my Christian friends had not intended for me."[15]

He continued to read books written by Christians and also to correspond with Christian friends in England. He found that some exponents of Christianity did not adhere to Christian theology and took a broader and deeper view of Jesus and his message. He started moving away from Christianity as preached by the missionaries. The missionaries, however, refused to give him up as a bad job and when he moved to Durban, "Mr. Spencer Walton, the head of the South Africa General Mission, found me out."[16]

The approach this time was softer. Mr. Walton never asked Gandhiji to embrace Christianity. He became Gandhiji's friend and introduced him to Mrs. Walton. Gandhiji liked them both for their "humility, preserverance and devotion to work."[17] At the suggestion of some other Christian friends, Gandhiji started attending the Wesleyan Church every Sunday. But he found the sermons "uninspiring" and the congregation "worldly-minded people who went to church for recreation and in conformity to custom."[18] On occasions, he fell into an "involuntary doze" and felt ashamed. He was relieved when he found that his neighbours in the Church "were in no better case."[19] Finally he gave up attending the Church.

Gandhiji had a standing invitation from a Christian family

14. *Ibid.*, 113.
15. *Ibid.*, p. 114.
16. *Ibid.*, p. 130.
17. *Ibid.*, p. 131.
18. *Ibid.*, pp. 131-32.
19. *Ibid.*, p. 132.

to join them for lunch every Sunday. "Once we began to compare," he writes, "the life of Jesus with that of Buddha. 'Look at Gautama's compassion,' said I. 'It was not confined to mankind, it was extended to all living beings. Does not one's heart overflow with love to think of the lamb joyously perched on his shoulders? One fails to notice this love for all living beings in the life of Jesus.' The comparison pained the lady." The contact came to an end soon after because Gandhiji tried to teach her son the superiority of vegetarian food over meat-eating. The lady felt dismayed and told Gandhiji that "my boy is none the better for your company." He took the hint and stopped the visits.[20]

Gandhiji had become a famous man by the time he left South Africa for good in 1915 and started working in India. He had not yet emerged as the Mahatma, nor risen to the supreme command of the national movement for freedom from British rule. Christian missionaries regarded him as a friend because of his proclaimed admiration for Jesus. Early in 1916 he was invited to address a Missionary Conference at Madras on the subject of Swadeshi. After having defined Swadeshi as "that spirit in us which restricts us to the use and service of our immediate surroundings to the exclusion of the more remote", he said that "in order to satisfy the requirements of the definition, I must restrict myself to my ancestral religion."[21] He advised the missionaries to "serve the spirit of Christianity better, by dropping the goal of proselytising but continuing their philanthropic work." He told them that Christ's message, "Go Ye Unto All the World", had been "narrowly interpreted" and that "in every case, a conversion leaves a sore behind it." At the same time he held up Hinduism as the embodiment of the Swadeshi spirit. That was the secret, he said, of its being the most tolerant religion.[22]

20. *Ibid.*

21. *Ibid.,*Volume 13, New Delhi, 1979 reprint, p. 219.

22. *Ibid.*, p. 220. The passege (Mark 16.15) is now recognised as an interpolation by Biblical scholarship. It is not found in "some manuscripts and ancient translations" of the gospel.

Christian missionaries had been propagating that the Reform Movement in Hinduism as well as Gandhiji's doctrine of satyagraha were influenced by the principles of Christianity. The proposition was presented to Gandhiji by Rev. Wells Branch in the latter's letter dated May 9, 1919. He wrote back on May 12 that "I do not think either has anything to do with Christian teaching." He held "modern civilisation and modern education" as responsible for the Reform Movement. As to satyagraha, he said that "it is an extended application of the ancient teaching."[23] In the same letter he rejected the "exclusive divinity of Jesus" while praising the Sermon on the Mount. Rev. Branch had come to believe that there were many "secret followers of Jesus" in India who were not coming out in the open because they feared persecution from Hindu society. Gandhiji replied, "I have moved among thousands upon thousands of Indians but I have not found any secret followers of Jesus."[24]

Thus by the time M. K. Gandhi emerged as Mahatma Gandhi and took command of the national movement for freedom in 1920, he had studied and reflected upon all aspects of Christianity and formed his views on them. He had watched the working of Christian missions from close quarters and understood their role vis-a-vis Hindu religion and culture. In years to come he would identify himself as a *sanātanī* Hindu fully satisfied with his ancestral faith. He would explain and elaborate his views on Christianity and Christian missions and defend the principles and practices of Hinduism which the missionaries held in contempt. But because he admired Jesus as a great teacher, he would continue to arouse fond hopes in Christian hearts.

Meanwhile, he had changed from a loyal citizen of the British Empire to its uncompromising opponent. The weapon he forged for fighting the British Raj in India was non-violent non-cooperation. The struggle for freedom was combined with a programme for socio-economic reconstruction in

23. *Ibid.*, Volume 15, New Delhi, 1979 reprint, p. 304.
24. *Ibid.*, p. 305.

which the abolition of untouchability was a major plank. His campaigns involved him in conflict not only with the British Government of India but also with Hindu orthodoxy.

While he was in Sabarmati Jail he was interviewed by a representative of *The Manchester Guardian* some time before March 18, 1922. *The Hindu* of Madras published the interview on August 15, 1922. The interviewer tried to pin him down by saying that non-cooperation was "contrary to Christ's teaching." Gandhiji replied, "Not being a Christian I am not bound to justify my action by Christian principles."[25]

While he was still in jail, the *Young India* of February 8, 1923 published an interesting item which deserves to be reproduced in full:

> Rev. Dr. Macarish, elected head of the Presbyterian Church Synod which recently met at Orillia in Canada referred to the incidental commercial advantages of religious missions in the following words:
>
> "One cry in the country had long been markets, wider markets, and since the introduction of the Fordney Bill, that cry has been louder and more insistent than ever. If the farmers and manufacturers desire to create a market, they would do well to get in touch with foreign missions, and we are assured that it would not be long till they received their money back with liberal interest.
>
> "Although the missionary went to the foreign fields to win souls for Jesus, the results of his labours also meant the extension of commerce. Trade would follow the banner of the Cross, as readily as it would the Union Jack, the Stars and Stripes, or any of the other national emblems, and usually it cost a good deal less.
>
> "It cost British Government £225,000,000 to make the Union Jack float over Pretoria; yet it is doubtful if the South African war did as much to promote trade, as missions there had previously done. In the past, the missionaries had been the best advertisers of heathen

25. *Ibid.*, Volume 23, New Delhi, 1967, p. 104.

countries. Dr. John G. Paton did more to advertise the South Sea Islands than the sandal-wood traders ever did, and who ever did more to advertise Africa than Livingston?

"Fifty years ago, it was said that when a missionary had been abroad for twenty years, he was worth £50,000 to British commerce; and it was probably not extravagant to say that one of our missionaries in India or China to-day was worth a similar sum to any great industrial centre in this country."

Gandhiji had launched his programme for abolition of untouchability soon after he came out of jail. He had made it clear to all concerned that untouchability was a Hindu problem and that Hindus alone should participate in the movement for its abolition. But Christian missions tried to jump into the fray. He received a letter from Mr. George Joseph of Travancore asking whether he could join the satyagraha at Vykom which was going on for securing to the Harijans the right to travel on certain roads and enter Hindu temples for worship. Gandhiji advised him on April 6, 1924 to "let the Hindus do the work" and referred him to the Nagpur resolution of the Congress which "calls upon the Hindu members to remove the curse of untouchability." At the same time he drew Mr. Joseph's attention to the untouchability practised by the Syrian Christians.[26] He also told the Hindus not to seek the support of non-Hindus in the Vykom satyagraha. "If you are fighting as an enlightened against the bigoted Hindu," he wrote to K. Madhavan Nair on May 6, 1924, "it is your bounden duty not only not to seek but respectfully to reject all support from non-Hindus."[27] He was aware that Christian missionaries were not above exploiting the situation to the disadvantage of Hinduism.

A "retired Indian police officer" in England wrote in *The*

---

26. *Ibid.*, p. 391. Non-Hindus continue to meddle in Hindu affairs with the tacit support of secular editors and the Government, whether it concerns Sati or temple-entry.

27. *Ibid.*, p. 545.

Manchester Guardian that Christian missionaries had done commendable work for the uplift of Harijans. Gandhiji thought that the article deserved his comment. He wrote a Note under the heading 'Ignorance' in the *Young India* of July 13, 1924. "The writer brings up for commendation," he said, "the Christian work among untouchables; I must not enter into the merits of Christian work in India. The indirect influence of Christianity has been to quicken Hinduism into life. The cultured Hindu society has admitted its grievous sin against the untouchables. But the effect of Christianity upon India in general must be judged by the life lived in our midst by the average Christian and its effect upon us. I am sorry to have to record my opinion that it has been disastrous. It pains me to have to say that the Christian missionaries as a body, with honourable exceptions, have actively supported a system which has impoverished, enervated and demoralised a people considered to be among the gentlest and the most civilized on earth."[28]

Gandhiji had the leisure to read and look through a large number of books, mostly on religion, while he was in Sabarmati Jail. Some of these books had been sent to him by Christians in India and abroad, who wanted to enlighten him about Christianity. Commenting on these books in the *Young India* of September 4, 1924, he wrote, "I must confess that whilst I recognized their kind motive, I could not appreciate the majority of books they sent. I wish I could say something of their gifts that would please them. But that would not be fair or truthful if I could not mean it. The orthodox books on Christianity do not give me any satisfaction. My regard for the life of Jesus is indeed very great... But I do not accept the orthodox teaching that Jesus was or is God incarnate in the accepted sense or that he was or is the only son of God. I do not believe in the doctrine of appropriation of another's merit... I do not take the words 'Son' and 'Father' and 'the Holy Ghost' literally... Nor do I consider every word in the

28. *Ibid.*, Volume 24, New Delhi, 1967, p. 476.

New Testament as God's own word. Between the Old and the New there is a fundamental difference. Whilst the Old contains some very deep truths, I am unable to pay it the same honours I pay the New Testament. I regard the latter as an extension of the Old and in some matters rejection of the Old. Nor do I regard the New as the last word of God... I would therefore respectfully urge my Christian friends and well-wishers to take me as I am. I respect and appreciate their wish that I should think and be as they are even as I respect and appreciate a similar wish on the part of my Mussalman friends. I regard both the religions as equally true with my own. But my own gives me full satisfaction. It contains all that I need for my growth. It teaches me to pray not that others may believe as I believe but that they may grow to their full height in their own religion."[29] He added, "That which I would not have missed was the *Mahabbarata* and the Upanishads, the *Ramayana* and the *Bhagavata*."[30]

Mahadev Desai has recorded in his Diary dated November 3, 1924 that a Swiss missionary met Gandhiji and apologised for his broken English. Gandhiji put him at ease by telling him that English was a foreign tongue for him also. The missionary told him, "Every one knows you all over Europe. In Germany and Switzerland, you are quite a name because you are an excellent Christian." Gandhiji laughed and said, "But I am not a Christian." The missionary persisted, "But you follow Christian principles in life faithfully." Gandhiji pointed out, "Yes, that is true. But those principles are found in my religion as well." The missionary "was a little put out" but insisted, "But in Christianity specially so." Gandhiji observed, "That is doubtful. I think all religions enjoin certain general commandments — 'speak the truth', 'harm nobody', etc. But personally my own religion gives me peace; if I got it from any other I would certainly embrace that religion." The missionary "did not seem to appreciate this

---

29. *Ibid.*, Volume 23, New Delhi, 1967, pp. 85-86.
30. *Ibid.*, p. 86.

remark", and left.[31]

The *Navajivan* dated December 7, 1924 recorded an interview which Gandhiji gave to two American professors. One of them asked, "Do you believe in Christ as the Saviour of humanity through His vicarious suffering?" Gandhiji replied, "I am not much impressed with the concept." The professor enquired, "Are you shocked?" Gandhiji said, "No, not shocked either... I do not believe at all that one individual can wash off the sins of some other and grant him redemption. It is a psychological fact that one individual may feel pained at the sins and sorrows of another and the consciousness that the former is grieved may lead to the moral uplift of the latter. But I cannot accept the idea that one man die for the sake of the sins of millions and save them."[32]

The missionary machine, however, kept grinding in the same old grooves. Its campaign among the Harijans kept on maligning Hinduism. Gandhiji was pained. "Lots of people," he said at the Antyaja Conference on January 16, 1925, " will come and tell you that your Hindu religion is all wrong, as you are not allowed to go to school or enter the temple. To such people you should say, 'We shall settle accounts with our Hindu brothers ; you may not come between us as you may not intervene in quarrel between father and son or among relatives.' And you should remain steadfast to your religion... Many Christian friends ask me to turn Christian. I tell them there is nothing wrong with my religion. Why should I give it up? I have joined the *Antyajas* and if for that reason Hindus persecute me, do I cease to be a Hindu? Hinduism is meant for me and my soul."[33]

Mahadev Desai records in his Diary dated May 30, 1925 that when Gandhiji was in Darjeeling he was invited by Miss Roland, a Christian missionary, to address an audience at the "Bengali teaching school" for missionaries. About "a hundred

31. Mahadev Desai, *Day-to-Day with Gandhi*, Volume 4, Varanasi, 1969, p. 86.

32. *Ibid.*, Volume 5, Varanasi, 1970, p. 39.

33. *The Collected Works*, Volume 26, New Delhi, 1967, pp. 8-9.

or hundred and fifty European men and women were present."[34] He said, "Conversion to a religion is like passing one's Entrance Examination, standing at the gateway to Heaven. Whether you accept one religion or another is of no consequence. All that God wants us to say is whether what we profess with our lips, we but believe in our hearts. There are thousands of men and women in India who do not know Jesus or his amazing sacrifice, but are far more God-fearing than many a Christian who knows the Bible and feels he follows the decalouge." He had no use for nominal Christians. "In my humble opinion," he continued, "a man is not 'converted' the moment he renounces his own faith and embraces another. I can quote a number of examples of Indians and Zulus who have turned Christians, but have not the faintest idea of the law of love or the sacrifice of Jesus or his message."[35]

He acknowledged "the debt we owe to missionaries for service to vernacular languages and literatures — Gujarati, Marathi and Bengali." He mentioned Pope and Taylor for what they did for Tamil and Gujarati. "But in this," he said, "you have touched but a fringe. You will serve India best when you pick up the poorest of Indians and that only when you identify yourselves with them."[36] He regretted what Bishop Heber had said about these poor people — Where every prospect pleases, and man alone is vile. "He was wrong. Let God forgive him," Gandhiji added.[37]

During the same visit to Bengal, Gandhiji was invited to speak before a meeting of missionaries held at the Y.M.C.A. in Calcutta on June 28, 1925. He started by telling them of his association with Christians since his student days in London.

---

34. Mahadev Desai, *op. cit.*, Volume 7, Varanasi, 1972, p. 50.

35. *Ibid.*, p. 52.

36. *Ibid.*, pp. 53-54.

37. *Ibid.*, p. 55. The full text of Bishop Heber's hymn is given in the Appendix at the end of this chapter. It is only one of the many specimens of contempt which Christians have shown for Hindus. The hymn was included in the official hymns of the Anglican Church in England and elsewhere.

"In South Africa," he said, "where I found myself in the midst of inhospitable surroundings, I was able to make hundreds of Christian friends." He made them laugh when he told them, "There was even a time in my life when a very sincere friend of mine, a great and good Quaker, had designs on me. He thought that I was too good not to become a Christian. I was sorry to have disappointed him. One missionary friend of mine in South Africa still writes to me and asks me, 'How is it with you?' I have always told this friend that so far as I know, it is well with me."[38]

Next, he told them about his meeting with Kali Charan Banerjee. "In answer to promises made," he said, "to one of these Christian friends of mine, I thought it my duty to see one of the biggest of Indian Christians, as I was told he was, — the late Kali Charan Banerjee. I went over to him — I am telling you of the deep search that I have undergone in order that I might leave no stone unturned to find out the true path — I went to him with an absolutely open mind and in a receptive mood, and I met him also under circumstances which were most affecting. I found that there was much in common between Mr. Banerjee and myself. His simplicity, his humility, his courage, his truthfulness, all these things I have all along admired. He met me when his wife was on her death-bed. You cannot imagine a more impressive scene, a more ennobling circumstance. I told Mr. Banerjee, 'I have come to you as a seeker', — this was in 1901 — 'I have come to you in fulfilment of a sacred promise I have made to some of my dearest Christian friends that I will leave no stone unturned to find out the true light.' I told him that I had given my friends the assurance that no worldly gain would keep me away from the light, if I could but see it. Well, I am not going to engage you in giving a description of the little discussion that we had between us. It was very good, very noble. I came away, not sorry, not dejected, not disappointed, but I felt sad that even Mr. Banerjee could not convince me."

38. *The Collected Works,* Volume 27, New Delhi, 1968, p. 434.

Passing on to his present position, he said, "Today my position is that though I admire much in Christianity, I am unable to identify myself with orthodox Christianity. I must tell you in all humility that Hinduism as I know it, entirely satisfies my soul, fills my whole being and I find a solace in the Bhagavad Gita and Upanishads that I miss even in the Sermon on the Mount. Not that I do not prize the ideal presented therein, not that some of the precious teachings in the Sermon on the Mount have not left a deep impression upon me, but I must confess to you that when doubts haunt me, when disappointments stare me in the face, and when I see not one ray of light on the horizon I turn to the Bhagavad Gita, and find a verse to comfort me; and I immediately begin to smile in the midst of overwhelming sorrow. My life has been full of external tragedies and if they have not left any visible and indelible effect on me, I owe it to the teaching of the Bhagavad Gita."[39]

His love of Hinduism did not mean disrespect for other religions. "I must add," he said, "that I did not stop at studying the Bible and the commentaries and other books on Christianity that my friends placed in my hands; but I said to myself, if I was to find my satisfaction through reasoning, I must study the scriptures of other religions also and make my choice. And I turned to the Koran. I tried to understand what I could of Judaism as distinguished from Christianity. I studied Zoroastrianism and I came to the conclusion that all religions were right, but every one of them imperfect — imperfect naturally and necessarily, — because they were interpreted with our poor intellects, sometimes with our poor hearts, and more often misinterpreted. In all religions, I found to my grief, that there were various and even contradictory interpretations of some texts..."[40]

He chided the missionaries for misrepresenting Hinduism. "You, the missionaries," he said, "come to India thinking that

39. *Ibid.*, p. 435.
40. *Ibid.*, p. 436.

you come to a land of heathens, of idolaters, of men who do not know God. One of the greatest of Christian divines, Bishop Heber, wrote the two lines which have always left a sting with me: 'Where every prospect pleases, and man alone is vile.' I wish he had not written them. My own experience in my travels throughout India has been to the contrary. I have gone from one end of the country to the other, without any prejudice, in a relentless search after truth, and I am not able to say that here in this fair land, watered by the great Ganges, the Brahmaputra and the Jumna, man is vile. He is not vile. He is as much a seeker after truth as you and I are, possibly more so... I tell you there are many such huts belonging to the untouchables where you will certainly find God. They do not reason but they persist in their belief that God is. They depend upon God for His assistance and find it too. There are many stories told through the length and breadth of India about these noble untouchables. Vile as some of them may be, there are noblest specimens of humanity in their midst."[41]

And this nobility was not confined to the 'untouchables' of India. "No. I am here to tell you," he continued, "that there are non-Brahmins, there are Brahmins who are as fine specimens of humanity as you will find in any place on the earth. There are Brahmins today in India who are embodiments of self-sacrifice, godliness, and humility. There are Brahmins who are devoting themselves body and soul to the service of untouchables, but with execration from orthodoxy. They do not mind it, because in serving pariahs they are serving God. I can quote chapter and verse from my experience. I place these facts before you in all humility for the simple reason that you may know this land better, the land to which you have come to serve. You are here to find out the distress of the people of India and remove it. But I hope you are here also in a receptive mood and, if there is anything that India has to give, you will not stop your ears, you will not close

41. *Ibid.*

your eyes and steel your hearts, but open up your ears, eyes and, most of all, your hearts to receive all that may be good in the land. I give you my assurance that there is a great deal of good in India. Do not flatter yourselves with the belief that a mere recital of that celebrated verse in St. John makes a man a Christian. If I have read the Bible correctly, I know many men who have never heard the name of Jesus Christ or have even rejected the official interpretation of Christianity will, probably, if Jesus came in our midst today in the flesh, be owned by him more than many of us. I therefore ask you to approach the problem before you with open-heartedness, and humility."[42]

Gandhiji told the missionaries that they stood isolated from the people of India because they "come to India under the shadow, or, if you like, under the protection of a temporal power, and it creates an impassable bar."[43] He said that he was not impressed by the "statistics that so many orphans have been reclaimed and brought to the Christian faith." He asked them to identify themselves with the masses and find out what the masses need most. "You cannot," he said, "present the hungry and famished masses with God. Their God is their food."[44]

A missionary asked him, "Do you definitely feel the presence of the living Christ within you?" Gandhiji replied, "If it is the historical Jesus, surnamed Christ, that the inquirer refers to, I must say I do not. If it is an adjective signifying one of the names of God, then I must say I do feel the presence of God — call him Christ, call him Krishna, call him Rama. We have one thousand names of God, and if I did not feel the presence of God within me, I see so much of misery and disappointment every day that I would be a raving maniac and my destination would be the Hooghly."[45]

An Englishmen "defended Bishop Heber's song on the

---

42. *Ibid.*, p. 437.
43. *Ibid.*, p. 438.
44. *Ibid.*, p. 439.
45. *Ibid.*

ground that the song did not refer to Indians but to Christians" and that "they described themselves in their songs very often as the worst of sinners." Gandhiji "put his defence out of court." He quoted "those parts of the song which said that India, Africa and such other countries were inviting the Christians to spread their light in these lands, and that it was there that nature's prospect pleased but only man was vile, because the heathen was worshipping wood and stone in his blindness." At the end he asked, "Is it not strange, that a song written ages ago is still sung in Christian circles?"[46]

On August 12, 1925 Gandhiji delivered another speech before the Y.M.C.A. at Calcutta. He started by giving an account of his association with Christianity and Christians. He mentioned Principal S. K. Rudra and C. F. Andrews as among his best friends. Coming to the duty of Indian Christians, he said, "In my humble opinion a Christian Young Indian owes a double duty — to those whose religion he has given up and to those whose religion he has adopted... The Indian Christian's duty to the religion he has given up is to retain all the good that belongs to it and impart it to the new he has taken. Contrarily, he takes the best of the new religion and transmits it to those whom he has left or who have banished him. But that never happens in a majority of cases. With deep grief that has to be noted. And in Madras you go to different quarters altogether, but by no means a congenial surroundings. You will find there vice double-distilled and no gain on either side."[47]

Instead, the Indian Christians had invited a double tragedy. They did not mix with Indians, and Europeans would not mix with them. "I tried to talk," he said, "as I kept walking on the Ellisbridge [in Ahmedabad] to young girls walking to their seminary. They did not even return my salaams. I attended a service also. You will be surprised to see that I was sitting in a corner hoping to exchange a

46. Mahadev Desai, *op. cit.*, Volume 7, p. 155.
47. *Ibid.*, pp. 161-62.

word — without avail, not even a glance. Excuses there may be, but that should not be the case. You cut yourself away from your kith and kin..."[48]

Another great mistake the converts to Christianity were making was to neglect their native languages and try to learn the English language alone. "They are passing through schools and colleges," he said, "like so many pieces of a machine — but they don't think, don't originate, forget their mother tongue. They try to learn the English language, succeed in making a hash of it, and trying to think in a foreign tongue, become paralysed... There is something radically wrong in a system which has brought about such helplessness." He commended to them the example set by Madhusudan Datta who had "enriched his mother tongue" and Kali Charan Banerjee and S. K. Rudra who had retained their Indianness after becoming Christians. "If the Indian Christians," he concluded, "want to serve their country, are to serve the religion they profess, it will be necessary to revise a great deal of what they are doing today."[49]

He was happy when the speakers who preceded him at a congregation of the Baptist Church on August 20, spoke in their mother tongue. "The man who discards his mother-tongue," he said, "gives up thereby his parents, his friends, his neighbours and his country as well. The man who is capable of snapping such ties of love becomes unfit for doing any good to humanity or to anybody whatever. And the man unfit to serve the world is unfit to know or serve God."[50]

He upheld the same spirit of Swadeshi in other spheres of life. "During my travels," he continued, "I find a general belief that to turn a Christian is to turn European; to become self-willed, and give up self-restraint, use only foreign cloth, dress oneself in European style and start taking meat and brandy. But I think the fact is, if a person discards his country, his customs and his old connections and manners when

48. *Ibid.*, p. 163.
49. *Ibid.*, p. 164.
50. *Ibid.*, p. 184.

he changes his religion, he becomes all the more unfit to gain a knowledge of God. For, a change of religion means really a conversion of the heart. When there is a real conversion, a man's heart grows. But in this country one finds that conversion brings about deep disdain for one's old religion and its followers, i.e., one's old friends and relatives. The next change that takes place is that of dress and manners and behaviour. All that does great harm to the country. In my view your object in changing your religion should be to bring about the prosperity of your country."[51]

He told them that conversion should not mean license in conduct. He drew their attention to what the Bible teaches about one's conduct towards one's neighbours. "Christian friends tell me," he said, "that when they change their faith, there remains no need for them to observe any restraint. They say, 'You can do anything you like when you become a Christian.' I respectfully say that this is a wrong notion. I shall give you an instance to prove my contention. There is a common belief that while some food is forbidden and some allowed in Hinduism, once you become a Christian, you get a license to eat anything you like and drink even liquor. Hence there are a lot of Christians who disregard their neighbour's feelings and do what they like at the cost of hurting them. But I was told the other day that the Bible condemns such conduct."[52]

A student doing post-graduate studies in the U.S.A. wrote to Gandhiji asking for his "frank evaluation of the work of Christian missionaries in India." He wanted to know if "Christianity has some contribution to make to the life of India" and if India could "do without Christian missionaries." Gandhiji said, "In my opinion Christian missionaries have done good to us indirectly. Their direct contribution is probably more harmful than otherwise. I am against the modern methods of proselytising. Years' experience of proselytising both in

---

51. *Ibid.*
52. *Ibid.*, pp. 185-86.

South Africa and India has convinced me that it has not raised the general moral tone of converts who have imbibed the superficialities of European civilization, and have missed the teaching of Jesus. I must be understood to refer to the general tendency and not to brilliant exceptions. The indirect contribution, on the other hand, of Christian missionary effort is great. It has stimulated Hindu and Mussalman religious research. It has forced us to put our house in order. The great educational and curative institutions of Christian missions I also count among indirect results, because they have been established, not for their own sakes, but as an aid to proselytising."[53]

A Christian Indian domiciled in Ceylon (now Sri Lanka) but studying in the U.S.A. sent to Gandhiji a number of questions on behalf of students associated with the Y.M.C.A. One of the question was, "What is your attitude towards the teachings of Jesus Christ?" Gandhiji published his reply in the *Young India* of February 25, 1926: "They have an immense moral value for me, but I do not regard everything said in the Bible as the final word of God or exhaustive or even acceptable from the moral standpoint. I regard Jesus Christ as one of the greatest teachers of mankind, but I do not consider him to be the 'only son of God'."[54]

An English translation of Gandhiji's autobiography was being serialised in the *Young India* from December 3, 1925 onwards. When the account of his first encounter with Christianity appeared in the weekly, he received a letter from Rev. H. R. Scott, "at present stationed at Surat." Gandhiji published the letter in the *Young India* of March 4, 1926. "I was the only missionary in Rajkot during those years (from 1883 to 1897)," wrote Rev. Scott, "and what you say about Christian missionaries in Rajkot standing at a corner near the High school and pouring abuse on Hindus and their gods fills me with painful wonder. I certainly never preached 'at a corner near the

53. ***The Collected Works***, Volume 29, New Delhi, 1968, p. 326.

54. ***Ibid.***, Volume 30, New Delhi, 1968, p. 47.

High school'; my regular preaching station was under a banyan tree in the Pan Bazar; and I certainly never 'poured abuse on Hindus and their gods.' That would be strange way to win a hearing from Hindus. Then you say that a well-known Hindu was baptised at that time, and that 'he had to eat beef and drink liquor, and to change his clothes, and go about in European clothes, including a hat.' No wonder that such a story got on your nerves, if you believed it. Well, I have been over 42 years in India, and I have never heared of such a thing happening; and indeed I know it to be quite contrary to what all missionaries with whom I am acquainted teach and believe and practise. During my time in Rajkot I baptised a number of Brahmins and Jain sadhus. They certainly had not to 'eat beef and drink liquor', either at the time of baptism or at any other time... I know of course that this kind of story is told about converts to Christianity in Kathiawad and elsewhere in India. It is obviously the wilful invention of people who wish to prevent the spread of Christianity in India and hope thereby to frighten young Hindus who show an inclination to learn the truth about Christianity, and no doubt it has had its results in deterring many such honest inquirers as yourself. But surely you must have had many opportunities since then of discovering that that particular libel is without foundation, and as a sincere lover of truth you cannot lend the great weight of your authority to perpetuate such a wilfully malicious misrepresentation of Christian missionaries."[55]

Gandhiji commented, "Though the preaching took place over forty years ago the painful memory of it is still vivid before me. What I have heard and read since has but confirmed that impression. I have read several missionary publications and they are able to see only the dark side and paint it darker still. The famous hymn of Bishop Heber's — 'Greenland's icy mountains' — is a clear libel on Indian humanity. I was favoured with some literature even at the

55. *Ibid.*, Only excerpts from Rev. Scott's letter are given in this Volume. In fairness to the missionary, we have reproduced the letter at some length from M.K. Gandhi, *Christian Missions*, Ahmedabad, 1941, pp. 12-13.

Yervada prison by well-meaning missionaries, which seemed to be written as if merely to belittle Hinduism. About beef-eating and wine-drinking I have merely stated what I have heard and I have said as much in my writing. And whilst I accept Mr. Scott's repudiation, I must say that though I have mixed freely among thousands of Christian Indians, I know very few who have scruples about eating beef or other flesh meats and drinking intoxicating liquors. When I have gently reasoned with them, they have quoted to me the celebrated verse 'Call thou nothing unclean' as if it referred to eating and gave a licence for indulgence. I know many Hindus eat meat, some eat even beef and drink wines. They are not converts. Converts are those who are 'born again' or should be. A higher standard is expected of those who change their faith, if the change is a matter of heart and not of convenience."[56]

Gandhiji started giving a series of lectures on the New Testament to the students of the Gujarat National College at Ahmedabad from July 24, 1926 onwards. Some Hindus did not like it. He was accused of being a "secret Christian". They feared that reading the Bible to young boys was likely to influence them in favour of Christianity. "We need not dread, upon our grown-up children," wrote Gandhiji in the *Young India* of September 2, 1926, "the influence of scriptures other than our own. We libralize their outlook upon life by encouraging them to study freely all that is clean. Fear there would be when someone reads his own scriptures to young people with the intention secretly or openly of converting them. He must be biased in favour of his own scriptures. For myself, I regard my study of and reverence for the Bible, the Koran and other scriptures to be wholly consistent with my claim to be a staunch *sanatani* Hindu. He is no *sanatani* Hindu who is narrow, bigoted and considers evil to be good if it has the sanction of antiquity and is to be found supported in any Sanskrit book. I claim to be a staunch *sanatani* Hindu because though I reject all that offends my moral sense, I find

56. *Ibid.*, pp. 70-71.

the Hindu scriptures to satisfy the need of the soul. My respectful study of other religions has not abated my reverence for or my faith in Hindu scriptures. They have indeed left their deep mark upon my understanding of Hindu scriptures. They have broadened my view of life. They have enabled me to understand more clearly many obscure passages in the Hindu scriptures."[57]

"The charge of being a Christian in secret," he continued, "was not new. It is both a libel and a compliment — a libel because there are men who can believe me to be capable of being secretly anything, i.e. for fear of being that openly. There is nothing in the world that would keep me from professing Christianity or any other faith the moment I felt the truth of and the need for it. Where there is fear there is no religion. The charge is a compliment in that it is a reluctant acknowledgement of my capacity for appreciating the beauties of Christianity."[58]

Gandhiji's great regard for Jesus was misunderstood by some Christians. W. B. Stover wrote to him, "You have taken the Lord Christ for your leader and guide. There is none better." Gandhiji replied, "You do not mind my correcting you. I regard Jesus as a human being like the rest of the teachers of the world. As such he was undoubtedly great. But I do not by any means regard him to have been the very best. The acknowledgement of the debt which I have so often repeated that I owe to the Sermon on the Mount should not be mistaken to mean an acknowledgement of the Orthodox interpretation of the Bible or the life of Jesus. I must not sail under false colours."[59]

Gandhiji had a discussion with some missionaries on July 29, 1927. The questions asked by the missionaries and the replies given by him were reproduced in the *Young India* of August 11, 1927. He opened the discussion with an introduction

---

57. *Ibid.*, Volume 31, New Delhi, 1968, pp. 350-51.
58. *Ibid.*, p. 351.
59. *Ibid.*, Volume 34, New Delhi, 1969, p. 10.

on how he looked at the history of religion. "Christianity," he said, "is 1900 years old, Islam is 1300 years old. Who knows the possibility of either? I have not read the Vedas in the original but have tried to assimilate their spirit and have not hesitated to say that though the Vedas may be 13,000 years old — or even a million years old, as they well may be, for the word of God is as old as God Himself — even the Vedas must be interpreted in the light of our experience. The powers of God should not be limited by the limitations of our understandings."

Next, he commented on the role of the missionaries as teachers of religion and said, "To you who have come to teach India, I therefore say, you cannot give without taking. If you have come to give rich treasures of experiences, open your hearts out to receive the treasures of this land, and you will not be disappointed, neither will you have misread the message of the Bible." The missionaries asked, "What then are we doing? Are we doing the right thing?" Gandhiji replied, "You are doing the right thing the wrong way. I want you to compliment the faith of the people instead of undermining it... Whilst a boy I heard it being said, that to become a Christian was to have a brandy bottle in one hand and beef in the other. Things are better now, but it is not unusual to find Christianity synonymous with denationalisation and Europeanisation. Must we give up our simplicity, to become better people? Do not lay the axe at our simplicity."[60]

The missionaries posed their problem, "There are not only two issues before us, viz., to serve and to teach, there is a third issue, viz., evangelizing, declaring the glad tidings of the coming of Jesus and his death in redemption of our sins. What is the right way of giving the right news? We need not undermine the faith but we may make people lose their faith in lesser things." Gandhiji's reply was sharp. "It would be poor comfort to the world," he said, "if it had to depend upon a historical God who died 2,000 years ago. Do not then

60. *Ibid.*, p. 261.

preach the God of history, but show Him as He lives today through you... It is better to allow our lives to speak for us than our words."[61]

The missionaries then asked, "But what about animistic beliefs? Should they not be corrected?"[62] Gandhiji told them not to concern themselves "with their beliefs but with asking them to do the right thing." Finally, the missionaries came out with their dogma, "How can we help condemning if we feel that our Christian truth is the only reality?" Gandhiji saw the implied intolerance and said, "If you cannot feel that the other faith is as true as yours, you should feel at least that the men are as true as you. The intolerance of Christian missionaries does not, I am glad to say, take the ugly shape it used to take some years ago. Think of the caricature of Hinduism, which one finds in so many publications of the Christian Literature Society. A lady wrote to me the other day saying that unless I embraced Christianity all my work would be nothing worth. And of course that Christianity must mean what she understands as such. Well, all I can say is that it is a wrong attitude."[63]

Gandhiji had received a letter from an American lady who described herself as "a lifelong friend of India." He reproduced it in the *Young India* of October 20, 1927. "Believing that Christ was a revelation of God," she wrote, "Christians of America have sent to India thousands of their sons and daughters to tell the people of India about Christ. Will you in return kindly give us your interpretation of Hinduism and make a comparison of Hinduism with the teachings of Christ?" Gandhiji commented, "I have ventured at several missionary meetings to tell English and American missionaries that if they could have refrained from 'telling' India about Christ and had merely lived the life enjoined upon them by the Sermon on the Mount, India instead of suspecting them would have appreciated their living in the midst of her children and directly

61. *Ibid.*, pp. 261-62.
62. *Ibid.*, p. 262.
63. *Ibid.*, pp. 262-63.

profited by their presence. Holding this view, I can 'tell' American friends nothing about Hinduism by way of 'return'. I do not believe in people telling others of their faith, especially with a view of conversion. Faith does not admit of telling. It has to be lived and then it becomes self-propagating."[64]

Coming to Hinduism, he wrote, "Believing as I do in the influence of heredity, being born in a Hindu family, I have remained a Hindu. I should reject it, if I found it inconsistent with my moral sense or my spiritual growth. On examination, I have found it to be the most tolerant of all religions known to me. Its freedom from dogma makes a forcible appeal to me in as much as it gives the votary the largest scope for self-expression. Not being an exclusive religion, it enables the followers of the faith not merely to respect all the other religions, but it also enables them to admire and assimilate whatever may be good in the other faiths. Non-violence is common to all religions, but it has found the highest expression and application in Hinduism. (I do not regard Jainism or Buddhism as separate from Hinduism.) Hinduism believes in the oneness not of merely all human life but in the oneness of all that lives. Its worship of the cow is, in my opinion, its unique contribution to the evolution of humanitarianism. It is a practical application of the belief in the oneness and, therefore, sacredness of all life. The great belief in transmigration is a direct consequence of that belief. Finally, the discovery of the law of varnashrama is a magnificent result of the ceaseless search for truth."[65]

Gandhiji was on a visit to Ceylon (now Sri Lanka) in November 1927. The *Young India* dated December 8,1927 reported his speech at the Y.M.C.A., Colombo. "Gandhiji then took," said the report, "the case of modern China as a case in point. His heart, he said, went out to young China in the throes of a great national upheaval, and he referred to the anti-Christian movement in China, about which he had occasion to

---

64. *Ibid.*, Volume 35, New Delhi, 1969, p. 166.

65. *Ibid.*, pp. 166-67.

read in a pamphlet received by him from the students department of the Young Women's Christian Association and the Young Men's Christian Association of China. The writers had put their own interpretation upon the anti-Christian movement, but there was no doubt that young China regarded Christian movements as being opposed to Chinese self-expression." To Gandhiji the moral of this anti-Christian manifestation was clear. He proceeded to advise the Ceylonese Christians. "The deduction," he said, "I would like you all to draw from this manifestation is that you Ceylonese should not be torn from your moorings, and those from the West should not consciously lay violent hands upon the manners, customs and habits of the Ceylonese in so far as they are not repugnant to fundamental ethics and morality. Confuse not Jesus' teachings with what passes as modern civilization, and pray do not do unconscious violence to the people among whom you cast your lot. It is no part of that call, I assure you, to tear the lives of the people of the East by its roots. Tolerate whatever is good in them and do not hastily with your preconceived notions, judge them. Do not judge lest you be judged yourselves."[66]

He ended with a message for the Buddhists who were members of the Y.M.C.A. and present in the meeting, "To you, young Ceylonese friends, I say: Don't be dazzled by the splendour that comes to you from the West. Do not be thrown off your feet by this passing show. The Enlightened One has told you in never-to-be-forgotten words that this little span of life is but a passing shadow, a fleeting thing, and if you realize the nothingness of all that appears before your eyes, the nothingness of this material case that we see before us ever changing, then indeed there are treasures for you up above, and there is peace for you down here, peace which passeth all understanding, and happiness to which we are utter strangers. It requires an amazing faith, a divine faith and surrender of all that we see before us... Buddha renounced

66. *Ibid.*, p. 249.

every worldly happiness, because he wanted to share with the whole world his happiness which was to be had by men who sacrificed and suffered in search of truth."[67]

Gandhiji had a discussion with members of the Council of International Fellowship who stayed in his Ashram in January 1928. The discussion was reported in the *Young India* of January 19. Coming to questions about conversions, he said, "I would not only not try to convert but would not even secretly pray that anyone should embrace my faith... Hinduism with its message of ahimsa is to me the most glorious religion in the world — as my wife to me is the most beautiful woman in the world — but others may feel the same about their own religion. Cases of real honest conversion are quite possible. If some people for their inward satisfaction and growth change their religion, let them do so. As regards taking our message to the aborigines, I do not think I should go and give my message out of my own wisdom. Do it in all humility, it is said. Well I have been an unfortunate witness of arrogance often going in the garb of humility. If I am perfect, I know that my thought will reach others. It taxes all my time to reach the goal I have set to myself. What have I to take to the aborigines and the Assamese hillmen except to go in my nakedness to them? Rather than ask them to join my prayer, I would join their prayer. We were strangers to this sort of classification — 'animists', 'aborigines', etc., — but we have learnt it from English rulers. I must have the desire to serve and it must put me right with people. Conversion and service go ill together."[68] A member asked, "Did not Jesus Himself teach and preach?" Gandhiji replied, "We are on dangerous ground here. You ask me to give my interpretation of the life of Christ. Well, I may say that I do not accept everything in the gospels as historical truth. And it must be remembered that he was working amongst his own people, and said he had not come to destroy but to fulfil. I draw a great distinction between the

---

67. *Ibid.*, p. 250.

68. *Ibid.*, pp. 462-63.

Sermon on the Mount and the Letters of Paul. They are a graft on Christ's teaching, his own gloss apart from Christ's own experience."[69]

As Gandhiji's view of the Christian missions became known, the controllers of missions felt concerned. Here was a man whose very humility was putting Christianity in the wrong. John R. Mott was a leading American evangelist and fabulous fund-raiser for the Protestant missions. He came and met Gandhiji on March 1, 1929 and tried to fathom him. The interview was published in the *Young India* of March 21, 1929. After discussing some generalities such as the future of India, etc., Mr. Mott came to the question he had travelled all the way to pose before Gandhiji. He asked, "What then is the contribution of Christianity to the national life of India? I mean the influence of Christ as apart from Christianity, for I am afraid there is a wide gulf separating the two at present." Gandhiji replied, "Aye, there is the rub. It is not possible to consider the teaching of a religious teacher apart from the lives of his followers. Unfortunately, Christianity in India has been inextricably mixed up for the last one hundred years with the British rule. It appears to us as synonymous with the materialistic civilization and imperialistic exploitation by the strong white races of the weaker races of the world. Its contribution to India has been therefore largely of a negative character. It has done some good in spite of its professors. It has shocked us into setting our own house in order."[70]

Mr. Mott asked if Christians can help in the removal of untouchability. Gandhiji informed him that the " removal of untouchability is purely a question of the purification of Hinduism" and "can only be effected from within." Mr. Mott insisted that "Christians would be a great help to you in this connection." He cited Rev. Whitehead, Bishop of the Church of England, who had made "some striking statements about the effect of Christian mass movements in ameliorating the

69. *Ibid.*, p. 464.

70. *Ibid.*,Volume 40, New Delhi, 1970, pp. 58-59.

condition of the untouchables in the Madras Presidency." Gandhiji said, "I distrust mass movements of this nature. They have as their object not the upliftment of the untouchables, but their ultimate conversion. This motive of mass proselytisation lurking at the back in my opinion vitiates missionary effort."[71]

Mr. Mott now came to the point. "There are some who believe," he said, "that the untouchables would be better off if they turned Christians from conviction, and that it would transform their lives." Gandhiji was equally clear. "I am sorry," he said, "I have been unable to discover any tangible evidence to confirm this view. I was once taken into a Christian village. Instead of meeting among the converts with that frankness which one associates with a spiritual transformation, I found an air of evasiveness about them. They were afraid to talk. This struck me as a change not for the better but for the worse."[72]

Mr. Mott asked Gandhiji, "Do you disbelieve in all conversion?" Gandhiji replied, "I disbelieve in the conversion of one person by another." Mr. Mott repeated the age-old missionary slogan, " Is it not our duty to help our fellow-beings to the maximum of the truth we may possess, to share with them our deepest spiritual experience?" Gandhiji observed, "I am sorry I must again differ with you, for the simple reason that the deepest spiritual truths are always unutterable. That light to which you refer transcends speech. It can be felt only through the inner experience. And then the highest truth needs no communicating, for it is by its very nature self-propelling. It radiates its influence silently as the rose its fragrance without the intervention of a medium."[73]

Finally, Mr. Mott tried the last weapon in his armoury. "But even God," he said, "sometimes speaks through his prophets." Gandhiji replied, "Yes, but prophets speak not through the tongue but through their lives. I have however

71. *Ibid.*, p.59.
72. *Ibid.*, p. 60.
73. *Ibid.*

known that in this matter I am up against a solid wall of Christian opinion." Mr. Mott came down and said, "Oh no, even among Christians there is a school of thought — and it is growing — which holds that authoritarian method should not be employed but that each individual should be left to discover the deepest truths of life for himself. The argument advanced is that the process of spiritual discovery is bound to vary in the case of different individuals according to their varying needs and temperament. In other words they feel that propaganda in the accepted sense of the term is not the most effective method." Gandhiji welcomed the statement adding, "That is what Hinduism certainly inculcates."[74] The interview ended on a pleasant note, though it did not satisfy Mr. Mott. He came for two more rounds some years later.[75]

A Christian missionary from Vizagapatam, Mr. Abel, interviewed Gandhiji on May 1, 1929. "Is not Jesus Christ the only sinless one?" he asked. "What do we know", said Gandhiji, "of the whole life of Christ? Apart from the years of his life given in the four gospels of the New Testament — we know nothing of the rest of his life. As a man well-versed in the Bible you ought to have known that."[76]

February 23, 1931 was Gandhiji's day of silence. He wrote a note to Dr. Thronton, a Christian missionary, in reply to some points the latter has raised. "If the missionary friends," he said, "will forget their mission, viz., of proselytising Indians and of bringing Christ to them, they will do wonderfully good work. Your duty is done with the ulterior motive of proselytising. I was the first to raise a note of warning in this respect... Help certainly you have (brought), viz., what comes through contact with you and in spite of you, i.e., the spirit of inquiry about the shortcomings of our own religion. You did not want us to pursue the inquiry because you saw immorality where we saw spirituality. When I go to your institutions I do not feel I am going to an Indian institution.

74. *Ibid.*

75. Mr. Mott lived to publish a book, *The Larger Evangelism,* in 1944 and share the Noble Prize for Peace with Emily Queen Balch in 1946.

76. *Ibid.*, p. 315.

This is what worries me."[77]

Gandhiji gave an interview to the press in Delhi on March 21, 1931. "Asked if he would favour the retention of American and other foreign missionaries when India secured self-government", Gandhiji was reported to have said, "If instead of confining themselves purely to humanitarian work and material service to the poor, they do proselytising by means of medical aid, education, etc., I would certainly ask them to withdraw. Every nation's religion is as good as any other. Certainly India's religions are adequate for her people. We need no converting spirituality."[78]

This raised a furore in missionary circles in India and abroad. Gandhiji wrote an article, 'Foreign Missionaries', in the *Young India* of April 23, 1931 in which he was pained to note that "Even George Joseph, my erstwhile co-worker and gracious host in Madura, has gone into hysterics without condescending to verify the report." He said that what was reported in the press was "what a reporter has put into my mouth."[79] He corrected the press report to read as follows: "If instead of confining themselves to purely humanitarian work such as education, medical services to the poor and the like, they use these activities of theirs for the purpose of proselytising, I would certainly like them to withdraw. Every nation considers its own faith to be as good as that of any other. Certainly the great faiths held by the people of India are adequate for her people. India stands in no need of conversion from one faith to another."[80]

He proceeded to "amplify the bald statement", which, one must say, was not much of an improvement on his earlier statement. He made no concession to conversion by "modern methods" which "has nowadays become a business like any other." He was reminded of "a missionary report saying how much it cost per head to convert and then presenting a

---

77. *Ibid.*, Volume 45, New Delhi, 1971, pp. 233-34.

78. *Ibid.*, p. 320.

79. *Ibid.*, Volume 46, New Delhi, 1971, p. 27.

80. *Ibid.*, p. 28.

budget for the 'next harvest'." He also asked some very pertinent questions: "Why should I change my religion because a doctor who professes Christianity as his religion has cured me of some disease or why should the doctor expect or suggest such a change whilst I am under his influence? Is not medical relief its own reward and satisfaction? Or why should I whilst I am in a missionary educational institution have Christian teaching thrust upon me?" He did not rule out conversion but gave his own meaning to it. "Conversion in the sense of self-purification, self-realization," he wrote, "is the crying need of the hour. That, however, is not what is meant by proselytising. To those who would convert India, might it not be said, 'physician heal thyself'?"[81] On the same day he cabled a summary of his article to *The Daily Herald* of London.

The Christian opinion, however, was far from satisfied by his article. On April 11, 1931, James P. Rutnam of Ceylon put some questions to him. "In this great struggle for Swaraj ," he asked, "are we not fighting for liberty, liberty to worship our God as we please, liberty to convince our fellows who are willing to be convinced by our fellows who can convince us? Is India so bigoted as to think that within her are confined all the riches of the world, all the treasures of knowledge and human experience?"[82] Gandhiji was painfully surprised at this persistent misunderstanding. He wrote another article, 'Foreign Missionaries Again', in the *Young India* of May 7, 1931. After explaining that he included Christianity among the religions of India, he said, "The attack has therefore surprised me. not a little especially because the views I have now enunciated have been held by me since 1916, and were deliberately expressed in a carefully written address read before a purely missionary audience in Madras and since repeated on many a Christian platform. The recent criticism has but confirmed the view, for the criticism has betrayed intolerance even of

81. *Ibid.*, pp. 28-29.
82. *Ibid.*, p. 109.

friendly criticism. The missionaries know that in spite of my outspoken criticism of their methods, they have in India and among non-Christians no warmer friend than I. And I suggest to my critics that there must be something wrong about their methods or, if they prefer, themselves when they will not brook sincere expression of an opinion different from theirs. In India under swaraj I have no doubt that foreign missionaries will be at liberty to do their proselytising, as I would say, in the wrong way; but they would be expected to bear with those who, like me, may point out that in their opinion the way is wrong."[83]

He had to return to the theme on May 5, 1931 when he received a long letter from Rev. B. W. Tucker. The missionary was "in full agreement with you in your protest against the methods employed by Christian missions in their efforts to gain proselytes through education, medical services and the like."[84] He also welcomed Gandhiji's assurance that a swaraj government will not create "any legal enactment compelling missionaries to withdraw if they failed to give up their proselytising activities." But he registered a protest "against the implications of your statement that the religions of India are adequate for her."[85] Gandhiji wrote a short comment emphasizing that he still adhered "to the statement to which Rev. Tucker takes exception and which is, 'Religions of India are adequate for her'." He also made it clear that "What is resisted is the idea of gaining converts and that too not always by fair and open means."[86] He followed up by yet another article, 'Missionary Methods in India', in the *Young India* of June 6, 1931. A retired Deputy Collector had written to him citing various sources, including Indian Census Report for 1911, and stating that missionaries were using material inducements for gaining converts. "That collection of quotations from named sources," wrote Gandhiji, "should, instead of offending

83. *Ibid.*, p. 110.
84. *Ibid.*, p. 237.
85. *Ibid.*, p .238.
86. *Ibid.*, p. 239.

missionaries, cause an inward search. I have several other similar articles, some from Christian Indians. The writer will excuse me for withholding them. The controversy ought not to be prolonged."[87]

Three months later when Gandhiji was in London for attending the Second Round Table Conference, he was invited on October 8, 1931 to speak at the Conference of Mission Societies in Great Britain and Ireland. He started by trying to remove the misunderstanding created by the recent controversy about the place of Christian missions in India after attainment of independence. He ruled out "legislation to prohibit missionary enterprises." But he maintained firmly his position about proselytisation. He said, "The idea of converting people to one's faith by speech and writing, by appeal to reason and emotion and by suggesting that the faith of his forefathers is a bad faith, in my opinion, limits the possibilities of serving humanity."[88] He admitted his indebtedness to "Christian influence for some of my social work" such as a "fierce hatred of child marriage." But he made it clear that "Before I knew anything of Christianity I was an enemy of untouchability."[89]

Rev. Godfrey Philips of London Missionary Society posed a question before Gandhiji. "I wish we could understand one another better," he said, "with regard to what is happening amongst the 'untouchables' in connection with Christian missions... We have found in our experience that when the 'untouchable', the outcaste, is down and out, we can do nothing permanent except by implanting in his inmost heart something that has vitalizing power — in our experience that is fellowship with God in Christ."[90] Gandhiji replied that "in my own humble opinion it is an erroneous way" and that as "the rose would not have to speak, neither would the Christian missionary have to speak." If the Christian missionary believes

87. *Ibid.*, p. 314.
88. *Ibid.*, Volume 48, New Delhi, 1971, p. 121.
89. *Ibid.*, p. 122.
90. *Ibid.*, p. 124.

that "before he can come to the help of the untouchables, he must bring the message of God, or the message of the Bible, to the untouchables, how much more than to a man like me?" Gandhiji emphasised that "after having mixed with tens of thousands of untouchables", he was convinced that they do not understand the missionary's language. "They understand me better," he said, "because I speak their language. I speak to them about their degraded condition. I do not speak about God. I feel that I take the message of God to them in this particular manner just as to a starving man I take the message of God through the bread I give him. I have no axe to grind. I must not exploit him, I just give him the bread. If I want to convey God to the humble untouchable I must take Him the way that he needs."[91]

The next question, put by Rev. C. E. Wilson of the Baptist Missionary Society, was sharp. "Does Mr. Gandhi," he asked, "mean that it is not right for us to go to India or any place and try to make people disciples, to teach the supreme truth of Jesus Christ, if we believe him to be the highest that we know? Mr. Gandhi has been preaching to us today. Does he mean to exclude all preaching?"[92] Rev. W. H. G. Holmes of the Oxford Mission at Calcutta told an anecdote about the plight of untouchables which he had himself seen. He was extending support to Rev. C. E. Wilson. "Would we be right," he asked, "in going to teach them about this Father, who I told them loved them as dearly as he loved us, and would Mr. Gandhi encourage them to let us have land to build on in order to teach these people?"

Gandhiji replied, "Yes, I would, on one condition that you will teach them the religion of their forefathers through the religion they have got. Don't say to them: 'The only way to know the Father is our way.'... Show the 'untouchables' the Father as He appears in his own surroundings. Unless you are satisfied that we do not know the Father at all, and then of

---

91. *Ibid.*, pp. 124-25.
92. *Ibid.*, p. 125.

course it is your duty to say — 'What you know as Father is no Father at all. What you believe comes from Satan.' I sometimes receive letters saying that I am a good man, but that I am doing the devil's work. I feel I adore the same Father though in a different form. I may not adore him as 'God'. To me that name makes no appeal, but when I think of Him as Rama, He thrills me. To think of God as 'God' does not fire me as the name Rama does. There is no poetry in it. I know that my forefathers have known him as Rama. They have been uplifted by Rama, and when I take the name of Rama, I arise with the same energy. It would not be possible for me to use the name 'God' as it is written in the Bible. It is contrary to experience. I should not be attracted. I should not be lifted to the truth. Therefore my whole soul rejects the teaching that Rama is not my God."[93]

A member of the Conference "referred to the command for Christians to go out to all the world and preach the Gospel to every creature." Gandhiji said that "if the questioner believed that these were the inspired words in the Bible, then he was called upon to obey implicitly — why did he ask a non-Christian for his interpretation?" The meeting ended with the President, Rev. W. Paton declaring that "Mr. Gandhi had made it abundantly clear that the issue between him and the Christian missionary movement lay much deeper than was supposed."[94]

On his way back from London on board S. S. Pilsana, Gandhiji gave a talk on Christ on Christmas Day, 1931. "I shall tell you," he said, "how, to an outsider like me, the story of Christ, as told in the New Testament, has struck. My acquaintance with the Bible began nearly forty years ago, and that was through the New Testament. I could not then take much interest in Old Testament which I had certainly read, if only to fulfil a promise I had made to a friend whom I happened to meet in a hotel. But when I came to the New Testament

93. *Ibid.*, pp. 126-127.
94. *Ibid.*, p. 127.

and the Sermon on the Mount, I began to understand the Christian teaching and the teaching of the Sermon on the Mount echoed something I had learnt in childhood and something which seemed to be a part of my being and which I felt was being acted up to in the daily life around me."

He had no use for the Jesus of history. "I may say," he continued, "that I have never been interested in a historical Jesus. I should not care if it was proved by someone that the man called Jesus never lived, and that what was narrated in the Gospels was a figment of the writer's imagination. For the Sermon on the Mount would still be true for me." Finally, he came to Christianity as practised by Christians and as preached by the missionaries. "Reading, therefore, the whole story in that light," he concluded, "it seems to me that Christianity has yet to be lived, unless one says that where there is boundless love and no idea of retaliation whatsoever, it is Christianity that lives. But then it surmounts all boundaries and book-teaching. Then it is something indefinable, not capable of being preached to men, not capable of being transmitted from mouth to mouth, but from heart to heart. But Christianity is not commonly understood that way."[95]

One of the Hindu practices which Christians regard as gross superstition and sin is idol-worship. A Christian, F. Mary Barr, sought Gandhiji's opinion about it. In his letter dated November 30, 1932, Gandhiji wrote, "What must not be forgotten about me is that I do not consider idol-worship to be a sin, but I know that in some form or other it is a condition of our being. The difference between one form of worship and another is a difference in degree and not in kind. Mosque-going or Chruch-going is a form of idol-worship. Veneration for the Bible, the Koran, the Gita and the like is idol-worship and even if you don't use a book or a building but draw a picture of divinity in your imagination and attribute certain qualities, it is again idol-worship and I refuse to call the worship of one who has a stone-image a grosser

95. *Ibid.*, pp. 437-433.

form of worship... It would be both arrogant and ignorant to look down upon such worship as superstition... All this is a plea for a definite recognition of the fact that all forms of honest worship are equally good and equally efficient for the respective worshippers. Time is gone for the exclusive possession of right by an individual or a group."[96]

Gandhiji had received a letter dated November 17, 1932 from Chas. Peacock stating that he was an Indian Christian who wanted to work for the removal of untouchability in Andhra "without surrendering my Christ... and without trying to change his religion." He replied on December 10, 1932 stating that "Christians who have no desire to proselytise can render substantial help to the Anti-untouchability Movement by working under or with the ordinary Hindu organisations." At the same time he added, "I observe from the correspondence I am receiving from Christian friends that the Hindu movement has quickened the conscience of Indian Christians and they are impatient to get rid of the taint in their midst."[97] It was a hint that Mr. Peacock would do better to work for the removal of untouchability prevalent among Christians and leave Hindu untouchables to the Hindus.

He made the point abundantly clear in an interview to the Associated Press of India on January 2, 1933. He had received a letter from Colombo informing him that "non-Hindus consisting of a Buddhist, a Roman Catholic lady, a Christian and a few Muslims" had offered "what has been misnamed satyagraha" in order to secure temple-entry for Hindu untouchables. "I have no hesitation whatsoever," he told the press correspondent, "in saying that this could not be justified under any circumstances. It would be a most dangerous interference if non-Hindus were to express their sympathy by way of direct action. Indeed, I go as far as to say that direct action can be offered [only] by those caste Hindus who are entitled to enter the temple in regard to which such action is

96. *Ibid.*, Volume 52, New Delhi 1972, p. 96.
97. *Ibid.*, p. 164.

taken, and who being entitled, believe in temple entry."[98] In a letter to Horace Alexander written on January 5, 1933 he pointed out, "I get now and then piteous letters from Christian Indians who, being born of untouchable parents, are isolated from the rest of their fellows."[99]

Gandhiji received a letter from Amritlal Thakkar, a Malabar Christian, stating that "the Christian Harijan in Travancore is, in matter of civic or social rights and in abject poverty, absolutely the same as his Hindu Harijan brother." He wrote in the *Young India* of March 18, 1933, that 'Christian Harijans' should be a contradiction in terms because untouchability was regarded as a special curse of Hinduism. "The present movement," he said "is automatically helping Christian Harijans, but I should be surprised if advantage is not being taken of the movement to drive out untouchability from the Church."[100]

The epic fast which Gandhiji had undertaken in order to oppose the separation of Harijans from Hindu society as intended by Ramsay MacDonald's Communal Award, brought him many letters from the West. A majority of them were "full of goodwill and appreciation of it and the motive lying behind it." But some letters were critical of the fast. One of them which Gandhiji published in full in the *Harijan* dated July 22, 1933, was from America and downright denunciatory. The writer thought that the fast had accomplished nothing, not even the publicity it was aimed at. "India whose culture and civilization," said the writer, "goes back far beyond record, which was given the new tongue of Christ Jesus by Thomas, the disciple, in the first century, and in the centuries just past has been given many opportunities to face the light, still remains in pagan darkness, its caste system of society the greatest sore spot on the modern world."[101] The disciple of Jesus went ahead and repeated all the standard accusations

98. *Ibid.*, pp. 344-45.
99. *Ibid.*, p. 365.
100. *Ibid.*, Volume 54, New Delhi, 1973, pp. 106-107.
101. *Ibid.*, Volume 55, New Delhi, 1973, p. 284.

that had been hurled by Christian missionaries against India for years on end — India's women were "without soul", India's millions lived in "nauseating filth", India's 'Holy Men' sat "for years in some deformed position publicly torturing the body to liberate the soul", and India's "pagan religious rites" consisted of "striking the body full of nails, spears through the tongue, and other revolting tortures." He said he had not read Miss Mayo's *Mother India* but "am told on good authority that it is a compilation of facts — so horrible that I have known cases of extreme illness from reading it."

The letter proved, if a proof was needed, that neither the protest registered by Vivekananda nor the admiration for Jesus expressed by Mahatma Gandhi had helped orthodox Christians to emerge out of the self-righteous ignorance in which they had enveloped themselves and stop their vicious propaganda against Hinduism. Gandhiji commented that the writer "starts with a bias and ends with it", that he "repeats the exploded libel about the women of India", that he had "evidently read literature containing ignorant and interested distortions", and that he had indulged in "wild generalisations" about "the tortures which so-called yogis undergo." He concluded, "One can pity the readers, if there were any such, who made themselves sick by reading a book which opened the drains of India and made the readers believe that they were India."[102] He was mild as ever and left it to the readers to judge for themselves the mind from which the letter had emanated.

One of the ways by which the Catholic Church in India sought to alienate Hindus from their ancestral religion was to insist that the children of Hindu husbands and Catholic wives would be brought up as Catholics. It had been seen that most Hindu young men who fell in love with Catholic girls yielded easily to this demand. The issue came before Gandhiji when Manu and Elizabeth, both of whom were known to him,

---

102. *Ibid.*, pp. 286-87. Earlier, Gandhiji had described Miss Mayo as a drain inspector.

decided for a love marriage. He was never enthusiastic about love marriages which he had seen failing in most cases after the first few years. Moreover, he was opposed to marriages tearing away young people from their families and favoured marriages seeking the "approval and blessings of the elders."[103] So he expressed his views on the subject in a letter dated November 16, 1933 written to Efy Aristarchi, a friend of Manu and Elizabeth. "The most fatal objection, however," he said, "that I can see to this proposed match, is that Elizabeth desires, and from her own standpoint perhaps naturally so, that the progeny should be brought up in the Roman Catholic faith. I do not mind it at all. But, even though Manu may have no objection, his parents and his people whom he loves dearly will never be able to reconcile themselves to their grandchildren being brought up in a faith other than their own."[104]

His objection was based on his perception of "a conflict going on between Hindu culture and the Christianity of Indians." He had seen that "Christianity has become synonymous with Western culture" which, in turn, "may be fittingly described as Christian culture" because "the religion of the Western people is predominantly Christianity." On the other hand, "Indian culture would certainly be described as Hindu culture." He, therefore, thought it proper that "the progeny of Elizabeth must be brought up in entirely different surroundings unless Manu decides to tear himself away from his surroundings and lives an exclusive life or decides to settle down in the West."[105] He was of the firm opinion that "when husband and wife profess a different faith, the progeny should be brought up in the faith of the husband" and he had "sound religious and philosophic reasons for this proposition."[106]

As more and more Christian agencies were coming

---

103. *Ibid.*, Volume 56, New Delhi, 1973, p. 234.
104. *Ibid.*, pp. 234-35.
105. *Ibid.*, p. 235.
106. *Ibid.*, p. 236.

forward to work for the removal of untouchability, Gandhiji made his terms clear in a speech at the Leonard Theological College, Jabalpur, on December 7, 1993. While inviting these agencies to work in subordination to Hindu agencies set up for Harijan uplift, he said, "You may choose to work independently. You may have the conversion of Harijans to Christianity. You may see in the movement a chance for propaganda. If you work among the Harijans with such aim, you can see that the very end we have in view will be frustrated. If you believe that Hinduism is a gift, not of God, but of Satan, quite clearly you cannot accept my terms. You and I would be dishonest if we did not make clear to one another what we stand for."[107]

A group of Christian Harijans came to Gandhiji and the talk he had with them was published in the *Harijan* of February, 23, 1934. "We are in the same position," they said, "as Adi-Dravida Hindus. Are we to have any share in this movement?" Gandhiji told them, "You are getting indirect benefit. The Christian missionaries are wide awake and recognize that they should do something." They proceeded, "We have decided to face the oppressors boldly. We are thinking of changing our faith." Gandhiji said, "I cannot say anything about that. But I feel that oppression can be no reason for changing our faith." The Christian Harijans asked, "Shall we get any relief in future from this movement?" Gandhiji assured them, "Yes, I am absolutely certain that, if this movement succeeds untouchability in Christianity is also bound to go."[108]

Mahadev Desai recorded in the *Harijan* dated January 25, 1935 a talk which Gandhiji had with a friend who had reported to him that the progress of the anti-untouchability campaign had "disturbed some of our Missionary friends." The friend said, "Your campaign is taking away from the Missionary's popularity." Gandhiji replied, "I see what you

107. *Ibid.*, pp. 310-11.

108. *Christian Missions*, p. 301.

mean, but I do not know why it should disturb them. We are not traders trenching on one another's province. If it is a matter of serving oneself, I should understand their attitude, but when it is entirely a matter of serving others, it should not worry them or me as to who serves them."[109]

The friend posed the question another way. "But perhaps," he said, "the authorities in charge of a Mission hospital would rightly feel worried, if you sent your people to go and open a hospital in the same place." Gandhiji explained, "But they should understand that ours is a different mission. We do not go there to afford them simply medical relief or a knowledge of the three R's; our going to them is a small proof of our repentance and our assurance to them that we will not exploit them any more. I should never think of opening a hospital where there is already one; but if there is a Mission school, I should not mind opening another for Harijan children, and I would even encourage them to prefer our school to the other. Let us frankly understand the position. If the object is purely humanitarian, purely that of carrying education where there is none, they should be thankful that someone whose obvious duty it is to put his own house in order wakes up to a sense of his duty. But my trouble is that the Missionary friends do not bring to bear on their work a purely humanitarian spirit. Their object is to add more members to their fold, and that is why they are disturbed. The complaint which I have been making all these years is more than justified by what you say. Some of the friends of a Mission were the other day in high glee over the conversion to Christianity of a learned pandit. They have been dear friends, and so I told them that it was hardly proper to go into ecstasies over a man forsaking his religion. Today it is the case of a learned Hindu, tomorrow it may be that of an ignorant villager not knowing the principles of his religion. Why should Missionaries complain, if I open a school which is more liked by Harijans than theirs? Is it not natural?"[110]

109. *Ibid.*, p. 195.
110. *Ibid.*, pp. 195-96.

The friend asked, "But if it was a pure case of conscience?" Gandhiji replied, "I am no keeper of anybody's conscience, but I do feel that it argues some sort of weakness on the part of a person who easily declares his or her failure to derive comfort in the faith in which he or she is born."[111]

The *Harijan* dated March 29, 1935 published an interview which Gandhiji had given to a Christian missionary before March 22. The missionary "asked Gandhiji what was the most effective way of preaching the gospel of Christ, for that was his mission." Gandhiji replied, "To live the gospel is the most effective way — most effective in the beginning, in the middle and in the end. Preaching jars on me and makes no appeal to me, and I get suspicious of missionaries who preach. But I love those who never preach but live the life according to their lights. Their lives are silent yet most effective testimonies... If, therefore, you go on serving people and ask them also to serve, then they would understand. But you quote instead John 3, 16 and ask them to believe it. That has no appeal to me, and I am sure people will not understand it. Where there has been acceptance of the gospel through preaching, my complaint is that there has been some motive." The missionary said that "we also see it and try our best to guard against it." Gandhiji observed, "But you can't guard against it. One sordid motive vitiates the whole preaching. It is like a drop of poison which fouls the whole food. Therefore I should do without preaching at all. A rose does not need to preach. It simply spreads its fragrance... The fragrance of religious and spiritual life is much finer and subtler than that of the rose."[112]

The same issue of the *Harijan* published another interview given by Gandhiji to some missionary ladies, also before March 22. One of their questions was whether the Harijan Sangh was doing "anything for the spiritual welfare

---

111. *Ibid.*, pp. 196-97.

112. *The Collected Works,* Volume 60, New Delhi, 1974, p. 323. John 3, 16 says, "For God loved the world so much that he sent his only Son so that everyone who believes in him may not die but have eternal life."

of the people." Gandhiji replied that "with me, moral includes spiritual" and that setting up a separate department for spiritual welfare will "make the thing doubly difficult." The ladies said that they had "something to share with the others" and that was the Bible. "Now as for Harijans," they asked, "who have no solace to get from Hinduism, how are we to meet their spiritual needs?" Gandhiji replied, "By behaving just like the rose. Does the rose proclaim itself, or is it self-propagated? Has it an army of missionaries proclaiming its beauties?"[113] The ladies persisted, "But suppose someone asked us, where did you get the scent?" Gandhiji said, "The rose if it has sense and speech would say, 'Fool, don't you see that I got if from my maker?'"[114]

The *Harijan* dated May 11, 1935 published an interview given by Gandhiji to a missionary nurse before that date. The nurse asked him, "Would you prevent missionaries coming to India in order to baptise?" Gandhiji replied, "If I had power and could legislate, I should certainly stop all proselytising. It is the cause of much avoidable conflict between classes and unnecessary heart-burning among the missionaries.... In Hindu households the advent of a missionary has meant the disruption of the family coming in the wake of change of dress, manners, language, food and drink."[115] The nurse commented, "Is it not the old conception you are referring to? No such thing is now associated with proselytisation." Gandhiji was well-informed about missionary methods. He said, "The outward condition has perhaps changed but the inward mostly remains the same. Vilification of Hindu religion, though subdued, is there. If there was a radical change in the missionaries' outlook, would Murdoch's books be allowed to be sold in mission depots? Are those books prohibited by missionary societies? There is nothing but vilification of Hinduism in those books. You talk of the conception being no longer there. The other day a missionary descended

113. *Ibid.*, p. 325.
114. *Ibid.*, p. 326.
115. *Ibid.*, Volume 61, Ahmedabad, 1975, p. 46.

on a famine area with money in his pocket, distributed it among the famine-stricken, converted them to his fold, took charge of their temple and demolished it. This is outrageous. The temple could not belong to the converted, and it could not belong to the Christian missionary. But this friend goes and gets it demolished at the hands of the very men who only a little while ago believed that God was there."[116]

The nurse took shelter behind the Bible. "But, Mr. Gandhi," she asked, "why do you object to proselytisation? Is not there enough in the Bible to authorise us to invite people to a better way of life?" Gandhiji replied, "If you interpret your texts in the way you seem to do, you straightaway condemn a large part of humanity unless it believes as you do.... And cannot he who has not heard the name of Jesus Christ do the will of the Lord?"[117]

The *Harijan* dated May 25, 1935 published a discussion which Gandhiji had with Pierre Ceresole on May 16. He told Gandhiji about a book, *India in the Dark Wood,* which he had recently read and which wanted "the main framework of the dominant Hindu philosophy to be shattered." The author of another book, *Jesus : Lord or Leader?,* also read recently by Ceresole, on the other hand, "rejects the claim of Christianity as the final religion and pines for a 'fuller and richer faith than we have reached and to believe that God who has nowhere left Himself without witness, will use the highest institutions of other systems and many races to enrich the thinking and worship of mankind.' He sees definite gain in the abandonment of special claim for the inspiration of the Bible, and classes himself among those 'who humbly desire to follow Jesus as leader, though their view of truth will not allow them to worship him as Lord'." Gandhiji commended the second approach, saying "There is a swing in the pendulum."[118]

Gandhiji was carrying on a discussion with Mr. A. A. Paul

116. *Ibid.*, pp. 46-47.
117. *Ibid.*, p. 47.
118. *Ibid.*, p. 68.

of the Federation of International Fellowships "on the so-called mass conversion of a village predominantly or wholly composed of Harijans."[119] Mr. Paul asked him to "publish a statement giving your view of conversion?" Gandhiji replied that it would be easier for him if Mr. Paul could formulate some questions to which he could reply. So the Executive Committee of the International Fellowship in Madras sent to him nine propositions which he published in the *Harijan* dated September 29, 1935 with his own comments on them.

The first proposition was: Conversion is a change of heart from sin to God. It is the work of God. Sin is separation from God.[120] Gandhiji observed, "If conversion is the work of God why should the work be taken away from Him?... I often wonder if we are true judges of our own hearts... And if we know so little of ourselves, how much less we know of our neighbours and remote strangers who may differ from us in a multitude of things, some of which are of the highest moment?"[121]

The second proposition was: The Christian believes that Jesus is the fulfilment of God's revelation to mankind, that he is our Saviour from sin, that he alone can bring a sinner to God and thus enable him to live.[122] Gandhiji said, "The second proposition deals with the Christian belief handed to the believer from generation to generation, the truth of which thousands of Christians born are never called upon to test for themselves, and rightly not. Surely it is a dangerous thing to present it to those who have been brought up in a different belief. And it would appear to me to be impertinent on my part to present my untested belief to the professor of another which for aught I know may be as true as mine. It is highly likely that mine may be good enough for me and his for him."[123]

---

119. *Ibid.*, p. 456.
120. *Ibid.*, p. 455.
121. *Ibid.*, p. 456.
122. *Ibid.*, p. 455.
123. *Ibid.*, p. 456.

The third proposition was: The Christian, to whom God has become a living reality and power through Christ, regards it as his privilege and duty to speak about Jesus and to proclaim the free offer which He came on earth to make.[124] Gandhiji said, "The third proposition too, like the first, relates to mysteries of religion which are not understood by the common people who take them in faith. They work well enough among people living in the traditional faith. They will repel those who have been brought up to believe something else."[125]

The next five propositions stated that if a man wanted to repent and live a new life as a disciple of Jesus, the Christian regards it as his right to admit him to the Christian Church; that the Christian will do all in his power to test the sincerity of the convert and point out the consequences of conversion; that the Christian will try his best to prevent conversion for material considerations; that the Christian shall not be accused of using material inducements if the conversion results in the social uplift of the convert; and that the Christian was right in accepting as his duty the care of the sincere convert, body, soul and mind.[126] "The other five propositions," commented Gandhiji, "deal with the conduct of the missionary among those whom he is seeking to convert. They seem to me almost impossible of application in practice. The start being wrong all that follows must be necessarily so. Thus how is the Christian to sound the sincerity of the conviction of his hearers? By a show of hands? By personal conversation? By a temporary trial? Any test that can be conceived will fail even to be reasonably conclusive. No one but God knows a man's heart. Is the Christian so sure of his being so right in body, mind and soul as to feel comfortably 'right in accepting as his duty the care of the sincere convert — body, soul and mind'?"[127]

124. *Ibid.*, p. 455.
125. *Ibid.*, p. 456.
126. *Ibid.*, p. 455.
127. *Ibid.*, pp. 455-57.

The last proposition was: It shall not be brought against the Christian that he is using material inducements, when certain facts in Hindu social theory, out of his control, are in themselves an inducement to the Harijans.[128] Gandhiji said, "The last proposition — the crown of all the preceding ones — takes one's breath away. For it makes it clear that the other eight are to be applied in all their fullness to the poor Harijans. And yet the very first proposition has not ceased to puzzle the brains of some of the most intellectual and philosophical persons even in the present generation. Who knows the nature of original sin? What is the meaning of separation from God? Are all who preach the message of Jesus the Christ sure of their union with God? If they are not, who will test the Harijan's knowledge of these deep things?"[129]

"It is a conviction daily growing upon me," concluded Gandhiji, "that the great and rich Christian missions will render true service to India, if they can persuade themselves to confine their activities to humanitarian service without ulterior motive of converting India or at least her unsophisticated villagers to Christianity, and destroying their social superstructure, which notwithstanding its many defects, has stood now from time immemorial the onslaught upon it from within and without. Whether they — the missionaries — and we wish it or not, what is true in the Hindu faith will abide, what is untrue will fall to pieces."[130]

Extracts from a letter from a Christian friend of Gandhiji were reproduced in the *Harijan* dated April 18, 1936. He quoted Jesus as saying to the Jews, "If you believe not that I am He, you shall die of your sins" and "I am *the* way, *the* truth and *the* life, no man cometh into the Father, but by me." Next, he threw a challenge to Gandhiji, "You must either believe Him to have been self-deceived or deliberately false." Finally, he declared, "I pray daily that Christ may grant to you a revelation of Himself as He did to Saul of Tarsus, that... you

128. *Ibid.*, p. 455.
129. *Ibid.*, p. 457.
130. *Ibid.*, pp. 457-58.

may be used to proclaim to India's millions the sacrificial efficacy of His precious blood."[131] Gandhiji wrote, "This is a typical letter from an old English friend who regularly writes such letters almost every six months. This friend is very earnest and well known to me. But there are numerous other correspondents unknown to me who write in the same strain without arguing. Since I now cannot for reasons of health write to individual writers, I use this letter as a text for a general reply."[132]

"My correspondent," continued Gandhiji, "is a literalist.... My very first reading of the Bible showed me that I would be repelled by many things in it if I gave their literal meaning to many texts or even took every passage in it as the word of God. I should find it hard to believe in the literal meaning of the verses relating to the immaculate conception of Jesus. Nor would it deepen my regard for Jesus if I gave those verses their literal meaning... The miracles said to have been performed by Jesus even if I had believed them literally would not have reconciled me to anything that did not satisfy universal ethics... Jesus then to me is a great world-teacher among others. He was to the devotees of his generation no doubt 'the only begotten son of God'. Their belief need not be mine. I regard him as one among the many begotten sons of God."[133] Finally, he said, "The *Gita* has become for me the key to the scriptures of the world. It unravels for me the deepest mysteries to be found in them. I regard them with the same reverence that I pay to the Hindu scriptures. Hindus, Mussalmans, Christians, Parsis, Jews are convenient labels.

---

131. *Ibid.,* Volume 62, New Delhi, 1975, pp. 332-33. Jesus' bombast about himself — 'I am He', etc. — can be seen in John 14.6. Saul of Tarsus was a persecutor of Christians before his conversion to Christianity. He became Paul after his conversion, and a great persecutor of mankind at large. He is one of the darkest figures in human history. Some scholars have seen him as the real inventor of Christianity and the father of the criminal history of this creed.

132. *Ibid.*, p. 333.

133. *Ibid.*, pp. 333-34.

But when I tear them down, I do not know which is which."[134]

On or after May 10, 1936 Gandhiji had a discussion with Professor Rahm, a reputed biologist from Switzerland. Dr. Rahm said that he was "perplexed by the many warring creeds in the world and wondered if there was no way of ending the conflict." Gandhiji gave a very straight-forward reply. "It depends," he said, "on Christians. If only they would make up their mind to unite with the others! But they will not do so. Their solution is universal acceptance of Christianity as they believe it. An English friend has been at me for the last forty years trying to persuade me that there is nothing but damnation in Hinduism and that I must accept Christianity. When I was in jail, I got, from three separate sources, no less than three copies of the *Life of Sister Therese,* in the hope that I should follow her example and accept Jesus as the only begotten son of God and my Saviour. I read the book prayerfully but I could not accept even St. Therese's testimony for myself."[135]

Gandhiji proceeded to make his position quite clear vis-a-vis orthodox Christianity. "But today," he said, "I rebel against orthodox Christianity, as I am convinced that it has distorted the message of Jesus. He was an Asiatic whose message was delivered through many media and when it had the backing of a Roman emperor, it became an imperialist faith which it remains today. Of course there are noble but rare exceptions like Andrews and Elwin. But the general trend is the same."[136] For the first time he did not try to reinterpret Christianity for Christians. The obstinacy shown by the orthodox Christians had hardened his attitude.

A Polish student brought a photograph to Gandhiji and got it autographed by him. "There is," he said, "a school conducted by Catholic Fathers. I shall help the school from the proceeds of the sale of this photograph." Gandhiji took

---

134. *Ibid.*, p. 334.

135. *Ibid.*, p. 388. *St. Therese* or Terese is honoured as one of the great Christian mystics by the Catholic Church.

136. *Ibid.*, p. 388.

back the photograph from the student and said, "Ah, that is a different story. You do not expect me to support the Fathers in their mission of conversion? You know what they do?" The *Harijan* of June 27, 1936 which relates this incident, continues, "And with this he told him.... the story of the so-called conversions in the vicinity of Tiruchengodu, the desecration and demolition of the Hindu temple, how he had been requested by the International Fellowship of Faiths to forbear writing about the episode as they were trying to intervene, how ultimately even the intervention of that body composed mainly of Christians had failed, and how he was permitted to write about it in the *Harijan*. He, however, had deliberately refrained from writing in order not to exacerbate feelings on the matter."[137]

The *Harijan* dated July 18, 1936 published a discussion which Gandhiji had with Pierre Ceresole and some Christian missionaries. The dialogue deserves to be reproduced at some length because it shows most clearly the missionary mentality and Gandhiji's opposition to it:

> (Missionary Lady) I have not had the time or desire to evangelize. The Church at home would be happy if through our hospital more people would be led to Christian lives.
>
> (Gandhiji) But whilst you give the medical help you expect the reward in the shape of your patients becoming Christians.
>
> (M.L.) Yes, the reward is expected. Otherwise there are many other places in the world which need our service. But instead of going there we come here.
>
> "(G.) There is the kink. At the back of your mind there is not pure service for its sake, but the result of service in the shape of many people coming to the Christian fold.
>
> (M.L.) In my own work there is no ulterior motive. I care for people, I cannot do otherwise. The source of this is my loyalty to Jesus who ministered to suffering humanity.

137. *Ibid.*, Volume 63, New Delhi, 1976, p. 47.

At the back of my mind there is, I admit, the desire that people may find the same joy in Jesus that I find. Where is the kink?

(G.) The kink is in the Church thinking that there are people in whom certain things are lacking and that you must supply them whether they want them or not. If you simply say to your patients, 'You have taken the medicine I gave you. Thank God. He has healed you. Don't come again', you have done your duty. But if you also say, 'How nice it would be if you had the same faith in Christianity as I have', you do not make your medicine a free gift.

(M.L.) But if I feel I have something medically and spiritually which I can give, how can I keep it?

(G.) There is a way out of the difficulty. You must feel that what you possess your patient also can possess but through a different route. You will say to yourself, 'I have come through this route, you may come through a different route.' Why should you want him to pass through your university and no other?

(M.L.) Because I have my partiality for my Alma Mater.

(G.) There is my difficulty. Because you adore your mother you cannot wish that all the others were your mother's children.

(M.L.) That is a physical impossibility.

(G.) Then this one is a spiritual impossibility. God has the whole humanity as His children. How can I limit God's grace by my little mind and say this is the only way?

(M.L.) I do not say it is the only way. There might be a better way.

(G.) If you concede that there might be a better way, you have surrendered the point.

(M.L.) Well, if you say that you have found your way, I am not so terrifically concerned with you. I will deal with one who is floundering in mind.

(G.) Will you judge him? Have you people not floundered? Why will you present your particular brand of truth to all?

(M.L.) I must present to him the medicine I know.

(G.) Then you will say to him, 'Have you seen your own doctor?' You will send him to his doctor, ask the doctor to take charge of him. You will perhaps consult that doctor, you will discuss with him the diagnosis, and will convince him or allow yourself to be convinced by him. But there you are dealing with a wretched physical thing. Here you are dealing with a spiritual thing where you cannot go through all these necessary investigations. What I plead for is humility. You do not claim freedom from hypocrisy for the Christian Church?[138]

At this point Dr. Pierre Ceresole, who pretended to be a "liberal" Christian, intervened:

(P.C.) Most of us believe our religion to be the best and they have not the slightest idea what other religions have revealed to their adherents...

(G.) I tell you you have not read as many books on Hinduism as I have about Christianity. And yet I have not come to the conclusion that Christianity or Hinduism is the only way.[139]

The missionary friend wondered, "What exactly should be missionaries' attitude?"

(G.) I think I have made it clear. But I shall say it again in other words: *Just to forget that you have come to a country of heathens and to think that they are as much in search of God as you are; just to feel that you are not going there to give your spiritual goods to them, but that you will share your worldly goods of which you have a good stock. You will then do your work without mental reservation and thereby you will share your spiritual treasures.*[140] The knowledge that you have this reservation creates a barrier between you and me.

---

138. *Ibid.*, pp. 90-92.
139. *Ibid.*, p. 92.
140. Italics in source.

(P.C.) Do you think that because of what you call the mental reservation, the work that one could accomplish would suffer?

(G.) I am sure. You would not be half as useful as you would be without the reservation. The reservation means that you belong to a different and a higher species, and you make yourself unaccessible to others.

(P.C.) A barrier would be my Western way of living?

(G.) No, that can be immediately broken.

(P.C.) Would you be really happy if we stayed at home?

(G.) I cannot say that. But I will certainly say that I have never been able to understand your going out of America. Is there nothing to do there?

(P.C.) Even in America there is enough scope for educational work.

(G.) That is a fatal confession. You are not a superfluity there. But for the curious position your Church has taken you would not be here.

(P.C.) I have come because the Indian women need medical care to a greater extent than American women do. But coupled with that I have a desire to share my Christian heritage.

(G.) That is exactly the position I have been trying to counter. You have already said that there may be a better way.

(P.C.) No, I meant to say that there may be a better way fifty years hence.

(G.) Well we were talking of the present, and you said there might be a better way.

(P.C.) No, there is no better way today than the one I am following.

(G.) That is what I say is assuming too much. You have not examined all religious beliefs. But even if you had, you may not claim infallibility. You assume knowledge of all people, which you can do only if you were God. I want you to understand that you are labouring under a double fallacy: That what you think is best for you is

> really so; and that what you regard as the best for you is the best for the whole world. It is an assumption of omniscience and infallibility. I plead for a little humility.[141]

Gandhiji had a discussion with C. F. Andrews who had just returned from a visit to New Zealand, Fiji and Australia. He wanted to know Gandhiji's reaction to the attitude of the missionaries vis-a-vis Harijan uplift. The discussion was reported in the *Harijan* of November 28,1936. It also deserves to be reproduced at some length:

> Gandhiji: Their behaviour has been as bad as that of the rest who are in the field to add to their numbers. What pains one is their frantic attempt to exploit the weakness of Harijans. If they said, 'Hinduism is a diabolical religion, come to us', I should understand. But they dangle earthly paradises in front of them and make promises to them which they can never keep. When in Bangalore[142] a deputation of Christians came with a number of resolutions which they thought would please me. I said to them: 'This is no matter for bargain. You must say definitely that this is a matter to be settled by the Hindus themselves. Where is the sense of talking of a sudden awakening of spiritual hunger among the untouchables and then trying to exploit a particular situation?... It is absurd for a single individual to talk of taking all the Harijans with himself. Are they all bricks that they could be moved from one structure to another? If the Christian missions here want to play the game, and for that matter Mussalmans and others, they should have no such idea as that of adding to their ranks whilst a great reform in Hinduism is going on.'
>
> C.F.A.: Let me ask one question. I said in Australia that all the talk of Dr. Ambedkar and his followers was not in terms of religion, and I said also that it was cruelty to bargain with unsophisticated people like the Harijans as they are in most parts of India. Then came the London Missionary

141. *Ibid.*, pp. 92-94.
142. Gandhiji was in Bangalore from May 31 to June 13, 1936.

Society's statement that the Ezhavas[143] in Travancore had asked for Christian instruction. I said then that the Ezhavas were quite enlightened and if they had really asked to be instructed in Christianity, it would be an entirely different matter. Was I right?

Gandhiji: I do not think so. Whilst there are individual Ezhavas who are doctors and barristers and so on, the vast majority of them are just the same as the Harijans elsewhere. I can assure you that no one representing the body of Ezhavas could have asked for Christian instruction. You should ascertain the facts from our principal workers there.

C.F.A: I see what you mean. Only I wanted to say that the London Missionary Society was a liberal body and would not make an irresponsible statement.

Gandhiji: But they at the centre cannot know, as the Parliament cannot know the truth of what is happening in India.

C.F.A: But that apart, I should like to discuss the fundamental position with you. What would you say to a man who after considerable thought and prayer said that he could not have his peace and salvation except by becoming a Christian?

Gandhiji: I would say that if a non-Christian, say a Hindu, came to a Christian and made that statement, he should ask him to become a good Hindu rather than find goodness in change of faith.

C.F.A: I cannot go this whole length with you, though you know my own position. I discarded the position that there was no salvation except through Christ long ago. But suppose the Oxford Group Movement changed the life of your son, and he felt like being converted, what would you say?

Gandhiji: I would say that the Oxford Group may change the lives of as many as they like, but not their

143. A depressed section of Hindu society in Kerala.

religion. They can draw their attention to the best in their respective religions and change their lives by asking them to live according to them. There came to me a man, the son of Brahmin parents, who said his reading of your book had led him to embrace Christianity... I said to him that you had never through your books asked Indians to take up the Bible and embrace Christianity and that he misread your book — unless of course your position is like that of the late Maulana Mohamed Ali, viz., that a believing Mussalman, however bad his life, is better than a good Hindu.

C.F.A: I do not accept Maulana Mohamed Ali's position at all. But I do say that if a person really needs a change of faith I should not stand in his way.

Gandhiji: But don't you see that you do not even give him a chance? You do not even cross-examine him. Suppose a Christian came to me and said he was captivated by a reading of the *Bhagavata* and wanted to declare himself a Hindu, I should say to him, 'Now what the *Bhagavata* offers the Bible also offers. You have not yet made the attempt to find it out. Make the attempt and be a good Christian.'

C.F.A: I don't know. If someone earnestly says, that he will become a good Christian, I should say, 'You may become one', though you know that I have in my own life strongly dissuaded ardent enthusiasts who came to me. I said to them, 'Certainly not on my account will you do anything of the kind.' But human nature does require a concrete faith.

Gandhiji: If a person wants to believe in the Bible let him say so, but why should he disregard his own religion? This proselytization will mean no peace in the world. Religion is a very personal matter. We should by living the life according to our own light, share the best with one another, thus adding to the sum total of human effort to reach God.[144]

144. *Ibid.*, Volume 64, New Delhi, 1976, pp. 18-20.

Mahadev Desai recorded in the *Harijan* dated December 5, 1936 a discussion which Mr. Basil Mathew had with Gandhiji about Missionary Methods. "That is a question to which I have given great thought," said Gandhiji, "and I am convinced that, if Christian Missions will sincerely play the game, no matter what may be their policy under normal circumstances, they must withdraw from the indecent competition to convert the Harijans. Whatever the Archbishop of Canterbury and others may say, what is done here in India in the name of Christianity is wholly different from what they say. There are others in the field also, but as a devotee of truth I say that, if there is any difference between their methods, it is one of degree and not of kind. I know of representatives of different religions standing on the same platform and vying with one another to catch the Harijan ear. To dignify this movement with the name of spiritual hunger is a travesty of truth. Arguing on the highest plane I said to Dr. Mott, if they wanted to convert Harijans, had they not better begin to convert me? I am a trifle more intelligent than they, and therefore more receptive to the influences of reason that could be brought to bear upon me. But to approach the Pulayas and Pariahs with their palsied hands and paralysed intelligence is no Christianity. No, whilst our reform movement is going on, all religious-minded people should say: Rather than obstruct their work, let us support them in their work."[145]

Mr. Mathew asked, "Do not the roots of the reform movement go back to the missionary movement? Did not the missionaries wake up the reformers and make a certain amount of stir among the untouchables?" Gandhiji replied, "I do not think that the missionary movement was responsible for a stirring of the right kind. I agree that it stung the reformers to the quick and awakened them to their sense of duty." Mr. Mathew persisted, "You have spoken of some good work being done by missionaries. Should not we go on with it?" Gandhiji observed, "Oh, Yes. Do, by all means. But give

145. *Christian Missions*, pp. 211-12.

up what makes you objects of suspicion and demoralizes us also. We go to your hospitals with the mercenary motive of having an operation performed, but with no object of responding to what is at the back of your mind, even as our children do when they go to Bible classes in their colleges and then laugh at what they read there. I tell you our conversation at home about these missionary colleges is not at all edifying. Why then spoil your good work with other motives?"[146]

Finally, Mr. Mathew asked, "Where do you find the seat of authority?" Gandhiji said, "It lies here (pointing to his breast). I exercise my judgment about every scripture, including the Gita. I cannot let a scriptural text supersede my reason. Whilst I believe that the principal books are inspired, they suffer from a process of double distillation. Firstly they come through a human prophet, and then through the interpreters. Nothing in them comes from God directly. Matthew may give one version of one text and John may give another. I cannot surrender my reason whilst I subscribe to divine revelation."[147]

The Missionary Supremo, John R. Mott, who had been receiving reports about Gandhiji's uncompromising stand against conversion under any circumstances, thought that it was time he himself sounded the Mahatma once again. So he paid his second visit to Sevagram and had long talks with Gandhiji on November 13-14, 1936. Parts of the conversation were reported in the *Harijan* dated December 9, 1936.

Mott started by praising Gandhiji for his effort to raise the Harijans, discussed the Yervada Pact and then broached the subject dear to his own heart. "The importance of this movement," he said, "lies beyond the frontiers of India, and yet there are few subjects on which there is more confusion of thought. Take for instance the missionaries and missionary societies. They are not of one mind. It is highly desirable that

146. *Ibid.*, p.212.
147. *Ibid.*, pp. 213-14.

we become of one mind and find out how far we can help and not hinder. I am the Chairman of the International Missionary Council which combines 300 missionary societies in the world. I have on my desk the reports of these societies; and I can say that their interest in the untouchables is deepening. I should be interested if you would feel free to tell us where, if anywhere, the missionaries have gone along wrong lines. Their desire is to help and not to hinder."

Gandhiji replied, "I cannot help saying that the activities of the missionaries have hurt me. They with the Mussalmans and Sikhs came forward as soon as Dr. Ambedkar threw the bombshell,[148] and they gave it an importance out of all proportions to the weight it carried, and then ensured a rivalry between these organisations. I could understand the Muslim organisations doing this, as Hindus and Muslims have been quarrelling. The Sikh intervention is an enigma. But the Christian mission claims to be a purely spiritual effort. It hurt me to find Christian bodies vying with Muslims and Sikhs in trying to add to the numbers of their fold. It seemed to me an ugly performance and a travesty of religion. They even proceeded to enter into secret conclaves with Dr. Ambedkar. I should have understood and appreciated your prayers for the Harijans but instead you made an appeal to those who had not even the mind and intelligence to understand what you talked; they have certainly not the intelligence to distinguish between Jesus and Mohammed and Nanak and so on."[149]

Mott asked, "But must we not serve them?" Gandhiji said, "Of course, you will, but not making conversion the price of your service."[150] Mott moved to the patent Christian position. He quoted Christ about "Preach and Teach" and said, "The whole Christian religion is the religion of sharing our life, and

---

148. The reference is to the Yeola Conference called by Dr. B.R. Ambedkar in September 1935. The Conference had adopted a resolution which said, "The depressed classes must leave the Hindu fold and join some other religion that gives social and religious equality to them."

149. *The Collected Works,* Volume 64, p. 35.

150. *Ibid.*, p. 36.

how can we share without supplementing our lives with words." Gandhiji replied, "Then what they are doing in Travancore is correct? There may be difference of degree in what you say and what they are doing, but there is no difference of quality. If you must share it with the Harijans, why don't you share it with Thakkarbapa and Mahadev? Why should you go to the untouchables and try to exploit this upheaval? Why not come to us instead?"[151]

Mott came out with more quotations from Jesus. But C. F. Andrews, who was present, sensed Gandhiji's impatience and suggested a compromise. Gandhiji said. "I do not think it is a matter which admits of any compromise at all. It is a deeply religious problem and each should do what he likes. If your conscience tells you that the present effort is your mission, you need not give any quarter to Hindu reformers. I can simply state my belief that what the missionaries are doing today does not show spirituality."[152]

The talks were resumed next day. Mott made a typically American offer. "If money is to be given to India," he said, "in what ways can it be wisely given without causing any harm? Will money be of any value?" Gandhiji replied, "No, when money is given it can only do harm. It has to be earned when it is required. I am convinced that the American and British money which has been voted for missionary societies has done more harm than good. You cannot serve God and mammon both. And my fear is that mammon has been sent to serve India and God has remained behind with the result He will one day have his vengeance. When the American says, 'I will serve you through money', I dread him. I simply say to him, 'Send us your engineers not to earn money but to give us the benefit of their scientific knowledge.'"[153]

Finally, Mott presented his pet theory that "money is stored-up personality" and that "Christ is able to dominate both the money and the machine." Gandhiji observed, "I

151. *Ibid.*, p. 37.
152. *Ibid.*, p. 38.
153. *Ibid.*, pp. 39-40.

have made the distinction between money given and money earned. If an American says he wants to serve India, and you packed him off here, I should say we had not earned his services... It is my certain conviction that money plays the least part in matters of spirit."[154]

The Church Times of London published, on October 16, 1936, the news of a meeting of Christian denominations held in that city. The meeting was presided over by the Archbishop of Canterbury. The main speaker was Dr. J. W. Pickett, Bishop of a Methodist Episcopal Church in the U.S.A. He was the author of a book, *Christian Mass Movements in India*, which he said he had written after making studies "on the spot." He reported that "four and a half millions of the depressed classes in India have become disciples of our Lord" and that "even Brahmins have testified — albeit reluctantly — to the power of Christianity to transform the characters and lives of people whom they once thought incapable of religious feelings, and to whom they denied the right of entrance to temples of Hinduism." According to him, "900,000 people now profess the Christian faith" in the Telegu area and "a surprisingly high proportion of them speak of a sense of mystical union with God." He quoted "their Hindu neighbours" who, according to him, had "admitted that the religion of Jesus Christ had lifted them to a new standard of cleanliness of person and home, and made them a trustworthy people." As a result, he said, "high-caste people are now coming into the church, literally by dozens of hundreds, in areas where this transformation of life has occurred among the untouchables." He described this "mass movement" as a "miracle, one of the great miracles of Christian history."[155]

Gandhiji reproduced the news in the *Harijan* dated December 19, 1936 and made his own comment on the 'miracle'. "I have rarely seen," he said, "so much exaggeration in so little space. A reader ignorant of conditions in India

154. *Ibid.*, p. 40.

155. *Ibid.*, pp. 149-50.

would conclude that the figures relate to the conversions due to the movement led by Dr. Ambedkar. I am sure Dr. Pickett could not have made any such claim. He had in mind the figures to date commencing from the establishment of the first church in India hundreds of years ago. But the figures are irrelevant to the general claim said to have been advanced by the Bishop. Where are the 'multitudes in India who marvel' at the transformation in the lives of 'four and a half millions of the depressed classes'? I am one of the multitudes having practically travelled more than half a dozen times all over India and have not seen any transformation on the scale described by Dr. Pickett, and certainly none of recent date. I have had the privilege of addressing meetings of Indian Christians who have appeared to me to be no better than their fellows. Indeed, the taint of untouchability persists in spite of the nominal change of faith so far as the social status is concerned... I should like to meet the Brahmins 'who have testified... to the power of Christianity to transform the characters and lives of people whom they once thought incapable of religious feeling'... I must pass by the other generalizations. But I should like to know the hundreds of high caste Hindus who 'are now coming into the church in areas where this transformation of life has occurred among the untouchables'. If all the astounding statements Dr. Pickett has propounded can be substantiated, truly it is 'one of the greatest miracles of Christian history', nay, of the history of man."[156]

At the same time Gandhiji asked, "But do miracles need an oratorical demonstration? Should we in India miss such a grand miracle? Should we remain untouched by it?" Stating that "Miracles are their own demonstration", he drew the attention of the missionaries to the "miracle in Tranvancore" where 2000 temples had been opened to the Harijans who "would enter them in their hundreds without let or hindrance from the most orthodox Hindus." He concluded that "the learned Bishop" had made a caricature of Christianity which

156. *Ibid.*, pp. 150-51.

"hurts me."[157]

The story-tellers, however, did not stop at making tall claims. In the *Harijan* dated December 26, 1936, Gandhiji had to comment on a pamphlet published by the Church Missionary Society of England. It had given a call for an "emergency fund of £25,000 to enable extra grants to be made during the next five years to those areas where this big movement is taking place." The Society appealed to the "whole church to support this effort" for the "sake of the hundreds of thousands who are dimly groping after Christ and who are finding spiritual life and social uplift through the Gospel."[158] Some of the claims made by Dr. Pickett were repeated in the pamphlet which had "discovered" that "the campaign for the removal of untouchability" led by Gandhiji "had signally failed because he clung to the Hindu system which has been the cause of the trouble." More important, the future prospects for Christianity in certain areas were seen as very promising. It was stated that the Bishop of Dornakal in the Telegu region "reckons that about a million people in his diocese are moving Christward" and among the Ezhavas "850,000 have waited on the Bishop in Travancore, because they are anxious that their entire community should become Christians."[159]

Gandhiji commented that he was "utterly unconscious of 'signal failure'", and that he who had "travelled in Telegu areas often enough" had "never heard of forty thousand Harijans or any figure near it asking for baptism."[160] As for the Ezhavas, he observed, "The papers report them to have congratulated the Maharaja on his Proclamation."[161] He concluded, "There is no other way to deal with exaggerations of which the appeal is full than by living them down and by the truth working through the lives of the reformers."[162]

157. *Ibid.*, p. 151.
158. *Ibid.*, p. 176.
159. *Ibid.*, pp. 176-77.
160. *Ibid.*, p. 177 .
161. This proclamation had opened Hindu temples to Harijans.
162. *Ibid.*, p. 178.

Professor Krzenski, according to whom "Catholicism was the only true religion", had a discussion with Gandhiji on January 2, 1937. The dialogue was reported in the *Harijan* of January 16. Gandhiji made use of Socratic wit to disarm him completely:

> Gandhiji: Do you therefore say that other religions are untrue?
>
> Krzenski: If others are convinced that their religions are true they are saved.
>
> Gandhiji: Therefore you will say that everyone would be saved even through untruth. For you say that if a man really and sincerely believes in what is as a matter of fact untruth he is saved. Would you not also hold, therefore, that your own way may be untrue but that you are convinced that it is true and therefore you will be saved?[163]

Krzenski's claim that he had studied and compared all religions and found his own to be the best, did not impress Gandhiji for whom religion was not a matter of "intellectual examination." He told the professor that "your position is arrogant." The professor then "switched on to the next question, viz., that of fighting materialism." Gandhiji said, "It is no use trying to fight these forces without giving up *the idea of conversion, which I assure you is the deadliest poison which ever sapped the fountain of truth*."[164]

Before leaving, the professor said, "But I have great respect for you." Gandhiji observed, "Not enough. If I were to join the Catholic Church you would have greater respect for me." Krzenski agreed and said that in that case "you would be as great as St. Francis?" Gandhiji winked, "But not otherwise? A Hindu cannot be a St. Francis? Poor Hindu?"

Krzenski wanted to take a photograph of Gandhiji. He was dissuaded by Gandhiji's quick remark, "No, surely you don't care for materialism! And it is all materialism, isn't it?"[165]

---

163. *Ibid.*, pp. 202-03.
164. *Ibid.*, p. 203. Emphasis added.
165. *Ibid.*, pp. 203.

On January 19, 1937 Gandhiji gave an interview to two Bishops and some other Christians at Kottayam. He had gone there to extend his support to the Maharaja's proclamation on temple-entry for Harijans. Bishop Moore said he was "ready to remove misunderstandings" about missionary work in Travancore which had disturbed Gandhiji. Gandhiji referred him to Bishop Pickett's claim about conversions in the Telegu country and Travancore, and the Church Missionary Society's call for funds. Moore pleaded ignorance about the claim and the collection and agreed that exaggerated reports should not be circulated. He also stated that "during the last year they could record 530 persons as having been baptised into the Anglican faith." But Bishop Abraham asserted that "there was a tremendous awakening among even the middle class *savarnas*" in Telegu areas and that "he had addressed meetings which were attended by many of the high-caste people." Gandhiji said, "That means nothing. To say that hundreds attended meetings addressed by Christian preachers is very different from saying that hundreds have accepted the message of Jesus and from making an appeal for money in anticipation of people becoming Christians in large numbers." The Christians wanted to know if "Mr. Gandhi had any objection to their stimulating and responding to the spiritual hunger of the people." Gandhiji said that "the matter was quite irrelevant to the discussion which was entirely about extravagant statements made by responsible people."[166]

On the same day he addressed a public meeting in the town. "In the estimation of those who so believe," he said, "this Proclamation is an act which it would be their duty to resist and to show to the Maharaja that by issuing the Proclamation of liberation he is simply prolonging the agony and giving a new lease of life to a body of superstitions which were bound to die their natural death." He had the Christian missionaries and their Hindu mouthpieces in mind. "I know," he continued, "that many Christians throughout the length

166. *Ibid.*, pp. 285-86.

and breadth of India do not regard Hinduism as a fraud upon humanity or a body of bad usages and superstitions. A religion which has produced Ramakrishna, Chaitanya, Shankar and Vivekananda cannot be a body of superstitions." After explaining the "essence of Hinduism" with the help of "one incredibly simple *mantra* of the Ishopanishad"[167], he suggested to "my Christian and Mussalman friends that they will find nothing more in their scriptures."[168]

He declared that he had himself been fighting against whatever corruptions had crept into Hinduism and requested all non-Hindus not to exploit the temporary weaknesses of this great religion. "I felt," he said, "that I could not do justice to this great meeting, especially a meeting that is held in a Christian stronghold, unless I was prepared to utter a truth I held dear as life itself. We all consciously or unconsciously find and strive for peace on earth and goodwill amongst mankind. I am convinced that we shall find neither peace nor goodwill among men and women through strife among men of different religions, through disputation among them. We shall find truth and peace and goodwill if we approach the humblest of mankind in a prayful spirit. Anyway that is my humble appeal to Christians who may be present in this great meeting... As I have said so often elsewhere, whilst the hand that traced the signature on the Proclamation was that of the Maharaja, the spirit that moved him to do so was that of God."[169]

On March 5, 1937 Gandhiji had a discussion with R. R. Keithahn, an American missionary, about the equality of all religions. The missionary was "not quite sure what was at

---

167. *Ibid.*, p. 289. The *mantra* is the very first one of the Ishopanishad: *īśāvāsyamidam sarvam yatkiñcit jagatyām jagat / tena tyaktena bhuñjithā mā gridhaḥ kasyacit dhanam*. Gandhiji translated it as follows: "God pervades everything that is to be found in this universe. Therefore the condition of enjoyment or use of the necessities of life is their dedication or renunciation. Covet not anybody's riches."

168. *Ibid.*, p. 290.

169. *Ibid.*, p. 291.

the back of Gandhiji's mind when he said that all religions were not only true but equal." He felt that "scientifically it was hardly correct to say that all religions are equal." But he admitted that "it is no use comparing religions" and that "they were different ways."[170] Gandhiji said, "You are right when you say that it is impossible to compare them. But the deduction from it is that they are equal. All men are born free and equal, but one is much stronger or weaker than another physically and mentally. Therefore superficially there is no equality between the two. But there is an essential equality: in our nakedness. God is not going to think of me as Gandhi and you as Keithahn... inherently we are equal. The differences of race and skin and of mind and body and of climate and nation are transitory. In the same way essentially all religions are equal... Where is the use of scanning details and holding a religion to ridicule? Take the very first chapter of Genesis or of Matthew. We read a long pedigree and then at the end we are told that Jesus was born of a virgin. You come up against a blind wall. But I must read it all with the eye of a Christian."[171]

A Roman Catholic Father came to see Gandhiji on March 5, 1937 and proposed that "if Hinduism became monotheistic, Christianity and Hinduism can serve India in co-operation." Gandhiji replied, "I would love to see the co-operation happen, but it cannot if the present-day Christian missions persist in holding up Hinduism to ridicule and saying that no one can go to Heaven unless he renounces and denounces Hinduism... not so long as there is militant and 'muscular' Christianity."[172] The Father persisted, "But if Indians begin to believe in one God and give up idolatry, don't you think the whole difficulty will be solved?" Gandhiji put a counter question to him, "Will the Christians be satisfied? Are they all united?" The Father admitted that the Christian sects knew no unity. "Then you are asking," continued Gandhiji, "a theoretical

170. *Ibid.*, p. 419.
171. *Ibid.*, pp. 419-20.
172. *Ibid.*, p. 421.

question. And may I ask you, is there any amalgamation between Islam and Christianity, though both are said to believe in one God? If these two have not amalgamated, there is less hope of amalgamation of Christians and Hindus along lines you suggest. I have my own solution, but in the first instance I dispute the description that Hindus believe in many gods and are idolaters... The whole mischief is created by the English rendering of the word *deva* or *devata* for which you have not found a better term than 'god'. But God is Ishwara, Devadhideva, God of Gods. So you see it is the word 'god' used to describe different divine beings, that has given rise to such confusion. I believe that I am a thorough Hindu but I never believe in many Gods."

Next, Gandhiji proceeded to defend idol-worship. "As for idol-worship," he said, "you cannot do without it in some form or other. Why does a Mussalman give his life for defending a mosque which he calls a house of God? And why does a Christian go to a Church and when he is required to take an oath swear by the Bible? Not that I see any objection to it. And what is it if not idolatry to give untold riches for building mosques and tombs? And what do the Roman Catholics do when they kneel before Virgin Mary and before saints — quite imaginary figures in stone or painted on canvas or glass?" The Father made a distinction between 'veneration' and 'worship'. "When I worship God," he said, "I acknowledge Him as creator and greater than any human being." Gandhiji observed, "Even so, it is not the stone we worship but it is God we worship in images of stone or metal however crude they may be."[173] The Father said, "But the villagers worship stones as God." Gandhiji explained, "No, I tell you they do not worship anything that is less than God. When you kneel before Virgin Mary and ask for her intercession, what do you do? You ask to establish contact with God through a stone image. I can understand your asking for the Virgin's intercession. Why are Mussalmans filled with awe

173. *Ibid.*, pp. 421-22.

and exultation when they enter a mosque? Why is not the whole universe a mosque?... But I understand and sympathise with the Muslims. It is their way of approach to God. The Hindus have their own way of approach to the same Eternal Being. Our media of approach are different, but that does not make Him different."[174]

The Father now came to the patent Christian position. "But the Catholics believe," he said, "that God revealed to them the true way." Gandhiji replied, "But why do you say that the will of God is expressed only in one book called the Bible and not in others? Why do you circumscribe the power of God?" The Father brought in Jesus who "proved that he had received the word of God through miracles." Gandhiji pointed out, "But that is Mahomed's claim too. If you accept Christian testimony you must accept Muslim testimony and Hindu testimony too." The Father dropped the subject and became curious about the Congress "veering round Communism."[175] Gandhiji advised him not to confuse with Communism the Congress campaign against inequality.

Finally, the Father expressed his fear of Hindus coming to power in free India. "When Hinduism comes to power," he asked, "will it not make a united front against Christianity? There are all the signs of Hinduism coming to power. And if it happens here, as it is happening in Spain,[176] Indian Christians will be despised and persecuted and swept off." Gandhiji told him that his fears were imaginary. "There is no such thing," said Gandhiji, "as Hindu rule, there will be no such thing... Let me tell you that no Hindu in his wildest imagination ever thought of this... Hinduism was well able to destroy the first Christians that came. Why did it not do anything of the kind? Travançore is a brilliant example of toleration. I was asked while I was there to see the most ancient church where St. Thomas is said to have planted the

174. *Ibid.*, pp. 422-23.

175. *Ibid.*, p. 423.

176. At that time, Communists were waging a civil war in Spain and persecuting Christians wherever Communist power prevailed.

first cross. Why should he have been allowed to plant it?" The Father "revealed his bugbear — Arya Samaj." Gandhiji said, "I agree that the Arya Samaj represents a type of militant Hinduism, but they never believed in the cult of the sword. The worst thing they are capable of is to ask you to become a Hindu if you went and spoke on their platform!"[177]

A distinguished American clergyman, Dr. Crane, met Gandhiji on February 25, 1937 and asked him various questions. The interview was published in the *Harijan* dated March 6, 1937. The first question was about Gandhiji's attitude to Christianity. "For a time," said Gandhiji, "I struggled with the question, 'which was the true religion out of those I know?' But ultimately I came to the deliberate conviction that there was no such thing as only one true religion, every other being false. There is no religion that is absolutely perfect. All are equally imperfect or more or less perfect, hence the conclusion that Christianity is as good and true as my own religion... Therefore I am not interested in weaning you from Christianity and making you a Hindu, and I would not relish your designs upon me, if you had any, to convert me to Christianity: I would also dispute your claim that Christianity is the only true religion. It is also a true religion, a noble religion, and along with other religions it has contributed to raise the moral height of mankind. But it has yet to make a greater contribution. After all what are 2,000 years in the life of a religion? Just now Christianity comes to yearning mankind in a tainted form. Fancy Bishops supporting slaughter in the name of Christianity."[178]

Dr. Crane asked, "But, when you say that all religions are true, what do you do when there are conflicting counsels?" Gandhiji replied, "I have no difficulty in hitting upon the truth, because I go by certain fundamental maxims. Truth is superior to everything and I reject what conflicts with it. Similarly that which is in conflict with non-violence should

177. *Ibid.*, pp. 423-24.
178. *Ibid.*, pp. 397-98.

be rejected. And on matters which can be reasoned out, that which conflicts with Reason must also be rejected... Well then, given these three criteria, I can have no difficulty in examining all claims made on behalf of religion. Thus to believe that Jesus is the only begotton son of God is to me against Reason, for God can't marry and beget children. The word 'son' there can only be used in a figurative sense. In that sense everyone who stands in the position of Jesus is a begotten son of God. If a man is spiritually miles ahead of us we may say that he is in a special sense the son of God, though we are all children of God."[179]

The next question from the clergyman was, "Then you will recognize degrees of divinity. Would you not say that Jesus was the most divine?" Gandhiji said, "No, for the simple reason that we have no data. Historically we have more data about Mahomed than anyone else because he was more recent in time. For Jesus there are less data available, no judge should shoulder the burden of sifting all the evidence, if only for the reason that it requires a highly spiritual person to gauge the degree of divinity of the subjects he examines."[180]

The clergyman sought his view about conversion. "I strongly resent," said Gandhiji, "these overtures to utterly ignorant men. I can perhaps understand overtures made to me, as indeed they are being made. For they can reason with me and I can reason with them. But I certainly resent the overtures made to Harijans. When a Christian preacher goes and says to a Harijan that Jesus was the only begotten son of God, he will give him a blank stare. Then he holds out all kinds of inducements which debase Christianity."[181]

Dr. Crane asked him if he regarded Hinduism as a synthesis of all religions. "Yes," replied Gandhi, "if you will. But I would call that synthesis Hinduism, and for you the synthesis will be Christianity. If I did not do so, you would

---

179. *Ibid.*, p. 398.
180. *Ibid.*, pp. 398-99.
181. *Ibid.*, p. 400.

always be patronizing me, as many Christians do now, saying, 'How nice it would be if Gandhi accepted Christianity', and Muslims would be doing the same, saying, 'How nice it would be if Gandhi accepted Islam!' That immediately puts a barrier between you and me."[182]

Finally, there was a discussion about what Dr. Crane called the caste system. Gandhiji said, "Hinduism does not believe in caste. I would obliterate it at once. But I believe in varnadharma, which is the law of life. I believe that some people are born to teach and some to defend and some to engage in trade and agriculture and some to do manual labour, so much so that these occupations become hereditary. The law of varna is nothing but the law of conservation of energy. Why should my son not be a scavenger if I am one?" Crane was surprised and exclaimed, "Indeed? Do you go so far?" Gandhiji replied, "I do, because I hold a scavenger's profession in no way inferior to a clergyman's... For a scavenger is as worthy of his hire as a lawyer or your President. That, according to me, is Hinduism. There is no better communism on earth, and I have illustrated it with one verse from the Upanishads which means: God pervades all — animate and inanimate. Therefore renounce all and dedicate it to God and then live. The right of living is thus derived from renunciation. It does not say, 'When all do their part of the work I too will do it.' It says, 'Don't bother about others, do your job first and leave the rest to Him.' Varnadharma acts even as the law of gravitation. I cannot cancel it or its working by trying to jump higher day by day till gravitation ceases to work. That effort will be vain. So is the effort to jump over one another. The law of varna is the antithesis of competition which kills."[183]

Someone wrote a long letter to Gandhiji. Extracts from it were published in the *Harijan* of March 6, 1937. The letter said, "Your attitude towards religious conversion and particularly

182. *Ibid.*, p. 401.
183. *Ibid.*, pp. 425-26.

the hope you entertain for the Depressed Classes within the fold of Hinduism, overlooks the prevalent practices of Hinduism as it exists in India today..." He also pointed out that "any religion is judged by its fruits." Hindu temples and mutts, he continued, collected a lot of money from the devotees, but instead of being used for rendering service it was used for the "princely lives" led by the heads of mutts. Religious heads, Swamis and gurus were practising "popery in its worst days." Temples and mutts had become "weapons of superstition and oppression." On the other hand, "Bishops and priests of Christian religion...render humanitarian service unequalled by any other class of human beings who follow any other faith or no faith, and are approachable to all people."[184]

Gandhiji commented, "It is good to see ourselves as others see us... The grave limitations of Hinduism as it is today must be admitted... Humanitarian work done by Christian missions must also be admitted. But these admissions of mine must not be interpreted to mean endorsement of the deductions of the writer." The writer had admitted the "sublimity of Hinduism as expounded by Vivekananda and Radha-krishnan." Gandhiji pointed out that this admission "should have led to his discovery of its percolation down to the masses." He said, "I make bold to say that in spite of the crudeness which one sees among the villagers, class considered, in all that is good in human nature they compare favourably with any villagers in the world. This testimony is borne out by the majority of travellers who from the times of Huen Tsang down to the present times have recorded their impressions. The innate culture that the villagers of India show, the art which one sees in the homes of the poor, the restraint with which the villagers conduct themselves, are surely due to the religion that has bound them together since time immemorial."[185]

184. *Ibid.*, pp. 401-02.
185. *Ibid.*, pp. 426-27.

Coming to service, Gandhiji wrote, "In his zeal to belittle Hinduism, the writer ignores the broad fact that Hinduism has produced a race of reformers who have successfully combated prejudices, superstitions and abuses. Without any drum-beating Hinduism has devised a system of relief of the poor which has been the envy of many foreign admirers... It is not the Indian habit to advertise charities through printed reports and the like. But he who runs may see the free kitchens and free medical relief given along indigenous lines." Missionary service institutions, on the other hand, "are established with a view to weaning Indians from their ancestral faith even as expounded by Vivekananda and Radha-krishnan."[186]

In his talk with Mr. John Mott and some other missionaries Gandhiji has compared the Harijans with the cow so far as understanding of Christian theology was concerned. The missionaries made much of it and went about propagating that Gandhiji had insulted the Harijans. He had explained in the *Harijan* of January 9, 1937 what he meant by the comparison.[187] But that did not stop the missionary campaign. So he returned to the theme in the *Harijan* of March 13, 1937. "This comparison," he wrote, "shocked my friends so much that the shock has travelled to America and I have begun to receive letters from America telling me how the comparison is being used to discredit me and my claim to serve Harijans. The critics seem to say, 'You can have little regard for Harijans if you compare them to the cow!'"

Gandhiji refused to be browbeaten and did not withdraw the comparison. He explained his simile once again and went farther. "Let my critics and credulous friends understand," he said, "that apart from the comparison, I stand on unassailable ground when I assert that it is a travesty of religion to seek to uproot from the Harijans' simple minds such faith as they have in their ancestral religion and to transfer their allegiance

186. *Ibid.*, p. 427.
187. *Ibid.*, p. 218.

to another, even though that other may be as good as and equal to the original in quality. Though all soils have the same predominant characteristics, we know that the same seeds do not fare equally well in all soils... But my fear is that though Christian friends nowadays do not say or admit that Hindu religion is untrue, they must harbour in their breasts the belief that Hinduism is an error and that Christianity as they believe it is the only true religion. Without some such thing it is not possible to understand, much less to appreciate, the C.M.S.[188] appeal from which I reproduced in these columns some revealing extracts the other day. One could understand the attack on untouchability and many other errors that have crept into Hindu life. And if they would help us to get rid of the admitted abuses and purify our religion, they would do helpful constructive work which would be gratefully accepted. But so far as one can understand the present effort, it is to uproot Hinduism from the very foundation and replace it by another faith. If the Christian world entertains that opinion about the Hindu house, 'Parliament of Religions' and 'International Fellowship' are empty phrases. For both the terms presuppose equality of status, a common platform. There cannot be a common platform as between inferiors and superiors, or the enlightened and the unenlightened, the regenerate and the unregenerate, the high-born and the low-born, the caste man and the outcaste. My comparison may be defective, may even sound offensive. My reasoning may be unsound. But my proposition stands."[189]

A joint manifesto, 'Our Duty to the Depressed and Backward Classes', was issued by "fourteen highly educated Indian Christians occupying important positions." It was published in full in the *Harijan* dated April 3, 1937, though Gandhiji "was disinclined to publish it in the *Harijan,* as after having read it more than once I could not bring myself to say anything in its favour and I felt a critical review of it might

188. Church Missionary Society based in London.

189. *Ibid.*, pp. 440-41.

serve no purpose." He thought it was an "unfortunate document." But as his criticism was "expected and will be welcomed", he decided to tender it. "They seem to have fallen between two stools," wrote Gandhiji, "in their attempt to sit on both. They have tried to reconcile the irreconcilable. If one section of Christians has been aggressively open and militant, the other represented by the authors of the manifesto is courteously patronising. They would not be aggressive for the sake of expedience. The purpose of the manifesto is not to condemn unequivocally the method of converting the illiterate and the ignorant but to assert the right of preaching the Gospel to the millions of Harijans."[190]

Para 7 of the manifesto had proclaimed, "Men and women individually and in family or village groups will continue to seek fellowship of the Christian Church. That is the real movement of the Spirit of God. And no power on earth can stem that tide. It will be the duty of the Christian Church in India to receive such seekers after the truth as it is in Jesus Christ and provide for them instruction and spiritual nurture. The Church will cling to its right to receive such people into itself from whatever religious groups they may come."[191] Gandhiji commented, "Men and women do not seek fellowship of the Christian Church. Poor Harijans are no better than the others. I wish they had spiritual hunger. Such as it is, they satisfy by visit to the temples, however crude they may be. When the missionary of another religion goes to them, he goes like any other vendor of goods. He has no special spiritual merit that will distinguish him from those to whom he goes. He, however, possesses material goods which he promises to those who will come to his fold. Then mark, the duty of the Christian Church in India turns into a right. Now when duty becomes a right, it ceases to be a duty... The duty of taking spiritual message is performed by the messenger becoming a fit vehicle by prayer and fasting.

190. *Ibid.*, Volume 65, New Delhi 1976, p. 47.

191. *Ibid.*, pp. 47-48.

Conceived as a right it may easily become an imposition on unwilling parties." Gandhiji saw the manifesto as "designed to allay the suspicion and soothe the ruffled feelings of Hindus." But, in his opinion, it "fails to accomplish its purpose" and "leaves a bad taste in the mouth." He concluded, "In the spiritual sphere, there is no such thing as right."[192]

Soon after Gandhiji made his comments on the manifesto, a missionary came to him seeking clarification. The discussion which Gandhiji had with him was published in the *Harijan* of April 17, 1937. "I wonder," said the missionary, "if those who made the statement were thinking of anything in the nature of *legal* right. It is, I think, a moral right they claim here rather than a legal one." Gandhiji replied, "My criticism would apply even if they had used the word 'moral right'. But it is clear that they mean a legal right because for one thing there is no such thing as a moral right, and secondly because in the very next para of the manifesto, in which they have referred to the Karachi Resolution of Fundamental Rights, they make it clear that they mean by 'right' legal right. A moral right, if there is any such thing, does not need any asserting and defending."[193]

The missionary came to his next question. "You have objected to Christian propaganda," he said, "on the ground that Harijans are illiterate and ignorant. What would you say of propaganda amongst non-Harijans?" Gandhiji replied, "I have the same objection because the vast mass of people of India do not understand the pros and cons of Christianity better than a cow. I use this simile in spite of the fact that it has been objected to. When I say that I do not understand logarithms any better than my cow, I do not mean any insult to my intelligence. In matters of theology, the non-Harijan masses can understand no better than the Harijans... Try to preach the principles of Christianity to my wife. She can understand them no better then my cow. I can, because of the

192 *Ibid.*, p. 48.
193. *Ibid.*, p. 79.

training I have had."

The missionary proceeded further. He said, "But we do not preach theology. We simply talk of the life of Christ and tell them what a comfort His life and teaching have been to us. He has been our guide, we say and ask others also to accept Him as their guide." Gandhiji observed, "Oh yes, you do say that. But when you say I must accept Jesus in preference to Ramakrishna Paramhamsa, you will have to go into deep waters. That is why I say, let your life speak to us, even as the rose needs no speech but simply spreads its perfume."[194]

The missionary shifted his ground. "But then," he said, "your objection is to the commercial aspect of Christian propaganda. Every true Christian will agree that no baits should be offered." Gandhiji asked, "But what else is Christianity as it is preached nowadays?... Why should students attending Mission schools and colleges be compelled or even expected to attend Bible classes?"[195] The missionary protested, "That was the old way, not the modern way." Gandhiji said, "I can cite to you any number of modern examples. Is not the Bishop of Dornakal a modern? And what else is his open letter to the Depressed Classes of India? It is full of baits." The missionary moved from education to medicine and said, "As regards hospitals, I think philanthropy without the dynamic of some religious teaching will not do." Gandhiji did not agree. "Then you commercialize you gift," he said, "for at the back of your mind is the feeling that because of your service some day the recipient of the gift will accept Christ. Why should not your service be its own reward."[196]

The missionary shifted his ground once more and said, "But then you must judge Christianity by its best representatives and not the worst." Gandhiji replied, "I am not judging Christianity as a religion. I am talking of the way Christianity is being propagated, and you cannot judge it by exceptions,

---

194. *Ibid.*, p. 80.
195. *Ibid.*, pp. 80-81.
196. *Ibid.*, p. 81.

as you cannot judge the British system of Government by some fine specimens of Englishmen. No, let us think of the bulk of your people who preach the Gospel. Do they spread the perfume of their lives? That is to me the sole criterion."

The missionary now wanted to "hear from you your attitude to the personality of Christ." Gandhiji gave him his settled view that Christ was "a great teacher of humanity" and not "the only begotten son of God."[197] The missionary was perplexed. "But don't you believe," he asked, "in the perfection of human nature, and don't you believe that Jesus had attained perfection?" Gandhiji replied, "I believe in the *perfectibility* of human nature. Jesus came as near to perfection as possible. To say that he was perfect is to deny God's superiority to man."

He anticipated the next assertion which the missionary was bound to make in order to prove that Jesus was perfect. "I do not need," he said, "either the prophecies or miracles to establish Jesus's greatness as a teacher. Nothing can be more miraculous than the three years of his ministry. There is no miracle in the story of the multitudes fed on a handful of loaves. A magician can create that illusion. But woe worth the day on which a magician would be hailed as the Saviour of humanity. As for Jesus raising the dead to life, well, I doubt if the men he raised were really dead... The laws of Nature are changeless, unchangeable, and there are no miracles in the sense of infringement or interruption of Nature's laws."[198]

In the *Harijan* dated April 17, 1937 Gandhiji published a letter which he had received from P. O. Phillip of the National Christian Council, complaining that Caste Hindus in Kerala were molesting Christians, particularly depressed class converts. He commented that he had received several other complaints of a similar nature. "The writers," he said, "claim that (1) the acts are not isolated; (2) they are perpetrated with the knowledge of influential Caste Hindus; (3) Caste Hindus

---

197. *Ibid.*, pp. 81-82.
198. *Ibid.*, p. 82 .

want to suppress, if possible, the progress of Christianity; (4) communal hatred is on the increase after the Temple Entry proclamation."[199] He advised the complainants to approach the Harijan Sevak Sangh for investigation of all cases. "I myself," he said, "will have no hesitation in denouncing the slightest departure by Caste Hindus from the strictest non-violence. It is difficult for me to see why communal hatred should be on the increase because of the Temple Entry Proclamation. Certainly I observed none during my recent tour in Travancore. And in so far as specific charges of molestation are concerned I would advise Shri Phillip's correspondent to file complaints in the local courts. I may mention that I have received complaints of a contrary nature from Caste Hindus alleging that Harijans living in or near Christian *cheris* were molested by Christians. I refused to publish the statements and referred the writers to the local courts. I would have likewise treated the foregoing postcard but for the very serious allegations contained in it. They could only be dealt with publicly and by a public investigation."[200]

A friend who had studied the work of the Salvation Army, sent to Gandhiji "an interesting note" which was published in the *Harijan* of June 12, 1937. He quoted the *Encyclopaedia Britannica* which said that the various social activities of the Army were actuated by the sole aim of proselytisation. General Booth, the founder of the Army, had himself written to his son that "the social work is the bait, but it is salvation that is the hook that lands the fish." Every soldier of the Army had to be a "Soul-winner."[201] Gandhiji commented, "Of course what is true of the Army is more or less true of all Christian Missions. The social work is undertaken not for its own sake but as an aid to salvation of those who receive social service. The history of India would have been written differently if the Christians had come to India to live their lives in our midst and permeate ours with their aroma if there was any... But say

199. *Ibid.*, pp. 91-92.
200. *Ibid.*, p. 92.
201. *Ibid.*, pp. 295-96.

some of them, 'If what you say had held good with Jesus there would have been no Christians.' To answer this would land me in a controversy in which I have no desire to engage. But I may be permitted to say that Jesus preached not a new religion but a new way of life."[202]

In the *Harijan* dated June 12, 1937 Gandhiji published a long extract from a letter he had received from an American sister who had worked for years as a missionary in India. "But as for Harijans themselves," she wrote, "I certainly do not agree that they are stupid, or unintelligent, or lacking in religious sense. They are not even unsophisticated. If we tried to use the 'high-pressure' methods of which you accuse us, I assure you we would get no results among them. To me they are just nice people very much like myself and my brothers and sisters and friends. To be sure they are oppressed and illiterate, even unkempt, but they are thoughtful, spiritual-minded, generous, kindly; in character they seem to me above, rather than below, the average of mankind. I like them better than Savarnas — but that is my bad taste, perhaps."

Next, she proceeded to tell Gandhiji that his attitude towards Harijans was superficial. "The only explanation," she continued, "that comes to my mind is that you either do not know them or you are insincere. The latter is unworthy of attention. The former might be true — for we sometimes know least those who live in the same house with us. May be, you still unconsciously have a little 'high caste' attitude.... It may be your city outlook. Whatever it is, you are not seeing them as I see them."[203]

She pleaded that she knew the Harijans better because she herself was a villager and had lived with them as one of them. "Our spiritual communion," she said, "was always on terms of equality. I received as much from them as I gave — may be more. At least I can testify that some of the deepest spiritual thinking, the most exquisite spiritual attainment, that

202. *Ibid.*, pp. 295-96.
203. *Christian Missions*, p. 80.

I have ever known, I have seen in the souls of Depressed Class Hindus — and I don't mean exceptional, educated ones, I mean illiterate villagers. But would I have seen it if I had been haggling them to become Christians? I assure you I would not!... To be sure they talk politics and economics, but it is only the spiritual interest that holds them till midnight, brings them back at dawn, and in the hot noonday, with the plea, 'If you knew how we want to hear that God loves us, you wouldn't want to rest.'"[204]

She also gave some advice to Gandhiji. "If you cannot meet that need," she concluded, "you cannot hold the Depressed Classes — if you can meet it, you will hold them. For that is what they are asking — yes, and Shudras, too, and even some merchants and Brahmans."[205]

Gandhiji rejected her suggestion that he did not know Harijans. "The writer," he said, "has no warrant for suggesting that I do not know or love Harijans sufficiently because I attribute to Harijans inability to receive Christian teachings. My attitude is not 'superficial' as she will have it to be. Whatever it is, it is based on deep experience and observation dependent not on a day's or even a year's contact, but on close contact for years with tens of thousands of India's masses, not as a superior being but feeling as one of them. But she is wholly right when she says, 'Whatever it is, you are not seeing them as I see them.' They are my kith and kin, breathing the same air, living the same life, having the same faith, the same aspirations, and the same earth sustaining us in life as it will in death! And for her?"[206]

He agreed with her that the spiritual needs of Harijans had to be met and that Caste Hindus had to treat them as equals. But he differed with her as regards the way to meet their spiritual needs. "But I am not so stupid as to think," he said, "that I or any single person can supply the spiritual

---

204. *Ibid.*, p. 103.
205. *Ibid.*, pp. 103-04.
206. *Ibid.*, p. 105.

needs of his neighbour. Spiritual needs cannot be supplied through the intellect or through the stomach, even as the needs of the body cannot be supplied through the spirit. One can paraphrase the famous saying of Jesus and say, 'Render unto the body that which is its, and unto the spirit that which is its.' And the only way I can supply my neighbour's spiritual needs is by living the life of the spirit without even exchanging a word with him. The life of the spirit will translate itself into acts of love for my neighbour."[207]

At the same time he was sure that Christian missions were not meeting whatever spiritual needs the Harijans had. "But to admit that Harijans," he concluded, "have the same spiritual need as the rest of us, is not to say that they would understand the intellectual presentation of Christianity as much as I would; for instance. I put them on the same level as my own wife. Her spiritual needs are no less than mine, but she would no more understand the presentation of Christianity than any ordinary Harijan would... Presentation, with a view to conversion, of a faith other than one's own, can only necessarily be through an appeal to the intellect or the stomach or both. I do maintain in spite of the extract I have quoted that the vast mass of Harijans, and for that matter Indian humanity, cannot understand the presentation of Christianity, and that generally speaking their conversion wherever it has taken place has not been a spiritual act in any sense of the term. They are conversions for convenience. And I have had overwhelming corroboration of the truth during my frequent and extensive wanderings."[208]

The same issue of the *Harijan* published a report which Gandhiji had received from Thakkar Bapa about the quality of Christian preaching in the Nizam's Dominions (the former Hyderabad State). The report said:

> About six months ago an event which took place at Karepally, Warangal District, Nizam's Dominions, describes

207. *Ibid.*, p. 104.
208. *Ibid.*, pp. 104-05.

> the methods adopted by the Christian missionaries to make conversions of Hindus and especially Harijans. Some days previous to the appointed date, the village teachers sent out news of the coming event into all the surrounding villages and made sure that the people of all castes of Hindus and especially Harijans were present on the occasion in large numbers. The pastor arrived at the place bringing with him a girl, about 12 years old, who he said would cure all that were presented to her of all sorts of diseases and also show them the real path to realization of God.
>
> The pastor then stood and said addressing those present, 'You believe in gods who are dead and gone. Your Rama was born, behaved and acted like an ordinary mortal and then died. So was the case with Krishna also, who had many more vices to his credit. Here is before you a person who is the very incarnation of Christ. Christ is in her now, which fact you can verify yourself by being cured of your diseases at the mere touch of her hands. Why believe in gods who are past and no more effective? You should all believe in and follow the path of Jesus Christ who was born to Virgin Mary, preached the Gospel which leads to salvation, died outwardly but rose again on the third day to redeem the sinning millions of the world.'
>
> A subscription of one anna per head and two annas for a metal cross were charged. They were told that, unless they wore the cross at all times and believed in the truth and efficacy of Christianity, there would not be any good effect in the case of diseased patients.[209]

Gandhiji made a brief comment. "If it is true," he said, "it stands self-condemned. I would like the Mission concerned to investigate the complaint and throw light on it."[210]

Another report which Thakkar Bapa sent was about the

209. *Ibid.*, pp. 106-07.
210. *Ibid.*, p. 107.

method of conversion employed by missionaries in the Shahabad District of Bihar. Gandhiji published it in the *Harijan* of June 19, 1937. "After having visited the village," said the report, "and having created familiarity with the Harijans they at once start a school and put it in charge of a Harijan teacher who either himself is an influential man or related to such a one. Whenever they come to learn that some tension or actual litigation is going on between the Harijans and other villagers they at once seize the opportunity to take up the side of the poor Harijans and help them with money and advice. They are thus hailed as saviours and conversion follows as if to repay the obligation. Whenever a village Harijan leader accepts the new faith almost all belonging to his clan follow him."[211] The report went on to point out that "In all cases of conversion, new or old, not a single instance can be found in which the acceptance of the new faith was due to any religious conviction... Those of the new and old who are still continuing as nominal Christians are willing to return to Hinduism if their grievances are removed." Finally, the report listed nine grievances of which "only one, namely, refusal of entry into temples was religious."[212]

Gandhiji wrote, "If what is said in the report about the conversions be true, it is from my standpoint reprehensible. Such superficial conversions can only give rise to suspicion and strife. But if a missionary body or individual choose to follow the methods described in the report, nothing can be done to prevent them. It is therefore much more profitable to turn the searchlight inward and to discover our own defects. Fortunately the report enables us to do so. Nine causes are enumerated to show why Harijans are induced to leave the Hindu fold. Seven are purely economic, one is social, and one is purely religious. Thus they are reduced economically, degraded socially and boycotted from religious participation. The wonder is not that they leave Hinduism, the wonder is

211. *The Collected Works,* Volume 65, pp. 316-17.
212. *Ibid.*, p. 317.

that they have not done so for so long and that so few leave their faith even when they do. The moral is obvious." He called upon the Harijan Sevak Sangh to find more workers for doing service to the Harijans and for "propaganda among the so-called caste Hindus, not in the shape of reviling them but showing them that religion does not warrant the treatment that is meted out to Harijans by them."[213]

A correspondent posed before Gandhiji four questions which were published in the *Harijan* of September 25, 1937. The first question was whether "Hindus who have once renounced their faith for some reason or other and joined Islam or Christianity" should be reconverted if they "sincerely repent and want to come back." The second question was about "Lakhs of Depressed Class people in South India" who "have joined Christianity wholesale but who "feel it worthwhile to readopt their ancestral faith." The third question was whether a Hindu who "was made to join another faith for certain material conditions" and "feels disillusioned" should be welcomed when he "comes and knocks at our door." The fourth question was as to what should be done with "Hindu boys and girls" who have been brought up and converted in Christian or Muslim orphanages and who now "approach us for *shuddhi*."[214]

Gandhiji's reply to all these questions was positive. "In my opinion," he observed, "they are not examples of real conversion. If a person through fear, compulsion, starvation or for material gain or consideration goes over to another faith, it is a misnomer to call it conversion. Most cases of mass conversion, of which we have heard so much during the past two years, have been to my mind false coin... I would, therefore, unhesitatingly re-admit to the Hindu fold all such repentants without much ado, certainly without any *shuddhi*... And as I believe in the equality of all the great religions of the earth, I regard no man as polluted because

213. *Ibid.*, pp. 317-18.
214. *Ibid.*, Volume 66, New Delhi, 1976, p. 63.

he has forsaken the branch on which he was sitting and gone over to another of the same tree. If he comes to the original branch, he deserves to be welcomed and not told that he had committed sin by reason of his having forsaken the family to which he belonged. In so far as he may be deemed to have erred, he has sufficiently purged himself of it when he repents of the error and retraces his step."[215]

Mr. John R. Mott who had come to India in order to preside over a conference of the International Missionary Council to be held at Tambaram in Madras Presidency from December 12 to 29, met Gandhiji on or before December 4, 1938. This was his third visit to the Mahatma. The discussion between the two went on for two days and was published in the *Harijan* of December 10. "This is a unique convention," Mott said, "where 14 councils of the younger churches of Asia, Africa and Latin America, and 14 of the older churches of Europe, America and Australia will be represented by over 400 delegates. We want this to be a help and not a hindrance to India... Am I, I ask, right in thinking that the tide has turned a little bit on the great things you impressed on me?" Gandhiji replied, "What I have noticed is that there is a drift in the right direction so far as thought is concerned, but I do feel that in action there is no advance. I was going to say 'not much advance' but I deliberately say 'no advance'. You may be able give solitary instances of men here and there, but they do not count."[216]

Some portions of the dialogue that followed are worth being reproduced at some length:

> J.M: Is not taking advantage of people's disabilities being avoided now? I must say I was terribly pained to read of the McGavran incident....[217]
>
> G: Even on this question, whilst some friends, I agree,

215. *Ibid.*, pp. 163-64.

216. *Ibid.*, Volume 68, New Delhi, 1977, pp. 165-66.

217. McGavaran had contributed to the missionary magazine, *World Dominion,* a fabricated report of a talk between Gandhiji on the one hand and Bishops Pickett and Azariah on the other.

are in earnest, so far as action goes, there has been no change.

J.M: You mean there is not action enough?

G: No, there is no action at all. I have plenty of evidence to prove what I say. I do not publish all the correspondence I get. Mr. A. A. Paul, whom you may know, convened a conference some time ago. The proceedings were revealing. Their resolutions were half-hearted. As far as I am aware, there was no unanimity about any definite action.[218]

J.M.: I was encouraged by a resolution of the National Christian Council which insisted on pure motives and pure practice.

G: You may cite the resolution but you will not be able to show corresponding action.

J.M: They are now talking of conversion of groups and families. I am not quite clear, though, as to what in certain cases the word 'group' implies.

G. I am quite clear. It is mass conversion called by another name.[219]

J.M: On the third question of the wise use of money I see signs of encouragement.

G: But it is making virtue of necessity. The Indian Christians are thinking aloud and doing things themselves. They are talking of their own responsibilities and saying, 'Thank God, American money can't come.'

J.M: How many missionaries and Christians in general help in constructive activities like the village industries movement, the new educational movement, and so on?

G: I am happy to be able to say that I have some valued Christian colleagues. But they can be counted on one's fingers. I fear that the vast bulk of them remain unconvinced... They evidently believe in industrialization and Western type of education. And missionaries as a

218. *Ibid.*, p. 166.
219. *Ibid.*, p. 167.

body perhaps fight shy of movements not conducted wholly or predominantly by Christians.[220]

But in spite of the best efforts of Christian missions to exploit the situation created by Gandhiji's call for abolition of untouchability, the tide was turning against conversions. This was admitted by the Tambaram Conference of the International Missionary Council presided over by Mr. J. R. Mott. "We have long held," proclaimed the Conference, "that the one serious rival for the spiritual supremacy of India that Christianity has to face is resurgent Hinduism, and recent happenings have deepened the conviction. The spirit of new Hinduism is personified in Mahatma Gandhi, whose amazing influence over his fellows is undoubtedly fed by the fires of religion and patriotism. Because he is a staunch Hindu and finds within the faith of his forefathers the spiritual succour he needs, he strongly opposes the Christian claim that Jesus Christ is the one and only saviour. This reminds us again that unless the great Christian affirmations are verified in Christian living, they beat ineffectively on Indian minds."[221]

By now the missionaries had realized that India was fast heading towards independence. That rang alarm bells in their mind. But they could not do anything about it except getting reconciled to new power equations. In years to come Christian missions would be forced to change their strategy and raise the slogan of Indigenisation. The Christian Ashram Movement of which we hear a lot these days, was one of the products of this new strategy. Some missionaries started planning to masquerade as Hindu sannyasins.[222] Meanwhile they started pestering Gandhiji with questions about the future of Christian missions in India. They wanted him to make some commitment.

The *Harijan* dated December 12, 1939 published extracts from a letter written to Gandhiji by an American missionary.

---

220. *Ibid.*, p. 170.

221. *Tambaram Series,* Volume 3, *Evangelism*, London, 1939, p. 126.

222. See Sita Ram Goel, *Catholic Ashrams:: Sannyasins or Swindlers?*, Second England Edition, Voice of India, New Delhi, 1994.

"Are you and the Congress," he asked, "generally neutral in regard to which religion a person belongs to?" He himself answered the question, saying, "I believe the Congress claims to be neutral, but my contention is that they are not." In proof of his assertion he cited two instances. "Your friend, the late Prime Minister of Madras,"[223] he stated, "sent a wire of congratulations to Christians who became Hindus. Is that being neutral? And just the other day, here near Bombay in Thana District, when about fifty hill people returned to Hinduism, the leaders in making them Hindus were Congress leaders of Thana District. So that plainly shows that Congress leaders favour Hinduism." He concluded by expressing fear about the fate of the "small minority" of Christians under *"Purna* swaraj" which he described as "Hindu raj".[224]

Gandhiji wrote back, "I am not aware of what Shri Rajagopalachari said. He is well able to take care of himself. But I can give my idea of neutrality. In free India every religion should prosper on terms of equality, unlike what is happening today. Christianity being the nominal religion of the rulers, it receives favours which no other religion enjoys. A government responsible to the people dare not favour one religion or another. But I see nothing wrong in Hindus congratulating those who having left them may return to their fold... I have already complained of the methods adopted by some missionaries to wean ignorant people from the religion of their forefathers. It is one thing to preach one's religion to whomsoever may choose to adopt it, another to entice masses. And if those thus enticed, on being undeceived, go back to their old love, their return will give natural joy to those whom they had foresaken."[225]

The missionaries, however, were loathe to give up. Another delegation came to Gandhiji with some new questions. The discussion was published in the *Harijan*

223. The reference is to C. Rajagopalachari who was Prime Minister of Madras from 1937 to 1939 when the Congress Ministry resigned.

224. *Ibid.*, Volume 71, New Delhi, 1978, p. 52.

225. *Ibid.*, p. 53.

dated January 1, 1939. One missionary who was a professor asked Gandhiji, "Will you under swaraj allow Christians to go on with their proselytizing activity without any hindrance?" Gandhiji replied, "No legal hindrance can be put in the way of any Christian or anybody preaching for the acceptance of his doctrine." The missionary wanted to know "whether the freedom they were having under the British regime would be allowed to them under the national Government without any interference." Gandhiji said, "I can't answer that question categorically because I do not know what is exactly allowed and what is not allowed under the British regime today. That is a legal question. Besides, what is permitted may not necessarily be the same thing as what is permissible under the law. All, therefore, that I can say today is that you should enjoy all freedom you are entitled to under the law today."[226]

The missionary continued, "Some of us are under an apprehension that they may have hereafter to labour under... disabilities. Is there any guarantee that such a thing would not happen?" Gandhiji replied, "As I wrote in *Harijan*, you do not seem to realize that Christians are today enjoying the privileges because they are Christians. The moment a person turns Christian, he becomes a *Sahib log*. He gets a job and position which he could not have otherwise got. He adopts foreign dress and ways of living. He cuts himself from his people and begins to fancy himself a limb of the ruling class. What the Christians are afraid of losing, therefore, is not their rights but anomalous privileges."[227]

Another missionary asked, "Why may I not share with others my experience of Jesus Christ which has given me such ineffable peace?" Gandhiji replied, "Because you cannot possibly say that what is best for you is best for all... And again, is it not superarrogance to assume that you alone possess the key to spiritual joy and peace, and that an adherent of a different faith cannot get the same in equal measure from a

---

226. *Ibid.*, p. 53.
227. *Ibid.*, pp. 79-80.

study of his scriptures? I enjoy a peace and equanimity of spirit which has excited the envy of many Christian friends. I have got it principally through the Gita." Coming to the obstinacy of Christians about their mission, Gandhiji added, "Your difficulty lies in your considering the other faiths as false or so adulterated as to amount to falsity. And you shut your eyes to the truth that shines in other faiths and which gives equal joy and peace to their votaries."

Finally, the missionary asked, "What would be your message to a Christian like me and my fellows?" Gandhiji said, "Become worthy of the message that is imbedded in the Sermon on the Mount and join the spinning brigade."[228]

A group of American teachers from the Ewing College and the Agricultural Institute, Allahabad, called upon Gandhiji on the eve of their return to America. The talk which Gandhiji had with them was published in the *Harijan* of January 7, 1939. One of the teachers asked, "What is the place of Christian missions in the new India that is being built up today? What can they do to help in this great task?" Gandhiji replied, "To show appreciation of what India is and is doing. Up till now they have come as teachers and preachers with queer notions about India and India's great religions. We have been described as a nation of superstitious heathens, knowing nothing, denying God. We are a brood of Satan as Murdoch would say. Did not Bishop Heber in his well-known hymn 'From Greenland's icy mountains' describe India as a country where 'every prospect pleases and only man is vile'? To me this is a negation of the spirit of Christ. My personal view, therefore, is that, if you feel that India has a message to give to the world, that India's religions too are true, though like all religions imperfect for having percolated through imperfect human agency, and you come as fellow-helpers and fellow-seekers, there is a place for you here. But if you come as preachers of the 'true Gospel' to a people who are wandering in darkness, so far as I am concerned you can have

228. *Ibid.*, p. 80.

no place. You may impose yourselves upon us."[229]

Gandhiji received a circular letter sent by the Secretary of the Seng Khasi Free Morning School stating that the Seng Khasi Free School Movement had been started in 1921 to break the missionary monopoly on education of the Khasi children and preserve national culture. The educational grants given by the British Government, said the circular, were used by the missionaries for printing Christian literature, including a Khasi translation of the Bible, and prescribing it in the school curriculum. The Deputy Inspector of Schools in Khasi and Jaintia Hills was a Christian. He insisted that the Seng Khasi Free Morning School should stick to the text-books prescribed by the missionaries. The School refused and was denied government aid. Gandhiji published the circular letter in the *Harijan* dated March 9, 1940 and commented, "If what is stated here is true, it enforces the argument often advanced by me that Christian missionary effort has been favoured by the ruling power. But I advertise the circular not for the sake of emphasizing my argument. I do so in order to ventilate the grievance of the secretary of the school. Surely he has every right to object to teaching proselytizing literature prepared by the missionaries... It is to be hoped that the school will not be deprived of the grant because of the secretary's very reasonable objection."[230]

Gandhiji had another discussion with Christian missionaries on March 12, 1940. As leaders of Christian thought, they asked for his guidance. "All I can say," said Gandhiji, "is that there should be less of theology and more of truth in all that you say and do." They requested him to explain. "How can I explain the obvious?" he said. "*Among agents of the many untruths that are propounded in the world one of the foremost is theology*. I do not say that there is no demand for it. There is a demand in the world for many a questionable thing." The missionary asked a supplementary question, "Are

---

229. *Christian Missions*, pp. 288-89.
230. *The Collected Works*, Volume 71, p. 219.

you sure that no great result has come through your own study of Jesus?' Gandhiji replied, "Why? There is no doubt that it has come, but not, let me tell you, through theology or through the ordinary interpretation of theologists. For many of them contend that the Sermon on the Mount does not apply to mundane things, and that it was only meant for the twelve disciples."[231]

Emily Kinnaird was 86 years old when she met Gandhiji on July 20, 1940. He addressed her as mother. A dialogue started when she observed that Gandhiji's advice to Britain and Denmark to offer non-violent resistance to Nazi Germany was no good. The dialogue, published in the *Harijan* of August 4, 1940, is being reproduced below because it is revealing:

G: What was the good of Jesus Christ laying down his life?

E.K: Oh, that was a different matter. He was the son of God.

G: And so are we!

E.K. No. He was the *only* son of God.

G: It is there that the mother and son must differ. With you Jesus was the only begotten son of God. With me He was a son of God, no matter how much purer than us all, but every one of us is a son of God and capable of doing what Jesus did, if we but endeavour to express the divine in us.

E.K: Yes, that is where I think you are wrong. If you accepted Christ in your heart and appealed to your people to do likewise, you could deliver your message with greater ease and far better effect. He is our salvation, and without receiving Him in our hearts we cannot be saved.

G: So those who accept the Christ are all saved? They need do nothing more?

E.K: We are sinners all, and we have to accept Him to be saved.

---

231. *Ibid.*, p. 328. Emphasis added.

G: And then we may continue to be sinners? Is that what you mean? You do not I hope belong to the Plymouth Brothers, do you?

E.K: No, I am a Presbyterian.

G: But you talk like some of the Plymouth Brothers I met long ago in Africa.

E.K: Yes, I am afraid you were so unfortunate in the Christian contacts you formed in Africa. You did not meet the right kind of people.

G: Surely you will not say that. I met a number of estimable people. They were all honest and sincere.

E.K: But they were not true Christians.

Gandhiji told her about Christians he met in South Africa "And old A. W. Baker," he said, "who must be over eighty now, is still at me. He writes to remind me time and again that unless I accept Christ in his way I cannot be saved."[232] The lady "wondered why we were so obtuse as not to see what was so obvious to her — the outstanding superiority of Christianity to any other message." She said that the Bible had been translated "into several hundred languages" and "God's message" made available to many people in their own dialects. Gandhiji observed, "That proves nothing." She ignored the remark and went on to say that "whereas fifty years ago there were so many hundred thousand Christians in India, there are today ten times as many." To that also Gandhiji replied, "Again that proves nothing. But why quarrel about labels? Can we not find a few hundred thousand Indians or Africans who live the message of Christ without being called Christian?"[233]

Gandhiji had a discussion with Harijan workers on January 8, 1942. One of the questions raised by them was how to deal with "temptations given by missionaries in the shape of books, school fees, etc., with a view to the boys' ultimate conversion." Gandhiji advised, "The missionaries have of

---

232. *Ibid.*, Volume 72, pp. 297-98.

233. *Ibid.*, p. 299.

course the right to preach the gospel of Christ and to invite the non-Christians to embrace Christianity. But every attempt to press material benefits or attractions in the aid of conversion should be freely exposed, and Harijans should be educated to resist the temptation."[234]

A Christian wrote to Gandhiji, "You oppose all conversion without conviction. But are you not inconsistent? You profess equal respect for all religions. Why then worry about how the conversion is brought about?"[235] Gandhiji gave a reply in the *Harijan* of March 29, 1942. "I have extracted the question," he said, "from your long and plausible letter, cleverly written. Conversion without conviction is a mere change and not conversion which is a revolution in one's life. You seem to forget that equal respect implies respect for my own faith as much as for yours or any other neighbour's. My respect for my own faith forbids my being indifferent to my children abandoning their parents' faith without conviction. And I should have little respect for you, if you led my children astray by making all kinds of worldly promises in which matters of the spirit had no play."[236]

Soon afterwards, Gandhiji became preoccupied with the Quit India Movement which led him to jail in August 1942. During this crises, the missionaries by and large were ranged on the side of the British. William Paton, Secretary of the International Missionary Council denounced the "moral imbecilities of Mr. Gandhi" in a letter he wrote on July 21, 1942 to L. S. Amery, the Secretary of State for India.[236a] But when he came out of jail in May 1944 after a fast which had weakened him considerably, four hundred Christians belonging to the National Christian Party gathered at Juhu (Bombay) where he was convalescing and offered prayer for his health. Gandhiji thanked them in a message dated May 28, 1944.[237]

---

234. *Ibid.*, Volume 75, New Delhi, 1979, p. 207.
235. *Ibid.*, p. 422.
236. *Ibid.*, p. 423.
236a. *The Transfer of Power*, London, Volume II, p. 552.
237. *The Collected Works*, Volume 77, New Delhi, 1977, p. 296.

On November 5, 1944 Gandhiji wrote a letter to the Metropolitan of Calcutta in response to some criticism the latter had offered. "Utmost frankness," he wrote, "is a sure test of friendship. I therefore appreciate your criticism, being that of a true friend." He added that "Religion should be a binding, not a disruptive force" and commended "the good work which some missionaries had done among the Frontier tribes."[238] On December 24, 1944 he sent a Christmas message and noted in his diary, "Today is Christmas Day. For us who believe in the equality of all religions, the birth of Jesus Christ is as worthy of veneration as that of Rama, Krishna, etc."[239]

Gandhiji's Christian disciple, J. C. Kumarappa, had written a book, *Practice and Precepts of Jesus*. He wrote a foreword to it on March 21, 1945. "It is a revolutionary view," he said, "of Jesus as a man of God. It is none the less revealing and interesting... Anyway, this reading of the Bible must bring solace to the Christians of India. If they will read the Bible as Prof. K. does, they need not be ashamed of their forefathers or their ancient faith."[240] On July 20, 1945, he wrote to Kumarappa, "I have distributed two copies of your book on Jesus to Indian Christians. Supply me with more books."[241]

Mrs. Clara Hopman, a Dutch artist, had made a statue of Jesus Christ measuring 6 ft. by 4 ft. It was priced Rs.10,000. The statue was to be installed in the premises of the All India Village Industries Association at Maganwadi. On October 28, 1945 Gandhiji wrote to Kumarappa, "You have good certificate about the sculpture. As soon as it is on view in Maganwadi, I shall set about collecting."[242]

The *Harijan* dated March 3, 1946 published a discussion which Gandhiji had with members of the Friends Ambulance Unit which had worked during the Midnapore cyclone in 1942 and the Bengal Famine in 1943. Prompted by Gandhiji's

---

238. *Ibid.*, Volume 78, New Delhi, 1979, pp. 269-70.
239. *Ibid.*, pp. 384 and 394.
240. *Ibid.*, Volume 79, New Delhi, 1980, p. 279.
241. *Ibid.*, Volume 80, New Delhi, 1980, p.9.
242. *Ibid.*, Volume 81, New Delhi, 1980, p. 432.

remark that even "converts to orthodox Christianity today are veering round", a member asked, "By 'veering' you mean going back?" He replied, "Yes, I mean going back to real Christianity, to Christ, not Western Christianity. They are beginning to realize that Jesus was an Asiatic. Having realized this, they are reading the Bible through Indian eyes. You should study the meaning of Indian Christianity through J. C. Kumarappa's book, *Practice and Precepts of Jesus*."[243]

Gandhiji's spirit of Swadeshi in respect of religion was not confined to India or Hinduism. He wanted to spread the message to the whole world. Some Black soldiers from West Africa came to him some time after January, 1946. He had a discussion with them which was published in the *Harijan* dated February 24, 1946. The first question they asked him was, "There are several religions in the world. They were all originated in foreign countries. Which one of these should Africa follow? Or should she discover her own religion? If so, how?" Gandhiji replied, "It is wrong to say that all religions were originated in foreign countries. I had fairly extensive contact with Zulus and Bantus and I found that the Africans have a religion of their own though they may not have reasoned it out for themselves. I am not referring to the rites, ceremonies and fetishes that are prevalent among African tribes but the religion of one Supereme God. You pray to that God. There are many religions, but religion is only one. You should follow that one religion. Foreigners might bring you Christianity. Christianity as exemplified in Europe and America today is a travesty of the teaching of Jesus. Then there are Hinduism, Islam and Zoroastrianism and so on. You should absorb the best that is in each without fettering your choice and from your own religion."[244]

Another question which the Africans asked was, "Everything

---

243. *Ibid.*, Volume 82, New Delhi, 1980, p. 155. In 1952, only four years after the Mahatma's death, Kumarappa became a drum-beater for Mao Tse-tung and his criminal gang. At the same time he saw Gandhi incarnate in Communist China. He turned out to be a crank of rare vintage.

244. *Ibid.*, Volume 83, New Delhi, 1981, p.11.

immoral and deadly is attributed to Africa. What steps should be taken to eradicate the foreign prejudice against us?" Gandhiji observed, "Many, perhaps most of the evils that are at the back of the prejudice against Negroes are the result of the nominal Christianity imported from America. They have learnt to drink, dance immoral dances and so on. Then there are evil African customs. You must eradicate these and thus disarm foreign prejudice. It is a laborious task but a joyous one. The epidemic of foreign prejudice will then die a natural death."[245]

On January 27, 1946 Gandhiji had a question and answer session with constructive workers who had come to attend a conference in Madras. A report of this session was published in *The Hindu* dated January 29. One of the questions "related to receiving assistance from Christian Missionaries in free India." Gandhiji said that "they could certainly accept help not only from Christian missionaries but from others also, if such help was offered sincerely and in a spirit of service to the country." He held up the example of C. F. Andrews. "India requires the help," he continued, "of all men of goodwill who were prepared to offer that help in a spirit of love and service." [246]

In the *Harijan* dated June 30, 1946, he described Jesus as the most active non-violent resister known perhaps to history.[247] The *Harijan* dated July 21, 1946, published his article, 'Jews and Palestine'. He held the Christians responsible for the Jews seeking a home in Palestine. "It is a blot on the Christian world," he wrote, "that they have been singled out, owing to a wrong reading of the New Testament, for prejudice against them. 'If an individual Jew does a wrong, the whole Jewish world is to blame for it.' If an individual Jew like Einstein makes a great discovery or another composes unsurpassable music, the merit goes to the authors and not to the community to which they belong."[248] He advised the

245. *Ibid.*, p. 12.
246. *Ibid.*, p. 39.
247. *Ibid.*, Volume 84, New Delhi, 1981, p. 372.
248. *Ibid.*, pp. 440-41.

Jews to follow the example of "Jesus the Jew" rather than resort to force in Palestine.

In the *Harijan* dated October 13, 1946 Gandhiji chided the Hindus of Jubbulpore for being rowdy and disturbing a Christian charity show in the town. The students of the local Christian convent had staged a drama at the end of which angels appeared before an orphaned girl and advised her to have faith in Jesus. A section of the audience had raised a hue and cry and demanded refund of the money they had paid for tickets. The organiser of the show had not been allowed to speak. Someone reported the incident to Gandhiji who wrote, "If what the correspondent says is true, the behaviour described was wholly unworthy. It betrayed extreme intolerance. Those who do not like things that do not coincide with their notions need not patronize them but it is ungentlemanly to behave like less than men when things are not to their taste."[249]

On June 7, 1947, Gandhiji had a discussion with some Christian missionaries. He told them, "The British and American missionaries in India have rendered no real service to the country. Their conception of service is to do work of compassion and serve the poor. But by establishing hospitals, schools and other institutions, they attracted our children and men, and our people left their own religion and embraced Christianity. Our religion is in no way inferior to Christianity."[250]

Gandhiji was in Rawalpindi on July 31, 1947 when the President of The Punjab Students Christian League asked him two questions. The interview was published in *The Hindustan Times* of August 3. The first question was if Christian missionaries would be asked to quit after India became independent. "Foreign missionaries," replied Gandhiji, "will not be asked to quit India. Indian Christians will be free to occupy high official positions in the Indian Dominion." The

249. *Ibid.*, Volume 85, New Delhi, 1982, p. 420.
250. *Ibid.*, Volume 88, New Delhi, 1983, p. 96.

second question was "if non-Christians in the Indian Dominion would have freedom to embrace Christianity." Gandhiji said that "he would be guided in this connection by the rules and laws framed."[251]

An Indian Catholic priest and a missionary came to Gandhiji with a report of "harassment of Roman Catholics at the hand of Hindus" in a village near Gurgaon, 25 miles from Delhi. Speaking at a prayer meeting on November 21, 1947, he said, "The persons who brought the information told me that the Roman Catholics were threatened that they would have to suffer if they did not leave the village. I hope this threat is unfounded and that the Christian men and women would be allowed to follow their religion and carry on their work without any hindrance. Now that we have freed ourselves from political bondage, they, too, are entitled to the same freedom to follow their religion and occupation as they had under the British."[252]

Gandhiji addressed a prayer meeting in New Delhi on December 24, 1947. It was the evening before Christmas. He said, "Tomorrow is Christmas. Christmas is to Christians what Diwali is to us... I do not regard Christmas as an occasion for people to indulge in drunkenness. Christmas reminds one of Jesus Christ. I offer greetings to Christians in India and abroad. May the new year bring them prosperity and happiness. It has never been my wish that the freedom of India should mean the ruin of Christians here or that they should become Hindus or Muslims or Sikhs. For a Christian to become a Hindu or a Muslim or a Sikh is a fate worse than death. According to my view a Christian should become a better Christian... I want that all the Christians in and outside India should become free in the true sense. Let them exercise self-restraint and pursue the path of sacrifice and martyrdom shown by Jesus Christ. Let them be free and increase the area of freedom in the world."[253]

---

251. *Ibid.*, p. 471.
252. *Ibid.*, Volume 90, New Delhi, 1984, p. 80
253. *Ibid.*, p. 293.

Summing up

The one thing that stands out in this long-drawn-out dialogue between Mahatma Gandhi and the Christians is that all along he identified himself as a staunch Hindu. In fact, he took considerable pride in this self-identification. Far from being a dirty word as it would soon become even for some Hindu leaders and organisations, the word "Hindu" conveyed to him all that was noble and elevating. He did not feel that he was being "communal" when he called himself a Hindu. Nationalism as he saw it came naturally to a Hindu of his definition. Nor did he ever try to impart to this word a merely geographical meaning by equating it with the word "*Bhāratīya*". On the contrary, he understood and interpreted it as the embodiment of what was for him the deepest spiritual message and the greatest cultural heritage. Hinduism for him was not merely "a way of life" as some Hindu leaders have started saying these days. For him, Hinduism was a vast spiritual vision beckoning man to rise to the highest heights.

In the many essays he wrote on the principles and practices of Hinduism, we find him affirming not only the fundamentals of Hindu spirituality but also the framework of Hindu culture and social philosophy. There is no symbol of Sanatana Dharma which does not stir him to his innermost depths and which he does not trace back to its inner and eternal spirit. He accords the highest honour to Hindu Shastras — the Vedas, the Upanishads, the Puranas,[254] the Gita,[255] the Mahabharata,[256] the Ramayana,[257] the Bhagavata.[258] He defends the "much-maligned Brahman" and entertains "not a shadow of doubt" that "if Brahmanism does not revive, Hinduism will perish."[259] He upholds the "spirit behind idol-worship" and is prepared "to defend with my life the thousands

254. Mahatma Gandhi, *Hindu Dharma*, Ahmedabad, 1950, p. 7.
255. *Ibid.*, p. 36.
256. *Ibid.*, pp. 20-21.
257. *Ibid.*, p. 178.
258. *Ibid.*, p. 22.
259. *Ibid.*,, pp. 391-92.

of holy temples which sanctify this land."[260] For him cow-protection "is the dearest possession of the Hindu heart" and "no one who does not believe in cow-protection can possibly be a Hindu."[261] The sacred thread has a "deep meaning for him" as it is "the sign of the second birth, that is spiritual." He says that *varṇāshrama* is "inherent in human nature, and Hinduism has simply made a science of it."[262] He never regards Buddhism, Jainism, Saivism, Vaishnavism, Shaktism, Sikhism, etc., as separate religions. All of them are for him schools of Sanatana Dharma which allows as many ways as there are seekers. His view of Hinduism was summed up in the *Young India* of September 17, 1925. "What the divine author of the *Mahabharata,*" he wrote, "said of his great creation is equally true of Hinduism. Whatever of substance is contained in other religions is always to be found in Hinduism, and what is not in it is insubstantial and unnecessary."[263] Earlier, he had foreseen a great future for Hinduism. "Hinduism," he had written in the *Young India* of April 24, 1924, "is a relentless pursuit after truth and if today it has become moribund, inactive, irresponsive to growth, it is because we are fatigued. As soon as the fatigue is over, Hinduism will burst forth upon the world with a brilliance perhaps never seen before."[264]

What has caused confusion and misunderstanding about his Hinduism is the concept of *sarva-dharma-samabhāva* (equal regard for all religions) which he had developed after deep reflection. Christian and Muslim missionaries have interpreted it to mean that a Hindu can go over to Christianity or Islam without suffering any spiritual loss. They are also using it as a shield against every critique of their closed and aggressive creeds. The new rulers of India, on the other hand, cite it in order to prop up the Nehruvian version of Secularism which is only a euphemism for anti-Hindu animus shared in

260. *Ibid.*, p. 73.
261. *Ibid.*, p. 297.
262. *Ibid.*, p. 374.
263. *Ibid.*, p. 4.
264. *Ibid.*

common by Christians, Muslims, Marxists and those who are Hindus only by accident of birth. For Gandhiji, however, *sarva-dharma-samabhāva* was only a restatement of the age-old Hindu tradition of tolerance in matters of belief. Hinduism has always adjudged a man's faith in terms of his *ādhāra* (receptivity) and *adhikāra* (aptitude). It has never prescribed a uniform system of belief or behavior for everyone because, according to it, different persons are in different stages of spiritual development and need different prescriptions for further progress. Everyone, says Hinduism, should be left alone to work out one's own salvation through one's own inner seeking and evolution. Any imposition of belief or behaviour from the outside is, therefore, a mechanical exercise which can only do injury to one's spiritual growth. Preaching to those who have not invited it is nothing short of aggression born out of self-righteousness. That is why Gandhiji took a firm and uncompromising stand against proselytisation by preaching and gave no quarters to the Christian mission's mercenary methods of spreading the gospel.

In any case, his *sarva-dharma-samabhāva* did not stop Gandhiji from processing Christianity in terms of reason and universal ethics. Christianity like Islam, he said, was born only yesterday and was still in the process of being interpreted. Christians should not, therefore, present their dogmas as if they were finished products. He found that Christianity had become an imperialist creed when it allied itself with a Roman emperor and that so it had stayed till our own times when it was working hand in hand with Western imperialism. He saw no sense in the Christian doctrine of the original sin and thought poorly of vicarious atonement. He placed Jesus very high as a moral teacher, but denied his virgin birth as well as the divinity accorded to him by Christian theology. Miracles of Jesus which have been the stock-in-trade of Christianity down the centuries, failed to impress him. He dismissed them as silly stories which did no credit to Jesus and were contrary to the unchangeable laws of Nature. And even as a moral teacher Jesus compared unfavourably with the Buddha when it came to universal compassion which for Gandhiji was the essence of spirituality. He spoke rather sharply about theology which Christianity prizes most but which according to him was an agent of a great many untruths known to human history. Thus very little was left of Christianity after Gandhiji had gone through it, claim by claim and dogma by dogma. The only part which survived unscathed was the Sermon on the Mount. Even this was seen by him as a Jewish rather than a Christian contribution. Jesus for him was a Jewish prophet par excellence. In any case, he saw no evidence that the Sermon had ever influenced Christianity as known from history. As for himself, the solace he found in the Gita was missing in the Sermon.[265]

A Christian scholar has summarised the dialogue which Gandhiji had with the Christian missionaries. He concludes: "The foregoing survey substantiates that, however unacknowledged, Gandhi did leave a stamp on missiological thought and practice in his life, for a time at least on the Indian scene. Most of his Christian missionary contacts being on the Protestant side, his influence too was largely confined to the Protestant side. Their liberal outlook, smaller structures and independent work were favourable to ideological and practical influence from without, though a fundamentalist approach to the Bible prevented a change in their dogmatic approach to non-Christian religions. The Catholic Church by its very size, hierarchically centralised structure and the sheer weight of its long tradition, was necessarily slow and cautious in opening to external influences. It was not before the Second Vatican Council in the early sixties that the new lines and influences in Catholic missiological thought were to receive

---

265. Modern research has discovered that the Sermon on the Mount can be found in Jewish sources quite some time before Jesus was born. It was by no means a characteristic contribution of Jesus. He had learnt it as a Jewish rabbi and preached it, if at all, in the same capacity. It is significant that the Sermon is missing from St. John's Gospel which imparts a divine status to Jesus and which Christian theology places above all other gospels.

official recognition in the Roman Church and find their place in the conciliar documents."[266] After giving some salient features of the Second Vatican Council, he continues, "The Council documents on the subject represent only the first step and the first official word in the new thinking on the subject. It will be long before we arrive at the last word if we arrive at all. But it would seem that since the Council itself giant strides have been made in missiology which if not avowedly due to Gandhi's influence do certainly represent the Gandhian and Hindu line of thinking."[267]

It is difficult to say whether the new formulations of the Second Vatican Council represented a change of heart or a change of strategy in the altered situation when Christianity was having a difficult time in the West and being forced to seek a new home in the East. If it was a change of strategy, one wonders whether it would have become a change of heart in case a continued pressure from "Gandhian and Hindu line of thinking" had been maintained after the passing away of the Mahatma. History does provide some instances when change of strategy has become a change of heart due to unyielding resistance from victims of aggression. Unfortunately, however, the class of people who came to power after independence had no use for the "Gandhian and Hindu line to thinking." They continued to swear by the Mahatma and even installed him as the Father of the Nation. But that was no more than an empty ritual. For all practical purposes no other country has bid goodbye to Gandhiji to the same extent as the country where he was born and from which he drew all his inspiration. In the world outside he is honoured as a great Hindu and an outstanding exponent of Hinduism at its best, both in word and deed. His philosophy of life, based on Hinduism, is inviting serious attention from the intellectual elite in America, Europe and Japan. In his own

---

266. Father I. Jesudasan, S.J., 'Gandhian Perspectives on Missiology', *Indian Church History Review*, July 1970, pp. 67-68.

267. *Ibid.*, p. 69.

country, however, he has been disfigured into the patron saint of a Secularism which decries Hinduism as "communalism" and goes out of its way to give protection to closed theologies of aggression, ideological as well as physical. Small wonder that the change of mission strategy has failed to become a change of heart.

Postscript

But, at the same time, it has to be admitted that Mahatma Gandhi's prolonged dialogue with Christian theologians, missionaries, moneybags, and the rest, left the Hindus at home more defenseless vis-a-vis the Christian onslaught than they had been ever before. Whatever laurels the Mahatma may have won abroad, he has proved to be a disaster for the Hindus in India. The sorry turnout can be traced to three basic infirmities from which his position vis-a-vis Christianity and its missions had suffered. Firstly, he coined and made fashionable the utterly thoughtless slogan of *sarva-dharma-samabhāva* vis-a-vis Christianity (and Islam). Secondly, he upheld an unedifying character like Jesus as a great teacher of mankind, and glorified no end the sentimental nonsense that is the Sermon on the Mount. Thirdly, he failed to see the true character of Christian missionaries, and nourished the illusion that he could tame them by his reasonableness and good manners. We are taking up the points one by one as they do call for some elaboration.

Sarva-dharma-samabhāva was unknown to mainstream Hinduism before Mahatma Gandhi presented it as one of the sixteen *mahāvratas* (great vows) in his booklet, *Maṅgala-Prabhāta*. It is true that mainstream Hinduism had always stood for tolerance towards all metaphysical points of view and ways of worship except that which led to *ātatāyī-āchāra* (gangsterism). But that tolerance had never become *samabhāva*, equal respect for all points of view. The acharyas of the different schools of Sanatana Dharma were all along engaged in debates over differences in various approaches to *Śreyas* (the Great Good). No Buddhist acharya is known to have equated the way of the Buddha to that of the Gita and vice versa, for instance. It is also true that overawed by the armed might of Islam, and deceived by the tall talk of the sufis, some Hindu saints in medieval India had equated Rama with Rahim, Krishna with Karim, Kashi with Kaba, the Brahmana with the Mullah, *pūjā* with *namāz,* and so on. But the sects founded by these saints had continued to function on the fringes of Hindu society while the mainstream followed the saints and acharyas who never recognized Islam as a *dharma*. In modern times also, movements like the Brahmo Samaj which recognised Islam and Christianity as dharmas had failed to influence mainstream Hinduism, while Maharshi Dayananda and Swami Vivekananda who upheld the Veda and despised the Bible and the Quran, had had a great impact. This being the hoary Hindu tradition, Mahatma Gandhi's recognition of Christianity and Islam not only as *dharmas* but also as equal to Sanatana Dharma was fraught with great mischief. For, unlike the earlier Hindu advocates of Islam and Christianity as *dharmas,* Mahatma Gandhi made himself known and became known as belonging to mainstream Hinduism.

It remains a mystery as to how Mahatma Gandhi came to regard Christianity and Islam as ways of spiritual seeking rather than as terrorist and totalitarian ideologies of predatory imperialism. Here we have doctrines with a deity who is exclusive and jealous of all other deities, who makes himself known to mankind not directly but through a proxy, who has chosen people with whom he enters into covenants for imposing him on the rest of mankind by means of force, who commands his chosen people to wage a permanent war on all other peoples, and who is most happy when his worshippers commit massacres, destroy whole civilizations root and branch, and plunder and enslave helpless men, women and children. Here we have histories stretching over hundreds of years and hailing as heroes and saints some of the most bloodthirsty gangsters and altogether despicable characters. Mahatma Gandhi's recognition of these ideologies as dharmas as good as Sanatana Dharma leads only to two conclusions. Either his own perception of Sanatana Dharma was not as deep as it sounds. Or the politician in him prevailed over his spiritual perception and he said what he did from the platform of *sarva-dharma-samabhāva* in the hope of winning over Christians and Muslims to the nationalist camp. In any case, the utter failure of his attempt to achieve this goal proves that the attempt was foolhardy. He failed to win any significant section of Christians or Muslims either to the nationalist cause or to the camp of *sarva-dharma samabhāva.* But in the process of popularising this slogan, he diluted the definition of *dharma* beyond recognition, and placed Hindu society permanently on the defensive. No other slogan has proved more mischievous for Hinduism than the mindless slogan of *sarva-dharma-samabhāva* vis-a-vis Christianity and Islam.

The Mahatma's heaping of admiration on Jesus and the Sermon on the Mount has proved no less mischievous. Before the Mahatma appeared on the scene, neither Jesus nor the Sermon on the Mount was known to Hindu society at large. It was only the small circle of Brahmo Samaj which had swooned on the name and the nonsense. But Mahatma Gandhi extolled them both, day in and day out, till they became household words, at least among the Hindu intelligentsia. It was a great solace to the Christian theologian and missionary that in the aftermath of Mahatma Gandhi he could silence all Hindu criticism of Christianity by merely mentioning these two magic names—Jesus and the Sermon. One wonders whether the Mahatma knew what modern research had done to the myth of Jesus. In any case, he was not at all called upon to lend his helping hand in the building up of a mischievous myth in this country. As regards the Sermon on the Mount, it has only to be referred to a Vyasa or a Valmiki or a Confucius or a Socrates, and it will be laughed out of court as bogus ethics devoid of discriminative wisdom. Mahatma Gandhi was not called upon to sell this mindless clap-trap as the sum and substance of the highest moral code.

In any case, the Christian missionaries themselves had never known the beauties of the Sermon on the Mount till Mahatma Gandhi discovered it for them. Now onwards they could strut around with superior airs.

Finally, Mahatma Gandhi's meeting the Christian missionaries again and again and wasting so much breath in talking to them on the same point, namely, the uniqueness of Jesus and their right to convert in his name, made them respectable in the eyes of Hindus at large. Till the Mahatma started advertising the Christian missionaries in his widely read weeklies, Hindus had looked down upon them as an unavoidable nuisance deserving only contempt and ridicule. The Mahatma invested them with unprecedented prestige and made them loom large on the Indian scene. One wonders why he failed to consult a text-book of missiology and find out for himself that Christian missionaries are trained and employed as incorrigible casuits, crooks, liers, and practitioners of despicable frauds. He was certainly living in a fool's paradise if he hoped that Christian missionaries could become straight and honest and serve in a humanitarians way. By inviting them to be of unmotivated service to their victims, he bestowed on them an aura which they had never had before. The result has been an unprecedented strengthening and multiplication of the Christian missionary apparatus for subverting Hindu society and culture. He had done the same when he salvaged the Muslim mullahs from their ghettos and made them look like giants during the infamous Khilafat agitation.

APPENDIX

Bishop Heber's Hymn

From Greenland's icy mountians,
    From India's coral strand,
Where Africa's sunny fountains
    Roll down their golden sand;
From many an ancient river,
    From many a palmy plain,
They call us to deliver
    Their land from error's chain.
What though the spicy breezes
    Blow soft o'er Ceylon's isle,
Though every prospect pleases
    And only man is vile.
In vain with lavish kindness
    The gifts of God are strewn,
The heathen in his blindness
    Bows down to wood and stone.
Can we whose souls are lighted
    With wisdom from on high,
Can we to men benighted
    The lamp of life deny?
Salvation, oh, Salvation!
    The joyful sound proclaim,
Till each remotest nation
    Has learn'd Messiah's name.
Waft, waft, ye winds, His story,
    And you, ye waters! roll,
Till like a sea of glory
    It spreads from pole to pole;
Till over our ransom'd nature
    The Lamb for sinners slain
Redeemer, King, Creator
    In bliss returns to reign.

15

The Hoax of Human Rights

The next encounter between Hinduism and Christianity took place in the Constituent Assembly which started framing independent India's Constitution in 1947 and completed the work by the end of 1949. The dialogue centred round what the Christian participants proclaimed as the their fundamental human right, namely, to propagate their religion.

The Christians were quite clear in their mind as well as pronouncements that the "right to propagate" religion entitled them to 1) receive massive financial help from foreign sources; 2) maintain and multiply churches and missions; 3) train and mobilize an ever expanding army of missionaries, native and foreign; 4) enlarge the mission infrastructure of seminaries, social service institutions and mass media; and 5) convert an increasing number of Hindus to Christianity by every means including fraud and material inducements. They had been holding meetings and passing resolutions on all these points even before the Constituent Assembly was mentioned in the negotiations between the Congress leaders and the British Cabinet Mission.

The Hindu participants, on the other hand, did not grasp the full meaning of the "right to propagate religion". They did understand that the word "propagate" was only a substitute for the word "convert", and tried to hedge in the provision with various restrictions. But they did not realize or think it important that "propagation of religion" had employed and would employ a formidable organisational weapon forged almost entirely with the help of foreign money and controlled completely by foreign establishments including intelligence networks. Therefore, the points they raised in the course of the dialogue did not go to the heart of the matter.

Mahatma Gandhi had tried to put the Christian missions in a tight spot by proclaiming that proselytisation was morally wrong and spiritually sterile if not counter-productive. He had also appealed to the missions to employ their enormous resources for rendering humanitarian service to the poor without any motive for proselytisation. But that was tantamount to asking and expecting a man-eater to start living on vegetarian diet. The only point which had registered with the missions was his ruling out any legislation against proselytisation and his affirmation that they would be free to operate in independent India. The missionaries had continued to maintain that they could not withhold "sharing their spiritual riches" with the heathens. The Mahatma's infatuation with Jesus as a "great teacher" and his identification of Christianity with the Sermon on the Mount had only whetted their appetite for converts. It was not long before they leapt into renewed endeavour.

On the other hand, the leaders of the nation who were in charge of framing the Constitution behaved as if they had never heard what Gandhiji had said vis-a-vis proselytisation. His views on the subject were not even mentioned in the deliberations of the sub-committee entrusted with finalising the clauses on fundamental rights relating to religion. Nor did his views figure in the relevant debates in the Constituent Assembly. One wonders whether this silence was maintained on his own behest or whether he had been side-lined. He was alive and active when the first debate on the subject came up in the Constituent Assembly in May 1947.

It is also significant that the Christian leaders who had made it a point to pester Gandhiji in earlier years ignored him completely after India become independent. Either they had given him up as a hopeless job or were apprehensive that he might say something which could create difficulties for Christian missions. Instead, they concentrated on the leaders of the Congress Party for seeking assurances that Christian rights and interests would be safeguarded in the future set-up.

What helped the Christian lobbyists a good deal was the talk about fundamental human rights which filled the atmosphere at the time the Constitution was being framed. The San Francisco Conference had completed the framework of a United Nations Charter. A declaration of fundamental human rights was being proposed and discussed. The Christian missions were backed by powerful people and establishments in the West. They, therefore, exercised considerable influence in the United Nations and were able to ensure that this declaration included their right to wield organisational weapons in the countries of Asia and Africa for the conversion of non-Christians. The politicians who mattered in India were either unaware of the Christian game or did not understand the implications of the "fundamental right to propagate religion". They yielded easily when the Christian lobby pressed for inclusion of the word "propagate" in the clause which in its earlier version had allowed only freedom to profess and practise religion.

The controllers of Christian missions in Europe and America had foreseen quite early in course of the Second World War that the enslaved countries of Asia and Africa were heading towards freedom. The future of Christian missions in these countries was fraught with danger. The missions were an integral part of Western imperialism. Leading native freedom fighters did not look at them with favour. It was, therefore, felt that the future of these missions had to be rethought and replanned. They had to be presented in a new perspective in the post-war world.

In the past, propagation of Christianity and conversion of heathens with the help of organisational weapons, forged and financed by the West, had been propped up as a "divinely ordained" privilege. That was not going to work in the new world order which was emerging fast. Propagation of Christianity was, therefore, to be presented as a fundamental human right. Christian missions were to become champions of religious liberty and minority rights.

A early as 1941 church organisations in Britain and the USA had set up Commissions[1] for projecting a post-war world order from the Christian point of view. The Commissions "foresaw" great opportunities for "world evangelization" in the "just and durable peace" that was to be ensured in the wake of victory over the Axis Powers. More important, the Federal Council of the Churches of Christ in America and Foreign Missions Conference of North America had set up a Joint Committee on Religious Liberty with which the International Missionary Council was cooperating unofficially. The Committee completed its work at the end of 1944 and its findings were presented to the world at large in a 604-page book published by the International Missionary Council from New York in January 1945.[2]

Part I of book surveyed the whole world, country by country, in order to pin-point "the problems of religious liberty today." Coming to India under British rule, the book said, "The major difficulty is in lack of social liberty, rather than in deficiency of civil liberty legally formulated. It is extremely hard for members of most Indian groups to transfer their allegiance to Christianity or to any religion unless it be to the majority group of Hindus — or in some areas, of Moslems — among whom they dwell. Persecutions and disabilities are severe, especially in regard to employment and the use of land. They rest upon the fact that transfer of religious allegiance brings a loss of entire status in society, including family position, economic relationship in village or caste guild and opportunities of marriage in the natural grouping. Not only do these hindrances tend seriously to limit accession to Christianity, even from the 'depressed classes' who have little to lose and everything to gain, but they also serve to cut off Christians as a distinct body of persons largely dependent

1. The British body was the Commission on International Friendship and Social Responsibility. Its counterpart in the U.S.A. was the Commision on a Just and Durable Peace set up under the Chairmanship of Mr. John Foster Dulles, the future Secretary of State.

2. M. Searle Bates, *Religious Liberty: An Inquiry*, New York, 1945.

upon their own meager group for economic and social opportunity."[3]

The problem faced by Christian missions in some princely states of India was also noted. "Restrictions in certain Native States," it was pointed out, "are ominous, since they suggest what the full combination of political rule with religious community interest may hold for wide portions of India in the future. Despite considerable British persuasion and influence to the contrary, certain Indian states prohibit the preaching of Christianity and the entry of missionaries within their borders. Some states forbid the erection of church buildings, some prohibit schools, one is tolerant of a single denomination. Patna recently put severe difficulties in the way of change from Hinduism to any other faith, using the piquant title 'Freedom of Religion Act'."[4]

Looking to the future the book stated, "Rule by Indians is already well along in transition and is certain to be consummated, whether by gradual or by revolutionary change from the present mixed system in which British authority has long fostered the concept and the practice of self-government... The Congress Party has committed itself to religious freedom and the protection of minorities. But the restraints of British neutrality and British protection of minorities are irksome to the strenuous elements, and they may be swept away in the name of 'Indian unity' or even of 'Hinduism restored'. All that has been associated in fact or in the emotions of Indians, with foreign rule and its cultural connotations will be a target for attack."[5]

Finally, it came to the main culprit — Hinduism. "It is necessary," it said, "to consider further the basic nature of Hinduism, the system which controls the lives of a multitude half as numerous as all the peoples of Europe. *It is a totalitarian social and economic and cultural complex knit together with*

3. *Ibid.*, pp. 56-57.
4. *Ibid.*, p. 57. Patna was a princely state in Orissa.
5. *Ibid.*, pp. 57-58.

powerful religious sanctions. Every act of life, from birth till death, is directed by it. Race, caste, guild or occupational grouping, tribe or clan, family, gods, temple and pilgrimage, literature and legend, folklore and local superstitions, ethical and social prescriptions, community in all senses of the term: they are one pervasive, controlling force — Hinduism. How can one renounce it? If not impossible the thought is unnatural, impious. Withdrawal is an outlawing of self from all established institutions and from normal human fellowship. Such is the background for the Hindu view of conversion."[6]

Mahatma Gandhi invited pointed attention. "Gandhi," said the book, "less conservative and less vehement than many Hindu leaders, has nevertheless on many occasions spoken his hostility to any enterprise, good though it is in much of its spirit and service, which has as its purpose or result the change of an Indian's faith from Hinduism to another." He was pinned down as inconsistent because he was a party to the resolutions of the Delhi Unity Conference in 1924. One of the resolutions was quoted as having said that "every individual is at liberty to follow any faith and to change it whenever he wills, and shall not by reason of such change of faith render himself liable to any punishment or persecution at the hands of the followers of the faith renounced by him." Moreover, "Gandhi has been reminded in a friendly way that much of his own life has been an effort to influence the spiritual and moral outlook of all sorts of people 'by speech or writing, by appeal to reason and emotion'."[7]

The book laid down 15 "important issues on religious liberty recurrent in the contemporary scene."[8] Three of them were as follows:

> 12. Does the individual have liberty to learn of other forms of religion than that in which he is born and trained and the liberty to give his allegiance to one of them?

---

6. *Ibid.*, p. 59. Emphasis added.
7. *Ibid.*, p. 61.
8. *Ibid.*, p. 130.

13. Then there is the issue of the freedom of the religious believer, singly or in association, to express his faith in such manner as to seek the adherence of others to it. Such freedom is the converse of the foregoing liberty.

14. Are religious allegiance and the presentation of religion to be confined by state frontiers? May the believer seek religious truth and fellowship, or express his faith, or devote himself to religious service beyond the boundaries of his own state?[9]

In its part II — The Problem of Religious Liberty —, the book conceded that throughout its history Hindu society had solved its religious differences peacefully. At the same time, however, it pointed out that the problem of religious liberty had never been raised by Hindus and no guidance in this respect was available from Hindu history. "There is small evidence," it said, "in Hindu literature of persecution within Hindu society proper. There was much controversy, religious and philosophical, and a good deal of variety in organization. But vague and absorptive polytheism, whether ethnic and static or advancing by addition and syncretism, did not raise clear issues of compulsion or liberty. Jainism and Buddhism were deviations and reforms from some aspects of the early Aryan faith-tradition. Their rise and progress; the standardization of Jainism as a minor sect of ascetic tendencies; the extension, export, the decline of Buddhism within a society of Hinduism — all were essentially peaceful. The changes came by persuasion and by slow social pressures or movements, without clear conflict of group wills against other groups or against individuals."[10]

Religious intolerance and persecution, it was noted, came to India in the wake of Islamic invasion. The Portuguese also practised religious persecution. But "it is only in the political developments of recent years, in the missionary introduction

9. *Ibid.*, p. 131.

10. *Ibid.*, p. 267. Incidentally, what was an asset of Hindu culture in the context of religious tolerance became a liability in the context of religious liberty!

of fresh Christian undertakings, and in the social and intellectual change of the contemporary scene that the issue of religious liberty has become apparent." Hinduism was again held up as the main culprit because "The chief social persecution of Christians has come from Hindus" while "Christianity has had little significant contact with Islam in India."[11] The reasons for this lack of Christian contact with Islam were not given. The book withheld the stark truth that Islam was in the same sordid business as Christianity, and that Christian missionaries were murdered and mission stations burnt down whenever and wherever they came in "significant contact with Islam". The bandits were devising a strategy for attacking a soft target which Hindu society has been for quite some time.

Part III of the book posed the question: What is religious liberty? Definitions of religious liberty given by various individuals and organisations were surveyed. Finally, the "statement on religious liberty" given by the sponsors of the Joint Committee in 1944 was chosen "as a brief and working formulation of recent attitudes." The statement was as follows:

> The right of individuals everywhere to religious liberty shall be recognized and subject only to the maintenance of public order and security, shall be guaranteed against legal provisions and administrative acts which would impose political, economic, or social disabilities on grounds of religion.
>
> Religious liberty shall be interpreted to include freedom to worship according to conscience and to bring up children in the faith of their parents; freedom to preach, educate, publish, and carry on missionary activities; and freedom to organize with others, and to acquire and hold property, for these purposes.[12]

Part IV of the book — The Grounds of Religious Liberty — provided a scholarly discourse on Natural Law and Natural

---

11. *Ibid.*, p. 271. Whatever the context, credit must go to Christianity!
12. *Ibid.*, p. 309.

Rights, Religious Liberty and the Interests of Organised Community, Religious Liberty in Terms of Ethics and Philosophy, Religious Liberty in Terms of Christian Theology and Tradition, and the Position of the Roman Catholic Church. "The main historical record," it was admitted, "and the present map of intolerance suggest that Christianity does not carry within itself principles, teachings, and practices which automatically and generally secure religious liberty for all men under its influence. An ethic is there, some teachings and practices are there, which are potentially favourable to religious liberty. But religious and social tendencies toward intolerance prevail over the elements working toward liberty... Beyond question Christians need in far greater measure to recognize the wrong of their intolerances, to realize the liberty of the spirit necessary to the Christian life and inherent — but too often latent — in Christian history, and to make their needed contribution to liberty in a world essentially non-Christian."[13]

Part V of the book discussed Religious Liberty in Law. It was noted that "the Modern State, of whatever type, tends to assume jurisdiction over all persons in its territory" and that "The individual thus possesses *legal* rights only in so far as allowed by the state."[14] Nor could religious liberty be safeguarded by "international action" because "international relations are controlled by sovereign states."[15] The only way out, therefore, was to find out "*whether religious liberty is an inviolable right.*" [16] The search spread to the arena of international law. "The development of international law," it was discovered, "has been associated in history and in concept

---

13. *Ibid.*, pp. 431-432. Thus Christianity, with all its intolerance, was found to contain the seeds of religious liberty! But Hinduism, with all its tolerance, could not claim that credit! In simple language, what the learned exercise wanted to say was that religious liberty was a by-product of religious intolerance and consequent conflict. One had to be a bandit before one could hope to be a saint.

14. *Ibid.*, p. 474. Italics in source.

15. *Ibid.*, p. 475.

16. *Ibid.*, p. 476. Emphasis added.

with the growth of religious liberty. But there is no principle or consensus in international law asserting an obligation of each state to accord religious liberty to its inhabitants."[17]

The search for "consensus in international law" formed Part VI of the book. It contained the Joint Committee's "conclusions and proposals." To start with, the existing states were placed (or evaluated) in five main and three subsidiary categories "according to conditions of religious liberty."[18] India found its place in Category III(a) along with Anglo-Egyptian Sudan, Burma, Ethiopia and Nigeria. These states were found to have " freedom of religion limited in certain regions, with important social pressures."[19]

Next, the book provided fifteen "brief observations on important issues for religious liberty recurrent in the contemporary scene."[20] The core observations were as follows:

> (12) and (13): In order that development in religion may be possible in any society and that individuals or groups may follow the expressions of religious truth which seem likely to bring them to their highest spiritual development, without the risks of hypocrisy and cramping confinement, individuals should have liberty at least from adolescence to learn of other forms of religion than that in which they are born and trained — with liberty to give allegiance thereto. Conversely, religious believers should naturally have liberty to declare and to recommend their faith to others and to invite fully voluntary adherence to it. Where these opportunities do not freely exist, religious liberty is denied or limited, and monopoly or fixity is sought by means of enforced ignorance and group compulsion.
>
> (14): Religion confined by national frontiers is politically bounded and is in danger of becoming in some measure a tool or function of the State. Individuals and

17. *Ibid.*, p. 54.
18. *Ibid.*, pp. 546-54.
19. *Ibid.*, p. 547.
20. *Ibid.*, p. 549.

> groups should be free to receive the stimulus and challenge of spirit which may come from outside their state and free to be associated in religious concerns, subject, of course, to all proper duties of citizenship, with persons and groups resident in other states. Any great truth or conception of truth has a supra-local quality, and several of the world's major religions are rightly called universal. Similarly, the normal expression of religious faith in service and in commendation of the faith to others is not confined by political boundaries... The alternatives of such normal liberty are either the denial of spiritual contact, the nationalizing of culture, in patterns of hideous danger revealed by the sealed-off minds of the totalitarian states — primitive and sophisticated alike; or restriction and control for political ends, infringing religious liberty and limiting the benefits which should be expected from essentially free contacts on the religious level.[21]

In this context the book cited the recommendations made by the Commission on The Church and State in Post-War India set up by the National Christian Council of India in 1944. The Commission had proposed:

> The Church claims freedom to proclaim its Gospel, and to receive into its membership those who from sincere and honest motives desire to join it. The Church claims this freedom to commend its Gospel, because it can do no other in the light of the command of its Founder to preach the Gospel to every creature. This argument may not weigh with a non-Christian government; but it is best for the Church to admit frankly that it desires to preach the Gospel because of its conviction that fullness of life and truth cannot be enjoyed apart from Christ. On those who cannot accept such a reason it may urge that religion is such a personal matter that every individual should be given freedom to make his own decisions in the matter.

21. *Ibid.*, pp. 551-552. It was forgotten that the totalitarian states — Fascist, Communist, Nazi — were creations of the Christian ethos which had dominated Europe during preceding centuries.

To commend truth as one sees it is no infringement of the liberty of another, as he is free if he wishes to continue in the convictions which he already holds. Rather it is a recognition of the responsibility of each man to choose what he believes....

In pleading for freedom to commend the Gospel to all, we would disavow any methods of propaganda which would endanger public order or cause scandal and unnecessary offence. We disapprove all methods of propaganda which hold out material advantage as a motive for conversion. Furthermore, though conversion does increase the number of Christians, and such increase may strengthen the political influence of the Christian community, we disavow any desire for such influence. It is not our wish that Christians as a community should seek political influence for themselves; it is rather our wish that they should form a Church intent only on obeying the will of God. Again, we are of opinion that no minor under the age of eighteen should be admitted into the Christian Church without the consent of his parent or guardian. But in the event of parent or guardian becoming Christian, it is in our opinion better that division in families is as far as possible to be avoided.[22]

Finally, the book came out with its own recommendations. "First," it said, "there should be serious study and discerning advocacy of proposals for an International Bill of Rights or International Charter of Liberties."[23] The program suggested by the Commission to Study the Organisation of Peace was summarised: "We propose that measures be taken to safeguard human rights throughout the world by (1) convening without delay a United Nations Conference on Human Rights to examine the problem, (2) promulgating, as a result of this conference, an international bill of rights, (3) establishing at this conference a permanent United Nations

22. *Ibid.*, p. 563.
23. *Ibid.*, p. 573.

Commission on Human Rights for the purpose of further developing the standards of human rights and the methods for their protection, (4) seeking the incorporation of major civil rights in national constitutions and promoting effective means of enforcement in each nation, (5) recognizing the right of individuals or groups, under prescribed limitations, to petition the Human Rights Commission, after exhausting local remedies, in order to call attention to violations."[24]

The program was recommended to the United Nations which was in the process of formation. "The United Nations Declarations of January 1, 1942," concluded the book, "based their common action upon the necessity 'to defend life, liberty, independence, and religious freedom, and to preserve human rights and justice in their own lands as well as in other lands'.... The Dumbarton Oaks Agreements (Proposals for the Establishment of a General International Organization) of October 7, 1944 declare that 'the organization should facilitate solutions of international economic, social, and other humanitarian problems and promote respect for human rights and fundamental freedoms.' The proposals center responsibility for this task in an Economic and Social Council, under the authority of the General Assembly. Thus commitments of direction are already made. They can be actualized by determination and persistence."[25]

There was not a word in this big book about the right of the heathens to defend themselves against Christian aggression euphamised as "the right to propagate religion". None of the learned men who collaborated in the compilation of this study noted that the heathens stood wholly unarmed vis-a-vis the Christian missions. The heathens were in no position to mobilise the mammoth finances which Christian missions could do with considerable ease. The heathens had no seminaries where they could train missionaries of their own and meet the challenge of Christian legionaries. The heathens

24. *Ibid.*, p. 576.
25. *Ibid.*, p. 579.

commanded no mass media which could defend their faith against the Christian blitzkrieg on any comparable footing. Nor had the heathens developed a scholarship which could prostitute itself in the service of an imperialist enterprise masquerading as a defender of human rights.

Simultaneously with the publication of this pretentious book, the U.S. Commission met in Cleveland, Ohio, U.S.A. and set up a National Study Conference which suggested several improvements in the Dumbarton Oaks Proposals of October, 1944. The British Commission did the same. The suggestions were hailed by the churches in both countries and recommended to their governments for being taken up at the San Francisco Conference of the United Nations which was scheduled to meet in April-June 1945.

Meanwhile, a Foreign Missions Conference had met at Toronto from January 5 to 8, 1945. It was "attended by 485 delegates and visitors from every state and province of the U.S.A. and Canada" and represented "every major Protestant denomination and church affiliation." The Conference passed resolutions "earnestly petitioning its two governments of Canada and the U.S.A. to give immediate attention to their responsibilities in three matters basic to world organisation, security and peace." One of the three matters was "responsibility for religious liberty."[26]

The World Council of Churches and the International Missionary Council exhorted church organisation all over the world to "intercede" for the success of the San Franscisco Conference. The National Christian Council of India received a cable from New York stating that the American churches were planning special intercession on April 22 for the success of the San Francisco Conference and suggesting like action in "your constituency." *The National Christian Council Review* commented, "Momentous issues will face the delegates to the San Fanscisco Conference of the United Nations as they assemble on April 25... A supreme responsibility rests at this

26. *The National Christian Council Review*, August 1945, p. 137.

time on the Universal Church."[27]

What this "intercession" meant became clear when the U.S. monthly, *Christianity and Crisis,* published in its June issue a report about Christian influence at San Francisco. "The concern," it said, "which Church leaders have shown during the past decade for the development of a law-governed world has borne fruit... The State Department included in its group of advisers or consultants, representatives of certain Church organisations, Federal Council, Church Peace Union, Catholic Welfare, and others. These representatives had worked consistently and steadily to back the American delegates in giving what Mr. Dulles has called a 'soul' to the Charter. They had backed the recommendations for a commission on Human Rights and had urged the recognition of such in preamble and definition of the Assembly's work."[28]

It seems, however, that lobbying for "religious liberty" through government delegations was not enough. Pressure from outside had to be maintained. It was with this aim that the World Council of Churches and the International Missionary Council set up a Commission on International Affairs which held its first meeting in Cambridge, England, in August 1946. One of its aims was to make sure that "the Church should and will play an important part in promoting the work of the United Nations." According to a spokesman of the Church, "It is imperative that Christians develop an intelligent understanding of what the United Nations Organisation is, what its duties are and the manner in which these duties are to be discharged."[29] He added, "The American Church helped influence the shaping of the Charter. Upon invitation of the Department of State they had their consultants at San Francisco Conference. Plans are now being perfected whereby Churches may have 'observers' present at the public meetings of the major organs of the United Nations including

27. *Ibid.*, March 1945. p. 56.
28. *Ibid.*, December 1945, pp. 212-13.
29. *Ibid.*, February 1947, p. 56.

the General Assembly."[30]

Rest is history. The Universal Declaration of Human Rights adopted and proclaimed by the General Assembly of the United Nations in October 1948 included Article 18 which read: "Everyone has the right to freedom of thought, conscience and religion: *this right includes freedom to change his religion or belief*, and freedom, either alone or in community with others and in public or private to manifest his religion or belief in teaching, practice, worship and observance."[31] The renewed assaults to be mounted by Christian missions in post-war Asia and Africa had been camouflaged in clever language.

II

Christian missions in India were privy to these proceedings of their international patrons. They had gone into action even before the United Nations Organisation came into being. The Punjab Indian Christian Association held a meeting at Lahore on November 4, 1944 and adopted a resolution that "in view of Gandhiji's statement that 'conversion is the deadliest poison that ever sapped the fountain of truth'", this meeting, "urges the leaders of the community all over India to make it known to all concerned that 'To preach the gospel' is a definite command of our master and an integral part of the Christian Religion, and that therefore no constitution for India will be acceptable to the community which does not guarantee freedom to every citizen to propagate his faith and to every adult to change his religion at his own free will without any legal let or hindrance."[32]

Another meeting of "Christians of all denominations" held at Nagpur on November 25, 1944 considered "the right of freedom to convert people of other faiths as an integral part of the Christian religion and inalienable and unalterable right

30. *Ibid.*, p. 57.

31. *The United Nations and Human Rights*, published by the UNO, New York, 1984, p. 242. Emphasis added.

32. *The National Christian Council Review*, January 1945, p. 12.

of all Christians as individuals or as organized in Churches."[33] More conferences were held at Bombay, Calcutta, Lahore and Madras in January and February 1945 on the occasion of the visit to India of Dr. J. W. Decker, Secretary of the International Missionary Council. He had come in order to "discover major principles, methods and emphasis which the Christian movement should adopt in its plan for the post-war decade or decades with special reference to strengthening the Church and its effective witness and to the *collaboration and help desired from abroad.*"[34] They adopted similar resolutions on 'religious liberty'.[35]

The Executive Committee of the All India Council of Indian Christians was held in Bombay on October 27-28, 1945. It decided to start negotiations with "responsible Congress authorities" for the "legitimate protection in the coming constitution of India of their rights both as a minority community and as a body standing for freedom of conscience and the full and unfettered profession, practice and teaching of their religion."[36] On October 30, 1945 representatives of the Catholic Union of India and the All-India Council of Indian Christians formed a Joint Committee with Mr. M. Ruthnaswami, Vice-Chancellor of the Annamalai University, as its Chairman. The Committee adopted a resolution "suggesting that in the future constitution of India the free profession, practice and propagation of religion should be guaranteed and that a change of religion should not involve any civil or political disability." The Committee also appointed a sub-committee "to formulate proposals for a future constitution to be placed before the Constituent Assembly."[37]

On February 4, 1946 a Christian Deputation met the British Parliamentary Delegation which was visiting India at that time. Some members of the Delegation asked the Deputation

33. *Ibid.*, p. 31.
34. *Ibid.*, p. 14.
35. *Ibid.*, p. 81. Emphasis added.
36. *Ibid.*, January 1946, p. 32.
37. *Ibid.*, December 1945, pp. 239-41.

"whether Christians feared that they would suffer in a self-governing India." The Deputation saw "a possibility arising, specially in rural areas" but were "clear that they desired to have secured to them as to other religious communities — in the Constitution itself — the right to practise, teach and propagate their faith without obstruction or discrimination."[38]

The National Christian Council Review of March 1946 published an editorial on 'Religious Liberty' and announced that "a comprehensive and profound study of this whole subject has been completed recently by Dr. Searle Bates." The words of the Council which Bates had borrowed vis-a-vis India had become "profound" in the process of being played back. The same issue published a long article by Rev. K. F. Weller of the Baptist Missionary Society in Orissa pointing an accusing finger at certain "Native States" vis-a-vis 'religious liberty'. "These instances," he warned, "are symptomatic and the situation should be watched carefully for it is a challenge to religious liberty which may grow in intensity in future."[39] He was repeating what had been stated by Bates who, in turn, had repeated what the missionaries in India had told him.

Rev. Stanley Jones wrote an article, 'Opportunities for the Church facing Indian Nationalism', in the *Review* of April 1946. He mounted a straight attack on Mahatma Gandhi. "There is the obvious fear," he said, "which possesses many minds, Christian and Muslim, that the Congress is closely bound up with Hinduism; that the national renaissance and the renaissance of Hinduism have been simultaneous and synonymous; that the supremacy of the Congress will mean the supremacy of Hinduism. There is some basis for this fear, for the leader of the nationalist movement, Mahatma Gandhi, has been closely identified with the movement to regenerate Hinduism, especially as it concerns the outcastes... It is also to be regretted that he uses Ramrajya in speaking of the kind of India he wants to see. In his mind this is probably very

38. *Ibid.*, April 1946, p. 120.
39. *Ibid.*, March 1946, p. 81.

innocent and proper but nevertheless it has not helped in the winning of the Muslims to the nationalist cause, nor has it made it easy for the Christians to feel at home, for they do not want Ramrajya either."[40] These were exactly the charges which the Communist Party of India and the Indian Muslim League were heaping on the Mahatma at that time.

Jones had no doubt that "there will be attempts made to forbid evangelistic work in an independent India." But he felt sure that the attempts will fail. "I believe," he concluded, "that the presentation of a disentangled Christ will be allowed and welcomed in free India. If it is not, then I do not understand the soul of India."[41] He knew how to combine frowns with flattery. Moreover, he had his eyes on that powerful section in the Congress led by Pandit Jawaharlal Nehru which harboured a deep-seated animus against Hindus and Hinduism and which could be made to say or do anything in order to avoid being called 'Hindu communalists'.

The same issue of the *Review* had given the 'good news'. "It is equally assuring," it reported, "to read what Pandit Nehru said while exhorting Indian Christians of the U.P. to vote for the two Indian Christian Congress candidates who were standing for election to the U.P. Legislative Assembly: 'I am astonished to read some of the propaganda that is being issued by or on behalf of the opponents of the Congress.... The cry of religion in danger is used when everybody knows that the fundamental creed of the Congress is freedom of religion and all that goes with it... Christians form the third largest group in the country and it is absurd for anyone to imagine that their religious or other rights can be suppressed or ignored.'"[42]

The Congress Election Manifesto had proclaimed a charter

40. *Ibid.*, April 1946, p. 99.

41. *Ibid.*, p. 101. "Disentangled Christ" means Christ torn out of Christian history. That criminal history which had been created, without a doubt by Christ, the one and only saviour, had come under fire in an age which had, by and large, freed itself from Christian monolatry.

42. *Ibid.*, p. 93.

of fundamental rights. One of the clauses assured that "Every citizen shall enjoy freedom of conscience and the right freely to *profess and practise* his religion, subject to public order and morality."[43] What the Christians missed in it was their "inalienable and unalterable right to propagate religion." Pandit Nehru's assurance did not mention this specific right. But the assurance was ample enough to cover anything and everything. The *Review* made the point quite clear. "These utterances of persons in responsible positions in Indian politics," it said, "go a long way toward dispelling our fears that under Swaraj Christianity will be in danger. However, the events of the next few months will show whether or not Christians have justifiable cause for thinking that they may be in for severe persecution. We trust in any future constitution of India that may be drawn up by a Constituent Assembly, religious freedom will be guaranteed and no let or hindrance will be placed in the way of Christians living, *preaching and teaching* their religion and *taking into membership of their Church* those who honestly accept their way of life and belief."[44] The posture of being persecuted comes easily to those who are aggressive by nature.

Pandit Nehru removed all Christian apprehensions in the next assurance he gave them. The Delhi correspondent of *The Catholic Herald* of London had an interview with Pandit Nehru and asked him pointedly, "What is your view of the Indian Christian representatives' proposal to the Cabinet Mission that they should be free not merely to practise but also to propagate their religion?" Pandit Nehru replied, "It stands to reason that any faith whose roots are strong and healthy should spread, and to interfere with that right to spread seems to me to be a blow at the roots themselves... Unless a given faith proves a menace to public order, or its teachers attempt to thrust it down the unwilling throats of men of other persuasions, there can be no justification for measures

43. *Ibid.*, February 1946, p. 62. Emphasis added.
44. *Ibid.*, April 1946, p. 94. Emphasis added.

which deprive any community of its rights."[45] It was a habit with him to speak "generally of things in general", to use his own words. But those who knew his prejudices and preferences never missed the point. It was, of course, his privilege not to know the source from which Christianity derived its strength and not to care what that strength had done and was doing to its weak and defenceless victims.

So the Tenth Triennial Meeting of the National Christian Council of India, Burma and Ceylon was held in November 1946 in an atmosphere of confidence in the future of Christian missions in India. Once again, Christian missions and churches could plan their future programme in a mood of optimism. The proceedings of the Meeting were reviewed by Rev. C.E. Abraham of the Serampore Theological College, "Another impression," he wrote, "that was left on one was the immensity of the unfinished task of the Missions and Churches in India. A coloured map of India that was exhibited showing unoccupied areas... drew pointed attention to the huge proportions of the evangelistic task of the Church in India... Conditions in India, political and social, are changing quickly and sometimes changing beyond recognition. At such a time as this, foresight rather than caution, is what is demanded of missionary statesmen... Are future leaders being recruited in sufficient numbers? Are they being given sufficient training in India or abroad to assume responsibilities? Or is the shibboleth of 'self-support' being allowed to stifle initiative and to cover up complacency? These are questions that need to be pondered most conscientiously by Mission Boards in India and overseas."[46]

The Meeting set up a Commission for making recommendations on 'The Church in a Self-governing India'. The Commission advocated that churches and missions should be

45. *Ibid.*, November 1946, pp. 335-36.

46. *Ibid.*, January 1947, pp. 12-13. The proposal of some 'nationalist' Christians that the Church in India should be self-supporting in order to be independent, was not relished by most Christians, particularly the missionaries.

integrated. This was to ensure that foreign missions were not spotted separately. In any case, integration was not to hinder the flow of foreign money and manpower. "This matter of integration," said the Commission, "should not of itself involve the diminishing of assistance by old Churches in personnel, funds and counsel to the Churches in India. The National Christian Council is convinced that the Church in India will continue to need and to welcome as colleagues their brethren in faith from the older Churches to join with them in the building up of the Church in the fulfilment of the duty of sharing the evangel of Christ."[47]

Bishop C. K. Jocob read a paper in the Meeting. The Churches in India, according to him, were in a transition period. "Till the Churches are established on a firm footing," he said, "they should continue to receive financial aid from the old Churches in the West. Not only for the building up of the Church, but for extending the evangelistic work in areas not yet touched, funds are needed by every section of the Church."[48]

A message which the National Christian Council received from the Indian Christian Association of Bombay repeated the same recommendation. "The Church of Christ," said the message, "is a Universal Church and there can be no place in Christian work for any distinctions on lines of nationality, race or colour. We, therefore, emphatically disagree with the ill-conceived cry of 'Foreign Missionaries Quit India' raised in certain disgruntled and irresponsible quarters. Moreover, the Christian Church in India is not in a position to take over the complete responsibility for the conduct of the Christian enterprise in this country. We are therefore deeply conscious of the fact that we still need the help and cooperation of the Churches in the West — both in the shape of material resources and personnel."[49]

The March 1947 editorial of the *Review* was full of hope

47. *Ibid.*, p. 17.
48. *Ibid.*, p. 32.
49. *Ibid.*, February 1947, p. 52.

for the future. "That the Christians in India," it said, "will be called upon to play an important part in the national life of the country is becoming increasingly clear. Not very long ago Pandit Nehru in an interview with a representative of The *Catholic Herald* said, 'Indian Christians are part and parcel of the Indian people. Their traditions go to 1500 years and more and they form one of the many enriching elements in the country's cultural and spiritual life.'" It quoted "a leading Congressman" saying to Dr. Stanley Jones that "what was needed for India was a character producing faith and that there was no doubt that the impact of Christ upon life produced miracles in change of character."[50]

The same issue of the *Review* presented a pamphlet, *The Right to Convert*, written by two Christian scholars and published by the Christian Literature Society. The pamphlet which was being widely advertised in the Christian press defined conversion as "changes of faith, together with the outward expressions that such changes normally involve, and efforts to promote such changes." It held up the right to convert as a *fundamental human right* which could not be interfered with. It also gave "reasons and convincing answers" to objections against conversions, namely, "that the established position is true; that all religions are the same; that conversion denationalises; that conversion brings in denominations; that conversion is socially disruptive; that conversion involves religious controversy; that conversion uses abusive methods; and that conversion uses unfair methods." The reviewer thanked the writers for their "substantial contribution to the literature dealing with the problem of religious liberty in the context of the present situation in India."[51]

The *Review* of May 1947 published a report of the findings of an informal conference of Christian leaders held at Brindaban, U.P., in January 1947. The report started by

50. *Ibid.*, March 1947, p. 103. Fifteen hundred will become two thousand years in Pandit Nehru's next pronouncement about the presence of Christianity in India.

51. *Ibid.*, pp. 142-43.

recording "its gratitude to the missionary enterprise which has led the churches of the West to bring to India the wonderful blessing of the Gospel of our Lord Jesus Christ and which has promoted those activities — spiritual, moral, intellectual, social and economic — that have flowed therefrom." It also assured "the sending societies that there is no thought here that the churches in India will not for a long time to come continue to need and to welcome the help of the older and the richer churches in facing the enormous tasks of regeneration and reconstruction of life in India."[52] It informed the fund-raisers abroad that "a study is being made under the auspices of the National Christian Council of unoccupied fields and of the needs especially of the tribal areas in order that an appeal may be made to all concerned and the efforts of new workers in pioneer fields be directed to the best effect." It concluded by saying that "*In regard to religious liberty* it was agreed that while doing all possible through every channel to secure fundamental human rights for all, yet in every situation the church should go forward courageously and not be too much troubled by state action."[53]

III

Meanwhile, the Advisory Committee on Fundamental Rights, set up by the Constituent Assembly on January 24, 1947, had finalised the Draft Articles which included 'Rights relating to Religion'. As related earlier, the Election Manifesto of the Congress Party had assured to every citizen 'freedom of conscience and the right freely to *profess and practise* his religion subject to public order and morality'. The Advisory Committee on Fundamental Rights held its first meeting on February 27, 1947 and elected Sardar Vallabhbhai Patel as its Chariman. The Committee then set up a Sub-committee to deal specifically with Fundamental Rights as distinguished from Minority Rights, etc. Acharya J. B. Kripalani was elected

52. *Ibid.*, May 1947, p. 243.
53. *Ibid.*, p. 244. Emphasis in source.

its Chairman. Rajkumari Amrit Kaur was the Christian representative in the Sub-Committee.

On March 17, 1947 Shri K. M. Munshi presented to the Sub-committee a Note and Draft Articles on Fundamental Rights. The Rights to Religion under Article III included the following clauses among others:

> (1) All citizens are equally entitled to freedom of conscience and to the right freely to *profess and practise* religion in a manner compatible with public order, morality or health:
>
> Provided that the economic, financial or political activities associated with religious worship shall not be deemed to be included in the right to profess or practise religion.
>
> (6) No person under the age of eighteen shall be free to change his religious persuasion without the permission of his parent or guardian.
>
> (7) Conversion from one religion to another brought about by coercion, undue influence or the offering of material inducement is prohibited and is punishable by the law of the Union.[54]

Many meetings of the Sub-committee were held till its final report was submitted to the Advisory Committee on Fundamental Rights on April 16, 1947. The changes which the Draft Articles underwent on various dates are being narrated below.

March 26, 1947

> Article VI -- Clause (1): All persons are equally entitled to freedom of conscience and the right freely to *profess and practise* religion in a manner compatible with public order, morality or health.
>
> **Explanation II:** The right to profess and practise religion shall not include economic, financial, political

54. B. Shiva Rao, *The Framing of India's Constitution, Select Documents*, Volume II, Bombay, 1967, p. 76. Emphasis added.

or other secular activities associated with religious worship.[55]

March 27, 1947

Clause (6) of Article VI was accepted in the following form:

No person under the age of 18 shall be converted to any religion other than one in which he was born or be initiated into any religious order involving loss of civil status.

Clause (7) of Article VI was passed in the following form:

Conversion from one religion to another brought about by coercion or undue influence shall not be recognized by law and the exercise of such coercion or undue influence shall be an offence.[56]

March 29, 1947

Clause (1) of Article VI as revised on March 26, 1947 was decided to be amplified so as to read as follows:

All persons are equally entitled to freedom of conscience and the right freely to *profess and practise* religion in a manner compatible with public order, morality or health and with the other rights guaranteed by the Constitution.[57]

The numbering of clauses continued getting changed as they were arranged and rearranged under Chapter I. They stood as under on successive dates:

April 3, 1947

16. All persons are equally entitled to freedom of conscience and the right freely to *profess and practise* religion subject to public order, morality or health and to the other provisions of this chapter.

---

55. *Ibid.*, p. 124. Emphasis added. Explanation I relates to Sikhs and is not relevant in the context of Christianity.

56. *Ibid.*, p. 125.

57. *Ibid.*, p. 131. Emphasis added.

Explanation II: The right to profess and practise religion shall not include any economic, financial, political or other secular activities that may be associated with religious worship.

Explanation III: No person shall refuse the performance of civil obligations or duties on the ground that his religion so requires.

22. No person under the age of 18 shall be converted to any religion other than the one in which he was born or be initiated into any religious order involving a loss of civil status.

23. Conversion from one religion to another brought about by coercion or undue influence shall not be recognized by law and the exercise of such coercion or undue influence shall be an offence.[58]

April 14, 1947

Clause 16 was decided to be redrafted as follows:

"All persons are equally entitled to *freedom of conscience,* to *freedom of religious worship* and to *freedom to profess religion* subject to public order, morality or health and to the other provisions of this chapter."

Explanation II: The above rights shall not include any economic, financial, political or other secular activities that may be associated with religious worship.

Explanation III: No change.[59]

There was no discussion on Clauses 22 and 23 which were left unchanged.

April 15, 1947

Clause 22: For the words 'converted to' substitute the words 'made to join or profess'.

Clause 23: In the third line, omit the words 'or undue influence'. Dr. Ambedkar proposed that the clause should end with the words 'recognized by law' but this

58. *Ibid.*, p.140. Emphasis added.

59. *Ibid.*, p.165. Emphasis added.

was not accepted by the Committee.[60]

April 16, 1947

16. All persons are equally entitled to *freedom of conscience*, to *freedom of religious worship* and to *freedom to profess religion* subject to public order, morality or health and to the other provisions of this chapter.

Explanation II: The above rights shall not include any economic, financial, political or other secular activities that may be associated with religious worship.

Explanation III: No person shall refuse the performance of civil obligations or duties on the ground that his religion so requires.

21. No person under the age of 18 shall be made to join or profess any religion other than the one in which he was born or be initiated into any religious order involving a loss of civil status.

22. Conversion from one religion to another brought about by coercion or undue influence shall not be recognized by law and the exercise of such coercion shall be an offence.[61]

By now Clauses 22 and 23 had been renumbered as 21 and 22. This draft was referred by the Advisory Committee to the Sub-committee on Minorities and some more changes were made in it on different dates.

April 17, 1947

Meeting of the Sub-Committee on Minorities examined the draft clauses recommended by the Fundamental Rights Sub-committee.

Clause 16. Mr. Ruthnaswamy pointed out that certain religions such as Christianity and Islam, were essentially proselytizing religions, and provision should be made to permit them to *propagate* their faith in accordance with

60. *Ibid.*, p. 166.

61. *Ibid.*, pp. 173-74. Emphasis added.

their tenets.[62]

April 18, 1947

In the Sub-Committee on Minorities meeting:

Clause 21. Mr. Ruthnaswamy: Its provisions will break up family life. A minor should be allowed to follow his parents in any change of religion or nationality which they may adopt.

Clause 22. Mr. Rajagopalachari questioned the necessity of this provision, when it was covered by the ordinary law of the land, e.g. the Indian Penal Code.[63]

April 19, 1947

H. C. Mookerjee, Chairman of the Minorities Sub-Committee, made the following recommendations:

Clause 16: The clause may be redrafted as follows:

"All persons are equally entitled to freedom of conscience and the right freely to profess, practise and *propagate* religion subject to public order, morality or health and to the other provision of the chapter; and that in Explanation 2 for the words 'religious worship', 'religious practice' should be substituted."

Clause 21: This clause may be redrafted as follows:

"(a) No person under the age of 18 shall be made to join or profess any religion other than the one in which he was born, except when his parents themselves have been converted and the child does not choose to adhere to his original faith;

"Nor shall such person be initiated into any religious order involving a loss of civil status.

"(b) No conversion shall be recognized unless the change of faith is attested by a Magistrate after due inquiry."[64]

---

62. *Ibid.*, p. 201. Emphasis added.
63. *Ibid.*, p. 203.
64. *Ibid.*, pp. 208-09. Emphasis added.

April 21, 1947

In this meeting of the Advisory Committee the following discussion was held:

M. Ruthnaswamy: The word 'propagate' is a well known word. It includes not only preaching but other forms of propaganda made known by modern developments like the use of films, radio, cinemas and other things.

K. M. Munshi: The word might be brought, I think, to cover even forced conversion. Some of us opposed it. I am not in favour of it. So far as the 'freedom of speech' is concerned it carries sufficient authority to cover any kind of preaching. If the word 'propaganda' means something more than preaching, you must know what it is and therefore I was opposed to this introduction of the word 'propaganda'.

Alladi Krishnaswami Ayyar: Even in the American continent we do not have these practices as a special right, because we have freedom of speech. We have freedom of conscience. You have got the freedom of the press which is involved in the freedom of speech and writing. Therefore why place in the forefront of our country this propagation of particular religious faith and belief? I personally do not recognise the right of propagation.

Govind Ballabh Pant: At the worst it is redundant and as so many members want it we had better introduce it.

K. M. Munshi: It is not a redundant word.

Chairman: Let us take votes on it. Those who are in favour of retaining the word 'propagate' may raise their hands. (The amendment was accepted.)[65]

Clauses 21 and 22 were taken up after some time and the following discussion ensued:

Secretary: This has been redrafted by the Minorities Committee like this: (a) No person under the age of 18

65. *Ibid.*, pp. 267-68.

shall be made to join or profess any religion other than the one in which he was born except when his parents themselves have been converted and the child does not choose to adhere to his original faith; nor shall such person be initiated into any religious order involving a loss of civil status. (b) No conversion shall be recognized unless the change of faith is attested by a Magistrate after due inquiry.

Chairman: I consider these are matters to be left to legislation. (With the concurrence of the House) Clause 21 is deleted. We may take up clause 22. This clause too is unnecessary, and may be deleted. This is not a fundamental right.

Frank Anthony: These are matters which are absolutely vital to the Christians; clause 22 about conversion.

M. Ruthnaswamy: The deletion of the clause allows conversion.

Frank Anthony: You are leaving it to legislation. The legislature may say tomorrow that you have no right.

Chairman: Even under the present law, forcible conversion is an offence.

Syama Prasad Mookerjee: There is significance with regard to the civil law. If a person is converted by undue influence or coercion, the rights do not relate to the point at which he was converted.

Chairman: What you really want is that society will not recognize forcible conversions. It is for the society and not for the law.

Syama Prasad Mookerjee: Clause 22 should not be deleted. It may not be recognized by law. Let us be clear about facts. If a person is converted to another religion even by undue influence...

Chairman: Is not the exercise of such undue influence an offence?

Syama Prasad Mookerjee: I am talking about the first part. If there is conversion by coercion, it does not put back the civil rights of the person as before.

Chairman: We cannot have a fundamental right for every conceivable thing. We are not legislating.

Bakshi Tek Chand: Take the recent case of a Sikh who was forcibly converted in Rawalpindi District. The Sikh society took him back later. Now what is the position of his rights in between these two times?

Chairman: That was forcible conversion. Forcible conversion is no conversion. We won't recognise it. "Conversion from one religion to another brought about by undue influence shall not be recognised by law." We drop the last line.[66]

April 22, 1947

The meeting of the Advisory Committee decided as follows:

Clause 16 should be redrafted as:

"All persons are equally entitled to freedom of conscience and the right freely to *profess, practise and propagate* religion subject to public order, morality or health, and to the other provisions of this chapter.

"(**Note**: It was agreed that Messrs Rajagopalachari and S. P. Mookerjee should submit a draft proviso to this clause permitting social legislation which may affect religious practice.)

"Explanation 2: The above rights shall not include any economic, financial, political or other secular activities that may be associated with religious practice.

Explanation 3: The freedom of religious practice guaranteed in this clause shall not debar the State from enacting laws for the purpose of social welfare and reform.

"(**Note**: The decision to insert the words 'religious practice' was taken by a majority of 2 votes.)

"Clause 21: Deleted.

"Clause 22 should be redrafted as follows:

"Conversion from one religion to another brought

66. *Ibid.*, pp. 271-72.

about by coercion or undue influence shall not be recognized by law."[67]

April 23, 1947

The clauses were renumbered and finalised as follows:

13. All persons are equally entitled to freedom of conscience and the right freely to *profess, practise and propagate* religion subject to public order, morality or health, and to the other provisions of this chapter.

Explanation 2: The above right shall not include any economic, financial, political or other secular activities that may be associated with religious practice.

Explanation 3: The freedom of religious practice guaranteed in this clause shall not debar the State from enacting laws for the purpose of social welfare and reform.

17. Conversion from one religion to another brought about by coercion or undue influence shall not be recognized by law.[68]

By now Clause 16 had become Clause 13 and Clause 22 had become Clause 17.

Thus even before India attained independence, a criminal ideology had been recognized as a religion, a colony crystallized by Christian-Western imperialism had been accorded the status of a minority community, and gangsterism financed and controlled from abroad had received a new lease of life.

It is true that high pressure propaganda mounted by powerful establishments in Europe and America had contributed considerably to the success of this conspiracy. But Indian leaders were no less guilty of sponsoring the sin, for one reason or the other, as we shall see.

---

67. *Ibid.*, pp. 290-91 Emphases added.
68. *Ibid.*, p. 298. Emphasis added.

16

Debate in the Constituent Assembly

On April 29, 1947, Sardar Vallabhbhai Patel presented to the Constituent Assembly the interim report on Fundamental Rights as submitted by the Advisory Committee. Clause 13 and 17 among the 'Rights relating to religion' generated a debate which took place on May 1. It was started by Shri K. M. Munshi who moved an amendment for rewording Clause 17 to read as follows: "Any conversion from one religion to another of any person brought about by fraud, coercion or undue influence or of a minor under the age of 18 shall not be recognised by law."[1] Explaining the amendment with regard to "conversion of a minor", Shri Munshi said, "As a matter of fact, it was proposed by one or the other Committee in some form or other, and it is the general feeling that this clause should be restored in this form, — any conversion of a minor under the age of 18 shall not be recognised by law. The only effect of non-recognition by law would mean that even though a person is converted by fraud or coercion or undue influence or be converted during his minority he will still in law be deemed to continue to belong to the old religion and his legal rights will remain unaffected by reason of his conversion. The idea behind this proposal is that very often, if there are conversions by fraud or undue influence or during minority, certain changes in the legal status take place, certain rights are lost. This will have only this effect that the rights will remain exactly the same as at the moment a person was converted by fraud or coercion or undue influence and

1. *Constituent Assembly Debates*, Volume III, 1947, p. 488.

in the case of a minor at the moment of conversion."[2]

Mr. Frank Anthony rose to move an amendment to Shri Munshi's amendment. He said he wanted to add the words "except when the parents or surviving parents have been converted and the child does not choose to adhere to its original faith." In support of his suggestion, he said, "I agree that conversion under undue influence, conversion by coercion or conversion by fraud should not be recognised by law. I am only interested in this question, Sir, on principle. My community does not propagate. We do not convert, nor are we converted. But I do appreciate how deeply, how passionately millions of Christians feel on this right to propagate their religion. I want to congratulate the major party for having, in spite of its contentious character, retained the words 'right to practise and propagate their religion'. Having done that, I say that after giving with one hand this principal fundamental of Christian rights, do not take it away by this proviso, 'or of a minor under the age of 18'. I say that if you have this particular provision, or if you place an absolute embargo on the conversion of a minor, you will place an embargo absolutely on the right of conversion. You will virtually take away the right to convert. Because, what will happen? Not a single adult who is a parent, however deeply he may feel, however deeply he may be convinced, will ever adopt Christianity, because, by this clause you will be cutting off that parent from his children. By this clause you will say, although the parents may be converted to Christianity, the children shall not be brought up by these parents in the faith of the parents. You will be cutting at the root of family life. I say it is contrary to the ordinary concepts of natural law and justice. You may have your prejudices against conversion; you may have your prejudices against propagation. But once having allowed it, I plead with you not to cut at the root of family life. This is a right which is conceded in every part of the world, the right of parents to bring up their children in

2. *Ibid.*, p. 489.

the faith that the parents want them to pursue. You have your safeguards. You have provided that conversion by undue influence, conversion by fraud, conversion by coercion shall not be recognised by law. You have even given discretion to the child provided it has attained the age of discretion to adhere to its original faith. The wording is 'and the child does not choose to adhere to its original faith'. If both the parents are converted and if they want their children to be brought up as Christians, if these children have reached the age of discretion and say that in spite of the conversion of their parents, they do not want to be brought up as Christians, under the restriction which I have introduced, they will not be brought up in the Christian faith."[3]

He was clear in his mind that the "right to propagate" meant or included in its ambit the "right to convert" not only adults but minors as well. "I realise," he concluded, "how deeply certain sections of this House feel on this right. But I do ask you, having once conceded the right to propagate, to concede this in consonance with the principles of family law and in consonance with the principles of natural law and justice."[4]

The next member to speak was Shri R. P. Thakur. He said, "Sir, I am a member of Depressed Classes. This clause of the Fundamental Rights is very important from the standpoint of my community. You know well, Sir, that the victims of these religious conversions are ordinarily from the Depressed Classes. The preachers of other religions approach these classes of people, take advantage of their ignorance, extend all sorts of temptations and ultimately convert them. I want to know from Mr. Munshi whether 'fraud' covers all these things. If it does not cover, I should ask Mr. Munshi to re-draft this clause so that fraud of this nature might not be practised on these depressed classes. I should certainly call these 'fraud'."[5]

---

3. *Ibid.*, p. 489-490.
4. *Ibid.*, p.490.
5. *Ibid.*, pp. 490-91.

The rest of the debate is being reproduced below:[6]

The Hon'ble Rev. J. J. M. Nichols-Roy (Assam: General): Mr. President, Sir, it appears to me that the clause as it came out of the Advisory Committee is sufficient and should not be amended at all. The amendment seeks to prevent a minor, who is of twelve years of age, or thirteen years of age, up to eighteen years of age from exercising his own conscience. The age limit may be quite right in law. But to think that a youth under the age of eighteen does not have a conscience before God and, therefore, he cannot express his belief is wrong. That side of the question must be appropriately considered. There is a spiritual side in conversion which ought to be taken notice of by this House. Conversion does not mean only that a man changes his form of religion from one religion to another, or adopts a different name of religion, such as, a Hindu becomes a Christian. But there is spiritual aspect of conversion, that is, the connection of the soul of man with God, which must not be overlooked by this House. I know there are those who change their religion being influenced by material considerations, but there are others who are converted being under the influence of spiritual power. When a boy feels that he is called by God to adopt a different faith, no law should prevent him from doing that. The consciences of those youths who want to change their religion and adopt another religion from a spiritual standpoint should not be prevented from allowing these youths to exercise their right to change their legal status and change their religion. We know, Sir, in the history of Christianity, there have been youths, and I know personally, there have been many youths, who have been converted to Christianity, who are ready to die for their conviction and who are ready to lose everything. I myself was converted when I was about fifteen years old when I heard the voice of God calling me. I was ready to lose anything on earth. I was ready to suffer death

6. Procedural details have been left out.

even. I did not care for anything save to obey and follow the voice of God in my soul. Why should a youth who has such a call of God be prevented by law from changing his religion and calling himself by another name when he feels before God that he is influenced by the Spirit of God to do that and is ready even to sacrifice his life for that. This part of the amendment about minors is absolutely wrong when we consider it from the spiritual standpoint. From the standpoint of conscience I consider that it is altogether wrong not to allow a youth from the age of twelve to eighteen to exercise his own conscience before God. It will oppress the consciences of the youths who want to exercise their religious faiths before God. Therefore, I am against this amendment as it is. The youths should be allowed to follow their own conviction if they have any, and should not be forced to do anything against their own conviction. Why should the law not allow them if they themselves do not care for their former legal status? Why should they be prevented from changing their religion? Why should their consciences be oppressed? That is a very important point, Sir, to be considered by this House. This freedom I consider to be a Fundamental Right of the youths. No law should be made which will work against good spiritual forces. India, especially, is a country of religions, a country where there is religious freedom. If this amendment is carried in this House, it will only mean that in making a law to prevent the evil forces our minds lose sight of the real religious freedom which the youths of this land ought to have. Therefore, I am against this very principle of forcing the youths by not allowing them to exercise their religious conviction according to their consciences. I would suggest, Sir, that if in the amendment moved by Mr. Anthony the words 'or save when the minor himself wants to change his religion' are included, then I do not object to this amendment. I am against any conversion by undue influence or by fraud or coercion. When we make a law against all these evils we should be careful to see that law does not oppress the consciences of the youths who also need freedom.[7]

The Hon'ble Shri Purushottamdas Tandon (United Provinces: General): Mr. President, I am greatly surprised at the speeches delivered here by our Christian brethren. Some of them have said that in this Assembly we have admitted the right of every one to propagate his religion and to convert from one religion to another. We Congressmen deem it very improper to convert from one religion to another or to take part in such activities and we are not in favour of this. In our opinion it is absolutely futile to be keen on converting others to one's faith. But it is only at the request of some persons, whom we want to keep with us in our national endeavour that we accepted this. Now it is said that they have a right to convert young children to their faith. What is this? Really this surprises me very much. You can convert a child below eighteen by convincing and persuading him but he is a child of immature sense and legally and morally speaking this conversion can never be considered valid. If a boy of eighteen executes a transfer deed in favour of a man for his hut worth only Rs.100/- the transaction is considered unlawful. But our brethren come forward and say that the boy has enough sense to change his religion. That the value of religion is even less than that of a hut worth one hundred rupees. It is proper that a boy should be allowed to formally change his religion only when he attains maturity.

One of my brethren has said that we are taking away with the left hand what we gave the Christians with our right hand. Had we not given them the right to convert the young ones along with the conversion of their parents they would have been justified in their statement. What we gave them with our right hand is that they have a right to convert others by an appeal to reason and after honestly changing their views and outlook. The three words, 'coercion', 'fraud' and 'undue influence' are included as provisos and are meant to cover the cases of adult converts. These words are not applicable

7. *Ibid.*, pp. 491-92.

to converts of immature age. Their conversion is coercion and undue influence under all circumstance. How can the young ones change their religion? They have not the sense to understand the teachings of your scriptures. If they change their religion it is only under some influence and this influence is not fair. If a Christian keeps a young Hindu boy with him and treats him kindly the boy may like to live with him. We are not preventing this. But the boy can change his religion legally only on attaining maturity. If parents are converts why should it be necessary that their children should also change their religion? If they are under the influence of their parents they can change their religion on maturity. This is my submission.[8]

Mr C. E. Gibbon (C. P. & Berar: General): It is quite wrong.

The Hon'ble Shri Purushottamdas Tandon: I am speaking, Sir, as a Congressman. I say that the majority of Congressmen do not like this process of making converts (*interruption*), but in order to carry our Christian friends with us...

Mr. C. E. Gibbon: I do not think, Sir, that the Speaker is competent to speak for all Congressmen.

Some Hon'ble Members: Why not?

Shri Balkrishna Sharma (United Provinces: General): The Speaker has every right to speak on behalf of most of the Congressmen. He is most certainly entitled to do so.

The Hon'ble Shri Purushottamdas Tandon: I know Congressmen more than my friend over there. I know their feelings more intimately than probably he has ever had an opportunity of doing, and I know that most Congressmen are opposed to this idea of 'propagation'. But we agreed to keep the word 'propagate' out of regard for our Christian friends. But now to ask us to agree to minors also being converted is,

8. *Ibid.*, p. 492. English translation of speech in Hindustani.

I think, Sir, going too far. It is possible that parents having a number of children are converted into some other faith but why should it be necessary that all these children who do not understand religion should be treated as converts? I submit it is not at all necessary. The law of guardianship will see about it. Guardians can be appointed to look after these children, and when they grow up, if they feel that Christianity is a form of religion which appeals to their minds they will be at liberty to embrace it. That much to my Christian friends.

I understand, Sir, that it is possible that difficulties may be raised by some lawyers. What is the legal difficulty about this matter? The ordinary law of guardianship will see about this. When we say that minors cannot be converted, that implies that when parents go to another faith and they have a number of children to look after the law of the country will take care of those children. You can always enact a law of guardianship and you can, if necessary, add to the laws which at present exist on the subject so that in such cases the minors should be taken care of. I do not, Sir, therefore, see that there is any legal difficulty in the way of the amendment which Mr. Munshi has proposed being accepted. I heartily support Mr. Munshi's amendment...[9]

Shri Ramnath Goenka: My point of order is, Sir, that under clause 13 which we have passed, all persons are equally entitled of freedom of conscience. 'All persons' must necessarily include at least those persons who have attained the age of discretion. It is not necessary that they must attain the age of 18 before developing conscience. It may be at the age of twelve, fifteen, sixteen or seventeen. If we pass clause 17 and prescribe the age of 18, it will be inconsistent with clause 13 which we have just now passed.[10]

Shri Ananthasayanam Ayyangar: Sir, I want to oppose this point of order raised by Mr. Goenka in a different way. The mover of this point of order said he has no objection to

9. *Ibid.*, p. 493.
10. *Ibid.*, p. 494.

persons who are of the age of discretion being converted. But the age of discretion has not been defined anywhere. It is open to this Assembly to say that the age of discretion is eighteen. Therefore, there is really no point of order, or there is no point in this point of order.

Mr. D. N. Datta: Mr. President, Sir, I feel that the whole of this clause 17 should go to the Fundamental Rights Committee and I would be glad if the whole clause could be deleted. I know the reasons for enumerating this under the Fundamental Rights, because we are now working under the present setting. But as it is going to be enumerated in the Fundamental Rights, it has to be seen, Sir, whether the amendment of Mr. Anthony should be accepted. Mr. Anthony wants that the option of the minors to join the religion they like on attaining majority, should be retained, just as the choice is given to Mohammadan children given in marriage during minority to repudiate the marriage on attaining majority, — what we call the option of puberty. A similar right he intends to be given to the children of the parents who have been converted. On attaining majority the child shall have the right of declaring whether he adheres to his original faith or whether he will join the faith of his parents who were converted. I for myself, do not see any reason, why that right should not be given to the child on attaining majority. On attaining, he may declare, if he was a Hindu, that he will adhere to Hinduism or if his parents have taken to Christianity, whether he will become a Christian. I think this right should not be taken away. It should be given and how it is to be given, it is for the Drafting Committee, or better still, that it should go to the Fundamental Rights Committee to determine whether this clause should remain or how it should remain. And before I go, I must say that the remark of Mr. Tandon that the majority of the Congress members are not in favour of introducing the word 'propagate' in clause 13 is not correct. This matter was discussed yesterday and the majority were in favour of keeping the word 'propagate'. Therefore, the contention of Mr. Tandon is not correct.[11]

Rev. Jerome D'Souza (Madras: General): Mr. President, I regret, Sir, that this discussion should have taken a turn which makes it look as if it is almost exclusively a minority problem, and as a result of that, degree of heat has been imported into it which most of us regret very much indeed. Sir, when this matter was discussed at the committee stage, quite independently from the question of minorities, legal difficulties with which the question bristles were brought home to us by men of the highest authority like Sir Alladi. As far as the minority rights are concerned, I can only say this, that the way in which clause 13 has been handled by this House is so reassuring and so encouraging to the minorities that we have no reason at all to quarrel or to ask for stronger assurances. That attitude must provoke on the part of the minorities an equally trustful attitude which I hope will inspire future relations and future discussions. I appreciate Mr. Anthony's stand that this is a question of wider nature of principle and family authority. I assure you I am speaking from that point of view. This question of conversion of minors may affect not only majorities in relation to minorities but the minorities among themselves, — one Christian group in relation to another Christian group, as Catholics and Protestants, and so on. But among all sections, in regard to the authority of a man over his family, I think certain rights should be assured and must be part of fundamental rights. We have nothing in these fundamental rights that safeguards or encourages or strengthens the family in an explicit way, and indeed I do not think this is necessary at this stage, because that is not a justiciable right. There are certain constructions where the wish of the State to protect and encourage the family is explicitly declared. I hope in the second part, among these fundamental rights which are not justiciable, some such declaration or approbation of the institution and rights and privileges associated with family life will be introduced. It may perhaps be thought that in our

11. *Ibid.*, p. 495.

country such a declaration is not necessary because among us the strongest family feeling is universal; we have not merely individual or unitary families but we have also joint families. I believe the discussion on this point has been partly influenced by that background of the joint family system. I am sure that Tandonji if I may be permitted to refer to him by name, when he was speaking of the minor child of converted parents, was thinking really in terms of the joint family where there are people ready to take over and bring up such children. But we are legislating for all sections of our people, for those also who are not in joint families but in unitary families. We are legislating for them, and therefore, some provisions must be made which, in the last analysis, will safeguard the authority of the parent, both parents or the surviving parent, in particular, as Mr. Anthony has said, in regard to nannies in the arms of their mothers. To take them away from the mother or father who are one with them, practically identified physically and juridically with them, is to introduce into our legislation an element which certainly weakens the concept of the authority and sanctity of the family. On this ground, as well as on the legal implications to which attention has been drawn, I mean difficulties in connection with the death, the marriage, the succession rights, of these minors, I oppose Mr. Munshi's amendment as it stands. Take the question of marriage. Marriage is permitted before 18 years. Now Mr. Munshi has carefully explained that his amendment does not prevent the minor children from going with the parents. But if they are to be married, under what law, by the ceremonies of which religion will they be married? If they follow their conscience and the religion they have adopted, whether they be Hindus, Muslims, or Christians, the question of the validity of that marriage will come in. All this is bristling with legal and juridical difficulties, quite apart from those other considerations into which, as I said, I regret we have entered with undue warmth. While I want to support Mr. Anthony's motion, I am more inclined to support the suggestion of the speaker who immediately preceded me, and ask the House to refer the entire clause back to the Advisory Committee so that the wording of it may be most carefully weighed. It can be brought back to this House just as we have decided, to bring back three or four other controversial matters. That is my suggestion and I would request...[12]

Shri Algu Rai Shastri (U.P. : General): Mr. President, I stand here to support the amendment moved by Mr. Munshi. I believe that by accepting the amendment we shall be doing justice to those minors who have perforce to enter the fold of the religion which their parents embrace out of their greed. This practice is like the one prevailing in the transactions of transfer of land and which is that 'trees go with the land'. It is on some such basis that the minor children who do not understand what change of religion or coercion or religious practices mean, have to leave their old faith along with their parents. This evil practice has a very bad effect on the strength of our population. It is proper for us that we, who are framing the charts of Fundamental Rights, should safeguard their interests and save them from such automatic conversion. The dynamic conditions of our society make it more important than ever that we should incorporate such a provision in our Constitution as will prevent such practices. Such minors on attaining majority often regret that they were made to change their religion, improperly. Wherever the Europeans or the white races of Europe, who rule practically over the whole world, have gone, they have, as Missionaries. A study of the 'Prosperous India' by Digby shows that 'cross was followed by the sword.' The missionary was followed by the batons, the swords and the guns. It was in this way that they employed coercion for spreading their religion and for extending their Empire. At the same time, they put economic and political pressure on the indigenous tribes and consolidated the foundations of their dominion. We want such an amendment in this clause of Fundamental Rights that a

12. *Ibid.*, pp. 496-97

person who wants to change his religion should be able to do so only after he is convinced through cool deliberation that the new religion is more satisfactory to him than the old one. For example it is only when I am convinced that Sikhism is preferable to Hinduism, that I should be able to change my religion. This right I believe we have. But no one should change religion out of greed and temptation. When the followers of one religion employ sword and guns to attack a family consisting of a few members the latter have no option but to accept the religion of the aggressors in order to save their lives. Such a conversion should be considered void and ineffective because it has been brought about through coercion and undue influence. In view of such conditions which exist today, conversion brought about through temptation and allurement is, in fact, not a conversion in the real sense of the term. I have a personal experience extending over a period of 24 years as to how the elders of the family are induced through prospects of the financial gain to change their religion and also with them the children are taken over to the fold of the new religion. It appears as if some are taking the land physically in his possession and the helpless trees go with it to the new master.

One particular part of the country has been declared as an 'Excluded Area', so that a particular sect alone may carry on its propaganda therein. Another area has been reserved for the 'Criminal tribes'. Similarly, other areas have also been reserved wherein missionaries alone can carry on their activities. In Chattisgarh and other similar forest areas there are tribes which follow primitive faiths. There the Hindu missionaries cannot carry on their activities. These are called 'Excluded and partially Excluded Areas', and no religious propaganda can be carried on in these areas except by the missionaries. This was the baneful policy of the Government. We should now be delivered from this policy of religious discrimination. In his book 'Census of India-1930' Dewton writes that the Christian population of Assam has increased 300 times and attributes this increase to certain evils in Hindu

Society. It is these evils which gave other missionaries opportunities to make conversions. In his book 'Census of India-1911' Mr. S. Kamath has said that the missionaries of one particular religion are reducing the numbers of another by exploiting the evils of that group. They convert some influential persons by inducement and persuasion. The bitterness of the present is due to such activities. I am conversant with what Christian missions have done for the backward classes and I have also seen their work among such classes of people. I bow to them with respect for the way in which they (missionaries) have done their work. How gracious it would have been had they done it only for social service. I found that the dispute, if and when it occurs, between members of such castes as the sweepers or the *chamars* on the one side and the land-lords or some other influential persons on the other, has been exploited to create bitterness between them. No effort has been made to effect a compromise. This crooked policy has been adopted to bring about the conversion of the former. Similarly, people of other faiths have intensified and exploited our differences in order to increase their own numbers. The consequence is that the grown-up people in such castes as *Bhangies* and *chamars* are converted, and with them their children also go into the fold of the new religion. They should be affectionately asked to live as brothers. This is what has been taught by prophets, angels and leaders. But this is not being practised, today. We are in search of opportunities to indulge in underhand dealings. We go to people and tell them 'you are in darkness; this is not the way for your salvation'. Thus every body can realise how all possible unfair means have been adopted to trample the majority community under feet. It is in this way that the Foreign bureaucracy has been working here, and has been creating vested interests in order to maintain its political strangle-hold over the people. If we cannot remove this foundation whom are we going to give the Fundamental Rights? To these minors who are in the lap of their parents? If we permit minors to be transferred like trees on land with the newly embraced religion of their parents, we would be doing an injustice. Many fallacious arguments are offered to permit this. We must not be misled by these. We know that our failure to stop conversion under coercion would result in grave injustice. I have a right to change my religion. I believe in God. If I realise tomorrow that God is a farce and an aberration of human mind then I can become an atheist. If I think that the Hindu faith is false, I, with my grey hair, my fallen teeth, and ripe age, and my mature discretion can change my religion. But if my minor child repeats what I say, are you going to allow him also a right to change his religion (at that age)? Revered Purushottam Das Tandon has said in a very appealing manner that if a child transfers his immovable property worth Rs.100 the transaction is void. How unjust it is that if a minor changes his religion when his parents do so, his act is not void? It has an adverse effect on innocent children. This attempt to increase population has increased religious bitterness. The communal proportion has been changed so that the British bureaucracy may retain its hold by a variation in the numbers of the different communities. I am saying all these things deliberately but I am not attacking any one community in particular. The sole interest of the government in the illusory web of census lies in seeing a balance in the population of the communities so that these may continue to quarrel among themselves and thereby strengthen its own rule. This amendment of Mr. Munshi is directed against such motives. Nothing can be better than that, and, therefore, I support it.

In my opinion this majority community should not oppress the minority. We respect and honour all and we give an opportunity to everybody to propagate his religion. Those who agree with you may be converted. But convert only those who can be legitimately converted. Improper conversions would not be right. You tempt the innocent little ones whom you take in your lap, by a suit of clothes, a piece of bread and a little toy and thus you ruin their lives. Later, they repent that they did not get an opportunity to have a religion of their choice. I, myself, am prepared to change my religion. But some one should argue with me and change my views and then convert me. Surely, I should have no right to change the religion of my children with me — specially children below a certain age. Those children are considered to be minors who are under teens, i.e., below eighteen.[13]

Mr. H. V. Kamath: (Under teens includes nineteen.)

Shri Algu Rai Shastri: However if it is nineteen, it is all the better. Even if it is not possible they should extend minority by a year of grace. The age limit fixed for minors and majors should be adopted in religious matter as well. They say that there would be no incentive for conversion if people have to forego their children. I hear that in Japan the father has one religion and the child another. What does religion mean? Does the mother feed her baby so that the child's religion might change? If the mother's love is true she will surely feed her baby. Does the mother's milk change the religion? We do not wish to snatch away the child from the mother's lap, but we wish to give to the baby a right to record his (natal) religion in the report of the Census and any other government records, till he attains majority and declares his (new) religion. We give him this right in this amendment. Parents need the company of their children. If they have changed their religion discreetly, let them educate their children. But the change in the religion of the children may be considered (only) on their declaration at reaching majority. This is the purpose of this amendment and I support it, and I strongly oppose the view that this right should not be given to children.[14]

Mr. Jagat Narain Lal (Bihar : General): Mr. President, I was expecting that after the acceptance of Clause 13, no representative of any minority of this House will have any ground for any objection. Clause 13 lays down that — 'All

13. *Ibid.*, pp. 497-99. English translation of speech in Hindustani.
14. *Ibid.*, pp. 499-500. English translation of speech in Hindustani.

persons are equally entitled to freedom of conscience and the right freely to profess, practice and propagate religion subject to public order, morality or health or to the other provisions of this Chapter.'

This goes to the 'farthest limit'. If you look to any of the best of 'modern world' Constitutions, you will find that nowhere has this right to propagate been conceded. If you look at Article 50 of the Swiss Confederation, it lays down that 'the free exercise of religion is guaranteed within limits compatible with public order and morality.' It ends there. If you look at Article 44 sub-clause (2) 1 of the Irish Free State, you will find there — 'Freedom of conscience and the free profession and practice of religion are subject to public order and morality, guaranteed to every citizen.'

If you refer to Article 124 of the Constitution of the Union of the Soviet Socialist Republics you will find — 'In order to ensure to citizens freedom of conscience, the Church in the U.S.S.R is separated from the State and the school from the Church. Freedom of religious worship and freedom of anti-religious propaganda is recognised for all citizens.'

If I place before you all the clauses pertaining to 'Freedom of professing religion', it will tax your patience. I do not want to waste more of your time in this connection. My submission is that this House has gone to the farthest limit possible with regard to the minorities, knowing well the fact that there are a few minorities in this country whose right to carry on propaganda extends to the point of creating various difficulties. I do not want to go into its details. The previous speaker had referred to certain things in this connection. I submit that should be sufficient. Hon'ble Tandonji by his observation that on reading the mind of most of the Congress members of this House he did not want to keep 'right to do propaganda' (on the statute), has rightly interpreted the mind of most of us. The fact is that we desire to make the minorities feel that the rights which they had been enjoying till now shall be allowed to continue within reasonable limits by the majority. We have no d[illegible] to curtail them in any way. But we do not concede the right to do propaganda. I want to appeal to those who profess to speak for the minorities not to press for too much. They must be satisfied with this much. It will be too much to press for more. That would be taking undue advantage of the generosity of the majority. That will be very regrettable. It is difficult, rather impossible, for us to go to that limit. I think that the amendment tabled by Mr. Munshi becomes essential if the right to propagate is conceded. The House should, therefore, accept it. Various arguments have been advanced in the House, and so I do not want to comment upon them again. With these words I support Mr. Munshi.[15]

Dr. B. R. Ambedkar: Mr. President, Sir, I am sorry to say that I do not find myself in agreement with the amendment which has been moved by Mr. Munshi relating to the question of the conversion of minor children. The clause, as it stands probably gives the impression to the House that this question relating to the conversion of minors was not considered by the Fundamental Rights Committee or by the Minorities Sub-Committee or by the Advisory Committee. I should like to assure the House that a good deal of consideration was bestowed on this question and every aspect was examined. It was after examining the whole question in all its aspects, and seeing the difficulties which came up, that the Advisory Committee came to the conclusion that they should adhere to the clause as it now stands.

Sir, the difficulty is so clear to my mind that I find no other course but to request Mr. Munshi to drop his amendment. With regard to children, there are three possible cases which can be visualised. First of all, there is the case of children with parents and guardians. There is the case of children who are orphans, who have no parents and no guardians in the legal sense of the word. Supposing you have this clause prohibiting the conversion of children below 18, what is going to be the position of children who are orphans? Are they not going to

---

15 *Ibid.*, pp. 500-501. English translation of speech in Hindustani.

have any kind of religion? Are they not to have any religious instruction given to them by some one who happens to take a kindly interest in them? It seems to me that, if the clause as worded by Mr. Munshi was adopted, viz., that no child below the age of 18 shall be converted it would follow that children who are orphans, who have no legal guardians, cannot have any kind of religious instruction. I am sure that this is not the result which this House would be happy to contemplate. Therefore, such a class of subjects shall have to be excepted from the operation of the amendment proposed by Mr. Munshi.

Then, I come to the other class, viz., children with parents and guardians. They may fall into two categories. For the sake of clarity it might be desirable to consider their cases separately; the first is this: where children are converted with the knowledge and consent of their guardians and parents. The second case is that of children of parents who have become converts.

It does seem to me that there ought to be a prohibition upon the conversion of minor children with legal guardians, where the conversion takes place without the consent and knowledge of the legal guardians. That, I think, is a very legitimate proposition. No missionary who wants to convert a child which is under the lawful guardianship of some person, who according to the law of guardianship is entitled to regulate and control the religious faith of that particular child, ought to deprive that person or guardian of the right of having notice and having knowledge that the child is being converted to another faith. That, I think, is a simple proposition to which there can be no objection.

But when we come to the other case, viz., where parents are converted and we have to consider the case of their children, then I think we come across what I might say a very hard rock. If you are going to say that, although parents may be converted because they are majors and above the age of 18, minors below the age of 18, although they are their children, are not to be converted with the parents, the question that we have to consider is, what arrangement are we going to make with regard to the children? Suppose, a parent is converted to Christianity. Suppose a child of such a parent dies. The parent, having been brought up in the Christian faith, gives the Christian burial to the dead child. Is that act on the part of the parent in giving a Christian burial to the child, to be regarded as an offence in law? Take another case. Suppose a parent who has become converted has a daughter. He marries that daughter according to Christian rites. What is to be the consequence of that marriage? What is to be the effect of that marriage? Is that marriage legal or not legal?

If you do not want that the children should be converted, you have to make some other kind of law with regard to guardianship in order to prevent the parents from exercising their rights to influence and shape the religious life of their children. Sir, I would like to ask whether it would be possible for this House to accept that a child of five, for instance, ought to be separated from his parents merely because the parents have adopted Christianity, or some religion which was not originally theirs. I refer to these difficulties in order to show that it is these difficulties which faced the Fundamental Rights Committee, the Minorities Committee and the Advisory Committee and which led them to reject this proposition. It was, because we realised, that the acceptance of the proposition, namely, that a person shall not be converted below the age of 18, would lead to many disruptions, to so many evil consequences, that we thought it would be better to drop the whole thing altogether. (*Hear, hear*). The mere fact that we have made no such reference in Clause 17 of the Fundamental Rights does not in my judgement prevent the legislature when it becomes operative from making any law in order to regulate this matter. My submission, therefore, is that reference back of this clause to a committee for further consideration is not going to produce any better result. I have no objection to the matter being further examined by persons who feel differently about it, but I do like to say that all the three Committees have given their best attention to the subject. I have, therefore, come to the conclusion that having regard to all the circumstances of the case, the best way would be to drop the clause altogether. I have no objection to a provision being made that children who have legal and lawful guardians should not be converted without the knowledge and notice of the parents. That, I think, ought to suffice in the case.[16]

The Hon'ble Sardar Vallabhbhai Patel: Sir, this is not a matter free from difficulties. There is no point in introducing any element of heat in this controversy. It is well known in this country that there are mass conversions, conversions by force, conversions by coercion and undue influence, and we cannot disguise the fact that children also have been converted, that children with parents have been converted and that orphans have been converted. Now, we need not go into all the reasons or the forces that led to these conversions, but if the facts are recognised, we who have to live in this country and find a solution to build up a nation, — we need not introduce any heat into this controversy to find a solution. What is the best thing to do under the circumstances? There may be different points of view. There are bound to be differences in the viewpoints of the different communities, but, as Dr. Ambedkar has said, this question has been considered in three Committees and yet we have not been able to find a solution acceptable to all. Let us make one more effort and not carry on this discussion, which will not satisfy everybody. Let this be therefore referred to the Advisory Committee. We shall give one more chance.[17]

So Clause 17 was "referred back to the Advisory Committee."[18]

The indecision of the Constituent Assembly regarding Clause 17 provoked a strong Christian reaction. *The National*

16. *Ibid.*, pp. 501-502.
17. *Ibid.*, pp. 502-503.
18. *Ibid.*, p. 503.

Christian Council Review of June-July 1947 published an 'Open Letter' by L. Sen on the subject of 'Religious Liberty' "All this talk," said the writer, "about mass conversions being achieved by improper means is absolute balderdash... For several centuries Hindus have kept the so-called untouchables from their temples and still do so in most places. It is a curious mentality that excludes a homeless man from one's own house and will not allow him to enter someone else's... Mr. Gandhi's great objection to conversion is that all religions are equally good. But Christianity does not think so. Mr. Gandhi will call this being intolerant. Very well, then, on his own showing Christianity which is intolerant must be inferior to Hinduism. He should, therefore, try to convert others to this nobler faith. Assuming, however, that Mr. Gandhi is right about the equality of all religions, why is he so anxious to prevent conversions by restrictive legislation? Is his conception of what is right or what is wrong only going to prevail in free India? Man has certain inalienable rights which not even a majority vote can take away. One of these rights is that he is free to choose his religion or society, without his motive being impugned by government, whether fascist, communist or democratic."[19]

The same issue commented on the proceedings of the Constituent Assembly. "At this session," it said, "the all-important subject of the Fundamental Rights came up. Both in the Committee which presented the Report of Fundamental Rights, and on the floor of the Assembly a good deal of heated discussion took place. High tribute must be paid to the Committee for presenting a report which is marked by a true sense of justice and fair play. It is particularly gratifying to note that freedom of conscience — the right freely to profess, practise and propagate religion, in the defence of which the National Christian Council has often expressed itself, has been recognized. The proposed amendment, relating to the right of conversion, however, according to

19. *The National Christian Council Review*, June-July 1947, pp. 273-74.

which young people under the age of 18 will not be allowed to change their religion, seems to us to be an undue interference with that freedom which has been properly recognized in the report. If parents who are convinced of the need for a change of faith are prevented from doing so for strong reasons of affection and attachment to their children, then the freedom of conversion become a mockery. Other serious things might be said against the proposed amendment — and some of these have been said on the floor of the Assembly — but even this is enough to indicate the harm such an amendment is likely to do to the cause of religious liberty. We hope, therefore, that the clause relating to conversion will be allowed to remain as it is. The prevention of coercion and improper influence in the matter of conversion is right and necessary and has been amply provided for in the clause as it stands."[20]

The campaign was carried forward in the August issue of the monthly. *It advised the Congress members not to take to the path of Nazi Germany.* "The Congress members of the Constituent Assembly," it said, "who wish to make everything Hindu from top to bottom should take a lesson from history. Hitler created a kind of nationalism which brought about the ruin of the German nation. His nationalism created a narrow outlook, and a sense of racial superiority which produced hatred for other nationals, and racial stocks. He gave to the German people those things and ideas which made the Germans feel distinctly different from others, i.e. the Swastika and a special salutation."[21]

The same issue of the *Review* carried an article, 'Evangelism in Independent India', by Rev. Stanley Jones. "In many quarters," he wrote, "there is a good deal of pessimism. It reaches all the way from the simple Indian Christian who said to me: 'I hear that when independence comes we Indian Christians will be forced to go back to the different castes from which we came'; to the Indian Bishop who is saying in

---

20. *Ibid.*, p. 278.
21. *Ibid.*, August 1947, p. 343.

the West that the Christians are going to undergo persecution in an independent India, an attempt will be made to wipe them out. Another expressed this pessimism when he said, 'I hear all the missionaries are going to be sent out of India with the coming of independence.' A superintendent of police said to me, 'Now that the British are going, are you missionaries going too?'"

"Also there will be an attempt," he continued, "here and there to make it impossible for men to accept the Christian faith. In about 17 of the Native States there have been enacted laws which make it necessary for one to appear before a magistrate when he wants to change his faith, and after police investigation the magistrate decides whether he can or not. That makes it almost impossible to change one's faith. But that is in the Indian States. The place to watch is the Centre. For the attitudes of the Centre will gradually prevail in the States. It is the Centre that counts. In time all will have to fall in line with it."[22]

He related what he had discovered after meeting the top Congress leaders:

> So I went to Sardar Patel, the strong man of the Congress, and asked him what part the missionaries can play, if any, in this new India. I told him that I was going to the Kodaikanal and the Landour Conventions which are important missionary centers and I wanted some word to bring to them from the highest sources. He very thoughtfully replied, 'Let them go on as they have been going on — let them serve the suffering with their hospitals and dispensaries, educate the poor and give selfless service to the people. They can even carry on their propaganda in a peaceful manner. But let them not use mass conversions for political ends.' 'If they do this then there is a place for them in the new India?' I asked. 'Certainly,' he replied, 'we want them to throw themselves in with India, identify themselves with the people and

22. *Ibid.*, p. 351.

make India their home.' This was quite clear and straightforward and from the man who has to do with the question of who shall or shall not come into India, for he is the Home Member.

I then saw C. Rajgopalachariar and asked him the same question. His reply was that 'While I agree that you have the right of conversion, I would suggest that in this crisis when religion is dividing us it would be a better part of your strategy to dim conversions and serve the people in various ways until the situation returns to a more normal state. If you are not willing to do that then I would suggest that instead of 'Profess, practise and propagate' as suggested in the Committee, it should be 'Belief, worship and preach'.' Then I further asked, 'Will the missionaries be tolerated or welcomed as partners in this new India?' His reply was: 'If they take some of the attitudes I suggest, then they will not only be welcomed, they will be welcomed with gratitude, for what they have done and will do.'

The third man I saw was Maulana Abdul Kalam Azad, the gracious head of Education in the Central Government. I asked him whether missionaries could be tolerated or welcomed as partners in the making of this new India. His reply was: 'Do not use the word 'tolerate', there is no thought of that. You will be welcomed. There is no point at issue with the missionaries, except at one point: at the place of mass conversions where there is no real change of heart. We believe in the right of outer change where there is inner change, but when masses are brought over without any perceptible spiritual change then it arouses suspicions as to motives. But apart from that we have no point at issue. You will be welcomed gratefully for what you have done not only for India but for other parts of the world such as the Near East.'

The fourth man to whom I went was the man whom Gandhiji calls 'the uncrowned king of India', Jawaharlal Nehru, and when I asked him whether missionaries will be tolerated or welcomed as partners in the making of the new India his reply was: 'I am not sure as to what is involved in being looked on as partners. But we will welcome anyone who throws himself into India and makes India his home.'

The fact of the matter is that the greatest hour of Christian opportunity has come in India. I have never had such a hearing in forty years as I have had in these last six months in India. The tensions have been let down. The combativeness against the Christian faith has been eased into an attitude of wistful yearning hoping that the Christians have some answer to the problems that confront us.

The Christian Church must now search its own heart and set its own house in order. It must cease from *little irrelevancies* and give itself to *big things*. The big thing in India is to present Christ in such a way as to become inescapable in the India to be. And the Church itself must be the message — it must show itself the embodiment of the new order...

Then every Christian must become a witness on fire with the love of Christ. The whole body of Christians must now be ablaze with the divine passion to serve and to save. It must consume us. For the crucial hour of the Chruch has now come in India.[23]

The debate on Clause 17 was resumed on August 30, 1947:

The Honourable Sardar Vallabhbhai J. Patel: The Committee discussed this and there were several other suggestions made by the House and the clause was referred back to the Committee. After further consideration of this clause, which enunciates an obvious principle, the Committee came to the conclusion that it is not necessary to include this as a fundamental right. It is illegal under the present law and it can be illegal at any time.[24]

---

23. *Ibid.*, pp. 352-54. Emphasis in source.
24. *Constituent Assembly Debates*, Volume 5, 1947, p. 363.

Shri M. Ananthasayanam Ayyangar (Madras: General): It is unfortunate that religion is being utilised not for the purpose of saving one's soul but for disintegrating society. Recently after the announcement by the Cabinet Mission and later on by the British Government, a number of conversions have taken place. It was said that power had been handed over to Provincial Governments who were in charge of these matters. This is dangerous. What has religion to do with a secular State? Our minorities are communal minorities for which we have made provision. Do you want an opportunity to be given for numbers to be increased for the purpose of getting more seats in the Legislatures? That is what is happening. All people have come to the same opinion that there should be a secular State here; so we should not allow conversion from one community to another. I therefore want that a positive fundamental right must be established that no conversion shall be allowed, and if any occasion does arise like this, let the person concerned appear before a Judge and swear before him that he wishes to be converted. This may be an out-of-the-way suggestion but I would appeal to this House to realize the dangerous consequences otherwise. Later on it may attain enormous proportions. I would like this matter to be considered and the question referred back for a final draft for consideration at a later sitting.[25]

Shri R. V. Dhulekar: Mr. President, my opinion is that Clause 17 should be retained as it stands. In the present environment, all sorts of efforts are being made to increase the population of a particular section in this country, so that once again efforts may be made to further divide this country. There is ample proof, both within this House and outside that many who live in this country are not prepared to be the citizens of this country. Those who have caused the division of our land desire that India may be further divided. Therefore in view of the present circumstances, I think that this clause should be retained. It is necessary that full attention should

25. *Ibid.*, p. 364.

be paid to this. While on tour, I see every day refugees moving about with their children and I find them at railway stations, shops, hotels, bakeries and at numerous other places. The men of these bakeries abduct these women and children. There should be legislation to stop this. I would request you that an early move should be made to stop all this and millions of people would be saved.

I submit that we cannot now tolerate things of this nature. We are being attacked, and we do not want that India's population, the numerical strength of the Hindus and other communities should gradually diminish, and after ten years the other people may again say that 'we constitute a separate nation'. These separatist tendencies should be crushed.
Therefore I request that section 17 may be retained in the same form as is recommended by the Advisory Committee.[26]

The Honourable Sardar Vallabhbhai J. Patel: Much of this debate may be shortened if it be recognised that there is no difference of opinion on the merits of the case that forcible conversion should not be or cannot be recognised by law. On that principle there is no difference of opinion. The question is only whether this clause is necessary in the list of fundamental rights. Now, if it is an objective for the administration to act, it has a place in the Second part which consists of non-justiciable rights. If you think it is necessary, let us transfer it to the Second part of the Schedule because it is admitted that in the law of the land forcible conversion is illegal. We have even stopped forcible education and, we do not for a moment suggest that forcible conversion of one by another from one religion to another will be recognised. But suppose one thousand people are converted, that is not recognised. Will you go to a court of law and ask it not to recognise it? It only creates complications, it gives no remedy. But if you want this principle to be enunciated as a seventh clause, coming after Clause 6, in the Second Schedule, it is unnecessary to carry on any debate; you can do so. There is

26. *Ibid.*, p. 364. English translation of speech in Hindustani.

no difference of opinion on the merits of the case. But at this stage to talk of forcible conversion on merits is absurd, because there cannot be any question about it.[27]

At this stage Mr. Hussain Iman walked up to the rostrum to speak.

The Honourable Sardar Vallabhbhai J. Patel: Do you advocate forcible conversion?

Mr. Hussain Iman: No, Sir, I very much regret the attitude of certain Members who are in the habit of bringing in controversial matters without any rhyme or reason. It was really a most uncalled for attack which the last speaker made on the Mussalmans, without mentioning names. But I regret that in the atmosphere which we are trying to create of amity such intrusions should be allowed to intervene and mar the fair atmosphere.

Sir, what I came to suggest was that this is such a fundamental thing that there is no need to provide for it. According to the law everything which has been done under coercion is illegal. Anything done by reason of fraud can never stand. Forcible conversion is the highest degree of undesirable thing. But it is not proper, as the Sardar himself has admitted, to provide it in the justiciable fundamental rights. The only place which it can occupy is in the annals of High Court Judgments. Any number of judgements exist which have declared that anything done by reason of fraud or coercion is illegal. Therefore it is not justiciable and cannot be justified by any sensible person in the world. I strongly advocate that it is not necessary to put it in any of the lists of Fundamental Rights.[28]

The President of the Assembly put to vote the motion "that this should not be put in the Fundamental Rights" and the motion was adopted. Christian missions carried the day. Hindus were trying to lock the stable after the horse had been stolen.

27. *Ibid.*, pp. 364-65.
28. *Ibid.*, p. 365.

The October 1947 issue of *The National Christian Council Review* published a letter written by Austin David. It deserves to be reproduced in full:

> It is a matter of great relief and rejoicing for all citizens of the Indian Dominion that the Constituent Assembly has decided to drop the Clause 17, and the amendment of Mr. K. M. Munshi which sought to restrict the freedom of conscience in the matter of profession, practice and propagation of religion. Because of this proposed amendment there was a great uneasiness among the Christians all over India. All sorts of fears and doubts were arising in the minds of the people as to the future of minorities. The Church in India is first of all beholden to the Christian members of the Constituent Assembly for their tactful and firm handling of the matter, and to all the members of the Constituent Assembly for their just and fair treatment towards its citizens in the matter of religious liberty.
>
> We also owe a very heavy debt of gratitude to the National Christian Council of India, in sending a mission to Delhi, consisting of Bishop S. K. Mondol, Vice-President, and Mr. E. C. Bhatty, one of the secretaries. Their visit to Delhi greatly helped in mobilising opinion among the Christian members of the Constituent Assembly in favour of working as a team, and in making them feel that the Christian community expected them to present its case with force, and firmness. There were certain matters on which compromise could not be made. We also understand that they met some Cabinet ministers, and other leaders whom they asked for a greater measure of religious liberty. Both of these gentlemen deserve our gratitude. They are both known for their calm and tactful handling of things, and they have once again proved their ability. We are convinced that in the future we...require... as our leaders... men with true Christian character, with no guile and self-seeking, working for the good of the Church. We should therefore thank the N.C.C. for

choosing these two gentlemen this time.[29]

The same issue of the *Review* published "news from Korea" which spelled out what Christians meant by 'religious liberty':

> Rev. C. C. Amendt, a Methodist missionary who recently returned to Seoul from the United States, reports about the Church's possibilities in Korea. He has made a number of 'jeep trips' into the countryside and found a hearty welcome from the Koreans and their Churches. 'We are thankful for the progress that has been made,' he said, 'for the crowded churches and for the unparalleled opportunity before us today. This past week I did what I never thought I or anyone else would ever do in Korea — *I preached in a Shinto shrine, now a Christian church. Not long ago I preached in a thriving new church that had formerly been a Japanese Buddhist temple. The great Eastern union service for all denominations, Koreans and American G.I.'S, was on the site of the most famous Shinto shrine in the land — a symbol of the complete change and religious freedom that has come to the Korean people*. The challenge of such a time of fluidity and change is beyond the power of words to express.[30]

Clause 13 came up before the Constituent Assembly once again on December 3, 1948. It figured as Article 19 in the Draft Constitution and read as under:

> 19.(1) Subject to public order, morality and health and to the other provisions of the Part, all persons are equally entitled to freedom of conscience and the right freely to profess, practise and propagate religion.
>
> (2) Nothing in this article shall affect the operation of any existing law or preclude the State from making any law
>
> (a) regulating or restricting any economic, financial,

29. *The National Christian Council Review*, October 1947, p. 477.
30. Ibid., p. 512. Emphasis added.

political or other secular activity which may be associated with religious practice;

(b) for social welfare and reform or for throwing open Hindu religious institutions of a public character to any class or section of Hindus.[31]

The Vice-President of the Constituent Assembly presented Article 19 as a "motion before the House" and went over the amendments "one by one." Some parts of the debate that followed are being reproduced below:

Prof. K. T. Shah: Mr. Vice-President, I beg to move—

"That the following proviso be added to Clause (1) of article 19:

"Provided that no propaganda in favour of any one religion which is calculated to result in change of faith by the individuals affected, shall be allowed in any school or college or other educational institution, in any hospital or asylum, or in any other place or institution where persons of a tender age, or of unsound mind or body are liable to be exposed to undue influence from their teachers, nurses or physicians, keepers or guardians or any other person set in authority above them, and which is maintained wholly or partially from public revenues, or is in any way aided or protected by the Government of the Union, or of any State or public authority therein."

Sir, the main article gives the right of freedom of propaganda. I have no quarrel with the right that anybody professing any particular form of belief should be at liberty, in this Liberal State, to place the benefits or beauties of his particular form of worship before others. My only condition — and the amendment tries to incorporate that — is that this freedom should not be abused, as it has been in the past. In places or institutions, where people of tender age or those suffering from any bodily or mental infirmity, are exposed to undue influence, they are liable to be influenced more by the personality of those in authority above them than by the

31. B. Shiva Rao, *op.cit.*, p. 264

inherent advantages and unquestionable reasoning in favour of a particular religion, and as such result in conversion. That is not a genuine change of opinion, but is the result of undue influence that ought to be stopped.[32]

Shri Lokanath Mishra (Orissa : General): I would have been very glad if I had a chance to speak generally on article 19 and not move this amendment. To my mind, if article 13 of this Draft Constitution is a charter of liberty, article 19 is a Charter for Hindu enslavement. I do really feel that this is the most disgraceful article, the blackest part of the Draft Constitution. I beg to submit that I have considered and studied all the constitutional precedents and have not found anywhere any mention of the word 'propaganda' as a Fundamental Right, relating to religion.

Sir, we have declared the state to be a Secular State. For obvious and for good reasons we have so declared. Does it not mean that we have nothing to do with any religion? You know that propagation of religion brought India into this unfortunate state and India had to be divided into Pakistan and India. If Islam had not come to impose its will on this land, India would have been a perfectly secular State and a homogenous state. There would have been no question of partition. Therefore, we have rightly tabooed religion. And now to say that as a fundamental right everybody has a right to propagate his religion is not right. Do we want to say that we want one religion other than Hinduism and that religion has not yet taken sufficient root in the soil of India and do we taboo all religions? Why do you make it a Secular State? The reason may be that religion is not necessary or it may be that religion is necessary, but as India has many religions, Hinduism, Christianity, Islam and Sikhism, we cannot decide which one to accept. Therefore let us have no religion. No. That cannot be. If you accept religion, you must accept Hinduism as it is practised by an overwhelming majority of the people of India.

32. Constituent Assembly Debates, Volume 7, p. 820.

Mr. Vice-President: We shall resume the discussion on Monday. A request has come to me from my Muslim brethren that as today is Friday we should now adjourn. I think we ought to show consideration to them and adjourn now to meet again on Monday at Ten of the clock.

Mr. Misra may then deliver the rest of his speech.[33]

The debate was resumed on December 6, 1948.

Shri Lokanath Misra: Sir, it has been repeated to our ears that ours is a secular State. I accepted this secularism in the sense that our State shall remain unconcerned with religion, and I thought that the secular State of partitioned India was the maximum of generosity of a Hindu dominated territory for its non-Hindu population. I did not of course know what exactly this secularism meant and how far the State intends to cover the life and manners of our people. To my mind life cannot be compartmentalised and yet I reconciled myself to the new cry.

The Honourable Pandit Jawaharlal Nehru (United Provinces: General): Sir, are manuscripts allowed to be read in this House?

Mr. Vice-President; Ordinarily I do not allow manuscripts to be read, but if a Member feels that he cannot otherwise do full justice to the subject on hand, I allow him to read from his manuscript.

The Honourable Pandit Jawaharlal Nehru: May I know what is the subject?[34]

Mr. Vice-President: Mr. Lokanath Misra is moving an amendment to article 19. I ask the indulgence of the House because Mr. Lokanath Misra represents a particular point of view which I hold should be given expression to in this House.

---

33. *Ibid.*, p. 822.

34. Pandit Nehru knew very well what the subject was. But he had his own way of showing contempt for those who stood by Hinduism.

Shri Lokanath Misra: Gradually it seems to me that our 'a secular State' is a slippery phrase, a device to bypass the ancient culture of the land.

The absurdity of this position is now manifest in articles 19 to 22 of the Draft Constitution. Do we really believe that religion can be divorced from life, or is it our belief that in the midst of many religions we cannot decide which one to accept? If religion is beyond the ken of our State, let us clearly say so and delete all reference to rights relating to religion. If we find it necessary, let us be brave enough and say what it should be.

But this unjust generosity of tabooing religion and yet making propagation of religion a fundamental right is somewhat uncanny and dangerous. Justice demands that the ancient faith and culture of the land should be given a fair deal, if not restored to its legitimate place after a thousand years of suppression.

We have no quarrel with Christ or Mohammad or what they saw and said. We have all respect for them. To my mind, Vedic culture excludes nothing. Every philosophy and culture has its place but now the cry of religion is a dangerous cry. It denominates, it divides and encamps people to warring ways. In the present context what can this word 'propagation' in article 19 mean? It can only mean paving the way for the complete annihilation of Hindu culture, the Hindu way of life and manners. Islam has declared its hostility to Hindu thought. Christianity has worked out the policy of peaceful penetration by the back-door on the outskirts of our social life. This is because Hinduism did not accept barricades for its protection. Hinduism is just an integrated vision and a philosophy of life and cosmos, expressed in organised society to live that philosophy in peace and amity. But Hindu generosity has been misused and politics has overrun Hindu culture. Today, religion in India serves no higher purpose than collecting ignorance, poverty and ambition under a banner that flies for fanaticism. The aim is political, for in the modern world all is power-politics and the inner man is lost in the dust. Let everybody live as he thinks best but let him not try to swell his number to demand the spoils of political warfare. Let us not raise the question of communal minorities any more. It is a device to swallow the majority in the long run. This is intolerable and unjust.

Indeed in no constitution of the world right to propagate religion is a fundamental right and justiciable. The Irish Free State Constitution recognises special position of the faith professed by the great majority of the citizens. We in India are shy of such recognition. U.S.S.R. gives freedom of religious worship and freedom of anti-religious propaganda. Our Constitution gives the right even to propagate religion but does not give the right to any anti-religious propaganda.

If people should propagate their religion, let them do so. Only I crave, let not the Constitution put it as a fundamental right and encourage it. Fundamental rights are inalienable and once they are admitted, it will create bad blood. I therefore say, let us say nothing about rights relating to religion. Religion will take care of itself. Drop the word 'propagate' in article 19 at least. Civilisation is going headlong to the melting pot. Let us beware and try to survive.[35]

Mr. Vice-President: The clause is now open for discussion.[36]

Pandit Lakshmi Kanta Maitra (West Bengal : General): Sir, I feel myself called upon to put in a few words to explain the general implication of this article so as to remove some of the misconceptions that have arisen in the minds of some of my honourable Friends over it.

This article 19 of the Draft Constitution confers on all persons the right to profess, practise and propagate any religion they like but this right has been circumscribed by certain conditions which the State would be free to impose in the interests of public morality, public order and public

35. *Ibid.*, pp. 823-24.
36. *Ibid.*, p. 831.

health and also in so far as the right conferred here does not conflict in any way with the other provisions elaborated under this part of the Constitution. Some of my Friends argued that this right ought not to be permitted in this Draft Constitution for the simple reason that we have declared time and again that this is going to be a secular State and as such practice of religion should not be permitted as a fundamental right. It has been further argued that by conferring the additional right to propagate a particular faith or religion the door is opened for all manner of troubles and conflicts which would eventually paralyse the normal life of the State. I would say at once that this conception of a secular State is wholly wrong. By secular State, as I understand it, is meant that the State is not going to make any discrimination whatsoever on the ground of religion or community against any person professing any particular form of religious faith. This means in essence that no particular religion in the State will receive any State patronage whatsoever. The State is not going to establish, patronise or endow any particular religion to the exclusion of or in preference to others and that no citizen in the State will have any preferential treatment or will be discriminated against simply on the ground that he professed a particular form of religion. In other words in the affairs of the State the professing of any particular religion will not be taken into consideration at all. This I consider to be the essence of a secular state. At the same time we must be very careful to see that in this land of ours we do not deny to anybody the right not only to profess or practise but also to propagate any particular religion. Mr. Vice-President, this glorious land of ours is nothing if it does not stand for lofty religious and spiritual concepts and ideals. India would not be occupying any place of honour on this globe if she had not reached that spiritual height which she did in her glorious past. Therefore I feel that the Constitution has rightly provided for this not only as a right but also as a fundamental right. In the exercise of this fundamental right every community inhabiting this State professing any religion will have equal right and equal facilities to do whatever it likes in accordance with its religion provided it does not clash with the conditions laid down here.

The great Swami Vivekananda used to say that India is respected and revered all over the world because of her rich spiritual heritage. The Western world strong with all the strength of a materialistic civilisation, rich with the acquisitions of science, having a dominating position in the world, is poor today because of its utter lack of spiritual treasure. And here does India step in. India has to impart this rich spiritual treasure, this message of hers to the West. If we are to do that, if we are to educate the world, if we are to remove the doubts and misconceptions and the colossal ignorance that prevails in the world about India's culture and heritage, this right must be inherent, — the right to profess and propagate her religious faith must be conceded.[37]

I have listened to some of the speeches that have been made in connection with this article. It has been objected to and it has been said that the right to propagate should be taken away. One honourable Member suggested that if we conceded the right, the bloody upheaval which this country has witnessed of late would again recur with full vehemence in the near future. I do not at all share that pessimism of my honourable Friend. Apparently my honourable Friend has not given special consideration to the conditions that are imposed in this article. The power that this article imposes upon the State to intervene on certain occasions completely demolishes all chances of that kind of cataclysm which we have seen.

It has also been said, and I am very sorry that an observation was made by an honourable Member of considerable

37. Lakshmi Kanta Maitra gave great strength to the Christian case. He was a well known scholar and Ṣanskrit Pandit. One can be sure that he knew Vivekananda's position vis-a-vis Christian missions. Swamiji had accused them of spreading calculated misinformation about India's culture and heritage. But the Pandit had his own reasons — reasons which we cannot point out in print — for twisting Vivekananda in order to serve the Christian cause.

eminence and standing, that the Christian community in its proselytising zeal has sometimes transgressed its limits and has done acts which can never be justified. An instance of Bombay was cited in defence of his position.

Mr. Vice-President: I am afraid you are making a mistake there. No particular instance, so far as I remember, was cited.

Pandit Lakshmi Kanta Maitra: Anyway I believe that was at the back of his mind. I am sorry if I have not got at it correctly. I want to say that a good deal of injustice will be done to the great Christian community in India if we go away with that impression. The Indian Christian community happens to be the most inoffensive community in the whole of India. That is my personal opinion and I have never known anybody contesting that proposition. This Indian Christian community, so far as I am aware, spends to the tune of nearly Rs. 2 crores every year for educational uplift, medical relief and for sanitation, public health and rest of it. Look at the numerous educational institutions, dispensaries and hospitals they have been running so effectively and efficiently catering to all classes and communities. If this vast amount of Rs. 2 crores were utilised by this Christian community for purposes of seeking converts, then the Indian Christian community which comprises only 70 millions would have gone up to...

Mr. Vice-President: You are mistaken there: it is only 7 millions.

Mr. Lakshmi Kanta Maitra : I beg your pardon. From 7 millions it would have gone to 70 millions. But the point Mr. Vice-President, is not in the figures. The point of my whole contention is that the Christian community in India has not done that proselytising work with that amount of zeal and frenzy with which some of our friends have associated it. I am anxious to remove that misconception. Sir, I feel that every single community in India should be given this right to propagate its own religion. Even in a secular state I believe there is necessity for religion. We are passing through an era of absolute irreligion. Why is there so much vice or corruption in every stratum of society? Because we have forgotten the sense of values of things which our forefathers had inculcated. We do not at all care in these days, for all these glorious traditions of ours with the result that everybody now acts in his own way, and justice, fairness, good sense and honesty have all gone to the wilderness. If we are to restore our sense of values which we have held dear, it is of the utmost importance that we should be able to propagate what we honestly feel and believe in. Propagation does not necessarily mean seeking converts by force of arms, by the sword, or by coercion. But why should obstacles stand in the way if by exposition, illustration and persuasion you could convey your own religious faith to others? I do not see any harm in it. And I do feel that this would be the very essence of our fundamental rights, the right to profess and practise any particular religion. Therefore this right should not be taken away, in my opinion. If in this country the different religious faiths would go on expounding their religious tenets and doctrines, then probably a good deal of misconception prevailing in the minds of people about different religions would be removed, and probably a stage would be reached when by mutual understanding we could avoid in future all manner of conflicts that arise in the name of religion. From that point of view I am convinced that the word 'propagate' should be there and should not be deleted. In this connection I think I may remind the House that the whole matter was discussed in the Advisory Council and it was passed there. As such I do not see any reason why we should now go back on that. Sir, the clause as it is has my whole-hearted support, and I feel that with the amendments moved by my honourable Friend Dr. Ambedkar and Shrimati Durgabai this clause should stand as part of the Constitution.[38]

38. *Ibid.*, pp. 831-33.

Shri L. Krishnaswami Bharathi (Madras : General) : Mr. Vice-President, after the eloquent and elaborate speech of my respected Friend Pandit Maitra I thought it was quite unnecessary on my part to participate in the discussion. I fully agree with him that the word 'propagate' is intended only for the Christian community. But I think it is absolutely necessary, in the present context of circumstances, that we must educate our people on religious tenets and doctrines. So far as my experience goes, the Christian community have not transgressed their limits of legitimate propagation of religious view, and on the whole they have done very well indeed. It is for other communities to emulate them and propagate their own religions as well. This word is generally understood as if it referred to only one particular religion, namely, Christianity alone. As we read this clause, it is a right given to all sectional religions; and it is well known that after all, all religions have one objective and if it is properly understood by the masses, they will come to know that all religions are one and the same. It is all God, though under different names. Therefore this word ought to be there. This right ought to be there. The different communities may well carry on propaganda or propagate their religion and what it stands for. It is not to be understood that when one propagates his religion he should cry down other religions. It is not the spirit of any religion to cry down another religion. Therefore this is absolutely necessary and essential.

Again, it is not at all inconsistent with the secular nature of the State. After all, the State does not interfere with it. Religion will be there. It is a personal affair and the State as such does not side with one religion or another. It tolerates all religions. Its citizens have their own religion and its communities have their own religions. And I have no doubt whatever, seeing from past history, that there will not be any quarrel on this account. It was only yesterday His Excellency the Governor-General Sri Rajaji spoke on this matter. It is very necessary that we should show tolerance. That is the spirit of all religions. To say that some religious people should not do propaganda or propagate their views is to show intolerance on our part.

Let me also, in this connection, remind the House that the matter was thoroughly discussed at all stages in the Minorities Committee, and they came to the conclusion that this great Christian community which is willing and ready to assimilate itself with the general community, which does not want reservation or other special privileges should be allowed to propagate its religion along with other religious communities in India.

Sir, on this occasion I may also mention that you, Mr. Vice-President,[39] are willing to give up reservation of seats in the Assembly and the local Legislatures of Madras and Bombay, and have been good enough to give notice of an amendment to delete the clause giving reservation to the Christian community. That is the way in which this community, which has been thoroughly nationalist in its outlook has been moving. Therefore, in good grace, the majority community should allow this privilege for the minority communities and have it for themselves as well. I think I can speak on this point with a certain amount of assurance that the majority community is perfectly willing to allow this right. I am therefore strongly in favour of the retention of the word 'propagate' in this clause.[40]

The Honourable Shri K. Santhanam: Mr. Vice-President, Sir, I stand here to support this article. This article has to be read with article 13; article 13 has already assured freedom of speech and expression and the right to form association or unions. The above rights include the right of religious speech and expression and the right to form religious association or unions. Therefore article 19 is really not so much an article on religious freedom, but an article on what I may call religious toleration. It is not so much the words 'All persons are equally entitled to freedom of conscience and the right

39. The Vice-President, Mr. H.C. Mookerjee, was, a Christian.
40. *Ibid.*, pp. 833-34.

freely to profess, practise and propagate religion' that are important. What are important are the governing words with which the article begins, viz., 'Subject to public order, morality and health'.

Hitherto it was thought in this country that anything in the name of religion must have the right to unrestricted practice and propagation. But we are now in the new Constitution restricting the right only to that right which is consistent with public order, morality and health. The full implications of this qualification are not easy to discover. Naturally, they will grow with the growing social and moral conscience of the people. For instance, I do not know if for a considerable period of time the people of India will think that purdah is consistent with the health of the people. Similarly, there are many institutions of Hindu religion which the future conscience of the Hindu community will consider as inconsistent with morality.

Sir, some discussion has taken place on the word 'propagate'. After all propagation is merely freedom of expression. I would like to point out that the word 'convert' is not there. Mass conversion was a part of the activities of the Christian Missionaries in this country and great objection has been taken by the people to that. Those who drafted this Constitution have taken care to see that no unlimited right of conversion has been given. People have freedom of conscience and, if any man is converted voluntarily owing to freedom of conscience, then well and good. No restrictions can be placed against it. But if any attempt is made by one religious community or another to have mass conversions through undue influence either by money or by other means, the State has every right to regulate such activity. Therefore I submit to you that this article, as it is, is not so much an article ensuring freedom but toleration — toleration for all, irrespective of the religious practice or profession. And this toleration is subject to public order, morality and health.

Therefore this article has been very carefully drafted and qualifications are as important as the right it confers.

Therefore I think the article as it stands is entitled to our wholehearted support.[41]

Shri Rohini Kumar Chaudhari (Assam : General): Sir, I am greatful to you for giving me this opportunity for making a few observations on this very important article. It struck me as very peculiar that, although as many as four articles have dealt with religion, there is no mention of God anywhere in the whole Chapter. At first I considered it extremely strange, but after going through the matter more carefully, I found every justification for it. From the way in which the world is progressing, there is very little doubt that a time will come when we may be in a position to dispense with God altogether. That has happened in other more advanced countries and therefore I believe, in order to make room for such a state of things, the word "God" has been purposely avoided in dealing with religion itself.

Another point is the propagation of any religion. I have no objection to the propagation of any religion. If anyone thinks that his religion is something ennobling and it is his duty to ask others to follow that religion, he is welcome to do so. But what I would object to is that there is no provision in this Constitution to prevent the so-called propagandist of his religion from throwing mud at some other religion. For instance, Sir, in the past we remember how missionaries went round the country and described Sri Krishna in the most abominable terms. They would bring up particular activities of Sri Krishna and say, 'Look here, this is your Lord Krishna and this is his conduct.' We also remember with great pain how they used to decry the worship of the idols and call them names. Sir, in the new Constitution we must make it perfectly clear that no such thing will be tolerated. It is not necessary in the course of propagating any particular religion to throw mud at other religions, to decry them and bring out their unsatisfactory features according to the particular supporters of a particular religion. There should be a provision in the

41. *Ibid.*, pp. 834-35.

law, in the Constitution itself that such conduct will be met with exemplary punishment.[42]

Shri T. T. Krishnamachari (Madras: General): Mr. Vice-President Sir, I am here to support the motion before the House, viz., to approve of article 19. Many speakers before me have emphasised the various provisions of this particular article and the background in regard to the framing of this article. What I would like to stress is this: Sir, we are not concerned here with compromises arrived at between the various communities. We are not really concerned with whether some advantage might be derived from the wording of this article later on by certain communities in regard to the furtherance of their own religious beliefs and practices, but I think emphasis should be laid on the fact that a new government and the new Constitution have to take things as they are, and unless the status quo has something which offends all ideas of decency, all ideas of equity and all ideas of justice, its continuance has to be provided for in the Constitution so that people who are coming under the regime of a new government may feel that the change is not a change for the worse. In achieving that particular object, I think this article has gone a long way.

Sir, objection has been taken to the inclusion of the word "propagate" along with the word "profess and practise" in the matter of religion. Sir, it does not mean that this right to propagate one's religion is given to any particular community or to people who follow any particular religion. It is perfectly open to the Hindus and the Arya Samajists to carry on their Suddhi propaganda as it is open to the Christians, the Muslims, the Jains and the Buddhists and to every other religionist, so long as he does it subject to public order, morality and the other conditions that have to be observed in any civilised government. So, it is not a question of taking away anybody's rights. It is a question of conferring these rights on all the citizens and seeing that these rights are

42. *Ibid.*, pp. 835-36.

exercised in a manner which will not upset the economy of the country, which will not create disorder and which will not create undue conflict in the minds of the people. That, I feel, is the point that has to be stressed in regard to this particular article. Sir, I know as a person who had studied for about fourteen years in Christian institutions that no attempt had been made to convert me from my own faith and to practise Christianity. I am very well aware of the influences that Christianity has brought to bear upon our own ideals and our own outlook, and I am not prepared to say here that they should be prevented from propagating their religion. I would ask the House to look at the facts so far as the history of this type of conversion is concerned. It depends upon the way in which certain religionists and certain communities treat their less fortunate brethren. The fact that many people in this country have embraced Christianity is due partly to the status that it gave to them. Why should we forget that particular fact? An untouchable who became a Christian became an equal in every matter along with the high-caste Hindu, and if we remove the need to obtain that particular advantage that he might probably get — it is untouchability a very important advantage, apart from the fact that he has faith in the religion itself — well, the incentive for anybody to become a Christian will not probably exist. I have no doubt, Sir, we have come to a stage when it does not matter to what religion a man belongs, it does not matter to what sub-sect or community in a particular religion a man belongs, he will be equal in the eyes of law and in society and in regard to the exercise of all rights that are given to those who are more fortunately placed. So I feel that any undue influence that might be brought to bear on people to change their religion or any other extraneous consideration for discarding their own faith in any particular religion and accepting another faith will no longer exist; and in the circumstances, I think it is only fair that we should take the status quo as it is in regard to religion and put it into our Fundamental Rights, giving the same right to every religionist, as I said before, to propagate his religion and to convert people, if he felt that it is a thing that he has to do and that it is a thing for which he has been born and that it is his duty towards his God and his community.

Subject to the overriding considerations of the maintenance of the integrity of the State and the well-being of the people, — these conditions are satisfied by this article — I feel that if the followers of any religion want to subtract from the concessions given herein in any way, they are not only doing injustice to the possibility of integration of all communities into one nation in the future but also doing injustice to their own religion and to their own community. Sir, I support the article as it is.[43]

Shri K. M. Munshi (Bombay : General) : I have only a few words to say with regard to the objections taken to the word "propagate". Many honourable Members have spoken before me placing the point of view that they need not be afraid of the word "propagate" in this particular article. When we object to this word, we think in terms of the old regime. In the old regime, the Christian missionaries, particularly those who were British were at an advantage. But since 1938, I know, in my part of Bombay, the influence which was derived from their political influence and power has disappeared. If I may mention a fact within my knowledge, in 1937 when the first Congress Ministry came into power in Bombay, the Christian missionaries who till then had great influence with the Collectors of the Districts and through their influence acquired converts, lost it and since then whatever conversions take place in that part of the country are only the result of persuasion and not because of material advantages offered to them. In the present set up that we are now creating under this Constitution, there is a secular State. There is no particular advantage to a member of one community over another; nor is there any

43. *Ibid.*, pp. 836-37. The business empire which T. T. Krishnamachari built in the pre-and post-independence period had and has been helping Christian missions in various ways — for reasons which cannot be discussed here.

political advantage by increasing one's fold. In those circumstances, the word "propagate" cannot possibly have dangerous implications, which some of the Members think that it has.

Moreover, I was a party from the very beginning to the compromise with the minorities, which ultimately led to many of these clauses being inserted in the Constitution and I know it was on this word that the Indian Christian community laid the greatest emphasis, not because they wanted to convert people aggressively, but because the word "propagate" was a fundamental part of their tenet. Even if the word were not there, I am sure, under the freedom of speech which the Constitution guarantees it will be open to any religious community to persuade other people to join their faith. So long as religion is religion, conversion by free exercise of the conscience has to be recognised. The word "propagate" in this clause is nothing very much out of the way as some people think, nor is it fraught with dangerous consequences. Speaking frankly, whatever its results we ought to respect the compromise. The Minorities Committee the year before the last performed a great achievement by having a unanimous vote on almost every provision of its report.

This unanimity created an atmosphere of harmony and confidence in the majority community. Therefore, the word "propagate" should be maintained in this article in order that the compromise so laudably achieved by the Minority Committee should not be disturbed. That is all that I want to submit.[44]

Having become aware of the inclinations of the High Command, Congress members of the Constituent Assembly were quick to fall in line. Article 19 was "added to the Constitution" with two minor amendments accepted by Dr. B. R. Ambedkar, who was piloting the Constitution in the Constituent Assembly. The right of Christians "to propagate religion" had become their "right to convert other people".

44. *Ibid.*, pp. 437-38.

And the "people" included minor children.

After a revision of the draft articles, Article 19 became Article 25 of the Constitution. And so it stays today. The right of Christians to convert non-Christians including minors stands fully protected.

Christians heaved a sigh of relief after months of hectic activity. Their spontaneous reaction was, "Pandit Nehru proves himself a gentleman."[45] Pandit Laxmi Kant Maitra, Mr. Krishnaswamy Bharati and Mr. T. T. Krishnamachari were congratulated for "their noble and courageous defence of the rights of a minority."[46]

Meanwhile, on August 15, 1948, exactly one year after attainment of independence, India had "recognized the unique position of the Catholic Church by establishing diplomatic relations with the Vatican." While presenting his credentials to the Pope, "Mr. Dhirajlal Desai, the first Indian Ambassador to the Holy See, testified to India's great reverence for Christ." India, according to Desai, was a new state "created by the sacrifices of the people, guided by one who sought to mould his life according to the message of Christ" and who had "affirmed the oneness of God and the greatness of the religious ideal proclaimed in the Sermon on the Mount."[47]

Mahatma Gandhi was dead by that time. His views on Christ, Christianity, One God of Biblical theologies and the Sermon on the Mount, however, had been expressed not so long ago. Moreover, those views had been compiled in a book, *Christian Missions: Their Place in India,* published in 1941. One wonders whether Mr. Desai or those in the External Affairs Ministry who prepared his brief, were aware of those views or tried to find them out before presenting Mahatma Gandhi to the Pope as a follower of Christ. No one

---

45. Felix Alfred Plattner, *The Catholic Church in India: Yesterday and Today,* Allahabad, 1964, p. 1. The book was first published in German from Mainz, West Germany, in 1963.

46. *Ibid.,* p. 6.

47. *Ibid.,* p. 8.

thought of presenting him as a great Hindu. The praises he had heaped on Jesus and the Sermon on the Mount had come in handy as nails in his coffin.

17

Missions Since Independence

The Constitution of independent India adopted in January 1950 made things quite smooth for the Christian missions. They surged forward with renewed vigour. Nationalist resistance to what had been viewed as an imperialist incubus during the Struggle for Freedom, broke down when the very leaders who had frowned upon it started speaking in its favour. Voices which still remained 'recalcitrant' were sought to be silenced by being branded as those of 'Hindu communalism'. Nehruvian Secularism had stolen a march under the cover of Mahatma Gandhi's *sarva-dharma-sambhāva.*

The followers of Mahatma Gandhi were the first to forget what their Master had said repeatedly on the subject of proselytization. Some of them found berths in the new power set-up and fell in line with Pandit Nehru. Some others who felt frustrated for one reason or the other became fascinated by Mao-tse Tung and started seeing the Mahatma reincarnated in Red China. Constructive workers of the Gandhian movement gave priority to economic programmes and sidelined all social and cultural problems. A new breed of 'Gandhians' became busy floating Voluntary Agencies and looking forward to being funded by Western Foundations. Some of these foundations were avowedly dedicated to promoting only Christian causes. Small wonder that these 'Gandhians' became, in due course, active or passive accomplices of the Christian missions.

The worst crisis, however, overtook those who became known as Hindu leaders in post-independence India. So long as the Mahatma was alive they had prospered by accusing him of promoting 'Muslim and Christian causes' at the cost of 'Hindu interests'. Now that he was no more, they did not really know what to do. Some of them continued to live in the past, deriving satisfaction from cursing the Mahatma for misleading the country for all time to come. Others revised their attitude towards him but they did so more out of convenience than conviction. *Sarva-dharma-samabhāva* acquired a new meaning for them. Criticism of Christian dogmas became a 'negative' approach. The 'positive' approach, they started saying, should match the missionary effort in the fields of education, medicine and social services. It did not occur to them that Hindu society being poor and bereft of a state of its own was in no position to run the race. The 'positive' approach thus became, for all practical purposes, an excuse for not facing the problem at all.

The bright sunshine in which Christian missions started basking can be reported best in the words of a Jesuit missionary. "The Indian Church," writes Plattner, "has reason to be glad that the Constitution of the country guarantees her an atmosphere of freedom and equality with other much stronger religious communities. Under the protection of this guarantee she is able, ever since independence, not only to carry on but to *increase and develop her activity as never before without serious hindrance or anxiety*."[1] The number of foreign missionaries registered an unprecedented increase. "One must admit," continues Plattner, "that the number of missionaries who came to India soon after independence had perceptibly increased. During the war years very few of them ever reached India. So a kind of surplus was building in Europe with corresponding lack of personnel in India... At the same time the Communists were expelling thousands of missionaries — mainly members of the American sects — from China. Some of them were then transferred to India but not all of them could adapt themselves to Indian conditions."[2]

1. Felix Alfred Plattner, *op. cit.*, p. 6. Emphasis added.
2. *Ibid.*, p. 10.

Far more foreboding than this forward march of the Christian missions, however, was the fact that they were able to take in their stride two serious exposures of their character and activities made during the fifties. The first jolt they received was from a book by K. M. Panikkar published in 1953. The second was the publication, in 1956, of the Niyogi Committee's report on missionary activities in Madhya Pradesh. The powers that be — the Government, the political parties, the national press and the intellectual elite — either protected the missions for one reason or the other or shied away from studying and discussing the exposures publicly for fear of being accused of 'Hindu communalism', the ultimate swear-word in the armoury of Nehruvian Secularism.

Panikkar's study was primarily aimed at providing a survey of Western imperialism in Asia from A.D. 1498 to 1945. Christian missions came into the picture simply because he found them arrayed, always and everywhere, alongside Western gunboats, diplomatic pressures, extra-territorial rights and plain gangsterism. Contemporary records, consulted by him, could not but cut to size the inflated images of Christian heroes like Francis Xavier and Matteo Ricci. They were found to be not much more than minions employed by European kings and princes scheming to carve out empires in the East. Their methods of trying to convert kings or commoners in Asia were fraudulent or conspiratorial or morally questionable. Seeing that "missionary activities... were connected with Western political supremacy in Asia and synchronised with it",[3] Panikkar had concluded, "It may indeed be said that the most serious, persistent and planned effort of European nations in the nineteenth century was their missionary activities in India and China where a large scale attempt was made to effect a mental and spiritual conquest as supplementing the political supremacy already enjoyed by Europe."[4]

3. K. M. Panikkar, *Asia and Western Dominance*, London, 1953, p. 15.
4. *Ibid.*, p. 481.

What hurt the missionaries most, however, was Panikkar's observation that "the doctrine of the monopoly of truth and revelation is altogether alien to the Asian mind" and that "practically every educated Asian who seriously and conscientiously studied to understand the point of view of the missionary, from Emperor Kang Hsi to Mahatma Gandhi, has emphasised this point."[5] He had knocked the bottom out of the missionary enterprise. No monopoly of truth and revelation, no missions. It was as simple as that.

The missionaries were up in arms. "To prove his point," they said, "Panikkar picks and chooses historical facts and then deals with them one-sidely." But none of them came out with facts which could redeem or even counterbalance those presented by Panikkar. Efforts to explain them away or put another interpretation on them, also remained a poor exercise. Fr. Jerome D'Souza had jibed, "A very fine narrative Mr. Panikkar, but you must not call it history."[6] He or his missionary colleagues, however, never bothered to tell what was that history which Panikkar had not taken into account. Subsequent Christian writings show that missionaries have not been able to stop smarting from the hurt caused by Panikkar's study.

The message that Panikkar had tried to convey to Asians, particularly his own countrymen, was that the history of Christianity was, for all practical purposes, a running commentary on the Christian doctrine. Christian missions were quick to understand it although they have never acknowledged the debt. Ever since, Christian historians have been making herculean efforts to salvage the doctrine from the history it had created. By now there is a plethora of Christian literature which bemoans 'the colonial handicap' that has stood in the way of Christ scoring over Rama and Krishna. And there has been a determined effort to present to the Indian people what Stanley Jones has described as the 'disentangled

5. *Ibid.*, p. 455.
6. Felix Alfred Plattner, *op. cit.*, p. 14.

Christ'. It is only India's politicians and intellectual elite who have failed to grasp what Panikkar had revealed about the character of the Christian doctrine.

Thus howsoever serious the flutter which Panikkar's book caused inside missionary dovecotes, the atmosphere outside continued to be favourable for them. Of course, 'narrow minded Hindus and fanatical Communists' provided some pen-pricks off and on. But they came to nothing in every instance. "The question was raised in Parliament," narrates Plattner, "as to whether the right to propagate religion was applicable only to Indian citizens or also to foreigners residing in India, for example the missionaries. In March 1954, the Supreme Court of India expressed its opinion that this right was a fundamental one firmly established in the Constitution and thus applied to everyone — citizen and non-citizen alike — who enjoyed the protection of India's laws. With this explanation the missionaries were expressly authorised to spread the faith, thus fulfilling the task entrusted to them by the Church."[7]

In 1955 a bill came before Parliament "which if passed would have seriously handicapped the work of missionaries", because it "provided for a strict system of regulating conversions." The issue was conversions brought about by force, fraud or material inducements. But no less a person than the Prime Minister of India, Pandit Nehru, came to the rescue of Christian missions and persuaded the Parliament to throw out the bill. "I fear that this bill," said Pandit Nehru, "will not help very much in suppressing evil methods but might very well be the cause of great harassment to a large number of people. We should deal with those evils on a different plane, in other ways, not in this way which may give rise to other ways of coercion. Christianity is one of the important religions of India, established here for nearly two thousand years. We must not do anything which gives rise to any feeling of oppression or suppression in the minds of our Christian friends and

7. *Ibid.*, pp. 6-7.

fellow-countrymen."[8]

The signing of the defence pact between the U.S.A. and Pakistan in 1954 had, however, made the Government of India somewhat strict about granting of visas to foreign, particularly American, missionaries. "The Catholic Bishops of India," writes Plattner, "found it very difficult to reconcile themselves to this new turn of affairs, which they considered highly unpleasant and unjustifiable. In March 1955 a delegation under the leadership of Cardinal Gracias of Bombay requested an interview with Prime Minister Nehru and Home Minister Pandit Pant, who had succeeded Dr. Katju."[9] Pandit Nehru, according to the Secretary of the Catholic Bishops' Conference of India, was "sympathetic but pointed out that the problem was political and national, not religious." Pandit Pant, on the other hand, gave a practical advice which proved very helpful to the missions in the long run. "He could not understand," continues Plattner, "why the Catholic Church, which had a long and historic existence in the country, had not succeeded in training Indian priests and professors for seminaries. The interview helped us to realise that in every sphere we have to recruit locally and train selected candidates for responsible positions."[10] The Home Minister of India, it seems, had no objection to the sale of a narcotic provided the vendors were native. Nor did he see any danger in the spread of a network financed and controlled from abroad. The lesson that the East India Company had subjugated the country by training and employing native mercenaries, had

---

8. Quoted in *Ibid.*, p. 7. There is no record that Pandit Nehru ever gave any thought to the 'different plane' or 'other ways' of dealing with 'those evils'. It remained his life-long privilege "to talk vaguely and generally about things in general", as he himself had said. His patent way of showing disapproval was to talk of a 'different plane' and 'other ways'. Those who understood his language took the hint and fell in line.

9. Christians were unhappy with Dr. Katju because in April 1953 he had made a statement in Parliament that "for a long time he had been in possession of information about questionable proselytising activities of missionaries in Central India" (*Ibid.*, p. 10).

10. *Ibid.*, p. 12

not been learnt.

What the network was doing was revealed soon after by the report of an Enquiry Committee appointed by the Government of Madhya Pradesh. "In the words of the Secretary of the Catholic Bishops' Conference of India," reports Plattner, "it created a sensation everywhere in India. For the Committee roundly condemned the efforts of Catholic and Protestant missionaries among the aboriginal tribesmen of the State's remote rural areas. The converts, it was alleged, were estranged from the ways of their own country with the express purpose of creating a 'State within a State'. It expressed the fear that one day the Christian community would assert its right to form a separate state as the Moslems of Pakistan had done."[11]

The appointment of the Committee was occasioned by "the activities of some Mission organisations in the recently Merged States of Raigarh, Udaipur, Jashpur and Sarguja" where trouble had been reported soon after their merger in Madhya Pradesh. "This strip of land," recorded the Committee, "comprising Surguja, Korea, Jashpur, Udaipur, Chang-bhakar and some other small States of Orissa is surrounded by Bihar and Orissa States and is inhabited by a very large percentage of aboriginals. The tract is full of forests and mineral resources. Foreign Missionaries from Belgium and Germany had established themselves in Bihar and Orissa and also in Jashpur in 1834 and had succeeded in converting a very large number of people to Christianity. In order to consolidate and enhance their prestige, and possibly to afford scope for alien interests in this tract, the Missionaries were reported to be carrying on propaganda for the isolation of the Aboriginals from other sections of the community, and the movement of Jharkhand was thus started. This movement was approved by the Aboriginals, local Christians and Muslims and the Missionaries sought to keep it under their influence by excluding all the nationalist elements from this movement.

11. *Ibid.*, p. 11.

The demand for Adiwasisthan was accentuated along with the one for Pakistan in 1938. The Muslim League is reported to have donated Rs. One Lakh for propaganda work. With the advent of political independence in India, the agitation for Adiwasisthan was intensified with a view to forming a sort of corridor joining East Bengal with Hyderabad, which could be used for a pincer movement against India in the event of a war between India and Pakistan."[12]

The missionaries had not welcomed the merger of these states with Madhya Pradesh. "On the integration of the States," according to the Committee, "Missionaries became afraid of losing their influence. So they started an agitation, playing on the religious feelings of the primitive Christian converts, representing the Madhya Pradesh Government as consisting of infidels and so on. Some of the articles published in Missionary papers, such as 'Nishkalank', 'Adiwasi' and 'Jharkhand' were hardly distinguishable from writings in Muslim papers advocating Pakistan, before the 15th of August 1947. The Missionaries launched a special attack on the opening of schools by Madhya Pradesh Government under the Backward Area Welfare Scheme."[13]

Simultaneously, Mr. Jaipal Singh, member of the Constituent Assembly and President of the All India Adiwasi Mahasabha, "accused the Bihar Government with failure to serve the people by not insisting on the integration of those states with Bihar." A pro-Bihar agitation was started in November 1947 and some Congressmen from Bihar were roped in. These Congressmen, however, became wise when they saw what the agitation was aimed at. They "brought to the District Superintendent of Police's notice that there was a conspiracy between Pakistan and some American and German missionaries to instigate the aboriginals to take possession

---

12. *Report of the Christian Missionary Activities Enquiry Committee, Madhya Pradesh* (known and henceforward referred to as the Niyogi Committee Report), Nagpur, 1956, Part I, p. 9.

13. *Ibid.*, p. 7.

of their own land commonly known as Jharkhand."[14] The *Jharkhand News* reported on March 6, 1949 a controversy "between Shri Jaipalsingh and Professor Hayward, his secretary, as regards the person who had received the amount of 50,000 from the Muslim League."[15]

The Government of Madhya Pradesh had to take notice of the agitation worked up by Christian missionaries. It had already led to violence in the adjoining States merged with Orissa. The missionaries had become too powerful in Madhya Pradesh to be ignored any longer. "It must be noticed," recorded the Committee, "that about 30 different Missions are working in Madhya Pradesh with varying number of centres in each district. Almost the entire Madhya Pradesh is covered by Missionary activities and there is hardly any district where a Mission of one denomination or the other is not operating in some form or the other. More than half the people of Madhya Pradesh (57.4 percent) consist of members of the Scheduled Castes, Scheduled Tribes and Other Backward Classes and it is amongst these that Missionary activities are mostly confined."[16]

The appointment of the Committee was announced on April 16, 1954 by a press note of the Government of Madhya Pradesh which said, "Representations have been made to Government from time to time that Christian Missionaries either forcibly or through fraud and temptations of monetary and other gain convert illiterate aboriginals and other backward people thereby offending the feelings of non-Christians. It has further been represented that Missions are utilised directly or indirectly for purposes of extra-religious objectives. The Christian Missionaries have repudiated these allegations and have asserted on the other hand that their activities are confined solely to religious propaganda and towards social, medical and educational work. The Missionaries have further alleged that they are being harassed by

14. *Ibid.*, p. 10.
15. *Ibid.*, p. 50.
16. *Ibid.*, p. 23.

non-Christian people and local officials. As agitation has been growing on either side, the State Government consider it desirable in the public interest to have a thorough inquiry made into the whole question through an impartial Committee."[17]

The Committee had seven members including the Chairman, Dr. Bhawani Shankar Niyogi, retired Chief Justice of the Nagpur High Court. Mr. K.C. George, a professor in the Commerce College at Wardha, represented the Christian community. It started by studying the material in government files. As a result it was led to enlarge its terms of reference to include political and extra-religious activities also. "The material gathered in the initial stages of the enquiry revealed to the Committee that its significance far transcended the bounds of any one country or region in the world and that it was calculated to have world-wide repercussions. That compelled the Committee to view the subject as an integral part of a larger picture on the broad canvas of world history. The Committee had to consult a number of published books, pamphlets and periodicals for determining the nature and form of their recommendations."[18]

The terms of reference enabled the Committee to evolve a Questionnaire which was sent to such individuals and organisations as could help in the investigation. It received 385 replies to the Questionnaire, 55 from Christians and 330 from non-Christians. Besides, the Committee toured 14 districts in which it visited 77 centres, contacted 11,360 persons, and received 375 written statements. Hospitals, schools, churches, leper homes, hostels, etc., maintained by various missions were among the Christian institutions visited by the Committee. The persons interviewed came from 700 villages.

"In all these places," recorded the Committee, "there was unanimity as regards the excellent service rendered by the Missionaries in the fields of education and medical relief. But on the other hand there was a general complaint from the

17. *Ibid.*, p. 169.
18. *Ibid.*, p. 4.

non-Christian side that the schools and hospitals were being used as means of securing converts. There was no disparagement of Christianity or of Jesus Christ, and no objection to the preaching of Christianity and even to conversions to Christianity. The objection was to the illegitimate methods alleged to be adopted by the Missionaries for this purpose, such as offering allurements of free education and other facilities to children attending their schools, adding some Christian names to their original Indian names, marriages with Christian girls, money-lending, distributing Christian literature in hospitals and offering prayers in the wards of in-door patients. Reference was also made to the practice of the Roman Catholic priests or preachers visiting new-born babies to give 'ashish' (blessings) in the name of Jesus, taking sides in litigation or domestic quarrels, kidnapping of minor children and abduction of women and recruitment of labour for plantations in Assam or Andaman as a means of propagating the Christian faith among the ignorant and illiterate people. There was a general tendency to suspect some ulterior political or extra-religious motive, in the influx of foreign money for evangelistic work in its varied forms. The concentration of Missionary enterprise on the hill tribes in remote and inaccessible parts of the forest areas and their mass conversion with the aid of foreign money were interpreted as intended to prepare the ground for a separate independent State on the lines of Pakistan."[19]

To start with, Christian missions put up a show of cooperation with the Committee. But they realized very soon that the Committee was well-informed and meant business. "The authorities and members of the Roman Catholic Church cooperated with the Committee in their exploratory tours in Raigarh, Surguja, Bilaspur, Raipur and Nimar districts. Shri G. X. Francis, President of the Catholic Regional Council, and Shri P. Lobo, Advocate, High Court, Nagpur, associated themselves with the Committee. But subsequently the Catholic

19. *Ibid.*, p. 3.

Church withdrew its co-operation, not only filing statement of protest, but also moving the High court for a Mandamus Petition (Miscellaneous Petition No. 263 of 1955)."[20]

The Petition was dismissed by the High Court on April 12, 1956, "holding that it was within the competence of the State Government to appoint a fact-finding Committee to collect information and that there had been no infringement of any fundamental rights of the petitioner." At the same time the High Court made some adverse remarks about certain questions in the Questionnaire. The Committee considered the remarks and "informed the petitioner and the public that none of the questions represented either the views of the Committee or any individual member thereof and our anxiety to have information on various points was due to our desire to find out to what extent, if any, could any activity be considered to infringe the limits of public order, morality and health imposed by the Constitution."[21]

The Report of the Committee, published in July 1956, presented the "history of Christian missions with special reference to the old Madhya Pradesh and Merged States."[22] Coming to the agitation for Jharkhand, it gave the background. "The separatist tendency," it said, "that has gripped the mind of the aboriginals under the influence of the Lutheran and Roman Catholic Missions is entirely due to the consistent policy pursued by the British Government and the Missionaries. The final segregation of the aborigines in the Census of 1931 from the main body of the Hindus considered along with the recommendations of the Simon Commission which were incorporated in the Government of India Act, 1935 apparently set the stage for the demand of a separate State of Jharkhand on the lines of Pakistan."[23]

The subsequent formation of the Adiwasi Mahasabha and the Jharkhand Party followed in stages as the separatist forces

20. *Ibid.*, p. 5.
21. *Ibid.*
22. *Ibid.*, Part II, Chapter II.
23. *Ibid.*, p. 49.

gathered strength. "This attempt of the Adiwasis," observed the Report, "initiated by the Christian section thereof is a feature which is common to the developments in Burma, Assam and Indo-China among the Karens, Nagas and Amboynes. This is attributed to the spirit of religious nationalism awakened among the converted Christians as among the followers of other religions. But the idea of change of religion as bringing about change of nationality appears to have originated in the Missionary circles... Thus while the Census officer isolates certain sections of the people from the main bodies, the Missionaries by converting them give them a separate nationality so that they may demand a separate State for themselves."[24]

Next, the Report considered "Christian post-war world policy,"[25] and quoted from several Christian sources. The aim of this policy in India was three fold: "(1) to resist the progress of national unity... (2) to emphasise the difference in the attitude towards the principle of co-existence between India and America... (3) to take advantage of the freedom accorded by the Constitution of India to the propagation of religion, and to create a Christian party in the Indian democracy on lines of the Muslim League ultimately to make out a claim for a separate State, or at least to create a 'militant minority'."[26]

The newly adopted Constitution of India, according to the Committee, had encouraged the controllers of Christian missions in Europe and America to concentrate on India. "Although Europe itself," observed the Report, "required 're-Evangelisation and re-Christianisation, because of the spread of the Gospel of Communism according to Marx, the W.C.C.[27] and I.M.C.[28] turned their attention to India and other colonial countries. They were encouraged by the promulgation of our

24. *Ibid.*, pp. 50-51.
25. *Ibid.*, Chapter III.
26. *Ibid.*, pp. 59-60.
27. World Christian Council.
28. International Missionary Council.

Constitution which set up a secular State with liberty to propagate any religion in the country. They noted that the Churches in India were growing steadily in number partly by natural increase, partly from evangelisation and that the mass or community movements to Christianity did not die out though slowed down, but that the spiritual life of the congregation was low and that the Indian Church lacked economic maturity. Though India has the most highly organised *National Christian Council* it had to be largely *paid for from abroad*. Even the institutional activities of Missions, viz., schools, colleges and hospitals were dependent upon foreign support. Even the ordinary congregational life and pastoral duty still required some form of foreign aid."[29]

The Report surveyed the state of religious liberty in various countries in the past and at present. It cited High Court judgements in India to the effect that religious liberty is "not an absolute protection to be interpreted and applied independently of other provisions of the Constitution."[30] Then it turned to "missionary activities in Madhya Pradesh since independence as disclosed by oral and documentary evidence."[31] This was the most substantial as well as the most revealing part of the Report. It laid bare what the Christian Missions had been doing not only in Madhya Pradesh but all over India in the name of exercising religious liberty.

There was a detailed account of "how this programme of mass proselytisation was inspired and financed by foreigners"[32] and how the paid *pracharaks* of various missions had fanned out in the rural and tribal areas. The *pracharaks* were particularly noticeable in the erstwhile Native States which had kept missionary operations under control before their merger in Madhya Pradesh. "It is thus indisputably clear," recorded the Report, "that financial assistance from abroad had been extended in far more liberal manner than even before

---

29. *Ibid.*, p. 54. Italics in source.
30. *Ibid.*, p. 94.
31. *Ibid.*, Part III, Chapter III, pp. 95-129.
32. *Ibid.*, p. 99.

the Constitution of India was promulgated, and that it is mainly with this help that Mission organisations are carrying on proselytisation amongst backward tribes, especially in areas freshly opened."[33]

This greatly extended scale of missionary operations was dressed up ideologically in a new theological concept. "It may be recalled," commented the Report, "that the expression 'Partnership in Obedience' came into vogue at the meeting of the Committee of the International Missionary Council held at Whitby in 1947 (page 94, World Christian Handbook, 1952) and it has a bearing on the expression 'need of particular churches to be rooted in the soil and yet supranational in their witness and obedience' (page 29, ibid.). These particular churches are in the old Mission fields 'which are touched by new nationalisms independent in temper and organisation and yet needing help from other churches' (page 29, ibid.). The expression 'Partnership in Obedience' was being interpreted variously and it was after discussion at a meeting of the Lutheran World Federation Executive and also of the Executive of the World Council of Churches held at Geneva in 1951, that it came to be interpreted as implying full and unreserved co-operation between the old and the younger churches in the effort of extending the Kingdom of God."[34] In plain language, the pompous proclamation meant that missions and churches in Europe and America which provided the finance would continue to plan, direct and control missionary activities in India.

The Report quoted Christian sources to show the extent to which Christianity in India was dependent on foreign finance. Rolland Allan had written in his book, *The Spontaneous Expansion of the Church,* published in 1949, that "it is money, money everywhere, all the time, everything depends on money." In another book, *Missionary Methods : St. Paul's or Our's,* published by the same author in 1953, he had felt "sad to sit and watch a stream of Christian visitors

33. *Ibid.*, p. 102.
34. *Ibid.*, p. 100.

calling upon a Missionary and to observe that in nearly every case the cause which brings them is money." *Christianity in the Indian Crucible* by Dr. E. Asirvatham had been published in 1955. "One chief reason," he had observed, "why Indian Christians in general still welcome foreign Missionaries is economy; it is an open secret that the Indian Church is not yet out of the swaddling clothes, so far as its economic support is concerned. To give an extreme illustration only Rs. 6,000 of the total income of Rs. 1,12,500 of the National Christian Council of India... is from Indian sources and the rest comes from the Mission Boards abroad."[35] It was curious that Christianity was presented as a two-thousand years old banyan tree when it came to its right to spread its tentacles, and as a tender seedling when it came to its capacity for growing up on its own.

The Report provided details of how much had been contributed by which Western country to the total of Rs. 29.27 crores received by Christian missions in India from January 1950 to June 1954:

Country	Amount in Rs.
U.S.A.	20,68,63,000
U.K.	4,83,89,000
Canada	1,67,56,000
Sweden	64,41,000
Denmark	33,91,000
Norway	27,97,000
Rest of Sterling Area	25,29,000
Switzerland	15,77,000
Aid from non-Sterling Area	14,72,000
Germany	11,72,000
France	7,61,000
Belgium	6,47,000
	29,27,000 [36]

35. *Ibid.*, p. 102.
36. *Ibid.*, p. 96.

The Report revealed that the bulk of this foreign money received ostensibly for maintaining 'educational and medical institutions' was spent on proselytisation. "It has been contended," said the Report, "that most of the amount is utilised for creating a class of professional proselytisers, both foreign as well as Indian. We have not been able to get the figures of the salaries which the foreign Missionaries receive for their service in India. Only Rev. Hartman (Amravati No. 1) was pleased to declare that his salary was 63 dollars per month paid from Home, plus free quarters and vehicle allowance. One can have some idea of the scale of salaries of American Missionaries from the fact that in the American Evangelical and Reformed Church there are 28 Missionaries on the India roll and under the head of Missionary salaries and appurtenances the figure comes to 90,072,23 dollars (American Evangelistic and Reformed Church Blue Book, 1955, pages 56,60). They are supplied with well-furnished bungalows, and they command resources in vehicles and other things."[37] At the same time it noted a great disparity between the scales of salaries and allowances paid to foreign missionaries on the one hand and to their native mercenaries on the other.

There were 480 foreign missionaries working in Madhya Pradesh at that time. Out of them as many as 236 were Americans. The Report gave a count of foreign missionaries, Americans and others, stationed in the 22 districts of the then Madhya Pradesh. "Besides those," it added, "included in the number given by the National Christian Council in the Christian Handbook of India 1954-55, it appears from the statement of Rev. R. C. Das that there is a large number of unattached evangelists. Rev. Das's statement receives support from the remark made in the Compiler's introduction to the Christian Hand-Book of India 1954-55 that the increased personnel has occurred in the smaller Missions most of which do not yet have any organised Churches."[38]

37. *Ibid.*, p. 103.
38. *Ibid.*, p. 105.

The methods of proselytisation had remained the same as in days of old. The Report gave concrete instances of how mission schools were used to influence the minds of young people. Harijan and 'Adivasi' students came in for special attention. They were "given free boarding, lodging and books" provided they attended Christian prayers. Bible classes were made compulsory by treating as absent for the whole day those students who failed to be present in those classes. School celebrations were used for showing the victory of the cross over all other symbols. Hospitals were used for putting pressure on poor class patients to embrace Christianity. The richest harvest, however, was reaped in mission orphanages which collected orphans during famines and other natural calamities such as floods and earthquakes. "No wonder," observed the Report, " that the largest number of converts are from such backward classes living in areas where due to various causes only Mission schools and hospitals exist. Most conversions have been doubtless insincere admittedly brought about in expectation of social service benefits and other material considerations."[39]

Another device employed for proselytisation was money-lending. Roman Catholic mission had specialised in this field. Poor people often approached the local missionary for loans which are written off if the debtor became a convert; otherwise he had to repay it with interest which he often found difficult. Protestant missionaries and others cited before the Committee instances of how this method worked. One of the conditions for getting a loan, for instance, was that the recipient agreed to chop off the top-knot (*chotī*), the symbol of his being a Hindu. "Some of the people," the Report noted, "who had received loans were minors and casual labourers. It also appeared that when one member of a family had taken a loan, all the other members of that family were entered in the book as potential converts. The rate of interest charged was 10 per cent and in a large number of

39. *Ibid.*, p. 113.

cases examined, one year's interest was deducted in advance. On being questioned, the people without any hesitation, said that their only purpose in going to the Mission had been to get money; and all said that without the lure of money none would have sought to become Christian."[40] Some other allurements such as the "promise of gift of salt, plough, bullocks and even milk powder received from abroad" were used to the same effect.[41]

There were several other ways of attracting converts. For instance, the new converts were employed as *pracharaks* on salaries ranging from Rs. 40/- to Rs. 100/- per month. This by itself proved an attractive proposition to those who were not in a position or qualified to earn even Rs. 20/-. Christians working in various government departments were exhorted and expected to participate in the game. Those who did not help were cursed in missionary publications. Christians placed in higher positions and missionaries who became influential members of the Janapad Sabhas put pressure on junior officers for influencing people in favour of Christianity.

The Report also noted "various methods of propagating Christianity."[42] Missionary publications "attacked idol worship in rather offensive terms." Dramas in which idol worship was ridiculed were performed in schools and elsewhere. Songs to the same effect were composed and sung. Rama was "described as a God who destroyed Ravan and was contrasted with Jesus who died for the wicked." Methods evolved for conveying Christianity in Hindu cultural forms were also in evidence. Some of them were plainly dishonest, as for instance, "the expression occurring in Tulsidas's *Ramayan*, viz. 'Girjapujan' was interpreted to the people as 'Girjaghar' i.e., a Church."[43] But, on the whole, preference was given to vicious attacks on Hinduism, which was held up as a false religion. "Such virulent and sinister

---

40. *Ibid.*, p. 115.
41. *Ibid.*, p. 116.
42. *Ibid.*, pp. 118-122.
43. *Ibid.*, p. 119.

attacks on Hinduism," observed the Report, "are in no way a departure from the manner which characterised the Christian preaching in the past, which Gandhiji referred to, particularly Bishop Heber's famous hymn, 'where every prospect pleases and only man is vile'."[44]

The Report contained a section on Mass Conversions brought about by material inducements. "If conversion is an individual act," it noted, "one would expect deep thought and study of the particular religion one wanted to embrace. But what we have found is groups of illiterate Adivasis, with families and children getting their top-knots cut and being shown as Christians. Most of them do not know even the rudiments of the new religion... The Government has supplied us with a list of persons recently converted in the Surguja district after the promulgation of the Constitution. A perusal thereof will show that about 4000 Uraons were converted in two years. Persons of varying ages from 60 years to 1 year are shown as converts and the list includes women and children also. We have met many Uraons in the course of our tours and we were struck very much by their total absence of religious feeling."[45]

The Committee had "reliable information that Mission organisations possess upto-date records of Baptisms."[46] But they refused to produce these records. "It would not be unsafe," concluded the Report, "to presume that the reluctance on the part of the Roman Catholic Mission organisations to produce such evidence was in no small measure due to the fear of the Truth being out... As a rule, groups have been converted, and we find 'individual conversion' has been an exception rather than the rule. We have come across cases of individual conversions only of persons who are village leaders and they have invariably been followed by 'Mass conversions' of the entire village soon after. We have not found it possible to accept the contention that the immediate

44. *Ibid.*, p. 121.
45. *Ibid.*, pp. 122-123.
46. *Ibid.*, p. 123.

material prosperity of these converted leaders bore no causal relation to their conversions."[47]

The Report expressed the view that conversions led directly to denationalisation. Greetings such as 'Ram Ram' and 'Jai Hind' were substituted with 'Jai Yeshu'. "The idea of the unique Lordship of Christ," recorded the Report, "is propagated in rural areas by the exhibition of the film 'King of Kings', which we had the pleasure of witnessing at Buldana. The supremacy of the Christian flag over the National flag of India was also depicted in the drama which was staged in a school at Jabalpur."[48] The missionary paper, *Nishkalanka*, had written, "Why does India desire that Portugal which has been exercising sovereignty for 400 years over Goa should surrender it? The fact is that a large majority of residents of Goa are quite contented with their present condition. Only a handful of Goans resident in Goa and in India are shouting for the merger of Goa with India. This attitude is not justified and those who are following this course are giving unrighteous lead to India."[49] The missions thus sided with Western imperialism and pooh-poohed India's aspiration to reclaim national territory under foreign occupation.

Finally, the Report found no substance in the Christian complaint that the Government of Madhya Pradesh was following a policy of discrimination against Christians. "The Government of Madhya Pradesh," it said, "have throughout followed a policy of absolute neutrality and non-interference in matters concerning religion and allegations of discrimination against Christians and harassment of them by Government officials have not been established. Such allegations have been part of the old established policy of the Missions to overawe local authority and to carry on propaganda in foreign countries."[50]

The Report was quite clear in its larger perceptions.

47. *Ibid.*, pp. 123-124.
48. *Ibid.*, p. 125.
49. *Ibid.*, p. 126.
50. *Ibid.*, p. 132.

"Evangelisation in India," it said, "appears to be part of the uniform world policy to revive Christendom for re-establishing Western supremacy and is not prompted by spiritual motives. The objective is to disrupt the solidarity of the non-Christian societies, and the mass conversion of a considerable section of Adivasis with this ulterior motive is fraught with danger to the security of the State."[51] The Christian missions were making a deliberate and determined "attempt to alienate Indian Christian Community from their nation."[52] The Community was most likely to become a victim of foreign manipulations in times of crisis.[53] The history of the Christian missions provided ample proof that religion had been used for political purposes.[54] Evangelization was not a religious philosophy but a force for politicisation.[55] The Church in India was not independent but accountable to those who paid for its upkeep. The concept of 'Partnership in Obedience' which covered the flow of foreign finances to the Church was of a piece with the strategy of Subsidiary Alliances which the East India Company had employed earlier for furthering and consolidating its conquests.[56] And conversions were nothing but politics by other means.[57]

The recommendations made by the Report followed logically from these perceptions. It recommended that (1) those missionaries whose primary object is proselytisation should be asked to withdraw and the large influx of foreign missionaries should be checked; (2) the use of medical and other professional services as a direct means of making conversions should be prohibited by law; (3) attempts to convert by force or fraud or material inducements, or by taking advantage of a person's inexperience or confidence or spiritual weakness or thoughtlessness, or by penetrating into

51. *Ibid.*
52. *Ibid.*, p. 144.
53. *ibid.*, p. 145-148.
54. *Ibid.*, pp. 148-149.
55. *Ibid.*, p. 149.
56. *Ibid.*, pp. 149-150.
57. *Ibid.*, pp. 151-152.

the religious conscience of persons for the purpose of consciously altering their faith, should be absolutely prohibited; (4) the Constitution of India should be amended in order to rule out propagation by foreigners and conversions by force, fraud and other illicit means; (5) legislative measures should be enacted for controlling conversion by illegal means; (6) rules relating to registration of doctors, nurses and other personnel employed in hospitals should be suitably amended to provide a condition against evangelistic activities during professional service; and (7) circulation of literature meant for religious propaganda without approval of the State Government should be prohibited.[58]

The Report which was accompanied by two volumes of documentation raised a storm in missionary circles in India and abroad. The missions were in no position to dispute the facts presented or contest the conclusions arrived at by the Enquiry Committee. All they could do was to raise the spectre of 'Hindu communalism' and warn against the 'danger of Hindu Raj'. It was said that "members of Hindu Mahasabha had begun to wield considerable influence" in the Government of Madhya Pradesh and that "their aim was to make one Hindu state out of India."[59]

The fact of missions in India seeking financial and other aids from missions abroad was equated with the Government of India seeking "foreign technical knowledge and the assistance of friends from many European and American countries in the development of the nation-building activities." The replacement of foreign missionaries was found impossible as the Government of India had "found impossible to replace foreign personnel with Indian personnel."[60] It was promised that "in the not distant future the coming of missionaries from abroad into India will be matched by the going out of Indian missionaries from this country."[61] The logic was quite in

58. *Ibid.*, pp. 163-64.
59. Felix Alfred Plattner, *op. cit.*, p. 10.
60. *The National Christian Council Review*, October 1956, p. 403.
61. *Ibid.*, p. 405.

keeping with the way the Church in India had come to look at itself.

If this self-image of the Church as a State within the State looked pretentious to some people, it could be accounted for only by their tendency towards totalitarianism. "There is a striking contrast," wrote a leading theologian, M. M. Thomas, "between the democratic idea of the State and the totalitarian idea of the State which is both implicit and explicit in the Recommendations of the Niyogi Report... The philosophy of State underlying the Report and advocated by it is unashamedly totalitarian. It therefore is a matter of vital concern to every one in this country whether Christian or non-Christian who believes in democracy."[62] The test of a state being democratic was that it recognised and honoured "supranational loyalties." In support of his proposition Dr. Thomas quoted Mahatma Gandhi who had "recognized truth and non-violence as realities demanding loyalty above the nation," and President Sockarno of Indonesia who had "stated that Nationalism should be limited by Humanism."[63] Thus servility to foreign financiers and controllers of missions in India became transformed into loyalty to universal moral values! "In deploring this," concluded Dr. Thomas, "and characterising supranationalism as 'extraterritoriality', the Niyogi Report has shown the kinship of its ideology with totalitarian Facism."[64]

The missions also tried to rally support from some persons of public standing in India. Dr. Hare Krishna Mahtab, then Governor of Bombay, obliged them readily. "We should not think," he said, "of closing our doors to anyone. If we think in terms of exclusiveness, we shall not make any progress."[65] But they found a hard nut in C. Rajagopalachari. "It seems," he wrote to a foreign missionary, "you expect from me an expression of my views on the specific question:

62. *Ibid.*, p. 395.
63. *Ibid.*, pp. 395-96.
64. *Ibid.*, pp. 396-97.
65. *Ibid.*, pp. 397.

What type of missionary workers are wanted in India, rather than on the question whether any missionary workers should come at all to India? I shall respectfully speak my opinion on the latter point. I feel it is not really possible on the ground of logic or on the evidence of miracles to hold that amongst the religions known as Hinduism, Buddhism, Islam, and Christianity, anyone is nearer the truth than any other. You will permit me to object to the exclusive claims for Truth made on behalf of any one of these faiths. If this my first point is granted, the only justification for missionary work is proselytism. But is it good on the whole for men and women to change from one religion to another? I think it is not desirable to make any effort at proselytism. I feel that such efforts undermine the present faith of the people, which is good enough for promoting right conduct in them and to deter them from sin. They tend to destroy family and social harmony, which is not a good thing to do."[66]

Rajagopalachari was repeating the views expressed very often and very forcefully by Mahatma Gandhi. But the men who ran the Government in New Delhi could not afford to defend the Father of the Nation. They had to defend their Secularism and Democracy which had come under shadow in the powerful Christian press in India and abroad. They found the recommendations of the Niyogi Report "in discordance with the fundamental rights of the Constitution" and "the Report was shelved."[67]

The Government of India's stand vis-a-vis the Report became clear within two months after its publication. In September 1956, "a question was raised in the Parliament about an alleged increase in the anti-Indian activities on the part of foreign Christian missionaries." The Minister of State for Home Affairs, B. N. Datar, came promptly to their defence. "There is no factual basis," he said, "for the assumption made in the question, according to the information available with the

66. *Ibid.*, December 1956, p. 490.
67. Felix Alfred Plattner, *op. cit.*, p. 11.

Government of India." At the same time he affirmed that "no steps would be taken to check the work of foreign missionaries."[68]

A Bill was introduced in the Parliament in 1960 for protecting Scheduled Castes and Tribes "from change of religion forced on them on grounds other than religious convictions." It was also thrown out because of resistance from the ruling party. "It was rejected," records Plattner, "after Mr. Datar declared in no uncertain terms that it was unconstitutional and that there were no mass conversions as alleged by the mover." The Minister went much further. "They were carrying on," he said, "Christ's mission by placing themselves at the service of mankind and such work was one of their greatest contributions to the world." He credited the missionaries with "the uplift of a large number of downtrodden people through their schools and social work."[69] It may be mentioned in anticipation that the same fate will meet the Freedom of Religion Bill which O. P. Tyagi will try to introduce in Parliament during the Janata Party regime.

"This attitude of Nehru and his government," concluded Plattner, "has inspired the Christians with confidence in the Indian Constitution."[70] Nehru had "remained true to his British upbringing."[71] Small wonder that the Catholic Bishops' Conference of India became quite optimistic about the future. "With the Indian Hierarchy well established," it proclaimed in September 1960, "and the recruitment of the clergy fairly assured, it may be said that the Church in India has reached its maturity and has achieved the first part of its missionary programme. The time seems to have come to face squarely the Church's next and more formidable duty: the conversion of the masses of India."[72]

There were good grounds for this optimism. Conversions

---

68. *Ibid.*, p. 7.
69. *Ibid.*, pp. 7-8.
70. *Ibid.*, p. 8.
71. *Ibid.*, p. 9.
72. *Ibid.*, p. 134.

to Christianity were on the increase as was soon indicated by the Census for 1971. "In India as a whole," wrote a Christian historian, "the Christian population increased by 64.9% between 1951 and 1971. This may be compared with a general population increase of 51.7% during the same period. In North East India the Christian population increased by 171.1% during the same period, compared with a general population growth in that region of 116.5%. Even these figures do not give the full picture because in 1971, 74.7% of the total North East India population was in Assam where the growth of the Christian community is the lowest. In the 1961-71 decade alone the growth of the Christian community in states and territories other than Assam was as follows:

State	Percentage Growth of Christians	Percentage Growth of General Population
Nagaland	76.29%	39.88%
Meghalaya	75.43%	31.55%
Manipur	83.66%	37.33%
Tripura	56.52%	36.28%

In the 1951-1971 period, the Christian growth in Nagaland was 251.6% and in Tripura 298.6%... According to the Census of 1901 Christians in the North East constituted 1.23% of the whole, by 1951 the proportion was 7.8% and in 1971, 12.5%. North East India now had 39.8% of the non-southern Christian population."[73]

A major part of this rich harvest in this region had been reaped by the Catholic Church. "Without question," continued the historian, "the most important post-war development has been the rapid expansion of the Roman Catholic Church. At the beginning of the war there were but 50,000 Catholics in the region; in 1977 there were 369,681. In part this was due to an extraordinary expenditure of resources both in terms of

73. F. S. Downs, *Christianity in North East India: Historical Perspectives*, Gauhati, 1983, pp. 3-4.

money and missionary personnel, including personnel brought in from other parts of India. But it was due also to the removal after independence of the restrictions the British had placed upon Catholic missions."[74]

This spate of conversions could be traced directly to the expansion of Catholic education. "The growth of Catholic educational programme in the North East," noted the historian, "was certainly phenomenal. While in 1935 they were operating 299 primary schools, 9 middle and high schools, and 2 colleges, by 1951 the numbers had increased to 591, 65 and 2 respectively. By 1977 there were 744 primary schools, 63 middle and high schools (a slight decrease) and 4 colleges... Altogether there were 811 educational institutions with 79, 891 students."[75]

The region reflected the expansion of Catholic education in the country as a whole. "The dawn of independence," wrote the Catholic educationist, T. A. Mathias, in 1971, "is a landmark in the development of Christian educational work in this country. Since 1947 there has been a fantastic expansion in the number of Christian institutions, chiefly among the Roman Catholics. Colleges have gone up from 42 to 114 and secondary schools from 500 to 1,200. The Catholic Directory, 1969, gives fairly accurate statistics for Catholic educational work. There are now 6000 elementary schools, 1200 secondary schools, 114 colleges, and 80 specialised institutions."[76]

The Catholic Directory for 1984 reported a still more phenomenal growth. The number of kindergarten (elementary schools) in 1981 had reached 2,550, the number of primary schools 6,183 and the number of secondary schools 2,986. The Directory does not give the number of colleges and specialised institutions, though it tells us that 1,141,787 students were studying in Catholic colleges and 35,519 in institutes for other studies.

The Catholic educational network, however, represents

---

74. *Ibid.*, pp. 151-52.
75. *Ibid.*, p. 154.
76. Quoted in *Ibid.*, p. 153.

only a part of the Catholic apparatus, though it is the most important from the missionary point of view. It alienates Hindu young men and women from their ancestral culture or at least neutralises them against missionary inroads if it does not incline them positively towards the promotion of Christianity. Schools at the lower levels and in rural and tribal areas win converts directly by forgoing tuition fees, providing free textbooks and stationery etc., housing students freely in hostels, and giving free meals to day scholars. Colleges provide many recruits to the higher echelons in government services besides executives in business houses. Most of them look quite favourably at the 'humanitarian services which Hindus have neglected'. Big sums flow into the coffers of the Catholic missions from bribes given by neo-rich parents looking forward to their children speaking English in the 'proper accent'. Convent educated girls are in great demand in the Hindu marriage market.

The other part of the apparatus comprises what are known as medical, social, and humanitarian service agencies. In 1984 the Catholic missions maintained 615 hospitals, 1529 dispensaries, 221 leprosoria, 309 homes for the aged and the handicapped, 1,233 orphanages and 1,271 centres for training people in various crafts and skills. That is also where work of conversion is carried on openly. These services are free or very cheap for those who show readiness to embrace 'the only true faith'. For others, they are quite expensive, particularly the hospitals furnished with imported equipment of the latest kind.

This apparatus was spread in 1984 over 17, 288 mission stations and manned by 49, 956 religious women, 4, 993 religious priests and 2, 801 religious men other than priests. The missionary personnel was grouped in 167 congregations of sisters, 39 congregations of priests and 19 congregations of brothers. The sisters functioned from more than 4000 houses maintained in different parts of the country by a personnel of more than 56,000. Corresponding figures for priests came to more than 700 houses and a personnel of nearly 14,000, and for brothers it was nearly 200 houses with a personnel of more than 2,000. Besides, there were 14 secular institutes with nearly 30 houses and a personnel of nearly 400. A majority of these congregations had their headquarters abroad — 97 of sisters, 25 of priests, 8 of brothers. Though they recruited their personnel for the most part from India, their control was completely in the hands of establishments abroad. As many as 26, 541 catechists were in the field for netting new birds and making them cram the Catholic creed.

There was a corresponding expansion of what is called the Catholic Hierarchy which the Pope had taken over, partly from the Portuguese, in 1886. The Hierarchy had grown apace till 1947 when it had 10 Archdioceses and 35 Dioceses. By 1984, a period of only 37 years, the number of Archdioceses had almost doubled to 19 and that of Dioceses more than trebled to 110. A record increase of 18 Dioceses in a single year took place in 1977 when the Janata Party was in power. Six of these were created in the sensitive areas of Madhya Pradesh where the State Government had stalled expansion of the Hierarchy after the Niyogi Committee had laid bare the missionary mischief in 1956. The Government of Madhya Pradesh in 1977, it may be noted, was dominated by the erstwhile Jana Sangh component of the Janata Party.[77]

The Hierarchy presided over 5,159 parishes and quasiparishes grouped in 110 ecclesiastical territories and manned by 7, 058 diocesan priests. The Catholic Directory gives the Latin names of Bulls and Decrees proclaimed by the Pope while creating new Dioceses and Archdioceses and appointing Bishops and Archbishops on advice from his Nuncio in New Delhi. Neither the Government of India nor any State Government has ever been consulted in the matter. In 1974, Prime Minister Indira Gandhi had started negotiations for a Pre-Notification treaty with the Vatican but the

77. I tried to find out from various bigwigs of the then Janata Party including the then Prime Minister Morarji Desai, the reason for this sudden spurt. I drew a blank. No one was even aware that this had happened. The Catholic Church alone knows and can reveal the secret.

Pope had stalled them on one excuse or the other. The Janata Party dropped even the negotiations when it came to power in 1977. The Pope was thus free to continue carving out a State within the State.

In addition, the Catholic apparatus controlled some 150 printing presses and more than 200 periodicals in English and Indian languages. Around 350 seminaries of all sorts were busy training missionaries, priests and other specialised functionaries for its missions. The number of students in these seminaries was 2,125 in 1984. In the same year, 3, 528 persons turned out by these seminaries were candidates for religious priesthood.[78]

We have not been able to obtain and analyse corresponding data regarding the expansion of the Protestant missions and churches. They stopped publishing consolidated figures quite some time ago. It can, however, be safely assumed that there has been a considerable expansion of the Protestant apparatus as well, though it might not have been as phenomenal as the Catholic. Missions from or financed by the U.S.A. and West Germany, we are told, have become particularly prosperous and are active over wider fields.

The cost of maintaining and expanding this huge missionary apparatus, Catholic and Protestant, should be considerable, though it is kept a closely guarded secret by the missions and churches concerned. The budgets for maintaining missions and church hierarchies are never made public. Not even a hint is available in Christian publications regarding how much money is received and from where. The Christian community in India is too poor to maintain this colossal and expensive edifice, not to speak of financing its widespread and multifarious operations. The logical conclusion that the apparatus is financed almost entirely from abroad, is confirmed by the budgets published by controllers of missions in Europe and America, as also by such figures of foreign remittances to

---

78. For full details, See Sita Ram Goel, *Papacy: Its Doctrine and History*, New Delhi, 1986. It is a Voice of India publication.

Christian organisations as are made known by the Government of India from time to time. "One billion dollars," says a recent and reliable report, "that is how much American Protestant Christian organisations spent last year [1988] trying to gain conversions from other religions, and the Catholic Church spent an equal amount. According to official Indian government reports US dollars 165 millions is sent to Christian missions in India each year."[79] This represents a staggering increase on the amount of foreign remittances noted by the Niyogi Committee for the period from January 1950 to June 1954.[80]

Thus it can be maintained no longer that the Portuguese and British imperialists alone were responsible for the expansion of Christianity in India. The native Indian rulers have proved far more helpful to the Christian missions. They have provided constitutional protection to Christian propaganda. They have made it possible for the missions to enter into areas from where the British had kept them out. What is most important, in the years since independence Christianity has come to acquire a prestige which it had enjoyed never before in this country.

It cannot be said that the country has not faced problems created by Christian missions. Converts to Christianity in the North East and Central India have constantly evinced separatist and secessionist tendencies. The Government of India has recognised the mischief potential of Christian missions by expelling from the country some well known missionaries who were found fomenting political unrest and promoting violence. But the larger lesson that Christian missions in general mean no good and much mischief to the country and its culture, has yet to be learnt.

Even before independence, some Christian missionaries had ganged up with the Muslim League and floated the scheme of a sovereign Christian State composed of tribal areas

---

79. 'The Big Business of Evangelisation', *Hinduism Today,* February 1989. As always, this article too is based on wide-ranging research.

80. See page 338 in this chapter.

in the North East and Central India. The two enclaves were to be linked together by a corridor passing through Bihar and Bengal. The Nizam of Hyderabad was expected to provide another corridor towards Christian populations in the Madras Presidency (Now Andhra Pradesh and Tamil Nadu) and the princely states of Travancore and Cochin (now Kerala). It was hoped that, in due course, these Christian populations would gravitate towards the sovereign Christian State and provide access to the Christian world outside via the Coromandal and Malabar coasts. The movement for an independent Travancore had drawn enthusiastic support from the local Christians. Cochin was expected to follow suit.

After independence, the hand of Christian missions has been manifest in violent secessionist uprisings in Nagaland, Mizoram, Manipur and Tripura. Christian missions in these areas have not been loathe to join hands with the Communists who have pursued the same aim in cooperation with Red China. It has cost India vast sums of money for meeting the menace militarily. Thousands of lives have been lost. And the fires lighted by the Christian missionaries are still smouldering under the surface in spite of concessions made in the shape of several Christian majority States.

Meanwhile, the Christian-sponsored agitation for a separate State of Jharkhand has been gaining strength. "A secret report of Intelligence Bureau," according to the *Indian Express* of January 13, 1989, "has claimed that some voluntary organisations who received foreign contributions had been 'covertly' helping the Jharkhand movement for a separate state comprising 21 districts of Bihar, West Bengal and Orissa. The organisations named by the report are: The Willian Carey Study and Research Centre (WCSRC), the Christian Institution for Study of Religion and Science (CISRC), the Liberal Association for the Movement of People (LAMP), the Gana Unnayan Parishad (GUP), and the Indian People's Welfare Society (IPWS). The Forum for the Concerned Rural Journalists (FCRJ) with its registered office at Jhargram, was also said to be a recipient of subsidy from WCSRC and CISRC."

Some of the foreign organisations from which finances flow to these "voluntary organisations" in India have also been named. "According to the report GUP, WCSRC etc., had been getting foreign contributions from several foreign agencies including 'EZE, ECCO and AGKED (West Germany), NAVIB Foundation (Netherlands). Swedish International Development Agency (SIDA), World Council of Churches (Geneva) and Bread for the World'."

The "voluntary organisations" know how to get around the laws of the land for serving their subterranean purposes. "These organisations, the report said, had their own techniques for circumventing Government regulations. The organisations receiving foreign contributions registered themselves with the Central Government, maintained an account of foreign contributions and kept records about the purpose and manner of utilisation of funds. But, while the annual returns of these organisations to the Reserve Bank of India showed that the money was spent on cultural, economic, educational, religious and social programmes, in reality, the report claimed, much less amount than that claimed in the returns was actually spent on the programmes, with the rest being either 'misappropriated' or 'clandestinely donated to designing organisations and elements to further their ulterior objectives'."

They also play hide and seek with the law enforcement agencies of the Government,. "They operate in cooperation with many other voluntary organisations. If one particular organisation comes to adverse notice it floats some other cover, and front organisations maintain close liason with organisations which have not come under the cloud. GUP and IPWS had thus been floated by the WCRSC and LAMP... WCSRC had been reportedly giving monetary help to the Jharkhand Coordination Committee, a common front with 49 cultural and political groups and mass organisations formed to give a new pitch to the Jharkhand movement... The organisation, the report said, encouraged 'struggles of working people, women, tribals, dalits, oppressed and children' of the Jharkhand region 'inciting' the organisations for a separate Jharkhand state."

Such a report in a leading national daily called for some comments from leaders of the nation, if not questions in Parliament. But it was not even noticed, least of all by those who pass as Hindu leaders, not to speak of politicians who swear by Secularism. The only response it elicited was some letters of protest from the functionaries of Christian organisations. In the letters-to-the-editor column of the daily they denounced the report as concocted. The editor maintained that the report emanated from reliable and responsible quarters. That was the end of the matter. The Christian missions in India had not a worry in the world except that caused by their own theological quibbles.

18

Dethroning Monotheism

Another dialogue between Hinduism and Christianity commenced with the publication of Shri Ram Swarup's magnum opus, *The Word As Revelation: Names of Gods,* in September 1980. It is still continuing.

The dialogue which Raja Ram Mohun Roy had started in the third decade of the nineteenth century stopped abruptly with the passing away of Mahatma Gandhi in January 1948. The Hindu leadership or what passed for it in post-independence India was neither equipped for nor interested in the battle for men's minds. It believed in 'organising' the Hindus without bothering about what they carried inside their heads. It neither knew nor cared to know what Hinduism stood for. Its history of India began with the advent of the Islamic invaders. The spiritual traditions, ways of worship, scriptures and thought systems of pre-Islamic India were beyond its mental horizon.

The Christian missions, as we have seen, had never had it so good. Unchallenged ideologically, they broke out of the tight corner in which Mahatma Gandhi had put them and resumed the monologue which had characterised them in the pre-dialogue period. A number of mission strategies were dressed up as 'theologies in the Indian context'. The core of the Christian dogma remained intact, namely, that Jesus Christ was the only saviour. The language of presenting the dogma, however, underwent what looked like a radical change to the unwary Hindus, particularly those in search of a 'synthesis of all faiths'.

In the days of old, the missions had denounced Hinduism

as devil-worship and made it their business to save the Hindus from the everlasting fire of hell. Now they abandoned that straight-forward stance. In the new language that was adopted, Hinduism was made a beneficiary of the Cosmic Revelation that had preceded Jehovah's Covenant with Moses. Hinduism was also credited with an unceasing quest for the 'True One God'. The business of the missions was to direct that quest towards Christ who was 'hidden in Hinduism' and thereby make them co-sharers in the final Covenant which Jesus had sealed with his blood. That was the Theology of Fulfilment. A number of learned treatises were turned out on the subject. The labour invested was perhaps praise-worthy. The purpose, however, was deliberately dishonest.

In the days of old, Hindu culture like Hindu religion was a creation of the devil. It had to be scrapped and the stage swept clean for the culture of Christianity to take over. In the new language, Hindu culture was credited with great creations in philosophy, literature, art, architecture, music, painting and the rest. There was reservation only at one point. This culture, it was said, had stopped short of reaching the crest because its spiritual perceptions were deficient, even defective. It could surge forward on its aborted journey only by becoming a willing vehicle for 'Christian truths'. That was the Theology of Inculturation or Indigenisation. It created another lot of literature. The missions, however, did not stop at the theoretical proposition. They demonstrated practically how Hindu culture should serve Jesus Christ. A chain of Christian Ashrams sprang up all over the country. A number of Christian missionaries started masquerading as Hindu sannyasins, wearing the ochre robe, eating vegetarian food, sleeping on the floor and worshipping with the accoutrements of Hindu *pūjā*. The sacrifice they made of comforts in the mission stations and monasteries was perhaps admirable. The purpose of the exercise, however, was perfidious.

The controllers of the missions were not exactly happy when they found that Communism was proving more attractive than Christianity for some of the missionaries.

Marxism was in the air and it was difficult to dissuade some theologians and field workers from seeing a social revolutionary in Jesus. So the controllers did what they thought to be the next best thing. They encouraged the hot-heads to hammer out another theology, complete with class struggle and the rest, and hurl it against the 'oppressive social system sanctioned by Hinduism'. It became the business of the Christian missions to help the 'have-nots of Hindu society' rise in revolt against their 'oppressors'. Hindu society was found to be brimful of caste discrimination, class coercion, degradation of women, neglect of children, untouchability, bonded labour, and so on. That was the Theology of Liberation. It also produced some literature. Malcontents from among the Hindus were hired to lend their names as authors. Never mind if the pamphlets were poorly written and badly printed. The pretence that they came from the 'deprived and the down-trodden section of Hindu society' had to be maintained.

The Christian press presented the quibbles among these competing theologies as if momentous matters were being discussed. Hindus were left with the impression that the house of Christianity stood divided from within. The controllers of the missions, however, had everything under control. They were experimenting with various strategies in order to find out which was likely to yield the best results in the long run. In any case, different strategies could be employed simultaneously by different flanks of the missionary phalanx. Each Hindu who came in contact with them could be served with the theology which suited his or her taste.

What helped the Christian missions a good deal from the outside was the rise of Nehruvian Secularism as India's state policy as well as a raging fashion among India's intellectual elite. The knowledgeable among the missionaries were surprised and somewhat amused. They knew that Secularism had risen in the West as the deadliest enemy of Christian dogmas and that it had deprived the churches of their stranglehold on state power. In India, however, Secularism was providing a smokescreen behind which Christianity could steal a march. Politicians of all parties including parties which passed as Hindu, leading journalists and academicians, and scribes of all sorts saw the spectre of 'Hindu communalism' whenever someone raised a voice, howsoever feeble and apologetic, about the foreign finances and subversive activities of the Christian missions. An informed critique of Christianity invited angry snarls from the same quarters. The missions did not feel quite comfortable with the guardians of India's Secularism; there were too many goddamned Communists, Royists, Socialists and Leftists of all sorts in that crowd. But that was a problem to be faced in the long run. In the short run, the deep hostility which Secularism in India entertained for Hinduism could be turned to Christianity's advantage. At the same time, Hindus could be frightened into entering a 'united front of all religions against the forces of Godless materialism'.

Mahatma Gandhi's *sarva-dharma-sambhāva* was providing grist to the same mill. The old man had tried to cure Christianity of its exclusiveness and sense of superiority. That was the substance of his objection to proselytisation. He had advised Christians in general and Christian missionaries in particular to be busy with their own moral and spiritual improvement rather than with the salvation of Hindus. In his own days, Christian theologians had resented his doctrine of *sarva-dharma-samabhāva* and repudiated it as destructive of the very basis of Christianity. But now that the doctrine had been turned into a mindless slogan by the Mahatma's own disciples and handed over to the watchdogs of Nehruvian Secularism as another bark against Hinduism, it was safeguarding Christianity's right to multiply its missions. The doubting Thomases among the Hindus could be told that Bapu stood for equality of all religions and their opportunity to flourish without let or hindrance.

This was the atmosphere in which Ram Swarup's book, mentioned at the beginning of this chapter, came out of the press. He had invested in it many years of meditation and reflection. Its subject was neither Christianity, nor its missions.

On the contrary, it was an attempt at understanding the spiritual consciousness which had manifested itself in a multiplicity of Gods, not only in India but in many other lands. Christianity came in for a brief examination when he evaluated Monotheism from the standpoint of the spiritual vision which has sustained religious pluralism among the Hindus down to the present day. But the premises from which he would subsequently develop his deeper critique of Christianity became clear in this book.

Before we take up Ram Swarup's critique of Christianity in some detail, it would be helpful if we survey briefly the history of how Monotheism came to India and how it acquired the prestige it enjoys at present in the eyes of the dominant and vocal section of the Hindu intelligentsia. It is not rarely that one meets Hindu thinkers who regard Monotheism as a distinct and major contribution made to religious thought by Christianity and Islam. Many Hindu thinkers disown as relics from a primitive past the multiplicity of Gods for which Hinduism is well known; they also denounce idol worship round which Hinduism has remained centred down the ages. Even those Hindu thinkers who do not disown the Hindu pantheon, consign it to an inferior status vis-a-vis the Great God who is 'One without a second'; if they defend idol worship, they do so only as a device meant for the 'spiritually underdeveloped' seekers who are supposed to be incapable of viewing God without the aid of visible forms.

Monotheism was unknown to Hinduism in ancient times, either as a religious doctrine or as a philosophical concept, not to speak of as a theology. The notion of the 'True One God' as opposed to 'False Many Gods' was unknown to the Vedas, the Upanishads, the Buddhist and Jain Shastras, the Epics and the Puranas, and the six systems of Hindu philosophy. "Indian spirituality," writes Ram Swarup, "proclaimed that the true Godhead was beyond number and count; that it had many manifestations which did not exclude or repel each other but included each other, and went together in friendship; that it was approached in different ways and through many symbols;

that it resided in the hearts of its devotees. Here there were no chosen people, no exclusive prophethoods, no privileged churches and fraternities and *ummas*. The message was subversive of all religions based on exclusive claims."[1] This spirituality was summed up in the Vedic *mantra*, They hail It as Indra, as Mitra, as Varuṇa, as Agni, and as that divine and noble-winged Garutmān. Truth (or Reality) is one; the wise ones speak of it in various ways, whether as Agni, or as Yama, or as Matarishvān.[2]

Monotheism came to this country for the first time as the war-cry of Islamic invaders who marched in with the Quran in one hand and the sword in the other. It proclaimed that there was no God but Allah[3] and that Muhammad was *the* Prophet of Allah. It claimed that Allah had completed his Revelation in the Quran and that Muslims who possessed that Book were the Chosen People. It invoked a theology which called upon the believers to convert or kill the infidels, particularly the idolaters, capture their women and children and sell them into slavery and concubinage all over the world, slaughter their sages and saints and priests, break or at least desecrate their idols, destroy or convert into mosques their places of worship, plunder their properties, occupy their lands, and heap humiliations on such of them as cannot be converted or killed either due to their capacity for fighting back or the need of the conquerors for slave labour. The enormities which the votaries of Islamic Monotheism practised on a vast scale and for a long time vis-a-vis Hindu religion, culture and society, were unheard of by Hindus in the whole of their hoary history. Muslim theologians, sufis and historians who witnessed or read or heard of these doings

1. Ram Swarup, Introduction to *Mohammed and the Rise of Islam* by D.S. Margoliouth, New Delhi, Reprint, 1985 and 1995, p. xix.

2. Rigveda, I. 164. 46.

3. This part of the *Kalima* is now being translated as "there is no god but God", which is not only mistaken but also mischievous. Allah has claimed unmistakably in the Quran that he is the god of the Muslims alone; the Quran never presents him as God of mankind.

hailed the doers as soldiers of Allah and heroes of Islam. They thanked Allah and the Prophet who had declared a permanent war on the infidels and bestowed their progeny and properties on the believers. They quoted chapter and verse from the Quran and the Sunnah of the Prophet in order to prove that what was being done to Hindus was fully in keeping with the highest teachings of Islam.

The mainstream of Hinduism drew the inescapable conclusion that Islam was not much more than glorified gangsterism, and closed its doors to any willing contact with the hated creed and its vicious votaries. There was, however, a somewhat different response from some marginal sections of Hindu society. We need not go into the objective and subjective factors which facilitated this response. The result was the same in every case. The doings of Islam were divorced from its doctrine and viewed as aberrations due to human failing. Its Monotheism was abstracted and absorbed as the doctrine of One God as against Many Gods. Finally, Islam was presented as good a religion as Hinduism. The saints who performed this feat are now known as the pioneers of the 'Nirguna school of Bhakti'. Most of them show symptoms of the deep inroad which Monotheism had made into their psyche.

In the prevalent lore of present-day Hindu scholarship, the Nirguna school of Bhakti has become a 'progressive movement of social protest' inspired by the message of human equality and brotherhood supposed to have been brought in by Islam. There are several other myths which, joined together, make this school sound like a radical, even a revolutionary departure from the mainstream of Hinduism. A study of the literature produced by this school, however, provides no evidence that its saints said anything which had not been said long ago and in a loftier language by the ancient sages of Sanatana Dharma, or which was not being said by the other and contemporary school of Bhakti. By and large, the Nirguna school, like the other school of Bhakti, was wedded to Vaishnavism and drew upon the Epics and the

Puranas, particularly the Bhagavata, for its devotional stories and songs. What made the Nirguna school sound different in its historical setting was the stress which most of its saints laid on the 'True One God (*sacchā sāhib*)' and the contempt they poured on idol worship (*pāthar-pūjā*). The Shaktas who worshipped the Great Mother were subjected to virulent attacks in the literature of this school. Allah of the Quran who brooked no partners, particularly of the female gender, and permitted no idol worship, had won a victory without his victims knowing it.

Some Jain monks succumbed to Monotheism in their own way. Jainism had no God who could be made exclusive, nor Gods and Goddesses who could be spurned. But it had its Tirthankaras whose idols were worshipped in its temples. There is evidence that the Sthanakavasi sect of the Svetambara school of Jainism renounced idol worship and turned its back on temples under the influence of Islam.

Islamic invasion was defeated in due course and Muslim rule disappeared from the greater part of the Hindu homeland. But Monotheism retained the prestige it had acquired during the days of Muslim dominance. This happened largely because medieval Hindu thinkers had refused or failed to study and understand Islamic Monotheism in all its ramifications and from its own sources.

Many Hindu writers and poets of the medieval period have left for posterity some graphic accounts of the Muslim behaviour pattern with all its essential ingredients — sack of cities and villages and massacre of whole populations, capture of women and children, humiliation of Brahmanas, breaking of sacred threads, burning of scriptures, slaughter of cows, desecration of idols, destruction of temples or their conversion into mosques, plunder of properties, and so on. But what we miss altogether in the whole of medieval Hindu literature is an insight into the belief system which produced this behaviour pattern. There is not even the hint of a curiosity as to why Muslims were doing what they were doing. No Hindu acharya — there were quite a few of this class during this period — is known to have had a close look at Allah or the Prophet or the Quran or the theology which sanctioned these dismal deeds. Islamic Monotheism was thus allowed to remain unchallenged as a religious doctrine.

Ram Swarup observes, "Hindus fought Muslim invaders and locally established Muslim dynasties but neglected to study the religious and ideological motives of the invaders. Hindu learning or whatever remained of its earlier glory, followed the old grooves and its texts and speculations remained unmindful of the new phenomenon in their midst. For example, even as late as the fourteenth century, when Malik Kafur was attacking areas in the far South, in the vicinity of the seat of Sri Ramanujacharya, the scholarly dissertations of disciples of the great teacher show no awareness of the fact."[4]

He continues, "Hindus were masters of many spiritual disciplines; they had many Yogas and they had developed a science of inner exploration. There had been a continuing discussion whether the ultimate reality was *dvaita* or *advaita*. It would have been very interesting and instructive to find out if any of these savants of Yoga ever met, on their inner journey, a Quranic being Allah (or its original, Jehovah of the Bible) who is jealous of other Gods, who claims sole sovereignty and yet whom no one knows except through a pet go-between, who uses the latter's mouth to publish his decrees, who proclaims crusades and *jihād*, who teaches to kill the unbelievers and destroy their temples and shrines and levy tribute on them and to convert them into hewers of wood and drawers of water."[5]

Monotheism which had survived the defeat of Islamic invasion was reinforced by Christianity which appeared on the Indian scene along with European Imperialism. Christian Monotheism was no different from that of Islam; both of them shared a common source in the Bible. Nor had Christian

4. Ram Swarup, Introduction to ***Mohammed and the Rise of Islam***, p. xvii
5. *Ibid.*, pp. xvii-xviii.

Monotheism lagged behind its Islamic variation in committing atrocities on a large scale, for a long time, and in many lands; in fact, Islam had followed in many respects the precedents set by Christianity. But in the Indian context, Christian Monotheism had an advantage over that of Islam. Hindus had no opportunity to see the fierce face of Christianity except in the small Portuguese and French enclaves for a short time. By the time Christianity was active in India on any scale, it had suffered a steep decline in the estimation of the dominant Western elite; the rise of modern science, rationalism and secularism had knocked the bottom out of Christian theology and deprived it of its stranglehold on the state. The British conquerors of India were not willing to back the Christian missions with state power to any great extent; the missions were not allowed to use their tried and tested methods for 'saving the Hindus from hell'.

Most Hindus felt offended when Christian missionaries used foul language vis-a-vis Hindu religion, culture and society and started making conversions. But few of them were equipped intellectually to identify the doctrine from which the language sprang and the attempts at conversion emanated. Christian missionaries were presenting themselves as worshippers of the 'True One God' and denouncing Hinduism as idolatry wedded to many Gods and Goddesses. Some Hindus defended their pantheon in the best manner they knew and continued to worship in their traditional temples. But others, particularly those who had benefited from English education, took the missionary accusation to heart and started ransacking their own scriptures in search of the 'True One God' who could stand shoulder to shoulder with the God of Christianity. They ended by disowning the multiplicity of Gods and denouncing idol worship. They gave out a call for purging Hinduism of its 'polytheism' so that Hinduism could be saved. That is how the Hindu reform movements started in the nineteenth century.

The psychology that was at work in the reform movements is illustrated best by the rise of Raja Ram Mohun

Roy to name and fame in a short time. He owed his fascination for Monotheism to his study of Islam. Hindus of Calcutta did not take to him kindly when he started denouncing polytheism and idol worship. It was only when he criticised the Christian doctrine of Trinity and the crude methods of Christian missionaries that the English educated gentry of Calcutta warmed up to him. He was hailed as a Hindu leader by this gentry when he discovered the 'True One God' in the Brahma of the Vedas and the Upanishads. The Brahmo Samaj he founded took the message to Madras, Malabar, Maharashtra. the North Western Provinces (now U.P.) and the Punjab.

The Arya Samaj, founded by Maharshi Dayananda, spread Monotheism over a larger area and among those sections of Hindu society which had never known it earlier. As a result, Hindu society seemed to acquire self-confidence. But the logic of what had been set in motion was remorseless. The wheel turned full circle in the Punjab where Neo-Sikhism forced the lives and sayings of the Gurus into the framework of Monotheism borrowed bodily and wholesale from Islam and Christianity. Nothing could have been more distorted and dishonest. But the exercise succeeded because by this time the dominant and vocal section of Hindu intelligentsia had become votaries of Monotheism. This section applauded when the Akalis drove out the Brahmana priests from the gurudwaras after accusing them of having installed idols of many Gods and Goddesses in places meant for the worship of the 'True One God'. Hindus who had retained their reverence for the idols had to collect and instal them elsewhere when they were thrown out of the gurudwaras. Mahatma Gandhi protested in vain when a temple inside the Harimandir at Amritsar was demolished; he was told that Sikhism did not permit idol worship in its holy places.

The Hindu reform movements had started with the best of intentions. They aspired to save Hindu society from the onslaught of Islam and Christianity. They also succeeded in stopping conversions. But in as much as they were rooted in reaction against Islam and Christianity rather than in a resurgence of the Hindu spiritual vision, they misfired in the long run. Instead of forging their own weapon of defence, they borrowed it from the adversary's armoury. Small wonder that it boomranged and turned out to the disadvantage of the cause they had espoused.

In disowning the multiplicity of Hindu Gods, the Hindu reform movements tended to disown the rich heritage of Hindu art, architecture, sculpture, music, dance and literature which had developed round these divinities and had no other *raison d'etre.* It was not long before they forgot the very purpose, namely defence of Hinduism, for which they had placed themselves in the vanguard of Hindu society. Worse still, the reform movements created an elite which looked down upon its own people and became progressively alienated from them in most of its perceptions. The wide gulf that yawns at present between the two sections of Hindu society is illustrated best by their respective response to the remains of Hindu temples destroyed by the Islamic invaders.

It is not unoften that Hindus in the countryside chance upon remains of temples which lie scattered on some site and which have escaped the notice of the Archaeological Survey of India. Invariably, they collect these remains, cleanse them, instal them under a tree or in an improvised temple, and start worshipping them. Experts from the Archaeological Survey who receive the report and visit the spot feel amused at the simplicity of these people. Sometimes the 'heap' consists entirely of the outer and decorative portions of a temple and does not contain a single figure of a God or Goddess, either in relief or in the round. But that does not make any difference to the worshippers. All they know and care for is that the remains came from a temple where their ancestors had worshipped at one time but which was subsequently destroyed by Muslims.

The story becomes entirely different when one visits the drawing rooms of the Hindu elite. One sees there an array of sculptures selected with care from the same ruins and installed on tasteful stands. But they draw no reverence from those who possess them. They are only antiques meant for interior decoration. One is expected to contemplate them for their lines and forms and place them properly in the history of Indian art. Woe betide the visitor who becomes curious as to how these idols which were once housed in some temple or temples have landed in a modern drawing room, and how they got mutilated or defaced or deprived of limbs. That sort of curiosity is most likely to be met with stunned silence or derisive smiles. One has exhibited one's utter lack of the aesthetic sense. This irrelevant digging into a dead past is simply not done in polished society. Or, worse still, one has betrayed one's inclination towards 'Hindu communalism', a dangerous disease in a society dedicated to Secularism.

It was not that voices in defence of Gods and their worship as idols were not raised while the Hindu reform movements surged forward. Some of these voices came from the tallest figures in the saga of India's re-awakening to her ancient heritage. Swami Vivekananda had said that if idol worship could produce a spiritual master like Sri Ramakrishna, all honour to it. Sri Aurobindo had expounded at length how the concrete images to which Vedic *rishis* addressed their hymns had emerged out of the deepest intuitions of spiritual consciousness. Mahatma Gandhi had avowed his reverence for idols and temples in unmistakable terms. But the voices, it seems, failed to impress the followers of these great men. The Ramakrishna Mission installed life-like statues of Sri Ramakrishna in the temples it built. Sri Aurobindo Ashram raised their own guru to the same status. Mahatma Gandhi has so far been spared that 'honour'. His followers, however, are not known for their fondness for Hindu idols or temples.

What was worse, the Ramakrishna Mission and the Sri Aurobindo Ashram imbibed the theology of Monotheism in another respect, namely, the cult of the latest and the best which will not be bettered. In the eyes of the Mission, Sri Ramakrishna is no more a saint who sought and verified in his own experience the truths of Sanatana Dharma; he has become a 'synthesis of all faiths' including Islam and Christianity such as has never been seen in the past and will not be witnessed again in future! The Ashram hails Sri Aurobindo not as a great yogin and sage who explored and explained to the modern world the deepest insights of the Hindu spiritual tradition, but as the highest manifestation of the Divine in human history! Shades of Christ and Muhammad.

The stalwarts of India's re-awakening never claimed to be founders of new religions. Nor were they interested in Hinduism because it carried some exclusive message made known to mankind by some Hindu at some point in time. For them, Hinduism was Sanatana Dharma, that is, a spiritual vision valid at all times, in all places and for all people, and directly accessible to all seekers without the help of an historical intermediary. To the Buddha, a new way was suspect. He described his own way as that on which the Buddhas of the past had walked and the Buddhas of the future will walk. And that is Ram Swarup's starting point in his book. He seeks the "higher meanings" of the Hindu pantheon not only because "it will add to our understanding of Hinduism, one of the most ancient and still one of the major world-religions" but also because, "it will throw light on the ancient Gods of many Asian and European countries, Gods by now so completely forgotten that we cannot study them directly."[6]

"The Hindu pantheon," observes Ram Swarup, "has changed to some extent but the old Gods are still active and are still understood though under modified names. Hindu India has a continuity with its past which other nations, which changed their religions at some stage, lack. It is known that the Hindu religion preserves many old layers and forms. Therefore, its study may link us not only with its own past forms but also with the religious consciousness, intuitions and forms that prevailed in the past in Europe, in Greece, in Rome, in many Scandinavian and Baltic countries, amongst the German and the Slavic peoples, and also in several countries of the Middle East. In short, the study may reveal a fundamental

6. Ram Swarup, *The Word As Revelation : Names of Gods*, New Delhi, 1980, p. 107.

form of spiritual consciousness which is wider than its Hindu expression."[7] This emergence of similar spiritual insights and forms over a vast area was not an accident.

The earliest Hindu expression of that spiritual consciousness is found in the Vedas, "humanity's oldest extant scripture."[8] Three things "stand out prominently" when we study the Vedic pantheon. Firstly, there is "a very large use of concrete images... many important Gods like *Surya, Agni, Marut* take their names after natural objects."[9] Secondly, "the spiritual consciousness of the race is expressed in terms of a plurality of Gods."[10] Thirdly, "all Gods have multiple names."[11] These are also features shared by the pantheons of many other peoples.

Ram Swarup starts with the Names of Gods which, in turn, lead him to an inquiry into the nature of language and the higher meanings of words. Taking up concrete images in the Vedic pantheon, he observes, "We have already seen that the physical and the intellectual are not opposed to one another. The names of physical objects become names of ideas, names of psychic truths, names of Gods; sensuous truths become intellectual truths, become spiritual truths... In fact, this is the only way in which the sense-bound mind understands something of the higher knowledge... This reverberating, echoing and imaging takes place up and down the whole corridor of the mind at all levels of abstraction. Here, as we traverse the path, we meet physical-forms, sound-forms, vision-forms, thought-forms, universal-forms, all echoes of each other. We meet *mantras* and *yantras* and icons of various efficacies and psychic qualities. In one sense, they are not the light above but they are its important formations. They invoke the celestial and raise up the terrestrial...[12] There is another

7. *Ibid.*, p. 108.
8. *Ibid.*, p. 5.
9. *Ibid.*, p. 109.
10. *Ibid.*, p. 110.
11. *Ibid.*, p. 115.
12. *Ibid.*, p. 110.

reason why images in the Vedas and the Upanishads are concrete. When the fever of the soul subsides, when the mind becomes calm, when the spiritual consciousness opens, things are no longer lifeless. In this state, things which have hitherto been regarded as ordinary are full of life, light and consciousness. In this state, 'the earth meditates as it were; water meditates as it were; mountains meditate as it were.'[13] In this state, no need is felt to separate the abstract from the concrete because both are eloquent with the same message, because both image one another. In this state, everything expresses the divine; everything is the seat of the divine; everything is That; mountains, rivers and the great earth are but the Tathāgata, as a Chinese teacher, Hsu Yun, proclaimed after his spiritual awakening."[14]

How did the Vedic sages see Gods in Nature's mighty phenomena like the earth, the sky, the sun and the stars? "They saw in them sources and springs of their own lives; they saw that these things were part of one Great Life; that they were meeting points of great spiritual truths; that they revealed what was concealed; that they prefigured a mighty design; that they were kith and kin, friends and lovers. But in order to yield their deeper meanings, they demanded continued fellowship. This the old sages gave ungrudgingly and joyfully. They filled their hearts and the fullness of their hearts broke out in songs of praise."[15]

Coming to the plurality of the Vedic Gods and their names, he comments, "The names of Gods are not names of external beings. These are the names of the truths of man's own higher self. So the knowledge of the epithets of Gods is a form of self-knowledge. Gods and their names embody truths of the deeper Spirit and meditation on them in turn invokes those truths. But those truths are many and, therefore Gods and their names too are many, though they are all

13. Chhandogya Upnishad, 7.6.1.
14. Ram Swarup, *The Word As Revelation*, pp. 111-12.
15. *Ibid.*, p. 117.

held together in the unity of a spiritual consciousness."[16]

Equipped with this perspective on the nature of spiritual consciousness and its inevitable expressions, Ram Swarup proceeds to examine Monotheism and Polytheism. He finds merit in both of them so long as they remain spiritual ideas and do not become intellectual concepts.

"The Spirit," he observes, "is a unity. It also worships nothing less than the Supreme. Monotheism expresses, though inadequately, this intuition of man for unity and for the Supreme[17]... When the urge for unity is spiritual, the theology of One God is no bar and the seeker reaches a position no different from *Advaita*, from *ekam sat*. He realizes that *God alone is,* and not that there is only One God. But if the motive for unity is merely intellectual, it helps little spiritually speaking. God remains an outward being and does not become the truth of the Spirit. It does not even help to reduce the number of Gods; instead it multiplies the number of Devils – if Christianity is any guide in the matter. We know Medieval Christianity was chockful of them. In fact, they occupied the centre of attention of the Church for many centuries to the exclusion of everything else. During these centuries it was difficult to say whether the Church worshipped God or these devils... The Church also abounded in Gods though they were not as plentiful as the devils. But these were not recognised as such because they appeared in the guise of angels, cherubims and seraphims."[18]

Coming to Polytheism, he comments, "If monotheism represents man's intuition for unity, polytheism represents his urge for differentiation. Spiritual life is one but it is vast and rich in expression. The human mind also conceives it differently. If the human mind was uniform, without depths, heights and levels of subtlety or if all men had the same mind, the same imagination, the same needs; in short, if all men were the same, then perhaps One God would do. But a man's

16. *Ibid.*, p. 116.
17. *Ibid.*, p. 126.
18. *Ibid.*, p. 127.

mind is not a fixed quantity and men and their powers and needs are different. So only some form of polytheism alone can do justice to this variety and richness. Besides this variety of human needs and human minds, the spiritual reality itself is so vast, immense and inscrutable that man's reason fails and his imagination and fancy stagger. Therefore this reality cannot be indicated by one name or formula or description. It has to be expressed in glimpses from many angles. No single idea or system of ideas could convey it adequately. This too points to the need for some form of polytheism."[19]

"The Vedic approach," concludes Ram Swarup, "is perhaps the best. It gives unity without sacrificing diversity. In fact, it gives a deeper unity and a deeper diversity beyond the power of ordinary monotheism and polytheism. It is one with the yogic and the mystic approach[20]... In this deeper approach, the distinction is not between a true One God and false Many Gods; it is between a true way of worship and a false way of worship. Wherever there is sincerity, truth and self-giving in worship, that worship goes to the true altar by whatever name we may designate it and in whatever way we may conceive it. But if it is not desireless, if it has ego, falsehood, conceit and deceit in it, then it is unavailing though it may be offered to the most true God, theologically speaking."[21]

Summing up, Ram Swarup says, "The truth is that the problem of One or Many Gods is born of a theological and not of a mystic consciousness. In the *Atharvaveda,* the sage Vena says that he 'sees That in that secret station of the heart in which the manifoldness of the world becomes one-form'... But in another station of man, where not his soul but his mind rules, there is opposition between the One and the Many, between God and Matter, between God and Gods. On the other hand, when the soul awakens, Gods are born in its

19. *Ibid.*, p. 128.
20. *Ibid.*, p. 128.
21. *Ibid.*, p. 129.

depths which proclaim and glorify one another. Gods are bound to appear when the spiritual consciousness awakens; though in another sense they also fall away, God as well as Gods, with all their outward, anthropomorphic forms, and along with all our conceptions of them, however sublime and exalted. Yes, even God falls away. For there is a spiritual consciousness which can do without God. Buddhism, Jainism, Sāṁkhya, Taoism and Zen confirm the truth of this observation. In fact, in Buddhism and Jainism, though Gods are plentiful, there is very little of One God. Yet in spiritual perception, insight and attainment, these religions are not less than those where One God rules the roost and is the sole cock of the walk."[22]

Monotheism as known to history is not born of spiritual seeking. Ram Swarup says, "Monotheism was not always a spiritual idea. In many cases it was an ideology. It was consolidated in wars and in turn it led to further wars... there was a larger association to create, an empire to consolidate, or other nations and tribes to conquer, and the idea of a 'One True God' was handy in the pursuit of this object. The diplomacy, the sword, systematic vandalism, all played their part in making a particular god supreme. From very early days, the One God of Christianity was bound up with the imperial needs of Rome. In more recent times, the Biblical God has tried to consolidate what the European arms and trade have conquered[23]... In the cultural history of the world, the replacement of Many Gods by One God was accompanied by a good deal of conflict, vandalism, bigotry, persecution and crusading. These conflicts were very much like the 'wars of liberation' of today, hot and cold, openly aggressive or cunningly subversive. Success in such wars played no mean role in making a local deity, say Allah of certain Arab tribes, win a wider status and assume a larger monarchical role[24]... This point needs stressing. For in the past, the controversy between One God and Many Gods

22. *Ibid.*, pp. 129-30.
23. *Ibid.*, p. 126.
24. *Ibid.*, p. 131.

or between My True God and Your False God led to many rolling of heads and much spilled blood, and even today there is no dearth of hot heads and the discussion still tends to polemics, bad blood, and frayed tempers. There are still organised churches and missions out to make war on the false Gods of the heathens."[25]

On the other hand, Polytheism "bred a spirit of religious tolerance and freedom" wherever it prevailed. "Ancient Rome, Greece and Egypt – all polytheistic cultures – were relatively free from religious wars... Rome, Alexandria and Athens were open places where different religions met and discussed freely. When St. Paul visited Athens, he was invited by the Athenians to speak about his doctrine. He did not avail himself of the opportunity but it is obvious that he did not feel at home in this atmosphere of free enquiry... St. Paul represented not the spirit's impatience with what is only cerebral but a passionate attachment to a fixed idea which is closed to wider viewpoints and larger truths of life. In polytheistic Rome too, men of different religious persuasions and sects met and built their temples and worshipped in their own way. But this freedom disappeared when Christianity, the religion of One True God, took over."[26]

Ram Swarup, therefore, calls upon the people of various countries in Asia, Africa, Europe and America to return to their ancient Gods which have been replaced by the semitic Gods in the recent past. "It would, therefore, be difficult," he writes, "to hold that the present Gods of semitic origin are superior to the now defunct pagan Gods. There was a time when the old pagan Gods were pretty fulfilling and they inspired the best of men and women to acts of greatness, love, nobility, sacrifice and heroism. It is, therefore, a good thing to return to them in thought and pay them our homage. We know pilgrimage, as ordinarily understood, as wayfaring to visit a shrine or a holy place. But there can also be a pilgrimage

---

25. *Ibid.*, pp. 133-34.
26. *Ibid.*, pp. 125-26.

in time and we can journey back and make our offerings of the heart to those Names and Forms and Forces which once incarnated and expressed man's higher life. They are holy Names and Symbols."[27]

Restoration of old Gods will restore among the people concerned a respect for their past. It will also fill the gap in their cultural history. "The present generations of many countries tend to regard their past as a benighted period of their history. A more understanding approach towards their Gods of old will work for a less severe judgement about their past and their ancestors. It will also fill the generation gap, not the one we talk about the most these days but a still wider one, the general rootlessness of a whole nation. Gods provide an invisible link between the past and the present of a nation; when they go, the link also snaps. The peoples of Egypt, Persia, Greece, Germany and the Scandinavian countries are no less ancient than the people of India; but they lost their Gods, and therefore they lost their sense of historical continuity and identity."[28]

Such a restoration is particularly relevant for the peoples of Africa and South America. "The countries of these continents have recently gained political freedom of a sort, but it has done little to help them and to give them a spiritual identity. If they wish to rise in a deeper sense, they must recover their soul, their Gods, their roots in their own psyche; there has to be a spiritual reassertion, a resurrection of their Gods. If they need any change, and there is no doubt they do, it must come from within themselves as a part of their own experience. If they do enough self-churning, then their own Gods will put forth new meanings in response to their new needs. They have to make the best of their own psychic and spiritual gifts and discover their own Gods within themselves. No people can import their Gods ready-made and rise spiritually under the aegis of imported deities,

27. *Ibid.*, pp. 131-32.
28. *Ibid.*, p. 132.

saviours and prophets."[29]

The old Gods are not dead; they have only withdrawn themselves. "If there is sufficient aspiration, invoking, and soliciting, there is no doubt that even Gods apparently lost could come back again. They are there all the time. For nothing that has any truth in it can be destroyed. It merely goes out of manifestation; but it could reappear under propitious circumstances. So could the old Gods come to life again in response to new summons."[30]

It was quite apt that a review of Ram Swarup's book which appeared in *The Times of India* dated March 29, 1981 described it as a call for "The Return of the Gods". The reviewer was the noted scholar from Santiniketan, Dr. Sisir Kumar Ghose. He was well-known as an exponent of Sri Aurobindo's thought.

Five years later, Ram Swarup examined Monotheism more concretely, that is, its unfoldment in the form of Islam and Christianity. "The spiritual equipage of Islam and Christianity," he wrote, "is similar; their spiritual contents, both in quality and quantum, are about the same. The central piece of the two creeds is 'One True God' of masculine gender who makes himself known to his believers through an equally favoured individual. The theory of mediumistic communication has not only a psychology; it has also a theology laid down long ago in the oldest part of the Bible in the Deuteronomy (18.19-20). The Biblical God says that he will speak to his chosen people through his chosen prophet: 'I will tell him what to say, and he will tell the people everything I command. I will punish anyone who refuses to obey him' (*Good News Bible)*. The whole prophetic spirituality, whether found in the Bible or in the Quran, is mediumistic in essence. Here everything takes place through a proxy, through an intermediary. Here man knows God through a proxy; and probably God too knows man through

29. *Ibid.*, p. 133.
30. *Ibid.*

the same proxy. The proxy is the favoured individual, a privileged mediator. 'No one knows the Son except the Father, and no one knows the Father except the Son and anyone to whom the Son chooses to reveal him,' says the Bible (Matt. XI. 27). The Quran makes no very different claim. 'This day I have perfected your religion,' says the Allah of the Quran through his last prophet (5.3)."[31]

He thought that the time had come for Hindus to evaluate Christianity and Islam in terms of Hindu spirituality. "Hitherto we have looked on Hinduism through the eyes of Islam and Christianity. Let us now learn to look at these ideologies from the vantage point of Hindu spirituality — they are no more than ideologies, lacking as they are in the integrality and inwardness of true religion and spirituality. Such an exercise would also throw light on the self-destructiveness of modern ideologies of Communism and Imperialism, inheritors of the prophetic mission or 'burden' in its secularised version of Christianity and Islam. The perspective gained will be a great corrective and will add a new liberating dimension; it will help not only India and Hinduism but the whole world."[32]

Respect for Hinduism, Buddhism, Taoism and Confucianism, and revolt against closed theologies was already growing in the world. "Dogmas are under a cloud; claims on behalf of Last Prophethood and Only Sonship, hitherto enforced through great intellectual conditioning, browbeating and the big stick, are becoming unacceptable. Religions of proxy are in retreat. More and more men now seek authentic experience. Men and women are ceasing to be obedient believers and are becoming seekers. They no longer want to be anybody's sheep, now that they know they can be their own shepherds. An external authority, even when it is called God in certain scriptures, threatening and promising alternately, is increasingly making less and less

31. Ram Swarup, Introduction to *Mohammed and the Rise of Islam,* pp. xvi-xvii.

32. *Ibid.*, pp. xix-xx.

impression; people now realize that Godhead is their own true, secret status and they seek it in the depths of their own being. All this is in keeping with the wisdom of the East."[33]

Ram Swarup completed his evaluation of the semitic creeds by locating them in their proper place on the map of the Samkhya-Yoga philosophy and psychology which are shared in common by all schools of Sanatana Dharma. He pointed out that the traditional commentators on Yoga had concentrated on the yogic or *ekāgra samādhi* and neglected treatment of non-yogic *samādhis*. It was, however, the non-yogic *samādhis* which held the key to an understanding of the psychic phenomena which do not have their source in the yogic *samādhi*. We shall quote him at some length:

> Considering that the two kinds of *samādhis* are not unoften confused with each other, it would have served the cause of clarity if both were discussed and their differences pointed out. After all, the Gita does it; in its last two chapters, it discusses various spiritual truths like austerity, faith, duty, knowledge in their triple expression and sharply distinguishes their *sāttvika* from their *rājasika* and *tāmasika* imitations.
>
> The elucidation of non-yogic *samādhis* or ecstasies has also its positive value and peculiar concern. It could help to explain quasi-religious phenomena which, sadly, have been only too numerous and too important in the spiritual history of man. Many creeds seemingly religious sail under false labels and spread confusion. As products of a fitful mind, they could not but make only a temporary impression and their life could not but be brief. But as projections of a mind in some kind of *samādhi*, they acquire unusual intensity, a strength of conviction and tenacity of purpose (*mūḍhagraha*) which they could not otherwise have.
>
> ...We may say that even the lower *bhūmis* (*kāma-bhūmis*) have their characteristic trances or *samādhis*,

33. *Ibid.*, p. xx.

their own Revelations, Prophets and Deities. They project ego-gods and desire-gods and give birth to *dvesha-dharmas* and *moha-dharmas,* hate religions and delusive ideologies. All these projections have qualities very different from the qualities of the projections of the yogic *bhūmi*.

For example, the God of the yoga-*bhūmi* of *Pātañjala Yoga* is free, actually and potentially, from all limiting qualities like desire, aversion, hankering, ego and nescience; free from all actions, their consequences, present or future, active or latent. Or in the language of *Pātañjala Yoga*, he is untouched by *klesha-karma-vipāka-āshaya.* But the god of the ecstasies of non-yogic *bhūmi* or *kāma-bhūmi* is very different. He has strong likes and dislikes and has cruel preferences. He has his favourite people, churches and *ummas* and his implacable enemies. He is also very egoistic and self-regarding; he can brook no other god or gods. He insists that all gods other than himself are false and should not be worshipped. He is a 'jealous god', as he describes himself in the Bible. And he 'whose name is Jealous' is also full of 'fierce anger' (*aph*) and cruelty. He commands his chosen people that when he has brought them to the promised land and delivered its people into their hands, 'thou shalt smite them, and utterly destroy them; thou shalt make no covenant with them, nor show mercy unto them... ye shall destroy their altars, and break down their images, and cut down their groves... For thou art an holy people unto the Lord...' (Deut. 7. I-6).

The Allah of the Quran exhibits about the same qualities. He is a god of wrath (*ghazb);* on those who do not believe in him and his prophets, he wreaks a terrible punishment (*azāb al-azeem*). In the same vein, he is also a mighty avenger (*azeez-ul-intiqām*). He is also a god of 'plenteous spoils' *(mūghanım kasīr,* 4.94). He tells the believers how he repulsed their opponents and caused them to inherit the land, the houses and the wealth of the disbelievers (33.27). He closely follows the spirit of Jehovah who promised his chosen people that he would give them 'great and goodly cities they builded not, and wells which they digged not, vineyards and olive trees they planted not' (Deut. 6.10-11).

No wonder this kind of god inspired serious doubts and questions, among thinking people. Some of his followers like Philo and Origen allegorized him to make him more acceptable. Some early Christian gnostics simply rejected him. They said that he was an imperfect being presiding over an imperfect moral order; some even went further and regarded him as the principle of Evil. Some gnostic thinkers called him 'Samael', a blind God or the God of the blind; others called him 'Ialda baoth', the son of Chaos.

He continues to offend the moral sense of our rational age too. Thomas Jefferson thinks that the 'Bible God is a being of terrific character, cruel, vindictive, capricious and unjust.' Thomas Paine (1737-1809) says of the Bible that 'it would be more consistent that we call it the work of a demon than the word of God.'

Hindus will buy any outrages if they are sold as Gods, Saints, or Prophets. They have also a great weakness for what they describe as 'synthesis'. In that name, they will lump together most discordant things without any sense of their propriety and congruity, intellectual or spiritual. However, a few names like Bankim Chandra, Swami Dayananda, Vivekananda, Aurobindo and Gandhi are exceptions to the rule. To Bankim, the God of the Bible is 'a despot' and Jesus's doctrine of 'eternal punishment' in the 'everlasting Fire' (Matt. 25. 41) is 'devilish'. Swami Dayananda remembering how the Biblical 'Lord sent a pestilence... and there fell seventy thousand men of Israel' (I Chr. 21.14), His Chosen people, observes that even 'the favour of a capricious God so quick in His pleasure is full of danger', as the Jews know it only too well. Similarly, the Swami argues, in his usual unsparing way, that the Allah and Shaitan of the Quran, according to its own showing, are about the same.

But to reject is not to explain. Why should a god have to have such qualities? And why should a being who has such qualities be called a god? And why should he have so much hold? Indian Yoga provides an answer. It says that though not a truly spiritual being, he is thrown up by a deeper source in the mind. He is some sort of a psychic formation and carries the strength and attraction of such a formation. He also derives his qualities and dynamism from the *chitta-bhūmi* in which he originates.

It will explain that the Biblical God is not peculiar and he is not a historical oddity. He has his source in man's psyche and he derives his validity and power from there; therefore he comes up again and again and is found in cultures widely separated. This god has his own ancestry, his own sources from which he is fed, his own tradition and principle of continuity, self-renewal and self-validation.

Not many know that a similar God, Il Tengiri, presided also over the life of Chingiz Khan and bestowed on him Revelations. Minhajus Siraj, the mid-thirteenth century historian, tells us in his *Tabqāt-i-Nāsiri,* that 'after every few days, he (Chingiz Khan) would have a fit and during his unconsciousness he would say all sorts of things... Some one would write down all he said, put (the papers) in a bag and sealed them. When Chingiz recovered consciousness, everything was read out to him and he acted accordingly. Generally, in fact always, his designs were successful.'

In this, one can see unmistakable resemblance with the revelations or *wahi* of the semitic tradition.

In actual life, one seldom meets truths of the *kāma-bhūmi* unalloyed. Often they are mixtures and touched by intrusions from the truths of the *yoga-bhūmi* above. This however makes them still more virulent; it puts a religious rationalization on them. It degrades the higher without uplifting the lower. The theories of *jihad*, crusades, conversions and *da'wa* become spiritual tasks, Commandments of God, religious obligations, vocations and duties of a Chosen People. 'See my zeal for the Lord', says Jehu, an army captain anointed as king at the command of Jehovah. Bound to follow His will, he called all the prophets, servants, priests and worshippers of rival Baal on the pretext of organising his service and when they were gathered, his guards and captains 'smote them with the edge of the sword' and 'they brake down the image of Baal, and brake down the house of Baal, and made it a draught house (latrine) unto this day' (2 Kings 10. 25,27)."[34]

This characterisation of the semitic creeds, their gods, their scriptures and their prophets was bound to bring about a radical change in the Hindu assessment of Christianity. More and more Hindu thinkers and scholars are going to primary sources rather than remain satisfied with the professions of the Christian missionaries. The dialogue initiated by Ram Swarup in 1980 has been carried forward in a series of publications from VOICE OF INDIA, a forum for presenting the Hindu point of view. The publications cover the doctrine of Christianity, its history, its heroes, its saints and its institutions.

34. Ram Swarup, Introduction to *Inner Yoga (Antaryoga)* by Anirvan, translated into English by S. N. Chatterjee, Voice of India, New Delhi, 1988, pp. viii-xi.

19

Sannyasins or Swindlers?

Hinduism Today, a bimonthly[1] published by the Saiva Siddhanta Church with headquarters in Hawaii, U.S.A., carried an article, 'Catholic Ashrams: Adopting and Adapting Hindu Dharma', in its issue of November-December, 1986. It noticed particularly the Saccidananda Ashram at Shantivanam in the Tiruchirapally District of Tamil Nadu. "The Shantivanam Ashram," it said, "looks like a rishi's home transported from Vedic times to the bank of sacred Cauvery River... A pilgrim's first impressions are strong, and very Hindu; the elaborately colorful Hindu shrine; the bearded, saffron-robed 'swami' seated cross-legged on a straw mat; devotees practising yogic meditation, even chanting Hindu scriptures. But these impressions gradually prove false. First, the eye detects that the courtyard shrine is for Saint Paul and that 'puja' is actually a daily mass, complete with incense, arati, lamps, flower offerings and prasadam. Finally, one meets the 'swami', learning he is Father Bede 'Dayananda' Griffiths, a Christian 'sannyasin' of impeccable British background."

The article raised an important question. "Are these places to be endorsed by Hindus as worthy attempts to share each other's spirituality? Or are they a spiritual oxymoron, a contradiction of terms, because Christians are interested in sharing — dialogue is the term they use — only as a means to conversions?" It also provided the answer by drawing a parallel. "A comparison," it observed, "might best illustrate Hindu concerns. Let us imagine that one day a Muslim missionary

1. It became a monthly from July 1987 onwards.

arrives in a poor section of America such as a part of the Catholic Hispanic (Mexican origin) section of San Francisco. Well supplied with zeal and petro-dollars from his own country, he learns Spanish, builds a Muslim cathedral along the lines of a Catholic building, outfitting it with pews, organs, choirs and so forth. Preaching from a Christian Bible appropriately edited according to the Koran, he puts on the clerical collar and black robes of a Catholic priest and holds Sunday services which look just like Mass, except that prayers are to Allah and Mohammed instead of Jesus. In ministering to the local people, he tells them that his Islamic faith is just a slight variation of Christianity, one which puts the crowning touches on it. Their fathers' religion, Catholicism was, he says, flawed but it is a good preparation for Islam. He gives loans to those in need, which need not be repaid if one joins his Church. He opens an orphanage and raises the children as Muslims though their parents are Christians. When accused of deceiving the people, he says he is only adapting his religion to the local context and expressing his Muslim charity and divine call to evangelize."

Soon after this article appeared, an interesting dialogue developed, independently, on the character and role of these "experiments in cross-cultural communication" or "contemplative hermitages that revolve round both Christian and Hindu ideals." The Hindu point of view was presented by Swami Devananda Saraswati of Madras. Fr. Bede Griffiths himself came forward to present the Christian point of view.

The dialogue started when the *Indian Express* of Madras published on March 18, 1987, the summary of a talk which a Christian theologian, Dr. Robert Wayne Teasdale, had delivered on March 12. Describing Fr. Bede Griffiths as "Britain's appropriate gift to India", Dr. Teasdale had applauded the Saccidananda Ashram as "a place of dialogue reconciliation and experience in depth" between Christianity and Hinduism. Shantivanam, he had said, was "the peace capital of the world." Between March 25 and April 30, the newspaper published five letters from its Christian readers. Three of them supported Fr. Bede Griffiths' experiment with Hindu symbols and sacred texts; the other two opposed it as a pollution and a move unauthorised by the Vatican. Finally, Dr. Teasdale came out with a rejoinder which was published in the *Indian Express* of June 1, 1987. He praised Fr. Bede Griffiths for the latter's study of "the Vedas, the Upanishads, and the Gita as well as other texts sacred to the Hindu tradition", and explained that he (Fr. Bede) had adopted "elements of Hindu ritual and prayer not to 'produce his own mix' but rather to express the Christian faith in terms intelligible to Indians."

It was at this point that Swami Devananda wrote a letter to the *Indian Express*. "Ten years ago," he said, "I suggested to a papal nuncio that I might don a friar's habit and preach Hinduism in the Italian countryside. I was promptly warned that I would be charged with impersonating a cleric and public mischief, as Roman Catholicism was the protected state religion and in full control of Italian education. Hinduism is neither protected nor India's state religion and we find priests like Bede Griffiths in the garb of Hindu sannyasis preaching Christianity in the Tamil countryside... Bede Griffiths has no grasp at all of the Indian psyche. It must be brought to his attention that he is meddling with the soul of a very old and sophisticated people by continuing his experiments at Shantivanam."

The *Indian Express* did not publish this letter. But its copy which had been endorsed to Fr. Bede Griffiths, elicited from him a reply on June 17. "The ochre robe," he said, "is the sign of sannyasa and sannyasa according to ancient Hindu tradition signifies renunciation of all worldly ties, the transcendence of all 'dharmas', that is, all social bonds, whether social or religious... Today we feel more than ever the need to go beyond the limitations of the different religions and seek for the source of unity which can unite them in the service of humanity. This is how we understand sannyasa in our ashram and why we feel justified in wearing the ochre robe. I may say that in all my more than thirty years in India I have never before known a Hindu sannyasi object to this... We see in this one way of bridging the gulf between Hindus and Christians and working towards that unity among religions for which the world is looking today."

Swami Devananda replied on July 21. After explaining how "the sannyasin is the very embodiment of *Sanatana Dharma,*" he said, "The Church does not recognise a priest outside of the apostolic succession of Peter, and we do not recognise a priest outside the Hindu *parampara.* In that you are a Roman priest and a Benedictine monk, you cannot possibly be a sannyasin; it is verily a contradiction in terms... Christianity, from its very inception to today, has subsumed and subverted the deities, symbols, rituals and philosophies of the peoples it wishes to conquer. This activity which is imperial and not spiritual, must cease before hostilities and mistrust will die; hostilities, by the way, that we never invited in the first place. By trying to justify your position as it is now, you impugn Hinduism, slur sannyasa, rout reason, ruin meaning, mutilate categories, transpose symbols, deny sacred convention and usage, profane principles, philosophise, and generally present an argument that is oxymoronic."

Fr. Bede Griffiths wrote back on July 23: "You are anxious to establish Hinduism as a separate religion with its own unique doctrine and symbols which differentiate it from other religions. But most Hindus hold the opposite view and maintain with Ramakrishna and Vivekananda that all religions are essentially the same and differ only in accidental characteristics which can be ignored. I have myself difficulties in accepting this position but I would have said that it is the prevailing view among educated Hindus to-day...[2] Perhaps my chief quarrel with you is that you are trying to institutionalise Hinduism, to turn it into a sectarian religion, which seems to me to be the opposite of its true character. I feel that you do the same to Catholicism. That Catholicism has a strong institutional

---

2. This shows the mischief created by Mahatma Gandhi's and Ramakrishna Mission's slogan of *sarva-dharma-samabhāva*. It also shows the depravity of the missionary mind. Fr. Bede is not at all ashamed of using a doctrine to which he does not subscribe.

character I do not deny, but I would say that there is something in Catholicism which transcends its institutionalised character as there is in Hinduism and that is what matters... Our search today is to go beyond the institutional structure of religion and discover the hidden mystery which is at the heart of all religion. It is this that sannyasa means to me." He quoted in his support what Swami Abhishiktananda (Fr. Henri la Saux), another 'Christian sannyasin' and his predecessor in the Saccidananda Ashram, had written about sannyasa.

Swami Devananda replied on July 30: "I would like to give you the benefit of the doubt (as do many of my brothers). I am not able to do so because the inherent tolerance and secularism of Hinduism has been abused by your kind too long. I appreciate that you do not want a sectarian Hinduism, for that would directly threaten your own vested interests... Church motives are always suspect when they are not openly vicious, and the means she employs to further her own wicked ends has never had any relationship to the ideals she preaches at others. You have been in India long enough to know that we idolaters are more interested in what we see than what we hear. We want action, right action, not words... You preach the transcendence of religion but remain yourself an official of a sectarian religion... And not only are you a Roman priest, but the moment you get into trouble you run to mummy Church for financial, emotional, moral, psychological, and doctrinal aid. How is this foreign and first allegiance going to bring about the Indianisation of Christianity, much less the transcendence of religion? Yet you have the insolence to suggest that Hinduism not organise herself in her hour of need. You will teach us religious transcendence from the very pit of religious institutionalism, a pit we have not fallen into in 10,000 years. I think your motives are clear; indeed, the idea is worthy of a Jesuit! We will transcend our dharma and the Roman Church will happily reap the benefits of our foolishness, being already on the scene to fill in the void we leave behind us. If you were remotely serious about the spiritual ideals expressed in your letter, you would renounce the Church forthwith and humbly place yourself in the hands of God. Hinduism has always been a commonwealth of religious and spiritual institutions, some highly sectarian, though we have avoided the curse of centralisation. There are times when centralisation is justified, when the Hindus of conviction must work together for a common goal. This is not sectarianism; it is common sense. I do think Dayananda and Vivekananda would agree with me here. Shankara himself institutionalised sannyas for the same reason that the institution must be revitalised today : to protect dharma. We have always maintained and practised the spiritual ideal of transcending institutional limitations, and have succeeded where others have failed because our spiritual disciplines demand that the correct means be employed. The first injunction observed by all seekers is that they do not interfere with, bastardise, or destroy the culture, traditions, symbols, and religion that support them on their journey, even when they have passed beyond these institutions. And passing beyond these institutions does not mean meddling with them on the way. God has always given us reformers when we need them. Do you qualify, Bede Griffiths?"

Fr. Bede Griffiths wrote back on July 31: "It is clear from all you say that you are a fundamentalist.[3] Whether Hindu or Christian or Buddhist or Muslim, a fundamentalist is one who clings to the outward forms of religion and loses sight of the inner spirit... Nothing could be further from the spirit of the great Hindus of the past, Ramakrishna, Vivekananda, Mahatma Gandhi, Sri Aurobindo, Ramana Maharshi or Ramalinga Swamigal. They remained firmly Hindu in their religion but were open to the spirit of truth in Christianity and in all other religions. I consider myself a Christian in religion

3. The word 'fundamentalist' was in the air as a pejorative term at that time. All sorts of secularists were bandying it around without ever explaining as to what it meant. An official of the Catholic Church calling a Hindu sannyasin fundamentalist sounds like a Stalinist naming Mahatma Gandhi as 'fascist'.

but a Hindu in spirit, just as they were Hindus in religion while being Christian in spirit...[4] It is obvious that we differ fundamentally in our understanding both of Hinduism and of Christianity and indeed of religion in general, so I will not continue this correspondence."[5]

But Swami Devananda did not give up. He wrote on August 7 : "I had hoped that when you took refuge in humbug jargon, I would at least rate above a superstitious fundamentalist. Chinmayananda is often dubbed a communalist, and I was looking forward to some dramatic monotheistic curse like Great Satan or Antichrist... It remains that you have avoided every specific issue, with generalisations and specious philosophising; it remains that you exploit our tolerance, secularism, and hospitality; it remains that you abuse and pervert our symbols and traditions to your own motivated missionary ends... You have not transcended religion and you have no intention of doing so, whatever your pious declarations. You have an overriding ambition to subvert and subsume us with our own spiritual concepts, just as Paul subverted and subsumed the Greeks with their's. As you see parallels in history, so do we, and we are thus forearmed. We will not be meekly sold down the river like Constantine !... I am not the protector of Sanatana Dharma; Narayana is the only protector of Dharma. This is an awful truth for you to admit, Bede Griffiths, and one that neither you nor I will escape."

The dialogue remained at a standstill for some days. It was resumed after Swami Devananda had studied the writings of Fr. J. Monchanin, the founder of the Saccidananda Ashram, who also had taken to the ochre robe and named himself Swami Param Arubi Anandam. He had written frankly and in a straightforward manner that Christianity should use Hindu philosophy and cultural forms in order to subvert

4. In this instance, Fr. Bede illustrates the Christian maxim of the Devil quoting the scripture.

5. The Christian missionary is always quick to run away from a dialogue if it does not develop as per rules laid down by him.

Hinduism. Swami Devananda brought these writings to the notice of Fr. Bede Griffiths. "I discover," he wrote on August 27, "that his writings directly confirm my suspicions about your motives and activities in India... This being the case, you have no moral authority to address or advise seekers of Truth."

Fr. Bede Griffiths replied on August 31: "Of course, if I held the same view as Father Monchanin, you would be justified in suspecting me of deception. But you must remember that Father Monchanin was writing forty years ago and immense changes have taken place in the Church since then. The Vatican Council introduced a new understanding of the relation of the Church to other religions and all of us have been affected by this. Swami Abhishiktananda (Fr. le Saux) in particular early separated himself from Fr. Monchanin, especially after his profound experience with Raman Maharshi at Tiruvanamalai...[6] You must realise also that the view which I hold is not peculiar to me. It is approved by the authorities of the Church both in India and in Rome. Many Catholics, of course, will not agree with it, but the understanding of the relation of the Church to other religions is only slowly growing and there are many different views in the Church today."

Swami Devananda's reply which he wrote on September 7, deserves to be quoted at some length. He said:

> There is no evidence that the Church has changed her wicked ways in the last forty years. On the contrary, since the checks placed on the Church by the British were

---

6. Here Fr. Bede was lying with a straight face. His writings as well as those of Fr. le Saux, penned years after the Vatican II, leave no doubt that they shared the strategy of Fr. Monchanin. The cat has now been brought out of the bag by no less a person than Raimundo Panikkar, the guru of the current mission strategy in India. Speaking at a seminar in Lyons, France, held on April 5-7, 1995, he said, "Monchanin is, with Le Saux, the founder of Shantivanam. Shantivanam lives on today in the tradition of the Trinity transmitted by its two founders and the last guru of the ashram, Father Bede Griffiths" (*Bulletin of the Abhishiktananda Society*, No. 17, January 1996, p. 115).

removed, she has been busy making hay in our tolerant secular sunshine. The methods of conversion have changed, but the Church's ancient ambition for world dominion has not changed. The Pope himself contributes over fifty million dollars a year towards missionary work worldwide, and this does not include the vaster sums of money available to Christian evangelists of all persuasions for their so-called charities. What has happened in the Church is that the term 'heathen' has been changed to 'non-Christian' (with the prayer that the 'non' will soon disappear). There have also been some unctuous platitudes uttered about our spiritual heritage at official functions. Rome, in her eternal conceit, thinks we will accept the facelift at face value and not probe into the heart of the person who wears the mask. This presumption itself is an example of patronising Christian arrogance. If the Church had in fact changed her ways then the dirty work of converting our poor and humble masses to Christianity would have long ago ceased!...

You do not need Church sanction to experiment with Hindu traditions and symbols or call yourself a sannyasin. You do need — and refuse to seek — the sanction of traditional Hindu authorities. Hindus do not recognise Church decrees vis-a-vis acts that affect them and their religious culture. Your declarations of Church approval is part bluff, part appeal. As we do not permit you to stand on our head, you seem to think we will permit the Church to stand there instead. This is exactly the message your bastard symbol of Omkara and cross conveys to us. We utterly reject both the symbol and the message...

Except as a psychological curiosity, I am no more interested in your personal beliefs than I am in those held by the political commissar at the local Russian consulate. Like him, you will argue that my beliefs compel me to respect your beliefs and thus accept your actions, even if they are detrimental to my traditions. I am very interested in your actions and how they affect Hinduism, and I do not accept them. I have said this before and it is what lies at the heart of my letters. In reply, you manifest that syndrome the Germans call *vorbeireden,* translated as 'talking-past-the-point'. This is a tactic to avoid contact with relevant issues. It often involves deceit and/ or self-deceit; but it does not mean that you misunderstand the situation. It is a verbose device to circumvent truth; and this, I concede sadly, is exactly what you have done. I really think it is time for some serious introspection.

I have read *Christ in India:* your expressed attitudes and ambitions for us are little different from Monchanin's."

In his book, *Christ in India*, written in 1966 and reprinted in 1986, only an year before this dialogue took place, Fr. Bede Griffiths had left no one in doubt that Hindu philosophies and cultural forms were to be used for conveying Christianity. Only his language was less straightforward than that of Fr. Monchanin. So was the language of Fr. Henry le Saux who was the successor of Fr. Monchanin at Saccidanand Ashram and who went about as Swami Abhishiktananda, proclaiming that he had reconciled Hinduism and Christianity in his experience of the Advaita!

A few more letters were exchanged. Finally, Fr. Bede Griffiths insisted on his right to use the Hindu symbol, OM, in his letter dated October 16. He said, "Of course, Om is by no means confined to Hinduism. It is found in Buddhism as well. Would you like to write to the Dalai Lama and tell him to stop the Tibetan people from using their most sacred mantra; Om mani padma hum?"[7]

Swami Devananda replied on October 21: "Apparently you know as little about Buddhism as you do about Hinduism, both of which are Sanatana Dharma. They have the same roots and traditions and usages and a mutual spiritual ideal that goes far beyond their differences. This is not true of the

---

7. Strictly speaking, "Om" is not a symbol but a *mantra*. It has, however, become one in usage over the last 20-30 years to identify Hinduism.

Semitic ideologies, which by their own definition, claim to be superior, unique and exclusive. Voltaire warned of these closed creeds when he wrote: 'The man who says to me, Believe as I do or God will damn you, will presently say to me, Believe as I do or I will kill you.' Think about this carefully, Father Bede, for you are the ordained representative of one of these creeds. And you seem to know even less about *mantra* than you do about Sanatana Dharma."

This dialogue about Christian missionaries masquerading as Hindu sannyasins continued, off and on, in the columns of the *Indian Express* of Madras. Some Hindus showed awareness of the true character of Christianity and its missionary methods. Others saw no harm in Christian missionaries taking to the ochre robe and using Hindu symbols in their worship; they felt that this was the way for the two religions to come together and work for common good. Goodwill, however, is no substitute for knowledge. And that is what most of our men of goodwill seem to lack. They will do well by reading some of the books in which Christian missionaries have expounded their strategies.

The article in *Hinduism Today* and the dialogue between Swami Devananda and Fr. Bede Griffiths alerted me, and made me look up the literature on Indigenisation (Acculturation) and the Christian Ashram Movement. Here I hit pay-dirt as they say in detective stories. The literature was quite frank about missionary intentions. I was now equipped to quote chapter and verse in proof of the stark truth that Indigenisation was no more than a mission strategy calculated to rope in Hindu philosophies, Hindu schools of Bhakti, and Hindu cultural forms in the service of Christianity. The Christian Ashram Movement, I discovered, was a predatory enterprise inaugurated in the early years of the seventeenth century by an abominable scoundrel, Robert Di Nobili of the Society of Jesus, who had masqueraded as a Brahmana from Rome, who had claimed to be in possession of the lost Yajurveda, and who had succeeded in baptising some Hindus before he was found out. The very fact that this scoundrel became and had remained the patron saint of Indigenisation was speaking volumes about its true character. Starting with Fr. Monchanin of the Saccidananda Ashram at Shantivanam, Fr. Henri le Saux and Fr. Bede Griffiths were in the same game. The book, *Christ in India*, by Bede Griffiths was giving a call which was loud and clear, namely, that Hindu civilization was to be taken over by 'Hindu Christians' as the 'Greek Fathers' of the Church had taken over the Greek civilization.

The outcome of this research on my part was a book, *Catholic Ashrams: Adopting and Adapting Hindu Dharma*, published by VOICE OF INDIA in 1988. It included four articles from *Hinduism Today* and the dialogue between Swami Devananda Saraswati and Fr. Bede Griffiths. A Preface was provided by me, documenting the Indigenisation strategy in some detail from impeccable Christian sources. Hindu readers found the book revealing. Christian missionary circles, on the other hand, felt upset. Christian Ashrams had been functioning so far without any fear of Hindus knowing their true character. Now on, they had the feeling that they were being watched by a vigilant Hindu society. Fr. Griffiths' stock fell even in Christian circles. The number of visitors to his 'Ashram' declined. He had been found out.

I happened to be the Treasurer of the Abhishiktananda Society in Delhi for a number of years. I had joined the Society at a time when I believed that the talk about Hindu-Christian dialogue was sincere. Now that I had exposed it as a strategy, my Christian friends in the Society felt pained, particularly at what I had written about Abhishiktananda after whom the Society was named. They tried to convince me that although Abhishiktananda had started as a missionary, he had changed in later years. One of them, Vandana Mataji who runs a Christian Ashram at Rishikesh and has written a book on the subject, protested, politely in my presence but vehemently elsewhere. It became her wont to describe me as a 'Hindu fundamentalist' in Christian publications in this country and abroad. I was also attacked as a 'Hindu fundamentalist' by a Catholic lady writer in a book published in Belgium in 1990. Some other notices of the same kind were reported by friends in a few other countries.

There was another sequel to the Devananda-Griffiths dialogue in early 1990. Shri Ram Swarup has the laudable habit of erring on the side of generosity. He had a distinct feeling that Swami Devananda and I had been unnecessarily hard on Fr. Bede Griffiths — Swami Devananda in his letters and I in my Preface to the book —, and that the man was after all not that bad. So he decided to try out Fr. Bede on his own. He sent to Fr. Bede a copy of his review of *The Myth of Christian Uniqueness: Towards a Pluralistic Theology of Religion* edited by John Hick and Paul F. Knitter and published in the USA in 1988. The review had appeared in *The Statesman* on 14 January 1990.

Fr. Bede thanked Ram Swarup in a letter dated 17 February 1990 and offered a few comments. "This openess to other religions," he said, "has always been present in Christianity from the beginning, though the opposite attitude of rejection has generally prevailed. The Bible itself, though it became more and more exclusive, always had an opening for the 'Gentiles'... The God of Izrael was always conceived as the God of all humanity, although interest centres more and more exclusively on Izrael. In the same way Jesus in the New Testament goes out of his way to proclaim the presence of God among other nations..." He also struck a personal note as he wrote, "When I was received into the Catholic Church in 1930 it was this belief in the presence of God among all nations that I accepted. Still I admit that it was rare and it was only at the Vatican Council in 1960 that it was officially acknowledged by the Church. For me this was only the formal acceptance of what I have always believed and practised." He concluded by saying that "we all have to learn how to be true to our own religion while we are critical of its limitations and to be equally true to the values of other religions while we recognize their limitations."

Ram Swarup replied on 31 March 1990 and commented

that Fr. Bede's "personal history is not merely interesting but it encourages me to make a personal confession." He went on to relate how he, like "all or most Hindus", had started by believing that "all religions say the same things", but had to "reflect deeply on the subject" after going through the following, among other books:

1. *The Encyclopaedia of Religions and Ethics* in 12 volumes.

2. Proceedings of a Seminar "held at Almora by Christians" most of whom were "connected with 'Ashrams' and 'Niketans'."

3. A book by Fr. Monchanin, the founder of Sccidananda Ashram, Shantivanam.

"It was my first contact with 'liberal' Christianity," proceeded Ram Swarup, "and I thought it was the old missionary 'war with other means'. After twelve years or so I wrote an article on 'liberal' Christianity. I am sending a copy of this article... I find that it also mentions you briefly." At the same time, Ram Swarup drew Fr. Bede's attention to how mainstream Christianity was continuing to wage a relentless war against other religions while maintaining the pretence of studying those religions and holding a dialogue with them. "They talk of 'dialogues' but they are determined that their victims should reach the same conclusions as they do. Their means are flexible, but their aims are fixed. The situation and the truth of the matter demands that we look, not on their arguments but on their mind." He enclosed another article with his letter. It was his review of *Seven Hundred Plans to Evangelize the World: The Rise of Global Evangelization Movement* by David B. Barrett and James W. Reapsome published in 1989 by the AD_2000 Series. The review had appeared in *The Statesman* dated 25 March 1990.

Fr. Bede was quick to come out in his true colours. "I am not quite sure," he barked in his letter of 6 April 1990, "what your purpose is in your attack on Christianity and Christian Missions. Is it simply to foment communal strife in India between Christians and Hindus, or have you some deeper purpose? If you want to attack Christianity itself, you will have to make a far deeper study of it than you have yet done. Above all you have to recognise the profound wisdom and goodness to be found in it, as all unbiased Hindus have done..."

I too had had some correspondence with Fr. Bede in 1988 before the first edition of *Catholic Ashrams* was published. I had found that the Father did not want Hindus to look into missionary methods but concentrate on the "evils in Hindu society" instead. In his reply of 6 April 1990 to Ram Swarup, Fr. Bede referred to this correspondence and said, "I suggested to Mr. Sita Ram Goel that you should both make a study of the shady side of Hinduism if you want to be honest... How do you account for the fact that with all its long tradition of wisdom and spirituality, India today is generally considered one of the most corrupt and immoral countries in the world?... I suggested to Mr. Goel that the Voice of India might well make a special study of various aspects of Hinduism. I suggested as a beginning the history of human sacrifice and temple prostitution from the earliest times to the present day... Another institution is the practice of sorcery and magic... Above all, of course, there is the problem of untouchability. Surely one of the greatest crimes in the history of religion. These things should be known and faced by those who defend Hinduism..."

It was the old story once again. The Christian missionary was telling the Hindus, "Please keep on with self-flagellation and breast-beating about the wicked society in which you live. We will take care of your salvation." In other words, the bandit wanted his victim to look the other way so that he could occupy the latter's house. The ruse had succeeded eminently. A whole battery of Hindu-baiters had come forward to play the Christian missionary's game. Some of them were employed by the missionary apparatus, while most of them were doing voluntary service to the same racket. It had become their whole time occupation to keep Hindus on the defensive, while the Christian missionary reaped his harvest of converts. It never occurred to these knaves and fools that the Christian missionary whom they were aping and helping was viewed in the modern West as a maniac whom it was better to dump abroad with a bag of money.

Fr. Bede had sent to Ram Swarup with his first letter of 17 February 1991 a copy of his Hibbert Lecture delivered in 1989. Ram Swarup had been impressed by it. But now he was face to face with a different Fr. Bede. He acknowledged Fr. Bede's letter of April 6 in his own letter of April 24, and wrote. "It is so different from your Hibbert Lecture which probably presented a more formal and public face, while the letter revealed a more conventional traditional-Christian or missionary visage. It was surprising that it took so little to surface so readily." Fr. Bede's accusation that Ram Swarup's articles were aimed at creating "communal strife between Christians and Hindus" was pinned down by him as "the language of blackmail and even threat to which Hindus are often subjected when they show any sign of stir."

He proceeded to point out that Fr. Bede had said "not a word" about "missionary Christianity, its theology, its apparatus and plans" with which the articles sent to him had dealt. "As a missionary," conceded Ram Swarup, "probably you think that the missionary apparatus is innocent and indeed we should be thankful to it for the spiritual aid it offers." At the same time he asked, "Why do you put on hurt looks if they [Hindus] do not take this apparatus at its Christian face value and look at it in the light of historical evidence and their own experience?"

Coming to Fr. Bede's advice that Ram Swarup had to "make a far deeper study" of Christianity in order to discover "the profound wisdom and goodness in it", Ram Swarup observed that he had studied Christianity for quite some time and from its most orthodox sources. "I must admit that to a scholar like you, my studies of Christianity must appear to be inadequate particularly when they have not led me to your conclusions. But I must beg you to take into consideration scores of others of impeccable Christian scholarship, whose scholarship is at least as good as your own, who have failed to find that 'profound wisdom and goodness' claimed by you in Christianity. On the contrary, they found in it arrogance, exclusive claims, contentious spirit, superstitions, lack of charity. Other scholars found that whatever was good and true in Christianity was found in other cultures and traditions as well but whatever was claimed to be special and unique to it — like virgin birth, resurrection, sole Sonship — was just make-believe and not of much worth..."

There was nothing new in Fr. Bede's charge that India today is generally considered one of the most corrupt and immoral countries in the world. "I have no means," commented Ram Swarup, "of ranking India in the moral scale, but I can readily believe that its place in the missionary world you inhabit must be very low, and it must also be low wherever the missionary influence reaches." Missionaries had been painting India black for several centuries. "Vivekananda had spoken of the mud which missionaries have thrown on India, an amount which not all the mud in the ocean-bed will equal." Many Christian networks in the USA at present were singing the same tune. Pat Robertson, a presidential candidate in the USA in 1989, had said, "Satan, beasts, demons. Destruction of soul in hell. That is what Hinduism is all about." Dayspring International had described India as "without spiritual hope" and quoted Mother Teresa as saying that Hindus were hungering for Jesus Christ.

Regarding Fr. Bede's advice about studies to be undertaken by VOICE OF INDIA, Ram Swarup wondered as to what was to be their scope. "Would the proposed study of human sacrifice, for example, include religions in which human sacrifice and even cannibalism form the central part of their theology and where they celebrate them daily in their most sacred rites?... Will it cover temple prostitutes, male and female, at Jerusalem often mentioned in the Bible?

Will it include nunneries and monasteries, and the whole system of 'consecration of virgins' where the morals are often described, not always without documentation, in the language you use for the Devadasi system?... You want a study of 'sorcery and magic'... You must be knowing that the first Christians pastors were known to be magicians and exorcists and that every church had its exorcists. Even now exorcism is central to baptism... John Wesley, the founder of Methodists, said that 'giving up witchcraft is in effect giving up the Bible'."

Finally, Ram Swarup informed Fr. Bede that VOICE OF INDIA "cannot undertake studies, you have proposed" and that Christian missionaries should stop dictating how Hindus should look at themselves. "Too often the missionaries have set our agenda for us. They taught us how to look at ourselves through their eyes. What they found wrong with us, we found wrong with ourselves. Voice of India wants that Hindus use their own eyes in looking at themselves and — also in looking at others."

Fr. Bede chose not to reply to Ram Swarup's letter and carry the dialogue further. He was not the first Christian missionary nor likely to be the last to run away when faced with stark facts and straight logic. But one thing must have become clear to him, namely, that Hindus were no more in a mood to take it lying down, and that Hindus had started seeing through the patent game of a predatory ideologies masquerading as religion.

Christian missionaries like Fr. Bede Griffiths have been trained in and practised double-think and double-speak for so long that they seem to know no more the difference between honesty and deceit. Their writings on mission strategy leave no doubt that they are out to undo Hinduism. But in their tactical writings, particularly in Hindu journals, they pretend to be better Hindus than the Hindus themselves. They themselves remain tied, hand and foot, to closed dogmas and authoritarian institutions. Yet they call upon Hindus to transcend everything and ascend into a startosphere where anything can mean anything. They themselves do not believe that all religions say the same things. Yet they try to silence Hindus by presenting this proposition. Readers of the earlier dialogues in this book know what Sri Ramakrishna, Swami Vivekananda and Mahatma Gandhi stood for. Yet our Bede Griffiths will have us believe that these great Hindus endorsed Christianity in the same way as they did Hinduism. A creed which breeds such dubious and double-faced characters raises many questions for which Hindus will have to find adequate answers.

The exchange between Ram Swarup and Fr. Bede Griffiths was included in the second and enlarged editions of *Catholic Ashrams* published in 1994. Meanwhile, more letters to the editor on the subject of Christian Ashrams and the mission strategy of Indigenisation had come to our notice. They were also included in the new compilation. The subtitle of the publication was changed from *Adopting and Adapting Hindus Dharma* to *Sannyasins or Swindlers?* to make it more appropriate.

20

A Hornet's Nest

One wonders whether it is a virtue or vice, but the Christian missionaries have been and remain compulsive record-keepers and plan-publishers. By now there are literally hundreds of thousands of publications providing details of what the Christian missions did or plan to do, where, to whom, in which manner and with what resources in money and manpower. "Each year," says a recent publication on the subject, "some 10,000 new books and articles on mission and evangelization are published, involving seventy or so major languages."[1] Besides, we have well-researched and thoroughly documented studies produced mostly by Western scholars, many of them believing Christians, on the spread of Christianity in the past. The story is blood-soaked. In America, Asia and Africa, Christianity has been an unashamed and active accomplice of Western imperialism.

The pious Christians who read this material do not question the validity of the Christian Mission. Nor do they bother their conscience with the morality of means employed by the soldiers of Christ. All they notice and care for is that so many heathens were 'saved' in the past and are expected to be 'saved' in the future. It never occurs to them that the heathens may question the validity of the Christian Mission itself and/or find fault with the means employed. They have a stock and ready reply to such questioning and objections: "According to our scriptures which are inspired, our divine saviour commanded us to teach and preach, and we cannot disobey him."

---

1. David B. Barrett and James W. Reapsome, *Seven Hundred Plans to Evangelize the World,* Birmingham, Alabama, U.S.A., 1988.

Now, anybody is free to write in a book what he pleases; all it costs is paper and ink. He is also free to believe that whatever has been written comes from a divine source; all he needs is renunciation of reason and a large dose of credulity. Again, he is free to convince himself that he is the better person and in a position to teach others; all he needs is self-righteousness combined with a certain amount of dense smugness. The trouble arises when he expects the others to agree with him and let him mount an aggression.

The Oxford University Press had published in 1982 the *World Christian Encyclopaedia* edited by David B. Barrett, "an ordained missionary of the Church of England, served 29 years in Africa, since 1970 an Anglican research officer." Ram Swarup reviewed this book in *The Times of India* dated 14 July 1985 under the caption 'Thy Kingdom in the Third World'.[2] He gave credit to Dr. Barrett for being "a quantifier and statistician *par excellence*" because "since the beginning of Christianity, every soul, dead and living, has been accounted for" and "a statistical picture of the Last Day of Judgement, of the souls that will be finally saved and finally damned" has been provided. But he refused to accept Dr. Barrett as "an impartial historian or a disinterested philosopher" because "he looks at everything from a missionary viewpoint." He cited the facts and figures compiled by Dr. Barrett to show how "the poor countries of the Third World which have been politically dominated till recently continue to be the special targets of missionary activities." The missions, he said, were concentrating on Third World countries because Christianity was losing heavily in Europe, North America, Australia and New Zealand. Dr. Barrett had tried to cover up this retreat at home and aggression elsewhere by stating that "the centre of gravity of Christianity is shifting from Europe and America to the Third World."

Christian readers of the newspaper were shocked. This

2. The review article is included in *Catholic Ashrams: Sannyasins or Swindlers?*, New Delhi, 1994, Appendix III, pp. 215-23.

was certainly a novel way of looking at the Christian missions. Hitherto the prevalent Hindu fashion had been to applaud the missions for the "great educational, medical and humanitarian services rendered by them." That is how Mother Teresa had been made into a myth. One could, of course, add in a footnote that it would have been better if the missions had done "all that splendid work without attempts at conversion." The missions disavowed this "undeserved accusation" and the "controversy" stood closed. This time, however, a dialogue looked like taking off. Only *The Times of India* editor did not allow it. Instead he published a few articles in praise of the Christian missions in order to redress the balance.

A dialogue in the columns of *The Times of India*, however, developed when Ram Swarup reviewed on March 13-14, 1988 another Christian publication, *Mission Handbook: North American Ministries Overseas*, published in the U.S.A. in 1986. The review was captioned 'Christianity for Export: God's Legionaries' and consisted for the most part of facts and figures which were given in the publication and which told their own story.[3] It quoted towards the end another publication (1980) in which a Christian missionary had asked the question as to why the missions had failed with the Buddhists of Burma and the Hindus of India when a single missionary had succeeded in converting 7000 animistic Karens within a few years. Ram Swarup posed a counter-question: "Thanks to the powerful missionary lobby in the United Nations, its universal declaration of human rights (1948) states that every individual has a right to embrace the religion or belief of his choice. But is there to be no charter that declares that countries and cultures and peoples of tolerant philosophies and religions who believe in live and let live, too, have a right of protection against aggressive, systematic proselytising? Are its well-drilled legionaries to have a free field?" Little did he know that he had raised a hornet's nest as was evident from

---

3. The review article is included in *Ibid.*, as Appendix IV, pp. 224-32.

the Christian response published by *The Times of India*.

In his letter published on April 1, 1988, Mr. Kuruvilla Chandy of Lucknow doubted "whether quotations have been verbatim and entire" and regretted that "it is also not clear in all cases what are the sources of the various 'facts and figures' given." He said that Christian missions need not "take cover under the Universal Declaration of Human Rights" because "there exists a fundamental right to propagate one's faith." The Constitution of India, he said, had also guaranteed this fundamental right in its Article 25. Religious proselytisation, he pointed out, was no different from that which "is constantly taking place in the realm of politics and commerce" where "the use of fraud is proverbial and even considered normal." He also accused the Government of India of practising proselytisation in favour of Hinduism by refusing to extend to the converts from scheduled castes and tribes the reservations and concessions that they enjoyed so long as they remained Hindus.[4]

In another letter published on the same date, Fr. L. F. Jose of New Delhi was "constrained to disagree with the tone and aim of the articles." He accused the reviewer of having "conveniently forgotten the fact that Christianity is an Oriental religion and Christ and his disciples were Oriental Jews." He asserted that "Christianity came to India even before Europe had heard about it" and that "the St. Thomas Christians of

---

4. While converting Hindus from scheduled castes and tribes, the Christian plea was that the 'Hindu caste system' did not allow them to improve their social and economic status. But the converts found out very soon that conversion to Christianity had in no way improved their position. In fact, they found themselves in a worse plight after leaving their ancestral society. The Christian missionaries forgot their earlier cliches about the 'Hindu caste system keeping some castes and tribes down and out'. They started a campaign that the benefits of reservations and the rest available to Hindu Harijans should be extended to 'Christian Harijans' as well. The campaign is bearing fruit. According to *The Times of India* dated 28 August 1995, "A consesus among political parties is emerging in favour of reservations for the 12 million dalits who form over a half of the country's Christian population and the government of India is under increasing pressure to amend Para Three of Presidential order of 1950..."

Kerala have a two-thousand year old history." Moreover, the latter-day Catholic and Protestant missionaries had "realised their folly and the thrust today is on 'inculturation,' etc."

Mr. K. N. Ninan of Bombay did not bother about facts or figures or logic. He went straight into the motives of the reviewer and pleaded against publication of such articles. "Mr. Ram Swarup's articles on Christianity," he said in his letter published on April 4, "show that he has an axe to grind against Christians and Christianity. This has also been evident from his previous regular, if sporadic, Christian-baiting treatises published in your daily. How can you afford to waste such precious space on crass irreverence born of frustration by a confirmed Christian-hater? Does this not amount to alienating the peaceful Christian community which has been doing invaluable work in the fields of education, medical care and social welfare, and which work has profited mainly the majority community?"[5]

In his letter published on April 7, Mr. John Vallamattam, President, Indian Catholic Press Association, found it painful that such articles should be published "at a time when there is so much talk of the need for communal harmony and inter-religious collaboration." He, however, granted goodwill to the writer out of "Christian charity" and hoped that the article would "help Christian communities to rid themselves of whatever is questionable in them." He promised to bring the article "to the attention of the concerned authorities in the Churches."

In his letter published on April 8, Mr. K. C. Thomas of Mugma (Bihar) accused the reviewer of having "collected a

5. The plea that information which is inconvenient to Christianity should not be published comes easily to Christian scribes and scholars. Christianity has had a long history of suppressing freedom of expression, and criminal persecution of those who do not toe the line of this or that church. In fact, the Christian bark becomes all the more ferocious if this part of Christianity's dark history is brought to public notice. It is very difficult for minds trained in totalitarian ways to appreciate facts and figures which go against their case. They do not like it at all that the skeletons in their cupboard be brought out and exposed to public gaze.

lot of questionable data in support of his view." The review was likely to find support among the "communal elements" in the majority community. "Export-oriented enterprises," he said, "are favoured by the government. Would our learned columnist be satisfied if the same export policy was enforced in the cases of Christianity and/or other minority religions in India? It might please the majority fundamentalist who cries wolf saying 'Hinduism is in danger'."

It was perhaps in keeping with the promise made by Mr. John Vallamatam that Mr. T. C. Joseph wrote an article, 'Is Christianity to Blame?', which was published on April 9. He thought that while Ram Swarup was "generous with statistics" his knowledge of Indian Church history was inadequate. The Church in India had not been helped by the British rulers who had "adhered to a strict policy of religious neutrality." It was not Ram Swarup's business to sympathise with the Latin Americans for the loss of their ancient faiths; the Latin Americans knew better what was good for them. The 6.2 million converts made in Africa every year was "no big number in a land of 500 million people." Nor was it significant that Hindus and Jains had lost 324,500 members to Christianity between 1970 and 1980; if Christianity was to make headway in India, it needed 15 million converts every year for the next hundred years. Christianity could not be blamed if "many of the lower castes" found in it "the opportunity to opt for a religion that freed them from the stigmas that stuck."[6] To see a Christian missionary behind "a separatist movement somewhere in the country is only a search for scapegoats." Mother Teresa and the missionary organisations had "to elicit compassion and solicit funds" by advertisements in the Western media because "India or, for that matter, any country in the Third World" was not "competent enough to look after its poor,

---

6. See footnote 4 above about the lower caste converts being 'freed' from the stigmas sticking to them while they were members of Hindu society. It is not unoften that 'Christian Harijans' are seen taking out demonstrations in protest against their plight in the various Christian churches.They held a demonstration when the Pope visited Madras in 1986.

sick or illiterate." The argument that "these services help in evangelisation" was "wafer-thin." He suspected that Ram Swarup had read "anti-Christian" books. He concluded by advising Ram Swarup "to search for the truth, and nothing but the truth, and read books of a different kind which too abound."

In his letter published on April 13, Mr. C. J. Chadwin of Chandigarh expressed "dismay at your editorial policy in allowing the publication of a skimpy and irresponsible article." He said that "two odd quotations lifted out of context from the Bible cannot purport to be the full and exact position of the Church universal." He admitted that in the past imperialistic powers had misused the Christian missions to serve their own interests. But that did not mean that "the basic aim of the missionaries worldwide and that of the Christian faith is to subdue peoples and cultures." The Church was actively involved in the "liberation of people in South America from dictatorships, in South Africa from the racist white regime and all over the world in liberation struggles of socially and economically oppressed people." Mother Teresa "never sought funds for conversion." She was only showing the "love of God in that dying and destitute whom we throw on the streets may have a chance to live and die with dignity."[7]

A Muslim from Indonesia, Mr. Ishtiyaque Danish, joined the dialogue at this stage. In his letter published on April 13, he said that Ram Swarup's article had "failed to throw enough light on how the huge amount of money is being used by the Christian missionaries." He continued, "No religion in the world permits or encourages its adherents to buy converts to

7. Christians never ask or allow to be asked the basic question as to how the people in Asia, Africa and South America became socially and economically depressed or the destitutes whom Mother Teresa is trying to 'help'. But history tells us that these people who were free and prosperous were reduced to this state by Western Imperialism of which the Christian missions were the most willing and vociferous accomplices everywhere. Break a person's bones and then come back with bandages and some gruel — that is the logic. Mother Teresa happens to be the foremost in this dirty and despicable Christian game.

their faith. But this is precisely what the Christian missionaries have been doing across the globe... I have no firm evidence if missionaries are involved in conversion-by-dollar business in India but this method is being practised in Indonesia on a wide scale. In an article contributed to a Christian-Muslim dialogue consultation held in 1976, Prof. Muhammed Rasjidi had remarked that 'the Church distributes rice, clothes and money among the poor people and uses these things to bring them closer to their mission. The Church lends money or natural manures and seeds to impoverished peasants on condition that they send their children to missionary schools... Distribution of water pumps, seeds of cloves and coconuts etc. is also being used to serve the same purpose... They (missionaries) shower gifts and provide certain facilities to isolated tribes. Then they put up a show of a census and ask these people to get themselves registered as Christians.'"

In a joint letter published on April 18, five Hindu readers from Delhi commented that none of the Christian correspondents had "controverted his [Ram Swarup's] data or argument or even kept to the subject"; instead, all of them had indulged in "irrelevant claims and unfounded allegations." They found Ram Swarup "highly informative and full of perspective." He embodied, they said, "a rare phenomenon in Indian journalism, indeed, on the Indian scene." He was "no hater of Christians." What had disturbed "certain well-organised, highly articulate and influential but hostile quarters" was the fact that he was "no hater of India and its age-long culture and religion and history." He had, however, "a vast audience which benefits by his writings and welcomes them." They looked forward to reading him more often in the columns of *The Times of India*.

Another letter published on the same day was from Harish Chandra of Delhi who said that history offered evidence opposite to the claims made by the Christian correspondents. He cited Pitrim Sorokin who had said, "During the past few centuries the most belligerent, the most aggressive, the most rapacious, the most power-drunk section of humanity has been precisely the Christian western world. During these centuries western Christendom has invaded all other continents; its armies followed by its priests and merchants have subjugated, robbed or pillaged most of the non-Christians. Native American, African, Australian, Asiatic populations have been subjugated to this peculiar brand of Christian 'love' which has generally manifested itself in pitiless destruction, enslavement, coercion, destruction of the cultural values, institutions, the way of life of the victims and the spread of alcoholism, venereal disease, commercial cynicism and the like." Small wonder, said Harish Chandra, that Christianity "was now trying to deny its imperialist link and claim for itself a brand-new identity."

Simultaneously, Anna Sujatha Mathai of Delhi called Ram Swarup's article "amazingly small-minded" and "petty visioned." She wondered why it had been given "the importance and space it did get." She claimed that Christianity stood for "loving your neighbour as yourself" while such articles "only add fuel to the already raging fires of violence and hate." She hoped that "Ram Swarup, a Christian hater, may like St. Paul who also hated Christians, one day be forced to face the blinding, dazzling truth of Christ's compassionate love."

Mr. S. G. Mampilli of Delhi said in his letter published on April 19, that the Constitution of India which gave protection to the Christian missions for propagating their faith had given the same right to the Hindus. Hindus, however, "are not willing to make sacrifices for sharing the treasures of their religion with people of other religions." Missionary work, according to him, was "a holy vocation for people who willingly choose it on the basis of their life-long commitment to chastity, the spirit of obedience and poverty which they joyfully accept and maintain till death." Christ had suffered and died and risen again from the dead "so that sinners may be saved from the circle of births, 'Punarjanm', as it is called in Hinduism." Ram Swarup had "intentionally ignored the positive side" in his "anxiety to expose the negative side of missionary work." Christianity had "an import aspect" besides its "export aspect." The people of India imported Christianity because "they were not satisfied with social evils like the caste system, untouchability, sati, child marriage, backwardness of women and so on which have no sanction in Christianity."

In his letter published on April 25, Judah S. G. Vincent of Delhi found Ram Swarup very successful "as a Christian baiter." He saw in Ram Swarup a "putative scholar" who had written a "one-sided article on what is obviously esoteric material" published by the "U.S. based Christian organisation *World Vision*." Christianity, he said, had a message for "a caste-ridden, superstition-bound, self-flagellating society." The missionaries were delivering that message through "their efforts at education, medicare and the like." Mr. Danish was right in saying that "it is abominable to buy converts." But he should know that "quite often the missionaries feel the need to support the nascent Christians materially for the reason that indigent people from the backward classes lose their special privileges under the constitution the moment they shift their allegiance to Christ." Thus, Mr. Vincent confirmed what Mr. Danish had only suspected.

Finally, in an article published on May 3, Mr. Sarto Esteves advised that "one should not go to a commercial handbook or a money-spinning publication to know the doctrine and teaching of Christ." Christianity should be learnt from the Bible where Christ himself was speaking to mankind. India should be glad that she had a Church organisation of 120 dioceses "manned by full-blooded, highly patriotic sons of India as bishops" and topped by two Cardinals. "Over 12,000 male priests and 50,000 religious women were running "institutes of higher learning, colleges, schools, hospitals, dispensaries, houses for the aged, the dying, the deserted and the rejected, orphanages, leprosaria, and asylums, to mention only a few." Liberation theology was being misunderstood. It only meant what Christ taught his followers long ago, namely, "to feed the hungry, clothe the naked, shelter the homeless, love one's enemies, offer the other cheek also to the one who strikes you."[8] This was the mission which "a minority which comprises 1.7 per cent of the total population of India" had undertaken.

Ram Swarup considered the points raised by the Christians and wrote a reply, 'Proselytisation as it is Practised', which was published in two instalments on May 23-24. "I did not realise," he said, "I was stirring a hornet's nest in reviewing the Mission Handbook. It invoked many rejoinders, most of them harsh. It helps inter-faith dialogue which the Church has recently invited." He found it interesting, though novel, that Mr. Kuruvilla Chandy had compared Christian proselytisation with proselytisation in politics. That is exactly what it was, with the difference that the Church had "always regarded it as a one-way traffic." It was to be remembered that so long as the Church was powerful, the penalty for renouncing Christianity was death.

"Perhaps a creed," continued Ram Swarup, "is best known by what it does when its holds political sway." He went on to cite some instances of what Christianity had done in Rome, Great Britain, Germany, Baltic countries, Mexico, etc. It was, therefore, wrong for Mr. Chandy to regard Christian proselytisation as "normal to life" because it was "a bigoted idea, a denial of God and his working in others." Mahatma Gandhi thought it to be "the deadliest poison that ever sapped the fountain of truth" and saw "no spiritual merit" in professional missionaries. In fact, for Gandhiji a missionary was "like any vender of goods"; he wanted to stop proselytisation by legislation.

"Social work" by Christian missions, said Ram Swarup, had become a myth and had to be examined. He cited how American Capuchin monks had seen "spiritual advantages of

---

8. The salesmen of 'Liberation Theology' never tell us that Jesus Christ himself sold his own brother, Judas Thomas, as "a slave skilled in carpentry", and that all Christian churches in Europe, Africa and the Americas were actively involved in slave trade till the early years of the nineteenth century.

famine and cholera" which brought to the missions many orphans. They were immediately baptised so that "baptismal water flows in streams, and the starving little tots fly in masses to heaven." Many of them did not survive. The book, *India and its Missions,* had stated clearly that "a hospital is a readymade congregation; there is no need to go into the highways and hedges and 'compel them to come in'." The Christian doctors and nurses were known for employing many subterfuges "with perfect satisfaction" in order to convert those who went to mission hospitals.

Apart from what missionary services were used for, the more important point was "who pays for these services." Ram Swarup cited Bishop Stephen Neil who had written after examining missionary education that "about a third of the cost of education was borne by private agencies, two-thirds by the Government." The Bishop had also observed that "even in independent India... the old order has continued without radical modification." So the Indians were paying not only for "missionary services" but also for maintaining the missionary apparatus which was used for converting them.

Much was being made of the "sacrifices" of the missionaries and "their love for Jesus and the natives in choosing their career." This was nothing more than "image-building" so that missionaries could become acceptable. The fact, however, was that the missions offered "a lucrative career" and people who joined them did so "in order to improve their social and financial status." Bishop Neil had observed that "missionaries of the last century were over-dressed and by the standard of the time lived in luxury, their stipend being £2000/- a year," while a great classical scholar and Regius Professor of Greek at Oxford, Benjamin Jowett, earned only £54/- a year in 1855-56.

Coming to mission finances, Ram Swarup said that Europe and America had remained the paymasters. The only difference was the recent policy of sending "more cash and less people." The new policy worked for economy as well as effectivity. The native missionary cost far less than his European or American counterpart and was less conspicuous. But he was also much more fanatic. "Not many white missionaries could outdo their brown counterparts." A Christian missionary of Indian origin but working in South Africa had written to President Botha that "the country would lose God's divine protection if Hinduism were allowed to flourish."

Ram Swarup found it difficult to understand why Christians felt hurt if Mother Teresa was viewed as just another missionary working for the promotion of Christianity. There was little doubt that she was "a true daughter of the Church in having her mind and heart closed to the religions of the countries of her labour and even adaptation." The other day when she was visiting the Vatican some Europeans wanted her to tell them about Vedanta as she was living in India. She had rebuked them for "betraying Christ." A comparison of her ways with those of Sister Nivedita told the truth. Sister Nivedita had helped India to "rediscover herself." She had given "national pride" to the Indian people. Mother Teresa, on the other hand, was never tired of presenting India as a land of poverty, disease and death. That was why the West was heaping her with money and honour. Sister Nivedita, "was not even remembered in the West, although the social work she did in the field of education, childcare and poor relief was no less commendable."

Ram Swarup saw no sense in the Christian hope that like St. Paul he might also stop being a "hater of Christians" and come to the "dazzling truth of Christ's compassionate love." He was no "hater of Christians." He was only asking them to look at their religion a little more critically and evaluate it in a more humane manner. Nor was St. Paul known for "compassionate love." Conversion to Christianity had made him "a greater persecutor, on a larger scale and a menace for centuries to come for other religions of the world." A wish for anyone to emulate St. Paul should not be expressed even by one's enemy.

Ram Swarup had been accused of reading "endless number of books available with an anti-Christian view" and advised to "read books of a different kind." He said he was "hardly aware of any anti-Christian books." On the other hand, he had read "the Bible, early Christian Fathers, Christian Catechisms, Christian encyclopaedias, Christian directories, orthodox accounts of Christian missionary activities, histories of Protestantism and the Catholic Church held in high esteem by them [the Christians]." He had found this literature "consistently anti-pagan" and did not know "what to think of a religion which teaches in and through its scriptures and its other literature written by its most devout, scholarly and pious sections such systematic hatred of all other religions and believes in a divine injunction to supplant them."

Christians, said Ram Swarup, should not divide books on Christianity in only two categories — pro-Christian and anti-Christian. There was a third category consisting of "critical and historical studies of the Bible and Christianity." They were "the most durable and solid" and had "proved the most damaging to Christianity." Similarly, "the work of scientists like Copernicus, Galileo, Linaeus, Buffon, Laplace, Lyell, Darwin and others" undermined the structure of Christian thought" which had a "limited conception of the universe." What, however, proved most subversive for Christianity was the "West's discovery of the East." Science had only discredited the dogmas of "virgin birth, resurrection and miracles." Eastern spirituality discredited "sole sonship, single revelation, special covenants, proxy atonement, exclusive salvation, chosen fraternity, single life, authorised saviours and mediators, etc." The deeper Western thinker and seeker had found "interiority, transcendence and universality" in Eastern thought. He had found in Eastern spirituality "not commandments of some arbitrary deity but truths of his own innermost being" and the "principle of tolerance, coexistence, benevolence and reverence which was new to him."

This particular dialogue came to a close with Ram Swarup's rejoinder. But only for the time being. It is bound to be resumed again and again till Christian theologians give up the dogma that Christianity holds a monopoly of truth and

Christian missions stop the subversion of other religions and cultures in the name of 'Christian compassion'.

It may be noted that some of the Christian correspondents objected to Ram Swarup's article being published in *The Times of India.* The plea sounds strange, to say the least. The Christians in this country own and control a large-sized press which includes several daily newspapers and many periodicals. The language which is used in this media vis-a-vis Hinduism is not always decorous; quite often, it is intemperate. Besides, the Christians get ample space in the press which is supposed to be owned and controlled by the Hindus. It is only once in a while that an article critical of Christian dogmas and/or missions, gets through. That, too, when the editor concerned finds that the facts cited and the conclusions drawn deserve the attention of his countrymen. The Christians who object to such articles being published at all have to think calmly and coolly whether their attitude reflects tolerance or otherwise. They have been telling us for many years now that they want and are prepared for a dialogue. We hope that the word "dialogue" in their current dictionary does not mean a monologue, as it did in past.

21

Exploding a Mischievous Myth

The history of Christianity, crowded as it is with crimes of the most horrendous kind, provides a running commentary on the Christian doctrine. And the biggest share in Christian crimes down the centuries can safely be alloted to the Roman Catholic Church, its head, its hierarchy, its theologians, its religious orders, and its missionaries.

There is, however, one criminal field in which the Roman Catholic Church has remained unrivalled. No other Christian denomination — these are as many as 23,000 of them — comes anywhere near the Roman Catholic Church when it concerns committing of blatant forgeries and foisting of pious frauds. It is no exaggeration to say that starting with Jesus Christ, the entire doctrinal and institutional edifice of Catholicism rests on a series of staggering swindles.

The Roman Catholic Church in India has remained true to the tradition. The literature it has produced during the last five centuries is full of lies of the filthiest sort, not only about Hindu religion and culture but also about its own 'religion' and role. And this garbage heap is topped by the hoax about the so-called St. Thomas.

We are told by Catholic 'historians' that Judas Thomas, a brother as well as an apostle of Jesus Christ, had landed in Malabar in 52 AD, founded the Syrian Christian Church, and travelled to Tamil Nadu for spreading the Good News when he was killed by the 'wily Brahmins' in 72 AD at the Big Mount (now called St.Thomas Mount) near Madras at the behest of a Hindu king named Mahadevan. The San Thome Cathedral on the beach in Mylapore is built on the spot where the saint is supposed to have been buried. This spot, like many others of the same spurious sort, has become a place of Christian pilgrimage not only for the flock in India but also for the pious Christians from abroad.

I had examined the story of St. Thomas in 1986 when I wrote a book on the Papacy during the Pope's visit to India.[1] I had discovered that while some Christian historians doubted the very existence of an apostle named St. Thomas, some others had denied credibility to the *Acts of Thomas*, an apocryphal work, on which the whole story is based. Even those Christian historians who had accepted the fourth century Catholic tradition about the travels of St. Thomas, had pointed out the utter lack of evidence that he ever went beyond Ethiopia or Arabia Felix. The confusion, according to them, had arisen because these countries were often mistaken for India by ancient geographers of the Graeco-Roman world.

I had also cited Bishop Stephen Neill who had spent many years in South India and who had examined the St. Thomas story as late as 1984. "A number of scholars," wrote Neill, "among whom are to be mentioned with respect Bishop A.E. Medlycott, J.N. Farquhar and Jesuit Dahlman, have built on slender foundations what can only be called Thomas romances, such as reflect vividness of their imagination rather than the prudence of historical critics."[2] And pained by the spread of spurious history he had observed: "Millions of Christians in India are certain that the founder of their church was none other than the apostle Thomas himself. The historian cannot prove it to them that they are mistaken in their belief. He may feel it right to warn them that historical research cannot pronounce on the matter with a confidence equal to that which they entertain by faith."[3]

Next, I had raised a question: "What difference does it

1. *Papacy: Its Doctrine and History*, Voice of India, New Delhi, 1986.

2. Stephen Neill, *History of Christianity in India: The Beginnings to 1707 AD*, Cambridge University Press, 1984, p. 27.

3. *Ibid.*, p. 49.

make whether Christianity came to India in the first or the fourth century? Why raise such a squabble when no one denies that the Syrian Christians of Malabar are old immigrants to this country?" I had also answered the question: "The matter, however, is not so simple as it sounds at first. Nor can the scholarly exercise be understood easily by those who have not been initiated in the intricacies of Catholic theology." The motives for manufacturing the myth were also detailed by me as follows:

> Firstly, it is one thing for some Christian refugees to come to a country and build some churches, and quite another for an apostle of Jesus Christ himself to appear in flesh and blood for spreading the Good News. If it can be established that Christianity is as ancient in India as the prevailing forms of Hinduism, no one can nail it as an imported creed brought in by Western imperialism.[4]
>
> Secondly, the Catholic Church in India stands badly in need of a spectacular martyr of its own. Unfortunately for it, St. Francis Xavier died a natural death and that, too, in a distant place. Hindus, too, have persistently refused to oblige the Church in this respect in spite of all provocations. The Church has had to use its own resources and churn out something. St. Thomas about whom nobody knows anything, offers a ready-made martyr.
>
> Thirdly, the Catholic Church can malign the Brahmins more confidently. Brahmins have been the main target of its attack from the very beginning. Now it can be shown that the Brahmins have always been a vicious brood, so much so that they would not stop from murdering a holy man who was only telling God's own truth to a tormented

4. Pandit Jawaharlal Nehru provides an excellent example of how some innocents abroad lap up lies sold by powerful organizations. "You may be surprised to learn," he wrote to his daughter, Indira, on April 12, 1932, "that Christianity came to India long before it went to England or Western Europe, and when even in Rome it was a despised and proscribed sect. Within 100 years or so of the death of Jesus, Christian missionaries came to South India by sea... They converted a large number of people" (*Glimpses of World History*, OUP reprint, Fourth Impression, 1987, p.87).

people. At the same time, the religion of the Brahmins can be held responsible for their depravity.

Fourthly, the Catholics in India need no more feel uncomfortable when faced with historical evidence about their Church's close cooperation with the Portuguese pirates in committing abominable crimes against the Indian people. The commencement of the Church can be disentangled from the advent of the Portuguese by dating the Church to a distant past. The Church was here long before the Portuguese arrived. It was a mere coincidence that the Portuguese also called themselves Catholics. Guilt by association is groundless.

Lastly, it is quite within the ken of Catholic theology to claim that a land which has been honoured by the visit of an apostle has become the patrimony of the Catholic Church. India might have been a Hindu homeland from times immemorial. But since that auspicious moment when St. Thomas stepped on her soil, the Hindu claim stands cancelled. The country has belonged to the Catholic Church from the first century onwards, no matter how long the Church takes to conquer it completely for Christ.[5]

But the leviathan which had ignored the serious doubts expressed by renowned Christian historians could not be expected to take notice of what an almost unknown Hindu had to say on the subject of St. Thomas. The Catholic Church in India went on spreading the myth merrily. Meanwhile, the Liberation Theology of the Church had added a new dimension to it. St. Thomas started being sold not only as the first founder of Christianity in India but also as the first to proclaim a new social message in this country. The *Express Weekend* of Madras dated 30 December 1989 presented this new portrait of the ancient Christian saint in an article written by C. A. Simon under the title, 'In Memory of A Slain Saint'.

Besides providing the standard Catholic 'history' of

5. *Papacy*, pp. 56-57.

St. Thomas and the cathedral at Mylapore, the article struck the following new note: "St. Thomas spent the last part of his life in Madras preaching the Gospel. A large number of people listened and embraced the way of life preached by him. *The oppressed and down-trodden followed him and claimed equal status in society as it was denied them by the prevailing social norms. He condemned untouchability and attempted to restore equal status to women.*" (Emphasis added).

The Christian scribe had written with great confidence because similar stuff, presented in a plethora of books as well as the popular press, had passed off without being challenged. He was not aware that Hindu scholars had started examining Christian claims about Christian doctrines and Christian saints, as also Christian calumny about Hinduism, Hindu society, Hindu culture, and Hindu history.[6] Nor did the editor of the *Express Weekend*, a Hindu by accident of birth, anticipate the spate of letters and articles which he soon had on his desk from knowledgeable Hindus. He did his best to suppress the true facts about the so-called St. Thomas and his so-called tomb at Mylapore.

The first Hindu salvo came from Ishwar Sharan of Madras. In a letter to the *Weekend Express* he pointed out what Christian historians such as R. Garbe, A. Harnack and L. de la Vallee-Poussin had stated long ago about the spurious character of the *Acts of St. Thomas*. He also cited Bishop Stephen Neill's warning to Christians against accepting the St. Thomas story as serious history. But what was more significant, he made known for the first time to the lay readers that the "St. Thomas Church stands on the ruins of a Jain Neminatha-swami temple and a Hindu Shiva temple which had a Nataraja shrine attached." The fact that Jain and Shiva temples stood at the site where the St. Thomas church stands now, stated Ishwar Sharan, was vouchsafed by inscriptions

6. C. A. Simon admitted subsequently that "I was not aware of the controversial version given by Sri Sita Ram Goel."

discovered in the church compound and recorded in a scholarly book, *Jain Inscriptions in Tamil Nadu*, compiled by A. Ekambarnath and C. K. Sivaprakasam and published from Madras in 1987. In another book, *Indiavil Saint Thomas Kattukkadai* written in Tamil by Ved Prakash and published from Madras in 1989, the Shiva temple that existed at Mylapore before it was replaced by the St. Thomas church, had been identified with the original Kapaliswara temple.

The *Weekend Express* published this letter in its issue of 13 January 1990 but suppressed its first and last paras. The first para had expressed astonishment that the "*Indian Express* allows its respected columns to be used to promote this Catholic romance as historical fact in this age of excellent and critical scholarship." The last para was about the two temples replaced by the St. Thomas church and the evidence from the inscriptions and Ved Prakash's book. This censorship was applied in spite of the fact that the *Weekend Express* had before it Ved Prakash's book which the author had sent to the weekly for review several months before C.A. Simon's article was flashed on its front page.

So Ishwar Sharan wrote a letter of protest on 16 January 1990 and sent it to the resident editor of the *Indian Express* in Madras. He pointed out how his letter had been truncated by a paper which had "given prime space" to a Catholic apologist to "tell his version of a controversial story." He brought to the resident editor's notice the articles which had been published earlier in the *Indian Express* about the destruction of Hindu temples by Muslims and that of some Jain and Buddhist temples by certain Hindu kings, and saw no reason why "Christians have escaped this review though they were the worst perpetrators of these kinds of deeds." He also pointed out that though Ved Prakash had sent as many as four copies of his book to the *Express Weekend*, the latter had not even acknowledged it in the "books received" column, not to speak of reviewing the scholarly study. Finally, he asked the resident editor that "when the Pope in Rome can no longer enforce the Index, how is it that the *Indian Express* can censor our reading material, obstruct a free access to information, and suppress discussion of a subject because it is controversial?"

The resident editor did not acknowledge this letter. And the *Indian Express* dated 29 January 1990 published on its city page an article, 'Madras — City Of Neglect', by Harry Miller denouncing the American evangelists for "disfiguring the city walls with their offensive posters" but repeating the St. Thomas story. Miller had reminded the Americans that "the very first evangelist — one Thomas by name — landed on our shores within a few years of the Crucifixion, some five centuries before America was 'discovered'" and that "we have never needed another." Ishwar Sharan wrote another letter to the *Indian Express* stating the facts which he had presented to the *Express Weekend* in his letter of January 13 and adding some more. He mailed a copy of it to Harry Miller as well. The *Indian Express* did not publish the letter. Nor did Harry Miller acknowledge or respond to it.

But Ishwar Sharan had taken care to circulate his 13 January letter among a number of Hindu scholars in Madras and elsewhere. Some of these scholars also wrote letters to the *Express Weekend* presenting the same facts in their own individual ways. They seemed to have forced the *Express Weekend* to have second thoughts on the subject. It published on 10 February 1990 a letter from Swami Jyotirmayananda which referred to the Tamil inscriptions and the book by Ved Prakash and stated: "There is reason to believe that St. Thomas church stands on the ruins of a Jain Neminathaswami temple and a Shiva temple which had a Nataraja shrine attached." The letter inferred correctly that the Shiva temple was the original Kapaliswara temple on the Mylapore beach but made a mistake in speculating that the original Kapaliswara temple "got eroded by the sea."

The mistake was corrected by Ved Prakash in a letter which the *Express Weekend* published on 3 March 1990. "Nowhere in the book," he pointed out, "do I mention that the Siva temple on the Mylapore beach was eroded by the sea. What is mentioned about the Siva temple is as follows: '...many evidences available in Santhome church show how there was a Siva temple and it was occupied, then step by step demolished and converted into a church." In support of his case, he cited a 12th century Chola inscription of 8 lines "found in the Cathedral" and an established Hindu tradition showing that the Kapaliswara temple "was there up to the 16th century" when the "Christians started demolishing it." He concluded that the present-day Kapaliswara temple did not stand on its original site and was built by Hindus at its new place "out of whatever they could salvage from the ruins of the old temple."

Ved Prakash's statement about destruction of the original Kapaliswara temple by Christians was confirmed by Dr. R. Nagaswamy, formerly Director of Archaeology, Tamil Nadu, and now Director of the Indian Institute of Culture in Madras. In an article, 'Testimony to Religious Ethos', published in *The Hindu* of 30 April 1990, he wrote: "A careful study of the monuments and lithic records in Madras reveals a great destruction caused by the Portuguese to Hindu temples in the sixteenth century A.D. The most important temple of Kapaleeswara lost its ancient building during the Portuguese devastation and was originally located near the Santhome cathedral... A few Chola records found in the Santhome cathedral and bishop's house refer to Kapaleeswara temple and Poompavai. A Chola record in fragment found on the east wall of the Santhome cathedral refers to the image of Lord Nataraja of the Kapaleeswara temple. The temple was moved to the present location in the sixteenth century and was probably built by one Mallappa... A fragmentary inscription, twelfth century Chola record, in the Santhome church region refers to a Jain temple dedicated to Neminathaswami."

Meanwhile, on 9 March 1990 Ishwar Sharan had sent to the *Express Weekend* a scholarly article, 'What the Historians Say About Saint Thomas', in reply to C.A. Simon's piece on the 'slain saint'. It carried citations from several impeccable sources, literary and archaeological, regarding the career and character of St. Thomas, the chronology of Christian presence in India, and the replacement of Hindu temples by churches at Mylapore. The article was neither acknowledged nor returned. Subsequent queries regarding the fate of the article also brought no response. So he addressed a registered letter to the resident editor on 1 June 1990 stating that his article had been "accepted by a respected publisher" to be published as book, and that "if you do not intend to publish the article... then the same should be indicated to me within the next two weeks..." The resident editor replied by a letter dated 11 June 1990 and said: "I find that *Express Weekend* carried on 13th January a letter from you on Mr. C.A. Simon's 'In Memory of a Slain Saint'. We have also published letters from Swami Tapasyananda and Mr. Ved Prakash on the same subject. It is not as if, therefore, the *Indian Express* refused to give space to your point of view. The availability of space being a severe constraint *Express Weekend* finds it very difficult indeed to publish long articles."

Ishwar Sharan decided to do some plain speaking to this editor who had equated a brief and censored letter to the editor with a grossly misleading front-page article. In his letter dated 25 June 1990, he said: "So the truth of the matter is that you do indeed have space to promote the ancient lie about St. Thomas coming to India to get killed by the wicked Hindus and especially the very wicked Brahmins, but you do not have space at all in your newspaper when somebody tries to unmask the fable... Swami Tapasyananda did not get a letter published in the *Express Weekend* as you have stated, but has written his own article in *The Vedanta Kesari*... What is really distressing is that you not only connive at this vicious lie being published in your paper to malign the Hindus but that you support it by suppressing the truth no matter how often or in what form it is presented to you." The resident editor did not care to reply.

Till this time, Ishwar Sharan did not know that Swami Tapasyananda of the Ramakrishna Mission in Madras had also sent an article to the *Express Weekend* and had received neither an acknowledgment nor a rejection. All he knew was that the Swami's article, 'The Legend of A Slain Saint To Stain Hinduism', had been published in the June 1990 issue of *The Vedanta Kesari*, the monthly of the Ramakrishna Mission in Madras. So it was a puzzle to him as to how the resident editor's letter had named Swami Tapasyananda as the writer of a letter which was never published. The cat came out of the bag when he referred the matter to the Swami, and learnt that the latter had indeed sent his article to the *Express Weekend* in the first instance.

Swami Tapasyananda's article being as detailed and documented as his own, Ishwar Sharan sent a copy of it to C.A. Simon whose address he had succeeded in obtaining from the *Express Weekend* after waiting for several months. The reply he received from C.A. Simon was revealing. Firstly, Simon disclosed the sources of his information about the story of St. Thomas. He referred to two modern books, a few leaflets, a stamp issued by the Government of India in 1972, and a speech by Dr. Rajendra Prasad, President of India. Secondly, he admitted that he was no scholar of the subject and "not aware of the controversial version" given by the other side. Finally, he prayed: "I learned that you are going to publish a book and intend to include my article as the Christian version. As I do not stand for any religious sect or group you may desist from doing so. Instead you may refer to more authoritative works on the subject if you feel so." The confidence with which he had written his article was gone as soon as he was made to know the difference between fact and fiction. What intrigued Ishwar Sharan, however, was the question: How had C.A. Simon come to know that Ishwar Sharan's article was going to be published as a book? Ishwar Sharan had not conveyed the information to him. The conclusion was obvious — C.A. Simon had learnt it from the resident editor of the *Indian Express*!

But in spite of all evidence presented to it regarding the myth of St. Thomas, the *Indian Express* persisted in promoting it. On 2 August 1990, it published a letter from Raju

Thomas, a learned Christian of Madras. The letter was about the plight of Scheduled Caste converts to Christianity. It rebuked the rich and powerful Christian Church in India for demanding reservations for these converts while itself doing nothing for them although they constituted 85 per cent of the Christian population in India. But it was prefaced by the old lie that Christianity had reached Kerala "in the first century before it went to Europe." Ishwar Sharan wrote another letter to the *Indian Express* on 3 August 1990 stating once again the true facts of the case. This letter was not published. But as a copy of the letter had been sent by him to Raju Thomas, the latter wrote a long letter to the *Indian Express* expressing doubts about the existence of Christianity in India in the first century AD. Raju Thomas' letter, too, was not published. Shri Ishwar Sharan came to know about it only when Raju Thomas wrote to him on 31 August 1990.

"You may ask me," said Raju Thomas in his letter to Ishwar Sharan, "if such is the case why did I assert that Christianity had come to India before it had reached Europe? My answer to this question is that I deliberately wanted an open debate and discussion on this subject... We will be able to challenge and question such falsified histories and traditional beliefs only when we take up such issues to the public and do not keep them as the top secrets. But the question is how many of our 'intellectuals' are ready to have open-minded debates and discussions?..." He was not quite correct in blaming the intellectuals alone. It is true that intellectuals who take pains to study every subject from its sources, are few and far between in this country. But it is also true that an intellectual culture cannot grow in an atmosphere where the media is controlled by purveyors of palpable falsehoods or bullied into abject surrender by the thought-police of Nehruvian Secularism.

That the intellectuals were hungry for correct information on an important subject, was proved when Ishwar Sharan's book, *The Myth of St. Thomas and the Mylapore Shiva Temple*, was published by VOICE OF INDIA in February

1991. The book sold very fast. It was reviewed in leading journals and commented upon favourably by well-known scholars. The main chapter in the book carried Ishwar Sharan's article submitted by him to the *Express Weekend* in reply to the one by C. A. Simon. The article had been expanded with additional material and informative footnotes. Besides, the book reproduced the articles by C. A. Simon, Swami Tapasyananda and Harry Miller. The letters which Ishwar Sharan had addressed to the *Express Weekend* on the subject of St. Thomas and the Santhome cathedral were also reproduced along with his exchanges with the resident editor of the *Indian Express* and Raju Thomas. The crowning piece in the book was the confession by C.A. Simon.

The most important development, however, was the stir which the book caused among the intelligentsia in Madras. The intelligentsia was aware that Christian missionaries had been using the St. Thomas story for maligning Hinduism and extolling Christianity. But it was not in a position to develop a dialogue because it lacked the correct information and the proper perspective. Now it was fully equipped and could hit back.

The International Institute of Tamil Studies, an academy sponsored and financed by the Government of Tamil Nadu, had published in 1985-86 a book titled *Viviliyam, Tirukkural, Shaiva Siddhantam Oppu Ayu*. The writer of the book was M. Deivanayakam, a Christian scholar supposed to be an expert on Tamil antiquities. The University of Madras had conferred a doctor's degree on the author for writing this dissertation. The thesis propounded by him was that the ancient Tamil saint, Tiruvalluvar, had become a disciple of St. Thomas and converted to Christianity. Stray sentences had been picked up from the Tamil classic, *Tirukkural*, and lined up with stray sentences from the Bible in order to prove the point that the Tamil saint owed his teaching to his contact with the Christian scripture.

Some scholars had written letters to Deivanayakam pointing out that his book was full of distortions and altogether misleading. But Deivanayakam had remained unrelenting. The Dharampuram Shaiva Math had invited the Christian scholar to a conference of Tamil scholars, and requested him to disown the thesis. He had come to the conference but refused to yield ground. Finally, the Math had prepared a book of refutation. It had been written by an eighty-five years old Tamil and Shaiva scholar, Arunai Vadivel Mudaliar. Ishwar Sharan's book on St. Thomas came as a shot in the arm of Mudaliar whose book was released by Sarojini Varadappa in a gathering of three hundred Tamil and Shaiva scholars held in a packed hall at Madras on 24 October 1991.

The meeting was presided over by Justice N. Krishnaswami Reddiar, a retired judge of the high court. He denounced Deivanayakam's book as "trash in the name of research." He quoted from Ishwar Sharan's book to point out that "the visit of St. Thomas to India was a myth", and wondered how a book like that by Deivanayakam could be published by an institute set up by the Government and honoured by a university with a doctorate. Dr. R. Nagaswami, eminent archaeologist, also censored the institute and the university for sponsoring a spurious thesis, and said that the St. Thomas story "was a ruse to spread Christianity in India." He cited what he knew from his own excavations at the Santhome church. Some other speakers, too, took Deivanayakam to task.

Meanwhile, Ishwar Sharan had discovered another Christian fraud. It came to light that Deivanayakam had collaborated with Dr. R. Arulappa, the Catholic Archbishop of Madras, in writing another but similar book, *Perinbu Villakku*, published in 1975. The Archbishop had also tried to prove that Tiruvalluvar had come in contact with St. Thomas during the latter's travels in South India, and converted to Christianity. But he had gone much further, and forged "evidence" on palm-leaf scrolls in support of his thesis. He had employed a Hindu scholar of Christianity, Ganesh Iyer, for this purpose, and paid him to the tune of 15 lakh rupees. The fraud had been exposed when someone put the police on the trail of Ganesh Iyer. The case had dragged on in the Madras metropolitan court from 1980 to 1986 when Ganesh Iyer was sentenced to ten months' imprisonment on various counts. But Dr. Arulappa had got him acquitted by means of a civil suit for compromise filed in the Madras High Court at the same time that the criminal case was going on. Ganesh Iyer had spilled the beans soon after.

Ishwar Sharan included the full story of this fraud in the revised and enlarged second edition of his book published by VOICE OF INDIA in 1995. The second edition included all the material published in the first edition and several other very informative articles, particularly those from Koenraad Elst and Leela Tampi. "What was originally an introduction to the study of the myth of St. Thomas and the destruction of a great Shiva temple" had now "begun to take the shape of a broader investigation into the Christian presence in India." It carried an introduction by Koenraad Elst. "In Catholic universities in Europe," wrote Elst, "the myth of the apostle Thomas going to India is no longer taught as history, but in India it is still considered useful. The important point is that Thomas can be upheld as a martyr and the Brahmins decried as fanatics."

Two conclusions emerged clearly from this particular Hindu-Christian encounter. Firstly, although the major print media in India is owned by Hindu moneybags, they have handed it over to Hindu-baiters of all sorts.[7] Secondly, there is no law in the country which can deal with intellectual crimes committed by Christian scribes ever so often. In fact, the existing law comes down heavily on those who expose those crimes; they are branded as Hindu communalists and accused of creating enmity between communities.

7. The *Indian Express* at Madras continues to spread Christian lies in a big way while sharing an occasional paragraph for mild or uninformed protests against them.

22

Plea for Rejecting Jesus as Junk

Jesus Christ has been the stock-in-trade of Christian missions down the ages. He has been packed in all shapes and sizes depending upon the gullibility of the clients to be duped. And he has been rammed down the throats of those who have refused to be hoodwinked by the hoax. As one surveys the history of Christian missions in lands where this hoax has been hawked or imposed, one comes across no end of force and fraud employed in its service by a variety of soldiers and salesmen most of whom are presented as saints. It can be said without exaggeration that if one is in search of a hardened criminal with a clean conscience, one should reach out for the first available Christian saint and one will not miss the mark. St. Francis Xavier, the Paron Saint of the East according to the Roman Catholic Church, provides an excellent example.

The Jesus shop in India was set up for the first time by the Portuguese pirates who started flocking in from 1498 AD onwards. But no buyers came forward to sample the merchandise except for some vagrants who took the bribes offered in exchange for baptism, and went back to live their lives as before. The garbage was then fed forcibly to helpless men and women and children whom the pirates had reduced to slavery and concubinage. The poor Parvas on the Pearl Fishery Coast had to purchase it because the Portuguese navy threatened them with a blockade of their catamarans in case they refused to come round. Meanwhile, some pirates dressed up as priests had started peddling the stock in the interior of Malabar, Tamil Nadu, Karnataka, Maharashtra and

Bengal. But Hindus everywhere had turned away with contempt and ridicule. Finally, Maharshi Dayananda had warned his countrymen against the fraud in words which were loud and clear. The hawkers of Jesus Christ were on the run after Swami Vivekananda exposed their methods in picturesque language, and invited them to have some sense of shame.

Jesus Christ would have continued to stink in Hindu nostrils but for another historical process which was simultaneously at work in this country. The long spell of Islamic terror had spawned a class of Hindus to whom superiority of armed might had come to mean superiority of religion and culture. They had started seeing exceptional merit in the Allah of Islam. They could not but see even greater merit in the Jesus of Christianity when the mailed fist of a Christian power overcame the Islamic marauder. Raja Ram Mohun Roy was a typical member of this double-distilled class. He had already passed under the spell of Allah when he came across Jesus. He took no time in jumping on the new bandwagon, and started presenting Jesus as an embodiment of virtues unknown to his countrymen. The Brahmo Samaj he founded continued to place Jesus on a higher and higher pedestal.

Mahatma Gandhi did not belong to this self-alienated class of Hindus. He came from the mainstream of Hinduism which had refused to be overawed by the bluff and bluster of both Islam and Christianity, and remained faithful to its age-old spiritual vision. Nor could the Mahatma be influenced either by the armed might or by the cultural arrogance of the latest conqueror. But due to a variety of reasons, he had developed a cult of his own and, like the medieval acharyas, identified the whole of Sanatana Dharma with this cult rather than see it as one of the strands in a vast fabric. Next, he had gone out in search of a similar cult in the scriptures of Islam and Christianity. He could not find what he was looking for either in the Quran or the Hadis. But some verses in one of the gospels made him dance with delight. He had hit paydirt!

This was the Sermon on the Mount which no Christian theologian or historian had so far noticed as something significant. In fact, Christian scholars had come to suspect the Sermon as an interpolation which was not at all in accord with the character and teaching of Jesus as found in the rest of the gospels. But what could these Christian worthies do in the face of the Mahatma's claim that he knew Christianity better than any Christian, dead or alive? In any case, the Mahatma's identification of Jesus' teaching with the Sermon was convenient for Christian missions in carrying forward their commerce farther afield.

Almost all other Hindu leaders and organisations followed the Mahatma's lead. They started vying with each other in praising Jesus to the skies. The Ramakrishna Mission all but replaced the Paramhamsa with this newly found fetish. Even those Hindus who looked askance at the activities of Christian missions could not help heaping fulsome praise on the Christian totem. It became a fashion with Hindu gurus, in India and abroad, to pay homage to Jesus before saying any thing else. And it was not long before Jesus was hailed as an avatar by many mainstream Hindus. Christian missions in this country had never had it so good. Now they had only to mention the magic name, and almost every English educated Hindu stood spell-bound. They went further and proclaimed that a Hindu who did not honour Jesus as a spiritual giant was no Hindu at all!

I myself had swallowed the Hindu version of Jesus — hook, line and sinker — while I was a college student. And that version stayed with me for forty long years — till I read Ram Swarup's critique of Monotheism in *The Word As Revelation: Names of Gods.* As a student of European history, I knew that the history of Christianity had been cruel and blood-soaked till recent times. But I had never thought that this history had been created by doctrines taught by Jesus in the gospels. Ram Swarup's critique made me sit up, and study Christianity in some depth. And I learnt with painful surprise that Jesus of the gospels was a vicious character. The viciousness of Christian history now stood fully and satisfactorily explained.

Another surprise for me was the findings of Christological research in the modern West. Book after book, written by Christian scholars, informed me that nothing was known — not even knowable — about the real Jesus if he existed at all, and that Jesus of the gospels was a theological statement rather than a historical character. So the historicity of Jesus, which is a fundamental tenet of Christianity, was a Big Lie.

The next thing that I learnt — now with considerable delight — was the steep decline of Christianity in its Western homelands due to the rise of humanism, rationalism, universalism, and science. It was only in the Afro-Asian countries, particularly Hindu-Buddhist lands, that Christian missions had found a flourishing market for Jesus. In fact, Christianity was trying to find a new home in the Hindu-Buddhist countries. The Western countries had no use for Jesus any more. But they were prepared to finance Christian missions to unload this junk elsewhere in exchange for services to be rendered by the missions in some other spheres — political, diplomatic, commercial, and subversive.

What pained me no end, however, was the fact that the Christological research in the modern West had remained unknown to Hindus by and large although it was readily available. Swami Vivekananda was the last Hindu leader who was fully acquainted with this research, and who had used it for blunting the thrust of Christian missions. One also got glimpses in Mahatma Gandhi's encounter with Christian missions to the effect that he was aware of this research to some extent, though he did not permit it to affect his evaluation of Jesus. But for the rest, Hindus had remained uninformed with the result that Christian missions had continued to sell Jesus of the gospels with great gusto, particularly the 'Jesus of history' with miracles and all. So I decided to present the findings of Christological research in a small booklet, *Jesus Christ: An Artifice for Aggression*, to serve as a companion volume to the revised and enlarged second edition of my major work on Christian missions, *Catholic Ashrams: Sannyasins or Swindlers*?

The first part of the book on Jesus presented the salient features of Christological research which had been summarised as follows by a scholar writing in 1986: "During the last thirty years theologians have come increasingly to admit that it is no longer possible to write a biography of him [Jesus], since documents earlier than the gospels tell us next to nothing of his life, while the gospels present the 'kerygma' or proclamation of faith, not the Jesus of history. Many contemporary theologians therefore regard the quest of the historical Jesus as both hopeless and religiously irrelevant — in that *the few things which can, allegedly, be known of his life are unedifying and do not make him an appropriate object of worship.*"

The second part of the book dealt with how the Jesus of Fiction had come increasingly to the fore in the modern West as the Jesus of History started fading fast. It listed and summarised quite a few books written by two schools. One school believes that notwithstanding his unknowability a man called Jesus did exist at some time. Many early sources as well as stray incidents in the gospels have been used to reconstruct the man and his doings. The outcome has been a spate of novels and speculative books which are entertaining rather than enlightening. Another school believes that no man named Jesus by Christianity ever existed, and that the Jesus of the gospels is a synthetic product for manufacturing which many cults prevalent in the Roman Empire in the first century AD have been used. The books produced by this school are fewer than those produced by the other school, but equally speculative.

The third part of the book came up with the latest Christian trickery, namely, how die-hard Christian theologians have invented the Jesus of Faith when they were deprived of the Jesus of History and faced with the Jesus of Fiction. This is a desperate attempt to resurrect the Jesus of the gospels. But the same research which has exploded the Jesus of History has nailed the Jesus of the gospels as a figure soaked in the blood of millions of innocents in many lands. In fact, the gospels are now regarded as the First Nazi Manifesto by knowledgeable historians, sociologists, and psychologists, and Christianity itself as a Big Lie.

The last part of the book provided statistics from authentic Christian sources for showing how Christianity had crumbled in the modern West, and how Jesus has been reduced to junk which the West is dumping on the East with the help of Christian missions. For the missions themselves, Jesus is only an artifice for mounting aggression against non-Christian societies and cultures, and no more an object of worship because they know the truth about what they are selling. Hindus should know that Jesus means nothing but mischief for their country and culture, and stop showing any weakness for him. Weakness for Jesus in a Hindu is the same as the weakness for dice in Raja Nala of epic fame. As Kaliyuga was able to enter Raja Nala and ruin him because of his weakness, weakness for Jesus helps in increasing the stranglehold of intelligence networks and foreign policy department of the West on the only Hindu homeland.

The book invited comments soon after it was published in April 1994. Most of the comments came from Hindus and objected to the language used in some parts of the book, particularly the description of Jesus as junk. But all writers agreed that the fact "revealed" from Christological research were "startling", and had put Jesus in his proper place as a monstrous myth. I told them that the criminal gangs of Christian swordsmen and missionaries had been waging a war against Hindu spiritual traditions, Hindu culture and Hindu nation, for the past five hundred years and with every weapon available to them at any time. Now that they had been worsted in their own homelands and forced to wear a soft face, they were trying to dictate the language we use for their totem. So long as Christianity refuses to revise its theology and withdraw its missions, there was no language which was strong enough for it and its hirelings.

Dr. K. Swaminathan of Madras, however, endorsed my language also. In a letter dated 2 June 1994, he wrote as follows to Swami Devananda Saraswati who had presented to him copies of the two books:

> "Jesus Christ: An Artifice for Aggression" takes my breath away. It is a devastating exposé of the myth of Jesus, besides which even the myth of St(?) Thomas pales into historical inconsequence, relatively speaking. The damage done by the latter is limited to South India only whereas that caused by Jesus has ravaged continents and destroyed civilizations in all parts of the world.
>
> I still cannot understand why Gandhiji had to extol Jesus, the person, to the skies (except perhaps his ignorance *at that time*) while condemning missionary work unequivocally although in understanding sweet language. Now I have come to the conclusion that Shri Goel's language, apparently strident and caustic at first look, is the *most appropriate* way (without mincing words) to deal with the sugar-tongued vipers that the Church and its missions have perfected themselves to be. Shri Goel has done immeasurable service to the Hindu cause and the Hindu awakening. His writings should be taught in the universities. What courage and perseverance he has displayed! I wish he were 20 years younger. What agony his heart must have gone through in fighting almost single-handedly a seemingly hopeless battle inspired by Ram Swarup. Thank the Lord Nataraja that he is now admirably supported by scholars like Shourie, Elst, yourself and a few others. I pray to the Lord that VOICE OF INDIA sweeps through our land in the coming years and causes a new Hindu Renaissance, jolting the so-called enlightened elite Hindus out of their fond illusions about Jesus and Prophet Mohammed into a realistic assessment of their lives. Till two years ago I believed in them myself!...
>
> "Catholic Ashrams" is indeed equally revealing about their modus operandi. I had all along thought Swami Abhishiktananda was a genuine Hindu Swami and a Yogi who fully followed Swami Gnanananda of Tapovanam

and Sri Ramana Maharshi and had rejected Christ totally after coming to India!

The Shantivanam Branch (Sathya Nilayam) in Mylapore still continues such fraudulent exercises. I recently came across one Father Thomas Marriet's books condemning Swami Vivekananda and Advaita... (Emphasis in original)

Shri B. M. Thapar of New Delhi, a devotee of Sathya Sai Baba, was more than annoyed by my description of Jesus as junk. He advised me against using the language I had used, and thought that my attack on Christianity could have been dexterous instead of being direct. I disagreed with him and told him that most of the time I had only cited what scholars in the West had said. Shri Thapar had, however, sent the two books — *Catholic Ashrams* and *Jesus Christ* — to some of his friends in the West. He sent to me copies of two comments he had received. In a letter dated 13 July 1994, Mr. Meads of Emporia, Kansas, USA, wrote:

And thank you for the books *Catholic Ashrams* and *Jesus Christ* . Being from a Christian Background, I was very interested in reading other's perspective of this major religion. Sita Ram Goel writes like a very angry fundamentalist, and I find that very unusual coming from a Hindu. It is quite obvious that he is not a Sai Baba devotee.

I found it a little disheartening to read the Jesus is junk paragraph in *Jesus Christ,* page 85. Baba said in his Christmas discourse 1978 (Sathya Sai speaks, vol X, chapter 45) that Jesus was a Karan-Janma, a Master born with a purpose — the mission of restoring love, charity, and compassion in the heart of man... I know nothing about the Catholic ashrams, very enlightening....

Mr. W. S. Cockburn of Bromley, Kent, England wrote on 19 July 1994:

The books have arrived safe and sound. 1) CATHOLIC ASHRAMS 2) JESUS CHRIST. Denise has already read

> No.2 from cover to cover and agrees with much. I think Sita Ram Goel is a clever man with quite a mind. His English is beautiful but he is so sharp and at times vicious. So Brij you have begun an interesting discourse. Denise and I feel like a couple of students about to read for our Ph.D. in CHRISTOLOGY.

While sending these comments to me, Shri Thapar himself wrote on 13 October 1994:

> I have completed reading "Jesus Christ — artifice for aggression"; when I previously wrote I had by chance read p. 85 only (viz. Jesus is junk etc.); your language made me uneasy. Now I have to thank you for alerting me to the subject of Christology; the documentation is such and so well done that it speaks for itself; I wholeheartedly agree with the spirit of your letter of 9/8/94 but feel I must part company with the language you have used on p. 85 and in a couple of sentences elsewhere...

I was late in air-mailing a copy to Dr. Winand Callewaert of Louvain, Belgium. He is an old India-hand who knows and speaks Hindi fluently, and has edited some medieval Hindi texts. I had met him some years ago, and a warm friendship had developed between us. But as soon as he saw some VOICE OF INDIA publications, he stopped even telephoning to me during his annual visits to Delhi. Back in Belgium, he started a whispering campaign against Koenraad Elst who, according to him, had been 'brain-washed by Sita Ram Goel'. I was, therefore, not altogether surprised when I received a long letter from him in November 1995:

Dr. Winand Callewaert,

Dept. Asian Studies
Blidje Inkonststraat 21
B - 3000 Leuven
Belgium
Leuven, 10th November 1995

Dear Sita Bhai,

A few weeks ago I received *Jesus Christ. An artifice for*

aggression.

It is a well written and well documented book, and without going into detail I can agree with many points you mention. I only take issue with the spirit in which it is written and the conclusions you draw. I worry about the aims you like to achieve, nourishing the feeling you have and that prompted you to write this book.

I have always had much respect for you, and affection, but I am very sorry that we got estranged. Let me explain. The ideas you have and the books you write about Christians (a tiny minority in India) are not a unique phenomenon. Most criticism you quote has been published by Christians themselves, and I can add plenty to it. No harm. That is a positive development. That is how a religion can evolve from institutionalisation and power-building to what it should be: give a dimension in life to those people who are in need of it. Let those who are not in need of it not bother about it.

But those ideas are not unique also in another way too. They occur in every religion and society as a negative phenomenon as well, in islam, in judaism, in christianity and unfortunately also in hinduism. At this level they do not have much to do with purifying the religion, but with another level of power, of politics. If you write in your book on p. 82 that Christianity in India is meant to destabilize the government, you no longer discuss the validity of the religious inspiration of Christianity. You discuss politics.

And that is the level where I am so scared of your publications.

It is all right with me if your publications help people, each one in his own religion, to purify his insight and his commitment. But it is dangerous if it brings about hatred among people. We are going to the 21st century and soon to a world with 5 billion people, whether we like or not. Too many people everywhere, whatever the reasons (and I surely disagree with the pope who plays a negative role here, using religion to impose some kind of ethics, but that is not the issue here).

In that kind of world my personal contribution I hope will be to bring people together. If you read my publications, you will ONLY find waves of understanding for hinduism or buddhism, not for the power bases (there too) that use religion for their own benefit, but understanding for the fine products of divine or whatever inspiration that has brought about outstanding literature and philosophy.

That is, dear Sita Ram, where I fear since several years, that our ways part. I can agree with much of the analysis you make about christianity (or islam), but where does it take one?

- The christian believer will be antagonized and turn against you. Result: feelings of hatred.

- The non-believer will say: of course religion exploits people for its own end, you see. Result: he will turn against the believing christians. Hatred.

- And the non-christians in India and elsewhere will only be too happy to find arguments in your books to say: of course this intelligent man has given proof that christianity is meant to exploit us. Let us suppress or throw out (if possible) the christians in India. Result: hatred.

I do not understand, Sita Bhai, how this can be your project.

What do you want to achieve?

- Prove that christianity is losing its power base in the west, because it was built on dogma and fear? Everybody knows that, but quite a few people-including myself-try to find a base in their life using the good elements in the christian inspiration, not bothering about the excesses, as much as hinduism too has offered plenty to me to define my purpose in life. And we are not alone.

- Increase a certain powerbase of so-called hindus, and therefore throw out from India whatever is not hindu? If that is your aim in life, it is not realistic.

See where the Ayodhya issue, or now Benares, is leading. To killing, hatred, communal feelings of one neighbour against the other. Politicians use your ideas to increase their own power, gundas and property pirates in Bombay use your or the Shiv Sena's ideology for their own aims. Is that what you hope to achieve?

- Do you want to defend a 'minority of hindus' against the oppression by islam and christianity. You cannot be serious about it. The real majority in India now is the oppressed classes, who for centuries have not had a chance in hindu society, and who were neatly kept in their place by a subtle religious system. Do not tell me that is not true. I am certainly in a position to know, but I do NOT make it my business to start attacking "hinduism" for that. What would I bring about then: useless hatred.

Interestingly, even in this area politicians have found food for their hunting, using the Dalits as a forceful votebank. Do you not see that? Some people are only too happy to see your publications. As much as in Belgium e.g. some people are only too happy to see anti-islamic publications, for their own political end.

Hatred brings about killings, as we saw recently in Israel.

If some think that there is no place for others, that is what you get. Israel, or south-Africa, or Belgium, or the US. In India too.

Sd/-
Winand

My reply to Dr. Callewaert is reproduced below:

28.2.1996

Dear Dr. Callewaert,

I hope you have received my acknowledgment of your letter dated 10 November 1995 which reached me on 29 November due to the mess prevailing in our postal system at that time.

Unfortunately, I was quite ill at the time I received your letter. I had to... remain bed-ridden for more than a month. It is only in the last few days that I have regained some strength and resumed work. I am now in a position to take up your letter, point by point, and present my own case.

I am glad you consider my book on Jesus "well written and well documented", and agree with many points I have made. I wish you had detailed those points for my enlightenment. Instead, you have gone ahead and nailed me for "the spirit in which it is written", the conclusions I have drawn, the aims I like to achieve, and the feelings I nourish. I will come to my conclusions and my aims in the paras that follow. Here I wish to say that your remarks about my spirit and feelings remind me of a fashion prevalent in India's politics — whenever a politician finds it difficult to pin down an opponent or a rival on specifics, he says, "I do not like the style of his functioning." Delving into the other person's psychology may sound deep but it hardly helps a healthy dialogue which should better be confined to facts and logic and value judgments.

My conclusions are clear enough, namely, that Jesus Christ and Christianity are junk which has been rejected by the modern West but which Christian missions are out to dump on the Third World countries with the help of Western wealth and media power, the same as in the case of many other commodities. The statistical evidence I have quoted about the steep decline of Christianity in its traditional homelands have not been cooked up by me; they have been compiled by a Christian organisation of impeccable credentials. Tell me where I have gone wrong. Or is it your case that what the West has come to know about Jesus Christ and Christianity should remain unknown in this part of the world? I beg to differ. There is no reason for my people to wallow in ignorance when knowledge is readily available.

My aims are also quite clear. I want Hindus to view

Christianity as a wicked ideology like Communism and Nazism, and not as a system of spiritual seeking like their own schools of Sanatana Dharma. My judgment is based on an extensive study of Sanatana Dharma classics and Hindu history on the one hand, and of the classics of Christianity and its history on the other. You may differ with my judgment, as I know you do. That is, however, a matter of dialogue which we want to have with our Christian friends but which the Christians whom I have known have chosen to avoid with a contemptuous smile.

That brings me to the next point, namely, your being "sorry that we got estranged". I wonder why you use the word "we" in this context. I have never felt estranged towards you. It is you who started avoiding me after having known and liked me for quite some time. The story is the same with several other Christian friends whom I have known and cherished for many years. None of you have had the decency to find out by means of a free and frank discussion with me as to why I have chosen to speak the way I have done. All of you have simply walked out of my life, hurling at me the base accusation that I am spreading hatred against the Christian community. Your present letter is brimful of this accusation.

I had the same experience when I started speaking against Communism after having been its votary for several years. Friends whom I had known and cherished for long became estranged without anyone of them trying to find out the reason for my rebellion. They simply started saying that I had been bought over by the CIA and was working not only against the poor and the downtrodden but also the freedom and integrity of my country. I have never been able to understand this behaviour pattern. I have had strong differences with many of my non-Christian and non-Communist friends without losing their love and esteem for me. The fact that I found the Christians and the Communists sharing this behaviour pattern in common confirms me in my conclusion that the two creeds are the same with a variation in verbiage. My studies of the histories of Christianity and Communism reinforce the same conclusion.

You state that "the ideas" I have and "the books" I write about Christians "are not a unique phenomenon". Before I come to the uniqueness part, I wish to point out the confusion you create by your loose language. Can you kindly quote a single sentence from any of my writings where I have said anything derogatory about Christians as such? I have said time and again that Christians in India are our own people who have been alienated from their ancestral society and culture by the divisive doctrine of Christianity. All my guns have always been trained on the doctrine of Christianity, none and never against Christians except the Christian missionaries. The same confusion prevails when I write about Islam. I am told that I am attacking Muslims. Let me tell you, as I have told many others, that I live in the world of ideas and not in that of human beings who are victimized (or ennobled) by those ideas. I make a clear distinction between propensities, good and bad, which are embedded in normal human nature and those which are imparted by ideas and ideologies.

In any case, your concern for the "tiny minority" of Christians in India is totally uncalled for in view of the long Hindu history of providing protection to all persecuted people from everywhere. We looked after the Jews and the Syrian Christians who were driven out of their homelands by the Catholic Church and the Zoroastrians of Iran. We took care of the Zoroastrians when they were driven out of Iran by Islam. We have provided shelter to the Buddhist Tibetans victimized by the Chinese Communists. All these refugee communities have lived and prospered in our land. And I assure you that our Christian countrymen will continue to flourish long after their present-day shepherds desert them, which they are bound to do in due course.

Now I come to the uniqueness of our critique. It is true that scholars in the West have written a lot in criticism of Christianity in its various aspects. But as I have pointed out, most of that criticism remains unknown in this country; so our effort is unique. More pertinently, the Western critique has been, most of the time, an operation aimed at salvaging Jesus Christ from the blood-soaked history he has created in many parts of the world and for centuries on end. I am sure you are familiar with the exercise named "the disentangled Christ". The diabolical crimes which can be traced, easily and logically, to doctrines preached by Jesus Christ have been blamed on Western imperialism in general and Spanish and Portuguese imperialism in particular. Or they have been explained away by being "placed in the concrete historical context". Our critique is unique because we have seen through this game and warned our people against being tricked and buying the big lie.

Our critique is unique in yet another way. Hindus have so far failed to view Christianity from the vantage point of Sanatana Dharma. On the contrary, they have been misled into viewing Sanatana Dharma from the vantage point of Christianity. The Brahmo Samaj, the Ramakrishna Mission, and the Gandhians have built up Jesus Christ into a spiritual giant and Christianity into a religion as good as, if not better than, Sanatana Dharma. The unique thing about our critique is our telling to Hindus that Jesus Christ is a very questionable character, and that Christianity is a cruel and predatory ideology like Communism and Nazism. Believe me that our books have caused a greater surprise and pain among Hindus who have been led to look reverentially at Jesus and think of Christianity as sharing a lot in common with Hinduism and Buddhism. Many of them are now trying to face and accept the unpleasant truths.

You also deny uniqueness to our critique on another count, namely, by stating that there is nothing new about publicizing the negative features of Christianity and Islam. I must say very emphatically that you are very much mistaken. Had you studied our critique as carefully as we have presented it, you would have discovered that it is preoccupied primarily and to a large extent with what are known as the most positive doctrines of these creeds — the character of Yahweh and Allah in the Bible and the Quran; the concepts of revelation, the only son, the last prophet, and covenant with the chosen people (the Church and the Ummah); the division of historical time into ages of ignorance and illumination, of the human family into believers and unbelievers, and of the inhabited world into lands of the blessed and the damned; the positing of a permanent war (Crusade and *Jihād*) to be waged by missions and military expeditions till the unbelievers are converted or killed; the imposition of a uniform code of conduct on the believers by a theocratic state; the second coming and the day of judgment; eternal heaven for the believers and eternal hell for the unbelievers. It is these positive doctrines of Christianity and Islam which have produced, logically and inevitably, what you name as the "negative phenomenon" — religious wars, massacres, genocides, rapine, iconoclasm, slave trade, and so on. I do not have to detail to you the histories of Christianity and Islam; they have been fully documented.

Next, we compare these positive doctrines of Christianity and Islam with the positive vision of Sanatana Dharma, and carry the same exercise in the field of history. That is the only way our people can be made to see the merits and demerits of the two radically opposed traditions — the Vedic and the Biblical. You have had in the West, and for a long time, a discipline known as the Science of Comparative Religion. We are fairly familiar with the exercise which always ends by showing Biblical Monotheism as the highest manifestation of religious consciousness. There is no dearth of Hindu scholars, even religious savants, who have lapped up this Western "science", and placed the Sanatana Dharma family of spiritual traditions on the defensive, all along the line. We have only reversed the exercise and shown Biblical Monotheism as a monstrous doctrine which has plagued mankind ever since it was spelled out by the Biblical prophets. I wonder if you are at all correct in labelling this scholarship as politics. Would it be acceptable to you if we describe as politics your Science of Comparative Religion? Please drop the accusation unless in your lexicon the word "politics" can cover anything and everything.

Of course, it is not for the first time that we have been accused of playing politics. The late Father Bede "Dayananda" Griffiths told us in so many words that Ram Swarup and I were trying to create communal riots between Hindus and Christians. Some other Christian friends have told us again and again that while they appreciate "religious Hinduism", they find it hard to understand "political Hinduism", meaning the kind of work we are doing. The point that all of you are trying to make is that Hindus should not stand up and speak in defence of their own religion and culture, that Hindus should not try to analyse and understand the factors and forces in the field around them, in short, that Hindus should remain at the receiving end for all time to come. We are sorry we have to reject your advice.

Nor are you alone in getting scared of our publications. The entire Christian establishment in this country and even its patrons abroad seem to be in the same state of mind. This is in spite of the fact that VOICE OF INDIA is, to use your own phrase, a tiny set-up as compared to the giant Christian establishment, not only in terms of resources and manpower but also in terms of reach. I do not have to read out the details to you; you know the facts as a specialist on the affairs of this country. What strikes me as interesting is that it was the same story when we started calling the bluff of Communism. We were only a few with no establishment worth the name. On the other hand, the Communist establishment in this country at that time was as big as the Christian establishment at present. What is more, the Communist campaign was backed by the official establishment which stood packed with fellow-travellers including the Prime Minister, Jawaharlal Nehru. But our publications created a scare not only in the Communist establishment in this country but also in the Soviet Union and Red China.

Again, the close parallel between Christianity and Communism has a message for us, namely, that those who build houses on fragile foundations get scared even by the slightest probe. On the other hand, we look at the edifice of sound spirituality and sterling culture built by Sanatana Dharma. It has survived the Islamic attack spread over more than thirteen hundred years, and the Christian attack sustained for five centuries. We were here long before Jesus Christ was born and hurled at an unsuspecting Pagan world. And I assure you we will be here long after the Bible starts selling as waste paper on pavements around the world. Recall the fate of Hitler's *Mein Kampf* and the *Collected Works* of Lenin and Stalin.

You speak of purifying religion. We are trying to purify Hinduism by rejecting the monotheistic poison it has imbibed under the impact of Islam and Christianity. We are asking Hindus to be proud of their Gods and Goddesses, of their temples and icons, of their sages and saints, of their cultural and social traditions, in short, of all that the Biblical creeds denounce as polytheism, pantheism, idolatry and superstition. And we call upon Christians and Muslims to have a close look at Yahweh and Allah, the only saviour and the last prophet, at missions and *da'wah*, in short, at every doctrine which sanctions exclusivism and aggression. Describing these calls as spreading hatred defies our imagination.

Many Christian friends I met have told me, "I do not like the missionaries." I told everyone of them that it was no use saying so to me in private, and that what I expected was a public protest. There has been no response. Dr. Raymond Panikkar advised me to join a common platform of all religions for opposing materialism, industrialism, consumerism, and technological totalitarianism. I told him that I was all for it provided the Christian and Muslim friends on the platform denounced the mission and the *da'wah*. He smiled and gave me up. I had to tell him that his advice was tantamount to making me look the other way so that my pocket could be picked. I am inviting you to create a platform in the West for protesting against the missions let loose upon us. Then alone I will accept as honest your plea of purifying religion. Charity should begin at home.

That takes me to the core of our critique. Let me assure you that we Hindus do not care at all about what the other people believe. Christians are welcome to believe in immaculate conception, virgin birth, resurrection, and the rest. Muslims are welcome to believe in Jibril and Miraj and the miracles of Muhammad. Both of them are welcome to worship whomsoever they view as God, in their own way. The trouble arises when Christians and Muslims try to impose their beliefs and ways of worship on other people by means of force and fraud masquerading as mission and *da'wah*. People cannot be brought together so long as this aggression continues. If objection to aggression means spreading hatred, we plead guilty.

The rest of your letter is irrelevant for me because you have missed the main point, namely, our audience, and mistaken us for a reform movement. Our audience is neither the Christians nor the Muslims, in India or elsewhere. Our audience is Hindu intelligentsia and Hindu intelligentsia alone. It has been a Hindu habit for long to resent the behaviour patterns of Christians and Muslims while praising Christianity and Islam as revered religions. Christians and Muslims cannot understand this Hindu habit. They say, and say it very rightly, that Hindus accept their religions only in theory while rejecting them in practice. We are asking Hindus to reverse the process. We are asking them to study Christianity and Islam in depth and see for themselves that Christian and Muslim behaviour patterns follow from the belief system of Christianity and Islam. We are telling Hindus that it is no use protesting against the behaviour patterns while remaining blind to the belief systems. That is the long and short of our effort.

In the case of Islam, our effort aims at raising the dialogue from the street level to the level of scholarly platforms. For a long time, Hindus have been flattering Muslims by seeing nothing wrong in the doctrine of Islam. For a long time, Muslims have been taking to the streets and shedding blood whenever and wherever Hindus object to their behaviour pattern. Muslims have never been asked by Hindus to reflect on the dogmas of Islam, and revise them wherever they go against peaceful coexistence. We are appealing to Hindus to start asking some questions about Islam so that Muslims are made to rethink. If asking questions with a view to holding a dialogue is provoking violence, we plead guilty again. Hindus had a long tradition of asking questions even about their own cherished doctrines. I wonder if you are well-acquainted with our acharyas — Brahmanic, Buddhist and the rest. It was only with the advent of Islam and, later on, Christianity that Hindus were terrorised into the habit of remaining silent when faced with wild claims and not asking any questions. We are trying to revive the ancient Hindu tradition.

Yours Sincerely
Sita Ram Goel

On the other hand, the response from another Christian quarters has been positive as well as ideological. A copy of my book on Jesus Christ had been sent for review to the Catholic monthly, *Jeevadhara*, published from Kottayam in Kerala.

The March 1996 (Vol. XXVI, No. 152) of the monthly is devoted to the theme discussed in my book. The book is not mentioned either in the Editorial or in the five article which comprise the issue. But its cover carries the title, 'The Historical Jesus', and a copy of it has been addressed to me by name. In any case, two articles in it refer to another VOICE OF INDIA publication, *Arun Shourie and his Christian Critic*, in which Arun Shourie has put a question mark on the historicity of Jesus.

The articles in the monthly travel tiresomely over the same well known territory which has been covered in my book on Jesus Christ. They flaunt the same tongue-twisting jargon as has always been characteristic of Christian apologetics. Christian theologians have always had any number of tricks up their sleeves. Reading the rigmarole between the lines, it is more than obvious that their totem continues to totter so far as its historicity is concerned. Their desperation on this score has become so acute as to make them blind to what they are admitting in another context. This becomes obvious in the very first article — 'Biblical Scholarship on Historical Jesus' — written by L. Legrand of St. Peter's Pontifical Seminary at Bangalore. After saying that the search for the Jesus of history had come to a dead halt for twenty years in the aftermath of Bultmann, the theologian proceeds:

> But now, in the last few years, the interest for the historical Jesus seems to have returned with a vengeance. The reason for this revival of interest can be attributed to the pendular movement of scholarly — or simply of human — attention. It is due also to the apparition of new factors.
>
> A first factor is the rediscovery of the Jewish roots and of the Israelite background of Jesus. The rediscovery itself resulted from the convergence of a variety of elements . An important ideological stimulus was the backlash of the Holocaust in Europe at the time of World War II. The massive scale of cruelty of this atrocious genocide induced a sense of shame and led to a reflexion on the

deep seated causes of antisemitism. *Christians theology and biblical exegesis had its share of the blame in so as it had dissociated Christian identity from its Jewish sources or even too often had expressed this identity in terms of antitheses of and opposition to Judaism.* The Declaration of *Nostra Aetate* of Vatican II on the Relations of the Church with non-Christian Religions has a long paragraph recalling "the spiritual bond that links the people of the New Testament with the descendants of Abraham" (S. 4). Positive as it was, it was none the less criticized for listing the "Jewish Religion" among non-Christian "religions". A huge input of biblical scholarship tends now to see Christianity and Judaism within the continuum of a single religious movement. Jesus did not "found" a new religion meanwhile proposing a radically new perception of belonging to Israel, and, if the Church is a "new Israel", it is so in the sense not of substituting the old one but of proposing a renewed vision of the irreversible call of God (p.97, emphasis added).

One wonders whether this exercise is going to restore historicity to Jesus. What one finds intriguing is, what will happen to his divinity once he is reduced to the status of a Jewish prophet howsoever high-grade? But before we come to the latest theological trick being played in this context, we like to draw attention to an outright confession made in the above statement, namely, that the Holocaust caused by the Nazis was a direct and inevitable outcome of anti-Semitism sponsored and spread by Christianity for centuries on end. As I have pointed out in my book on Jesus Christ, the anti-Semitism of Christianity proceeds straight from what the Jesus of the gospels says about the Jews.

Did the writers of the gospels — all of them Jews — realize what they were letting loose when they transferred from the Romans to the Jews the guilt of killing Jesus? Is Christianity today prepared to purge the gospels of those poisonous phrases which make them the First Nazi Manifesto vis-a-vis the Jews? And will Christianitv go further and revise its attitude towards other non-Christians as well?

These questions are inter-linked. For, the problem which Christianity has posed, and continues to pose, before mankind is not confined to its attitude towards the Jews alone. The other non-Christians are also bothered by its attitude towards them. The writer of the article from which I have quoted above makes it more than clear that we Hindus at least can expect no such change in Christianity's attitude towards us. Coming to the end of the article, he proclaims:

> In so far as India is concerned, these developments are also relevant. India knows very well the problem of the meaning of history, that is, of an eternal and abiding Truth immanent in the contigencies of a transient world. Can *Sath*, the real Being, be enmeshed within the fleeting realities of this world? In concrete terms, can a carpenter living in a remote backward province of the Roman Empire in the distant first century of our Era be really 'the Truth' as he claimed to be, for all times and all places? Attempts have been made to rescue the Christian claim by disconnecting the Galilean Jesus from the Risen Lord. Jesus of Nazareth, limited in space and time, confined to the narrow boundaries of Semitic culture and outlook, would be of restricted relevance for today's India. Only the Risen Lord in his Glory, image of God and First-born of Creation would be the Christ of India, the Lord which the Sages and the Rishis of old would have already met in their vision of the Absolute. But would not this be a strange Bultmannian solution? Liberationist perspectives, Dalit and Female Theology aptly remind us that the poor and their oppression are also very much part of the Indian landscape and that they cannot be dispossessed of the Jesus of Nazareth who shared in their toil and knows in the flesh what it means to live in a world of injustice and corruption. Indian hermeneutics has to face the complexity of the Indian situation, its culture and counter-cultures... (p.102).

The magic by means of which a mosquito is to be transformed into a mammoth remains a closely guarded Christian secret. But we know what it is. It is the formidable finance and media power of Christian missions.

This pompous passage is only an elaboration of what J. C. Manalel says in the Editorial:

> ...in a country all but lost in the mire of the vilest crimes and corruption, the Life-of-Jesus research can hold aloft the torch of Jesus' truth and justice and love and be a constant reminder of his shining example of self-sacrifice and self-gift to humankind (p.86).

Comment on this denunciation of India and the tall claims made for the Christian totem would be superfluous. These are age-old missionary slogans being shouted in a new idiom. In the days of yore, India used to be a land of heathenism, sin, and fornication with false gods. Now it is a land of crime and corruption, caste and sex discrimination. In the days of yore, Christianity was to save us from eternal hell-fire. Now it promises to save us from social oppression and injustice. In short, we remain the damned as ever, and Christianity the only saviour as before. The rest is blah blah, of which Christian missionaries are never is short supply. What beats us is that these guys never mention in this context the plight of Dalit Christians whom they have uprooted from their ancestral society and culture, and who are displayed prominently when it comes to demanding benefits available to Hindu Harijans. Brazen-faced lying! thy name is Christianity!

Coming to "the Sages and the Rishis of old", there is no gainsaying that they *have* met the likes of Jesus in their meditations. But unfortunately for the Christian theologians their description of these spectres happens to be quite different. Take the Buddha for instance. He gives a graphic description of *Māra* whom he met while meditating in his *Vajrāsana* under the Bodhi Tree at Gaya. If one reads the doings of *Māra* in the *Dīghanikāya* and the doings of Jesus in the gospels, one cannot miss the similarity between the two. The

Gita also provides ample details of the *asura-sampad* manifested by Jesus. There are many other stories of *devāsura-saṁgrāma* — the Hindu view of history in the classics of Sanatana Dharma — in which we meet malignant figures like that of Jesus. It is time for Christian missionaries to stop telling lies about India's Sages and Rishis. They should not force us to tell more truths about Jesus. We assure them that we have done plenty of Life-of-Jesus research.

That the house of Christianity rests on fragile foundations was proved by the letter which VOICE OF INDIA received from Fr. Werner Chakkalakal. He had ordered a copy of *Jesus Christ* by value payable parcel (VPP). But he did not honour the VPP. VOICE OF INDIA wrote to him a routine letter stating that the VPP had been sent in response to his explicit order in writing, and that by not honouring it he had wasted postage which a non-profit organisation of small means could ill afford. The letter which VOICE OF INDIA received in reply is reproduced below:

Dept. of Literacy & Value Education **Navchetana Communications**

M.P. Regional Centre for performing Arts,
Literacy, Value Education & Productions
Tel. & Fax: (0755) 531389

To
Voice of India
2/18 Ansari Road
New Delhi – 110 002 19.4.96

Dear Friends,

I understand that yours is not a commercial organisation, but one devoted to glorify a falsely understood "Hindutva" by spreading misinformation about those whom you perceive as rivals. Your very name claiming to be the "Voice of India" is symbolic of your pretensions.

I had the chance cursorily to go through your book "Jesus Christ: Artifice for Aggression", a typical example of scurrilous, mischievous and sophistic writing with a show of specious erudition. It is useless to answer such studied mischief, because there is no sincere love of truth in such propaganda. Hence I decided not to honour it with a rejoinder. Sincere Hindus will not change their minds about Christ, by reading your scurrillous literature.

Only I wish to advise you not to sponsor such humbug, which would only show up the hollowness of your enterprise.

But I respect your love of Hinduism, even though it is for the wrong reasons.

Sincerely Yours,
Fr. Werner Chakkalakal CMI

Postal address for letters: NAVCHETANA, P.B. No.47, BHOPAL – 462 001 (M. P.) INDIA. R. No. 952/95.
Street address: (also postal address for packets) NAVCHETANA CENTRE, VIP Road, LALGHATI, BHOPAL – 462 032.

The letter which VOICE OF INDIA wrote back is also reproduced:

To 25.4.96
Fr. Werner Chakkalakal CMI
Navchetana Centre,
VIP Road, Lalghati,
Bhopal - 462 032
Madhya Pradesh.

Dear Sir,

Many thanks for your letter of the 19th. You have bared a face which we have always suspected to be hiding behind the mask of amiableness.

Our postcard was only a routine complaint that you did not honour the VPP which was sent to you in response to your explicit order, and that not being a commercial organisation we can ill afford loss by way of wasted postage.

We do write such complaints whenever some customor does what you did. You could have kept quiet as some of them do, or apologised as some others have done. There was no occasion for you to let your spleen take over.

We are, however, happy to know that when you ordered the book you had planned to write a rejoinder. We wish you had not changed your mind. And we do look forward to a reasoned rejoinder from you or someone else in your set-up. After all it is *your* Church which has been claiming for quite some time that Christians are in a dialogue with adherents of other religions. The book you have denounced after only a cursory look at it, happens to be a Hindu contribution to the dialogue. Or is it your case that Hindus should not examine the dogmas you sell and have a close look at the totem by which you want them to swear?

In any case, the heavy artillery of awesome adjectives you have brought into action is not going to annihilate the large number of books on Christology written by outstanding scholars in the West. Some of these scholars happen to be renowned Christian theologians. The book on which you have frowned so frightfully claims no originality. It has only presented what the traditional homelands of Christianity have known about Jesus for years on end. You would have been within your rights as well as bounds of a healthy dialogue if you had pointed out where the book had misquoted a source, or quoted it out of context, or used logic which was not straight, or used a value judgment which was not valid. We feel sorry that instead of advancing arguments, you have chosen to hurl swear-words.

We are surprised indeed to see you reacting so violently to the modern Western view of Jesus and whatever else goes with that name. We wonder how you would react if you were to glance even cursorily at the Hindu view of Jesus as presented in some of our other publications. We shall present these publications to you if you feel interested and promise not to break out into another juvenile outburst.

You accuse us of glorifying "a falsely understood 'Hindutva'." It is gratifying to know that you do not reject Hindutva outright like many others in your profession together with the motley crowd of Nehruvian Secularists. You also announce that you respect our love for Hinduism. We now wait for you to tell us what the "truly understood" Hindutva of your perception happens to be. We shall be grateful for your guidance.

We, however, refuse to let you pass unchallenged when you flatter yourself by believing that we Hindus perceive Christianity as a rival to Hindutva. That is far from the truth. Do not be misled by the recent phenomenon of some Hindu leaders and organizations recognizing Christianity as a religion. The broad mass of mainstream Hindus have always despised Christianity as an *åsurika* creed brought in by alien invaders and imposed on some of our people by force, fraud and material inducements.

You object to our naming ourselves as "the Voice of India". That is because you do not know the premises from which we proceed. We believe that India is the homeland of Hindus and that the voice of Hindus is the Voice of India. We regard our Christian and Muslim compatriots as our own people who have been alienated from their ancestral society and culture by the divisive doctrines of Christianity and Islam. Voice of India speaks for these kidnapped Hindus as well. They have been enslaved and brainwashed and cannot speak for themselves. And we look forward to the day when they will speak for themselves rather than through some self-appointed shepherds.

Incidentally, your jibe at the name of our organisation has prompted us to have a look at the banner under which you sail — *Navchetana Communications: M.P.*

Regional Centre for Performing Arts, Literacy, Value Education and Productions. It is quite a mouthful. Kindly let us have a list of your publications and/or a write-up on your performance. Meanwhile, please pardon us for saying that we have found no music in the language of your letter, no rhyme in your reasoning, no value in your judgments, and no art or education in your performance as a whole. Let us not get away with the belief that that is all that you have to show by way of "Productions".

We are enclosing the latest list of our publications. There is nothing more that we can boast of at present. In fact, the work we are doing is very simple. You will understand it better if we put it in your own language — the language of a multinational corporation marketing the "only true faith" and the "only saviour from sin and eternal perdition". Here it is. We are organizing consumer vigilance and warning our people against buying counterfeit goods. It is no use resenting our presence in the field. The better course for you is to take the hint and stop selling your merchandise under false labels. In short, unless you desist from selling lies, we shall continue to tell the truth about you and your goods.

Jai Shri Rama,

Yours faithfully
For Voice of India
Sd.
(Sita Ram Goel)

Fr. Werner's letter shows what happens when the skeletons which Christian missionaries have been hiding are brought out of the cupboard. The missionaries feel rattled. It also shows the confidence which Hindu eulogization of Jesus has inspired in the missionary mind. They have come to believe that Hindus who reject Jesus are no Hindus at all. Here is a Christian missionary who believes that he and not Hindus know what true Hindutva means!

The encounters in this chapter highlight a few points. Firstly, Hindu intelligentsia is prepared to face unpleasant facts and draw the right conclusions; it is only Hindu scholarship which has failed again and again to study aggressive dogmas and present them as such. Secondly, there are people in the West who are prepared to listen provided Hindus present their case to them. Thirdly, there are elements in the West (as in India) who believe that an aggression once established cannot and should not be questioned, and who see scenes of civil war if the victims of aggression refuse to remain at the receiving end; that is what they mean when they extol "Hindu tolerance".

23

Encounter with Arun Shourie

Missiology is a meticulous discipline developed quite early in the history of Christianity as auxiliary to an exclusivist and aggressive doctrine — Jesus Christ is the only saviour; there is no salvation outside the Church; and infidels should be compelled to come in. By now the discipline has become rather rich with experience gained over several centuries and in all parts of the world. Many universities in Europe and the Americas teach Missiology in their faculties of Catholic and Protestant theologies. And there are a large number of Christian seminaries spread over many countries where Missiology is studied in great depth and detail by the soldiers of Christ before they commence their prowl in search of prey.

As one surveys the literature of Missiology, one is struck by its close similarity to the Communist literature on strategy and tactics for staging the Revolution. One can go further and compare the two literatures — Christian and Communist — with the literature on military science. Again, the close similarity is striking. One can, therefore, conclude quite safely that Missiology is simply another name for waging war on non-Christian societies and cultures with a view to conquer and convert them completely.

The war was hot and waged with whatever happened to be the most lethal weapons at any time, so long as the states in Europe served as the secular arm of the Church. In this first phase of a permanent war, there was no crime, howsoever horrendous, which Missiology did not prescribe or endorse, and which was not practised by the holy warriors with great glee and clean conscience. The blood-soaked history of

Christian missions which preceded or accompanied or followed the armies of European imperialism, has been narrated by the missionaries themselves. Men like Francis Xavier stand out in this record as hardened criminals masquerading as religious priests.

The hot war came to end only when the imperialist powers realized that their empires could be jeopardized if the sword was used overtly in the service of the cross, particularly in the countries of Asia where the infidels were proud of their religions and cultures and capable of coming out with armed resistance. Missiology was forced to devise methods of waging a cold war by manipulating human minds. Armed might was to be called into service only when missionary provocations enraged the natives and riots broke out. For the rest, massive finance and media power provided more effective weapons.

In this second phase of the permanent war, Christian missions mounted vicious campaigns of calumny against the religions and cultures of the conquered people so that the latter could be disarmed ideologically, deflated psychologically, and thrown on the defensive all along the line. At the same time, programmes of proslytization were launched for crystallizing in the heart of subjugated societies whole colonies of converts. Country after country was honeycombed with this bastardized breed always ready to serve as the fifth-column of Christian-Western imperialism. In most cases, the converts proved to be more faithful than their foreign masters.

The game was going on smoothly and satisfactorily when it was spoiled by the retreat of Western imperialism after the Second World War. What was more ominous for Christian missions, Christianity itself was found out and suffered a collapse in its traditional homelands. Missiology was now called upon to devise still more devious methods, not only for camouflaging the fangs of a criminal creed but also for finding a new home for it elsewhere, particularly in the Hindu-Buddhist countries. The lead for forging more sophisticated methods, was given by the Second Vatican Council after prolonged deliberations during 1962-65. The foremost among these new methods was described as "dialogue". The missionaries were directed to "discover whatever was of value in other religious traditions" and proclaim that "salvation was available" in those traditions as well. The fact that this concession rendered the Christian missions redundant was neither faced nor mentioned. The purpose of "dialogue" was far from honest.

In the context of "dialogue" with Hindus, the first purpose is quite obvious. Hindus who participate in it recognize explicitly or implicitly that Christianity is a religion and that those who are out to spread it have a legitimate place in this country. The second purpose of "dialogue" is to search for and locate segments of Hindu spiritual tradition which sound or can be made to sound similar to some Christian tradition. A "common ground" between Hinduism and Christianity can then be proclaimed and used for conveying Christianity in Hindu attire. The third purpose is to probe for points of resistance which Hindu mind may harbour vis-a-vis Jesus Christ, the Christian message and the Christian missions so that mission strategy can be suitably revised for overcoming the resistance.

Needless to say that Hindu participants have to be of different types for serving the different purposes of "dialogue". The Hindu who qualifies for the first purpose has to be more or less ignorant of Hinduism as well as of Christianity. The Hindu who suits the second purpose should be somewhat knowledgeable about Hinduism but an innocent abroad when it comes to Christianity. Hindus of both types are available easily and in plenty, particularly because the bait of foreign trips for holding "dialogue" in better places and with brighter people is always there. What has proved difficult is the search for a Hindu who can serve the third purpose of "dialogue".

So "dialogue" for serving its first two purposes has been going on for quite some time. Christian organizations qualified for holding "Hindu-Christian dialogue" have mushroomed all over the country in recent years. The proceedings are reported in the Christian press as well as in the publications of these organizations. Books on "Hindu-Christian dialogue" or "common ground" between Hinduism and Christianity have also been multiplying, particularly in Europe and the U.S.A. Periodicals devoted specifically to Hindu-Christian dialogue have also been launched.

A dialogue for serving its third purpose could be held only in January 1994 when Arun Shourie, the noted journalist and scholar, was invited by the Catholic Bishops' Conference of India (CBCI) to present a "Hindu assessment" of missionary work in India. But unfortunately for the managers of this "dialogue", it went out of hand and misfired. Ever since, the giant Christian establishment in India has been smarting with the hurt which Arun Shourie has caused. The uproar he has raised can be compared only with the uproar which had followed the publication of K. M. Panikkars' *Asia and Western Dominance* in 1953. Missiology has been mobilizing its arsenal of apologetics and polemics in order to control the damage that has been done to Christian claims and pretensions.

It is difficult to say why the CBCI chose Arun Shourie for "dialogue". All one can do is to infer from known missionary motives. Here was a Hindu, they must have thought, who was a man of stature, and known for his scholarship as well as pronounced sympathy for Hindu causes. His writings and speeches so far gave no indication that his commitment to the Hindu spiritual vision was profound, or that his knowledge of Christian doctrine and history was wide-ranging. He could, therefore, be expected to provide some clues to the current Hindu resistance to Christianity, and at the same time say something about Jesus Christ or Christianity which could be advertised to the advantage of Christian missions.

The CBCI was celebrating the 50th anniversary of its foundation, and holding a Seminar at Ishvani Kendra, a Catholic seminary in Pune. Almost all the Catholic big-wigs in India were present when Arun Shourie gave his talk on 5 January 1994. He had been given two Conference documents — 'Trends and Issues in Evangelization of India' and 'Paths of Mission in India Today' — which the Seminar was discussing. His critique was confined to missionary methods, more or less on the lines laid down by Mahatma Gandhi during his prolonged encounter with Christian missionaries. Some of those present asked some questions which also were similar to the questions the Mahatma had been asked earlier. The atmosphere was cordial all through. At the end of the session, its president remarked, "It has been a feast." After his return to Delhi, Arun Shourie received a letter dated 11 January 1994, from Augustine Kanjamala, Secretary to the Conference, thanking him for sparing time from his "busy schedule", and requesting him to "give a presentation in writing" so that it could be published along with the "talks of various speakers of the Conference."

Arun Shourie completed the paper pretty fast. He gave it the caption, 'Missionaries in India', and sent a copy of it to Kanjamala on 20 January 1994 with the request that it be published with the two Conference documents as annexures because it had references to and citations from them at several places. He received from Kanjamala a letter dated 9 February thanking him for "completing the work and sending it" promptly but pointing out that the paper was too long for "publication along with other contributors." Kanjamala asked him if it was possible to "cut it down to, say, 10,000 words." Finally, on 27 February 1994 Kanjamala came to meet Arun Shourie at the latter's home in New Delhi and informed him that his paper "would be published alongwith responses from six or so persons who were working on the matter."

In the two months that followed, Arun Shourie expanded his paper with material from the history of Christian missions in India during British rule. He highlighted the motives from which missionary work had proceeded, and the consequences it had entailed. He cited ample evidence to show how the work of undermining Hinduism and keeping

India enslaved had been shared between missionary scholars and scholar missionaries on the one hand and the British administrators on the other. And he pointed out how "the genes planted then had grown into the *fleurs de mal,* the flowers of evil which continue to poison the perceptions of our elite to this day." Finally, he offered an analysis of the two Conference documents to show how Christian missions had continued the same work of subversion in post-independence India with such adjustments as were dictated by the new situation.

By the time the paper was fully elaborated, it had acquired the size of a book. Arun Shourie published it in early May 1994 under the title, *Missionaries in India: Continuities, Changes, Dilemmas.*[1] The two Conference documents were included in it as annexures for purposes of ready reference. A copy of the book was sent to Kanjamala with compliments and thanks "for the invitation extended" and the opportunity given to the author "to delve into the subject." Meanwhile, Arun Shourie had written several articles on the subject in his syndicated column which appears in more than a score of newspapers published in several languages all over the country. The articles evoked a lively discussion in the *Maharashtra Herald* of Pune.

Kanjamala was quick to acknowledge receipt of the book by his letter dated 18 May 1994. But what followed the acknowledgment left Arun Shourie aghast. Firstly, Kanjamala accused Arun Shourie of publishing "our seminar material without permission", and enclosed "a corrected and revised version" to be included in a new edition of the book. Secondly, he sent an article, 'Hinduization or Christianization', and insisted that it be incorporated as a chapter in the new edition as per agreement arrived at "when we met each other in Delhi in February." Thirdly, he suggested that the cover page of the new edition should carry his name as co-author because his article and the two Conference documents

1. ASA Publications, New Delhi, 1994.

would together form one-third of the book. Finally, he requested Arun Shourie to let him know "when the next edition is coming out with the revised material", and promised to "promote" it.

Kanjamala had given away the game he was playing or was forced to play, when he confessed in the same letter that "some people are very displeased with me", and appealed to Arun Shourie to "appreciate my situation." Arun Shourie was prepared to sympathize with the man placed in plight, perhaps for no fault of his own. But he was not at all prepared to concede to that man the right to invent stories, tell lies, and let his fancy run a riot. So he chided Kanjamala in a long letter dated 24 May 1994. The letters which Kanjamala had written to him earlier were still in his file. He used them to put the record straight. He repudiated as a total lie Kanjamala's story that there was an agreement for including in the book a chapter written by Kanjamala. He turned down Kanjamala's suggestion regarding co-authorship as contrary to his nature and practice as a writer. And he pointed out that at no stage before or after his talk in Pune or in the letters written to him subsequently, he was given to understand that the two Conference documents were for private circulation. In fact, he had been given not one but two sets of the documents with the word "Draft" written clearly on top of the first page in each case.

Kanjamala wrote back that what he had conveyed in his letter dated 18 May 1994 was due to a "misunderstanding". Arun Shourie expressed his happiness to Kanjamala, and thought that the "cloud had blown over." But he had not taken into account the patent missionary methods. He found that a vituperative campaign had been launched against his book and against him personally. Articles started appearing in various newspapers and publications of the Church, attributing motives to him and misrepresenting as well as denouncing his book. Several Christian scribes had joined the campaign. But Kanjamala was in its forefront.

PRAJNA BHARATI, a forum for intellectual discourse and

discussion with headquarters in Hyderabad, invited several senior Churchmen to discuss *Missionaries in India* on a public platform with Arun Shourie. All of them excused themselves on one pretext or the other. At last the forum extended an invitation to Kanjamala. He agreed to participate in the discussion on the condition that he would present his critique before Arun Shourie gave an answer. Arun Shourie had no objection to Kanjamala having the first salvo.

The discussion took place on 4 September 1994 in a big hall at Hyderabad. The hall was packed to capacity. The discussion and the question-answer session that followed lasted for three and half hours. Kanjamala made the following points:

1. Literature showing Hindu antagonism to Christian missionaries is nothing new. The Arya Samaj had produced such literature in the past. Rashtriya Swayamsevak Sangh, Bharatiya Janata Party, Vishwa Hindu Parishad and many other organisations are producing it at present.

2. Arun Shourie has written the book for a specific readership in mind, namely, the people belonging to Hindu organizations, and with a specific purpose in view, namely, to present Christian missionaries as enemies of the nation.

3. The missionary and allied literature cited by Arun Shourie in support of his main argument pertains to the colonial period of India's history. It was written in a different context and is, therefore, dated and irrelevent in the present situation.

4. Conversations of Gandhi with Christian missionaries, writings of Vivekananda, and conclusions of the Niyogi Committee Report also belong to a bygone age. They relate to an antiquated world view, mission view, mission theology, concept of salvation, role of Christian missionaries and evangelization.

5. Arun Shourie's book is aggressive and his interpretation of data exaggerated. His strategy is negative. He has a hidden agenda because nowhere in his big book he

says anything positive about the work and contribution of Christian missionaries. He is preoccupied with missionary activities aimed at conversion. He has not even mentioned eminent Christian scholars such as Bede Griffiths, Klaus Klostermaier, Abhishiktananda, Sara Grant, Amalorpavadas, Amaloor, Raimundo Panikkar, M. M. Thomas etc. whose contributions to Indian thought are well-known.

6. Arun Shourie has not taken into account the lead given by the Second Vatican Council. He has quoted from CBCI documents which were only working papers of a seminar but not referred even once to the statement[2] issued by the CBCI at the end of the seminar.

7. Recent Christian thinking on missionary activities has a very positive attitude to all the world religions. The primary motive of these activities is not conversion. The old mission idea of salvation is on the way out.

8. Arun Shourie says that missionary activity should be subject to public scrutiny. But who will be the scrutinizer? India's parliamentary and judicial systems are in decline. Government of India is biased against Christian missions.

9. Conversion movement among Scheduled Castes, Scheduled Tribes and some backward communities is simultaneously a protest movement, and not necessarily a salvation movement. Hindu society has sections to whom social liberation has great appeal. Ambedkar had also led a similar protest movement.

10. Christian missions are blamed for trouble in the North-East. But the trouble is not due to religion; it is politics, the same as in Punjab and Kashmir. Why should

---

2. In his letter dated 18 May 1994, Kanjamala referred to the documents as "draft report" and to the statement as the "revised and corrected version" of the "draft report". He sent it to Arun Shourie after *Missionaries in India* was already in print. How could Arun Shourie refer to it in the book? Moreover, the statement reflected nothing of the "draft report", namely, the two Conference documents. It consisted entirely of stereotyped missionary claims and slogans.

Arun Shourie choose the North-East in particular?

11. The question is often asked that if salvation is possible in other religions, what is the usefulness of Christian missions? The answer at present is that missions witness and express God's love and promote love, justice, peace and human dignity.

12. Christianity is 2000 years old in India, while missionary work is only 500 years old. For a long time, the government in India was on the side of the missions; yet Christians remain an insignificant minority in this country. It should be obvious that Christianity poses no threat to Hinduism; yet Christians are being subjected to physical attack in all parts of the country, particularly in the Hindi belt.

13. The small Christian community, a mere two per cent of the total population, has made great contributions in the field of education, medical help, and care of the poor and the destitute. Christian missionaries like myself are always prepared to suffer great hardships and travel to distant places in order to render service.

14. Even a staunch critic of Christianity like K. M. Panikkar has admitted that clauses of the Indian Constitution which pertain to the welfare of Scheduled Castes and Tribes, are a Christian contribution. There are only a few people who are willing to stand on the side of the poor and the marginalised. Gandhi had tried his own experiment but failed. What remains now is the Christian missionary experiment.

15. Arun Shourie has spared not even Mother Teresa in his book. But she is the ideal for a majority of the missionaries.

Kanjamala ended his critique with a prayer of Mother Teresa, and another of St. Francis of Assissi.

Arun Shourie developed his rejoinder along the following lines:

1. Christian missionaries have made great contributions in many areas. Many missionaries have been dedicated

people. Nobody in India's public life is opposed to Christian propagation of faith. Kanjamala should not fight battles with imaginary enemies.

2. Christians in India are open to a dialogue, unlike the Islamic community which has stamped out dialogue by its verbal terrorism. The CBCI dignitaries deserve tribute for inviting discussion.

3. The book contains quite a few references to the positive contributions made by Christian missions. Kanjamala should have read the book with greater care. He has misrepresented the book in several other instances. He should read again pages so and so.

4. Missionary attacks on Hinduism were not mistakes; they were gross exaggerations and wholesale distortions made with a purpose. Swami Vivekananda and Gandhiji pointed out repeatedly that the motive of these attacks was to malign Hinduism. Even so it is admitted that these attacks helped to hasten the work of Hindu reformers.

5. Hindus by and large did not get converted to Christianity, not because the missionaries did not try but because Hindu society has always had inner strength.

6. It is wrong to say that missionaries could have used state power for effecting conversions. The fact is that state power was not available to them. By the time British rule became established in India, Christians in Europe had become humanised and overt use of state power was not allowed for conversions. Islam had used state power during its rule. Look at the result. If today the Indian Constitution is changed to say that Fundamental Rights guaranteed in Chapter III are available only to Hindus, you will see Christians and Muslims flocking to the Hindu fold.

7. Kanjamala says that Arun Shourie has not spared even Mother Teresa. But the book does pay handsome tributes to her. Kanjamala's comment, therefore, is not a good example of Christian honesty.

8. Kanjamala says that 85% of the Christian priests do

not want conversion. Yet conversions go on, covert and overt. The book provides evidence, not about methods of conversion used in the past but about methods which are being used at present.

9. It was only when the book was published that Kanjamala started proclaiming that the Conference documents reproduced in it were confidential. This is dishonest. On the other hand, the document which he offers as the final statement, is a whitewashed document. The author could have been held guilty if he had published some selected passages from the earlier documents. But he has published them in full at his own expense. He did so because unlike the "final statement", the earlier ones are candid and straight-forward.

10. Citations from old missionary literature are being dismissed by Kanjmala as belonging to a bygone age. But the sophisticated slander they carried has been internalized by the Indian elite. That is why our country stands bewildered today. That literature is, therefore, not yet dated. Moreover, Kanjamala's own articles in the press published recently prove that the sophisticated slander continues.

11. The book does discuss changes in missionary thinking and cites the Conference documents in this connection. Had it dealt with changes supposed to have been introduced by people like Bede Griffiths, the author would have landed in court on a charge of defamation.

12. The current missionary literature contrasts Jesus Christ with Rama, Krishna and Mahadeva, and says that while the former died and rose on the third day the latter died for good. The author can cite what the latest biblical scholarship says about Jesus. But he does not want to go into that at present. Even the gospels carry contradictory stories about Jesus.

13. Kanjamala says that Arun Shourie has a hidden agenda. Arun Shourie has no need to hide anything. He says openly that he wants to save the country from the

sweet poison which missionaries are spreading about Hindus Shastras, Hindu Gods and Goddesses, and Hindu Avatars. How would Kanjamala feel if somebody wrote the same way about Jesus and Mary Magdalene?

14. The world has to be grateful to Pope John for bringing back compassion in the Christian doctrine. But the CBCI Secretary's Report views this change with great concern. The Report mourns that the new doctrine has killed the motive for missionary work, namely, conversions. The Church in India finds it difficult to accept the change.

15. The fact is that the change has been brought about by the collapse of Christian belief due to progress of science and technology. The same thing has happened to Marxism. Islam is bound to meet the same fate.

16. Kanjamala refers to the Nazi persecution of Jews. It is, however, Christians who have persecuted Jews for 2000 years. That was because, by an act of fraud, the gospels shifted the responsibility for killing Jesus from Pontius Pilate to the Jews.

17. When the book refers to missionary subversion in the North-East, it quotes not some RSS source but a report of the Joint Intelligence Committee of the Government of India. The author has changed only the names of places and persons mentioned in the report. But the means and methods employed by the missions come out clearly. Kanjamala's own articles say how they are alienating converts in the North-East from the rest of India.

18. Christian missions claim that they have brought about a change in the social status of converts. But the CBCI's own report admits that there has been no change, and discrimination against Dalit Christians continues in the Church. Christian missionaries are now agitating for reservations for Dalit converts. All that the missions have succeeded in doing is to spread abominable superstitions among the Harijans and tribals.

19. Christian scholarship is quite mischievous. It has distorted India's history. For instance, the national heroes

of the 1857 rebellion against British rule are being presented as villains. This scholarship says that tribals are not Hindus. People should read the discussion in Census reports about how to describe the tribals. There was a deliberate attempt to name them as non-Hindus by inventing new terms like "animists" etc. Christian missionaries are continuing the fraud. The same method was used by missionaries like Macauliffe to separate Sikhs from Hindus. Ambedkar also fell into the missionary trap in respect untouchables when he demanded separate electorates for them. Kanjamala gives the recent example of Hindus converting to Buddhism at Patna. He does not mention the quarrel that arose when it was discovered that the show had been financed by a Christian group. Christian missions happen to be patrons of people like Rajasekhara Chetty and Kanshi Ram, and the poison they emit.

20. Kanjamala claims that Christian missions are working for the welfare of tribals. But when Sarvodaya workers or the RSS starts welfare activities such as schools in the tribal areas, the missionaries are up in arms. The fact is that they are not bothered about welfare of any people. All they are trying to do is to find a new home for Christianity in the poor countries because Christianity has collapsed in Europe and North America. Modernization has bankrupted the Church everywhere. That is why the Church is worried over untouchability dying out in India.

21. Christian missionaries should be honest when they try to convert anyone. The person should be informed about what the latest biblical scholarship says about Jesus Christ. He is no longer an historical figure. The convert should not be kept in the dark about the rationalist critique of Christianity and the Bible. Otherwise the convert is bound to suffer from tension when he or she learns the true facts later on.

Arun Shourie ended his answer by examining the prayers cited by Kanjamala. He found them full of "our", "I" and "me", meaning the Church and the Christians. Why pray for only one community? Why not for all people? The Upanishad prayers, he said, breath a different, a universal spirit.

There were some questions at the end. Kanjamala repeated the same arguments as earlier, though in a different way. Arun Shourie fixed him again with new quotations from missionary literature, and more facts about missionary work.

While I prepared for publication Arun Shourie's encounter with Kanjamala,[3] I noticed a few weaknesses in the former's argument.

Firstly, a Hindu does not have to subscribe to the negative-positive syndrome in respect of the work of Christian missions. There can be nothing positive about poison which is what Christian missions have been and remain. One need not subscribe to Mahatma Gandhi's preposition that Christian missions quickened Hindu conscience and expedited Hindu reform movements. Hindus had been reforming and renewing their society long before Christianity was born, and did not have to wait for Christian missions to stand up and perform. Moreover, the reform movements inspired by Christian missions have only derailed Hindu society and made it ape the Christian-Western model.

Secondly, Hindus are not called upon to do homage to a Christian hoax like Mother Teresa. She is a synthetic product manufactured by Christian media power and prize-distribution devices. All she has done is to portray Hindu society in nasty and negative colours. It is time that Hindus see through the humbug.

Thirdly, the Christian attempt to date its historical record should be viewed in the context of Christian dogma which has created that record. So long as the dogma remain constant, the record cannot be dated, no matter how soft the new verbiage happens to be. The Christian argument that old missionary writings should be overlooked as belonging to a bygone age, is absolutely phoney.

---

3. *Arun Shourie And His Christian Critic*, Voice of India, New Delhi, 1995.

Fourthly, there is no evidence that Pope John or the Second Vatican Council brought back compassion in the Christian doctrine. The statement implies that the Christian doctrine did have compassion to start with and had lost it at some stage. This is not true. The doctrine was cruel and aggressive at its very birth. Pope John can at best be credited with realism which made him see the collapse of Christianity in the West, and give a call for change of tactics so that Christianity could secure another home.

Meanwhile, another musketeer of the Christian Mission in India was trying to engage Arun Shourie into another duel. Vishal Mangalwadi with headquarters in Mussoorie, U.P., wrote ten letters to the author of *Missionaries in India* between 8 August 1994 and 21 September 1995. Arun Shourie glanced at the first letter and consigned it to where it belonged — the waste-paper basket. The others that followed remained unopened and met the same fate. He had better things to do than go through the garbage collected by a professional practitioner of *suppressio veri suggestio falsi.* Mangalwadi published his letters in the form of a book in early 1996. "I had hoped," he mourned, "that Mr. Shourie would reply to my letters, so that eventually we could publish our dialogue — perhaps jointly. However, since he chose not to, these letters are now placed before the reader as a monologue."[4]

In his 'letters', Mangalwadi tries to look very learned. He consumes a lot of verbiage but says very little. He cites many books like his own, and drops any number of names which nobody except his own tribe has ever heard. He also advertises that he has been on frequent trips abroad, and spoken on varied subjects in different countries. But none of it is likely to impress the reader who knows what the whole-time hirelings of Christian missions are doing normally and non-stop — spilling ink, trotting the globe, and blowing hot air — while dwelling on the one and only theme, namely, that

4. Introduction to *Missionary Conspiracy: Letters to a postmodern Hindu,* Mussoorie, 1996.

Christianity has a monopoly over Truth with capital T. "God has revealed the Truth," says Mangalwadi, "in His Word (the Bible)." Those who have read the Bible with the eyes of European Enlightenment, can only comment that Jehovah does not cease to be the Devil he is simply by being labelled as God, and that the most wicked book known to the history of mankind does not cease to be so simply by being sold as 'His Word'.

For the rest, Mangalwadi's 524-page monologue can be summarized in a few sentences. He wants us to believe that the Christian missions have been, and remain, "a conspiracy to bless India", and that the atrocities to which this country was subjected during the British rule should be blamed on people like Clive. It is the same stereotyped song which a whole tribe of Christian scribes has been singing over the last several decades in order to salvage Christianity from its horrible history. But unfortunately for the tribe, the history of Christianity and its missions everywhere has been documented in great detail by Western scholars. What is more, in days not very distant, the hawkers of "the only saviour" have themselves chronicled their gory deeds with considerable pride. These first-hand accounts leave little doubt that Christian missionaries were the most criminal elements in the colonial establishments of the West, and that the teaching which activated them came from Jesus Christ. Secular colonialists like Clive had caused only physical injuries to the conquered people, and robbed them merely of material wealth. The soldiers of Jesus Christ, on the other hand, uprooted their victims from the latter's spiritual habitat, and deprived them of their souls. Mangalwadi himself is an excellent example of what happens when a Hindu embraces Christianity.

A word about the jargon with which Mangalwadi starts his exercise. He dismisses Arun Shourie by pigeon-holing him as 'post-modern'. He does not know that Hinduism has its own view of Time, and that a person who serves Sanatana Dharma cannot be dated. Scholars like Arun Shourie belong neither to the past, nor to the present, nor yet to the future. They belong to a timeless span. By the same logic the history of Christianity cannot become dated so long as its basic theology remains intact. It is no use changing verbiage. What needs changing is the dogma, namely, that Jesus Christ is the one and only saviour.

24

Fixing a Christian Windbag

The United States of America is a land of sharp contradictions when it comes to matters of faith. On the one hand, it is the land of Thomas Jafferson, Tom Paine, James Madison and Mark Twain who distrusted or denounced or ridiculed the Christian dogma and scripture in unmistakable words. On the other hand, it is the land of the most fanatical and fundamentalist Christian sects each one of which will have not only the USA but the whole world exclusively for itself. On the one hand, it is a land where the spiritual vision of Hinduism and Buddhism finds ready audience, and flourishes. On the other hand, it is a land where blind belief systems like Christianity and Islam whine and whimper, and brainwash any number of victims. The key to understanding the scene lies in the history of this land.

Bloodthirsty fanaticism which characterises the biblical creeds was unknown to the Pagans who had lived for long and in peace with their environment and every variety of worship in the vast stretch which is now known as the United States. But the scene was disturbed from the early sixteenth century onwards when wave after wave of Christian sects from Europe poured in, destroyed the Pagans as well as Paganism, and occupied the whole place. Most of these sects were Protestants, the Puritans from England and elsewhere being the dominant element among them. They were fleeing from persecution in Europe at the hands of the Catholic Church and other Protestant sects. They viewed themselves as the chosen people and looked forward to creating a total Christian society in accordance with their own tenets in what they viewed as the promised land. But as has been usual with Christian sects throughout the history of Christianity, it was not before long that these sects fell out among themselves, and took to heresy-hunting and witch-burning.

The promised land was heading towards becoming another hell like Europe when fortunately for it the European Enlightenment entered it in the eighteenth century. The founding fathers of the Republic and the framers of the United States Constitution were secularists who believed in the freedom of religion and left the choice of belief to individual conscience. The warring Christian sects were thus kept at bay, and Deism and Atheism came to flourish with increasing speed. Buddhism, Confucianism, Taoism and Hinduism also entered the scene, significantly since the second half of the nineteenth century, and the US people started getting informed more and more about spiritual traditions which were radically different from Christianity. The USA became a melting pot of faiths as it had been a melting pot of races, peoples and cultures. It continued to be honey-combed with Christian sects and cults which multiplied fast and into thousands. But, by and large, it remained a land of liberal humanism..

Meanwhile, the USA was becoming a land of big money and big business, particularly during the twentieth century. Christianity followed suit and became a big business through the mechanism of missions sent out for saving the heathens in Asia and Africa. Huge amounts of money were collected from gullible Christian communities by portraying the heathens as starved in body and soul and hungering for Jesus Christ. Media power was used to the hilt. Missions provided lucrative careers to crude and illitrate cowboys trained for a few months in seminaries which went on multiplying. Multinational corporations also moved in to help the missions because the culture which the missions spread increased the demand for US manufactures. The State Department and the Pentagon saw the missions as useful agencies for gathering intelligence and planting misinformation. All in all, Christian sects could collect and spend billions of dollars and employ millions of people for selling Jesus Christ like fast foods and other items of modern consumerism. It is not unoften that we hear scandals about how some clever people embezzle big slices of money collected for missionary work.

Ram Swarup reviewed in *The Times of India* dated 13-14 March 1988 the *Mission Handbook: North American Missionaries Overseas* published in the USA in 1986. He quoted several books on how Hindus and Hinduism are viewed by some Christian sects in the USA. The Texas-based Gospel for Asia group looks down upon Hindus "as a living example of what happens when Satan rules the entire culture", and sees India as "one vast purgatory in which millions of people... are literally living a cosmic lie!" Dayspring International, a Virginia-based evangelical organisation, describes India as a land of "division, despair and death" in a television programme and quotes Mother Teresa in holding that India was "in dire need of Jesus." In fact, Mother Teresa is often quoted by and shown on Christian controlled electronic media in the USA for painting India in the darkest colours.

The top TV Evanglist, Pat Robertson, has become well-known in recent years for his loud-mouthed harangues against Hindus and Hinduism. He is leader of the Christian Coalition and represents the conservative Christian community as well as the Christian right-wing of the Republican Party in the USA. He is also a billionaire businessman whose empire has its tentacles in all corners of the world. He reaps rich rewards from diamond and gold mines and thousands of acres of rain forest in Zaire. President Mobutu of Zaire is notorious for human rights violations, and has been debarred from entering the USA. But Robertson has tried to pressurise President Bill Clinton for lifting the ban on Mobutu. Successive US ambassadors in Zaire have complained that Robertson is undermining US foreign policy in that part of the world. In any case, Robertson got shot into fame when he made a bid for the US presidency in 1988.

On 23 March 1995, Robertson appeared on the "700 Club" TV show which he controls, and started by saying that

Hinduism was devil-worship and despicable idolatry responsible for India's poverty and other ills. "Of all of India's problems," he proclaimed, "one stands out from the rest. That problem is idol worship. It is said that there are hundreds of millions of Hindu deities. All this has put a nation in bondage to spiritual forces that have deceived many for thousands of years." According to him, Hindus "are out to kill other human beings in the name of their God." And he appealed to his countrymen to keep Hindus and Hinduism out of the USA. "We are importing Hinduism into America," he mourned. "We can't let that stuff come into America" he warned. At the same time, he assured his audience that Hindus were hungering for and in desperate need of Jesus Christ.

I came to know of the whinings of this Christian windbag from an article in the monthly *Hinduism Today* which had given his address and advised Hindus all over the world to register protest. The first thing I did was to airmail to him a copy of *Jesus Christ: An Artifice for Aggression* in order to let him know what we Hindus think of the garbage he is out to sell. I followed it up with a letter dated 15 July 1995 which read as follows:

> Dear Mr. Robertson,
>
> Some friends in the USA — the country of Thomas Jefferson, James Madison, Walt Whitman and Mark Twain, and a land par excellence of liberal humanism — have drawn my attention to your recent fulminations against Hinduism, Hindus, and India.
>
> My first reaction was sheer amusement at this latest spectacle of patent Christian tantrums. I am familiar with what Christian theologians, missionaries and windbags have been saying about our religion, our people, and our country since the days of St. Hippolytus (230 AD), more particularly since 1542 AD when that Patron Saint of Pirates, Francis Xavier, reached our shores. Thousands of shelves in hundreds of Christian seminaries in India and abroad are laden with the pornography which soldiers of

the Only Saviour have produced down the centuries.

I also know that you have to make a living for yourself,[1] and collect money for maintaining the giant missionary apparatus in this country as well as keeping within your fold the rice Christians you have managed to collect during the past four hundred years. I can see that the only way you can do it is by selling to your gullible people the Big Lie that we are an accursed rabble hungering for Jesus Christ. You are neither the first nor likely to be the last in this cynical enterprise. I have witnessed how Mother Teresa has flourished and become a world figure by plying the same trade with a straight face.

On second thoughts, however, I have decided to pen the lines that follows.

Firstly, I plead that we are living in an age when sinners are coming forward to apologize to the sinned against. I cannot believe that you are unaware of how the Germans have apologized to the Jews and the Japanese to the Koreans. And I think it is high time for Christians to apologize to the Hindus. The crimes which Christian missionaries have committed in this country since the days of Francis Xavier have been documented by Christian scholars themselves.

Secondly, I wish to point out that you have got your priorities wrong. Instead of trying to save the Hindus, you should better try to save whatever has survived of the totem by which you swear. I have airmailed to you a copy of *Jesus Christ: An Artifice for Aggression* in which I have compiled the conclusions of Christological research in the modern West. It is too late in the day for you to exercise yourself about Hinduism and the Hindus. It may be more profitable for you to address your own dwindling flock in what was once known as Christendom.

Thirdly, I like to draw your attention to the fact that we

1. I did not know at that time that Robertson was a buisness tycoon and a big moneybag on his own.

Hindus are an ancient people and have survived many storms including those mounted by Islam and its elder blood brother — Christianity. We were here long before your Jehovah and Jesus were invented by the diabolical drives in human nature and hurled upon an unsuspecting humanity. And we will be here long after the Bible starts selling as waste paper on pavements around the world. Try to remember the fate of Hitler's *Mein Kampf* and the *Collected Works* of Lenin and Stalin.[2]

For, Hinduism is a spiritual culture which is intrinsic to the human species, and has never been in need of big battalions, or big money, or big media in order to back it up. Hinduism knows how to find its way to human hearts, no matter how desperate the effort of contrived creeds to shut them tight against all higher aspirations. Hinduism is Sanatana Dharma, the Perennial Wisdom and Virtue. It is no use spitting at the Sun.

Regards

Yours Sincerely
Sd.
Sita Ram Goel

Mr. Pat Robertson,
CBN, 977 Centerville Turnpike,
VIRGINIA BEACH, VA 23463-0001,
U.S.A.

Meanwhile, Shri Bharat J. Gajjar who lives and works in Washington had contacted Robertson's Christian Broadcasting Network and protested against the venom being vomited by its star performer. He received a letter dated 4 August 1995 from Robertson which said:

Dear Bharat,

Thank you for contacting CBN concerning our program

---

2. The last two sentences in this para comparing the Bible with the works of Hitler, Lenin and Stalin were censored out by most papers which published this letter; such is the awe inspired by this wicked book.

presentation on Hinduism. I appreciate this opportunity to respond to you.

I'm sorry you objected to my comments. It is not my intent to offend anyone because of their religion, and I want you to clearly understand that I do believe in religious freedom. It is guaranteed in the Constitution of the United States and everyone has the right to believe as they wish. However, though I respect the rights of others, please understand that I have a responsibility to speak the truth. The truth is that the Hindu faith has absolutely nothing to do with God! The Bible tells us that there is only one way to hit the mark and that is to come to Jesus Christ. Jesus said in John 14:6, "I am the Way, the Truth, and the Life: NO MAN COMES TO THE FATHER, BUT BY ME."

I don't make the rules — God makes the rules. He said if you don't come through Jesus Christ, there is no entrance into heaven. Those who believe they can come to God any other way, whether it be by New Age, Hinduism, Mohammed, or through any other person or thinking — are being deceived.

It is our continual prayer at CBN for all people to come to a saving knowledge of the truth of the Gospel of Jesus Christ. God is not willing that any should perish. Thank you again for this opportunity to respond to you.

Yours in Christ,
Sd.
Pat Robertson

A copy of Robertson's letter to Gajjar was received by Ram Swarup. He wrote the following article which was published in several US periodicals including *Hinduism Today:*

Mr. Robertson invited many critical comments from the Hindus. To one such Hindu critic, Bharat J. Gajjar, Robertson replied. This reply is as important to the American Hindus as his earlier TV statement which

HINDUISM TODAY reported [July, 1995]. The reply is in some ways more than a fulmination. It is a credo, an ideological statement and deserves a different kind of notice. Moreover, Robertson's mental blocks are not his alone but widely shared. Therefore, to discuss them would be all the more useful. I shall therefore reply to his reply here.

In his letter to Mr. Gajjar, Robertson says that he had no intent "to offend anyone," and that he wants it to be understood that he believes in "religious freedom" — this is reassuring after his previous performance. But he also adds that while he respects the rights of others, he has "a responsibility to speak the truth." He tells us that "the truth is that the Hindu faith has absolutely nothing to do with God!" He adds in lively Americanism that "there is only one way to hit the mark and that is to come to Jesus Christ. Those who believe they can come to God any other way, whether it be by New Age, Hinduism, Mohammed or through any other person or thinking — are being deceived." At the end, he modestly states, "I don't make the rules — God makes the rules."

The reply is brief but rich in traditional Christian theology. It reveals in a clear profile the unchanging face of Christianity, a Christianity which still lives in medieval times and refuses to change. It gives in a few sentences the most important elements of Christian theology: a single or exclusive God, an equally single and exclusive channel of reaching him and a conception of truth which requires no self-preparation, a truth which is ready-made and can be had by simply looking up a particular book.

Biblical God

First, about Hindus having no God, though they have more often been accused of having too much of it. Let us readily admit that Hindus do not have a God of the Biblical tradition, the God of Robertson's familiarity. Their God is not Jehovah, an exclusive God, a jealous God, a God that denies other Gods. In the *Vedas*, the oldest scripture of the Hindus, Gods are often invited to "come together." They are praised "conjointly" and it does not offend any one of them. *Vedic* Gods live in friendliness, they do not deny each other.

This approach was shared by the Chinese, Egyptians, Greeks, Romans and most other advanced cultures and peoples. The Greeks had no difficulty in recognizing their God in the Gods of the Hindus. It is the Semitic tradition which sees their devils in the Gods of others.

This negative view derives from another basic Biblical concept — that their God is the only one, the only true God. True, this view implies that there are other Gods, but it is freely and repeatedly stated that they are "false", they are "abominations", and they are to be dethroned.

Hindus have no God of this description. True, they too often describe their God as one, *ekam,* but they also call him many, *aneka*. Strictly speaking, Hindus do not believe in one God, they believe in one Reality, *ekam sat*. They do not say "there is only one God"; they say "God alone is." The unity of Hindu God is spiritual, not numerical. He pervades all. He is one in all and the same in all. He is also beyond all. Semitic religions have no such concept. Hindu spirituality is mystical and theological, not credal and ideological.

Exclusive Intermediary

Now we turn from an exclusive God to an exclusive savior. The two stand together. In this too, Robertson is saying nothing new, but repeating the old Christian doctrine of "No salvation outside the Church", now modified in this ecumenical age to "No salvation without Jesus Christ." In his support, he quotes the Bible as his authority. This is a curious way of arguing. You assume what you have to prove, put it in your own book and then cite it as your authority. It would be considered dull-witted in a sophomore, but in a Christian preacher it makes a bright and clinching argument.

Revelatory religions work through mediators and intermediaries. In these ideologies, first there is a God of strong preferences and hatred. He chooses a people, but even to them He does not reveal himself directly. He makes His will known to them through a favored intermediary who in turn has His apostles to broadcast His message. The next link in the chain are evangelists — read "televangelists" in the modern conditions. The message is received by one but preached and relayed by others who had no share in the revelation. Their merit is greater if they do it with strong hands and in perfect faith and are troubled by no intellectual scruples or conscience.

In this too the Hindu tradition differs completely. In this tradition, God resides in man's heart, and He is accessible to all who seek Him in sincerity, truth and faith. In this tradition, God is man's own innermost truth and the seeker finds Him in the cave of his heart. In this tradition, God reveals Himself directly to the seeker and needs no specially authorized savior, no go-betweens.

Here we may also make another point. Since Hindu spirituality recognizes God in man, it also recognizes great goodness in him. On the other hand, ideologies which deny man's sacred Godliness also deny his essential goodness. They find man basically sinful, and unfortunately also treat him so. Of course, no one need deny that there is much in man which is not Godly, but let us not make it into a dogma of the depravity of human nature. Let us also become aware of man's other dimension, his Godliness and goodness.

Soul Searching

Hinduism teaches that as one goes deeper into oneself, one meets deeper Gods. An external and impure mind gives only external Gods. This leads us to Robertson's idea of truth and his responsibility to speak it. In Hindu conception, one's truth cannot be greater than one's seeking. In this conception, truth does not lie in some quotable passages of a book. It has to be known through a culture of the spirit, through great seeking, *tapas,* purity and self-inquiry. Let Robertson himself find whether he fulfills this condition.

Hindu spirituality is *yogic*. It is found everywhere, though not always equally developed. It is found among the wise men of Egypt, Greece, Mexico and China. Today, it is in its most preserved form in Hinduism. Hinduism preserves the ancient wisdom of many nations and cultures, their Gods and their insights which they lost under the onslaught of monolatrous creeds. Spiritual humanity needs renascent Hinduism for its self-revival.

Robertson wants to keep out Hindus from America. But would he be able to keep out Hinduism from the seeking humanity? Hinduism resides in all seeking hearts and whenever man's seeking for Gods becomes spiritual, Hinduism, or the tradition of *Sanatana Dharma,* automatically comes in. In what way and how long could man's innermost truth be kept away from Him?

Several months have passed but Robertson has neither replied to my letter nor commented on Ram Swarup's article. Does he feel surprised by the discovery that Hindus can also hit back? For a long time, Christian warriors have been used to Hindus taking it lying down. Or does he feel confident that he can take in his stride the recent Hindu re-awakening as well? His predecessors in the Christian missionary enterprise had felt the same way.

We wonder.

25

Calling the Pope's Bluff

The Papacy started as a crimes cartel which it has remained throughout its long career. But the collapse of Christianity in the West and the retreat of Western imperialism has forced it to change its methods, and function more and more like a multinational corporation. Buyers for its stale and discredited merchandise — Jesus Christ, the only son of the only God and the only saviour from eternal perdition — are becoming increasingly scarce, and it is no more in a position to thrust the garbage down people's throats. Earlier, the pope spoke and the others had to listen. Now the pope is prepared to answer question. He is, however, not yet ready nor equipped to go beyond his copybook.

The Italian Radio and Television had requested Pope John Paul II to appear on its network for a question-answer session on the occasion of his completing fifteen years of his office in October 1993. The person chosen for putting the questions to him was Vittorio Messori, a media man and a believing Catholic. It was planned that the interview would he transmitted to electronic media around the world. The Pope had agreed but could not keep the appointment due to other preoccupations. A few months later Messori was asked to present his questions in writing. The Pope's answers were then published in the form of a book in 1994.[1] The book would have passed into history as another Catholic raving but for the storm it raised among the Buddhists of Sri Lanka. The Government of Sri Lanka had to mobilize thirty

1. His Holiness John Paul II, *Crossing the Threshold of Hope*, New York, 1994.

thousand policemen and an army squad in order to provide protection to the Pope during his visit to the island republic in 1995.

Messori has arranged his questions and the Pope's answers in an odd-sized (11 x 20 cm.) volume. The pages covered by the whole exercise number around 200, taking into account the large spaces left empty at the beginning and end of each chapter. It is printed in double-spaced lines and with wide margins on the right and the left. It has no table of contents. The chapters are not numbered so that it looks more like a travel guide or children's book than a dissertation on some august subject, except for the fact that it carries no illustrations.

Some of the chapters are devoted to the time-worn tenets of Christianity. They are as follows:

1. "The Pope": A Scandal and a Mystery.
2. Does God really exist?
3. "Proof": Is it still valid?
4. If God exists why is he hiding?
5. Is Jesus the Son of God?
6. Why is there so much evil in the world?
7. Why does God tolerate suffering?
8. What does "to save" mean?
9. Why so many religions?
10. Buddha?
11. Muhammad?
12. Judaism?
13. Is only Rome right?
14. Why divided?
15. Does "eternal life" exist?
16. What is the use of believing?
17. The Mother of God.

Other chapters relate to praying, centrality of salvation, Christians becoming a minority by the year 2000, the Church and the Council, qualitative renewal, reaction of the world to the Pope's claims, God's hand in the collapse of Communism, hope for the young, new evangelization, search for the unity of churches, human rights, defence of every life, women, not being afraid, and the scope for hope in the future. These are either supplementary to the main subjects, or comments on current issues faced by the Catholic Church.

The Pope's answers are brimful of citations from the Bible. He quotes 35 verses from Genesis, 2 from Exodus, 4 from Job, 6 from Psalms, 2 from Proverbs, 10 from Isaiah, 2 from Ezekiel, 8 from Matthew, 15 from Mark, 33 from Luke, 123 from John, 15 from Acts, 33 from Romans, 30 from 1 Corinthians, 6 from 2 Corinthians, 8 from Galatians, 7 from Ephesians, 7 from Philippians, 10 from Colossians, 5 from 1 Timothy, 9 from 2 Timothy, 11 from Hebrews, 2 from 1 Peter, 7 from 2 Peter, 16 from 1 John, and 8 from Revelations — a total of 403 verses of which 59 are from the Old Testament and the rest from the New. He quotes some Church canons also and employs a few mystagogic Greek and Latin words. Thus the Pope's performance is no better than that of the meanest parish priest who has crammed the same scriptures and is quick to quote from them. In any case, it does not occur to him that the same authorities have been quoted by his predecessors for saying just the opposite of what he says now. Messori is awestruck simply because firstly he shares the Pope's conviction that the Bible is the Word of God, and secondly because as a believing Catholic he regards an audience with the pope a rare privilege.

Ram Swarup's attention to the Pope's performance was drawn by the happenings in Sri Lanka. And he himself wrote a book[2] as a contribution to the "dialogue" which Christians say they are now carrying on with non-Christians. The "dialogue" has been "guided" most of the time because, during the long period of its domination, Christianity "has conditioned our minds" not only about how we look at it but also about how we look at ourselves. But things have changed and now the others "have their own thoughts about it as well as about themselves."

2. *Pope John Paul II on Eastern Religions and Yoga: A Hindu-Buddhist Rejoinder*, Voice of India, New Delhi, 1995.

The Pope's book, according to Ram Swarup, "departs from the pre-colonial era" only in so far as it "discusses non-Christian religions." Earlier, the Church had seldom taken "any official notice of them", or dismissed them "as handiwork of the Devil." For the rest, the book "says nothing new" and "merely reiterates Catholics' traditional position." The Pope has advanced the same old "claims for Christianity's God, its founder, its Apostles, its Church, its officials, its rites." Only the language is new. The Pope believes that "old half-lies will make one new, whole truth."

The "copious documents" of the Second Vatican Council use the words "Hinduism" and "Buddhism" only once, though the Council is supposed to have inaugurated a new era in Christianity's view of non-Christian religions. Pope John Paul II is more generous and "devotes several pages" to "Buddhism and Eastern Yoga." But the "generosity" has been forced on him because Hinduism and Buddhism are now "better known among the Westerners, they attract the more educated, the more serious and seeking type among them." The concessions he seems to make amount to very little or nothing. There is only "a change of language and not of heart." Even the concession in language makes him feel "uncomfortable" so that "as soon as he makes the concession he takes steps to withdraw it."

Speaking of Buddhism, the Pope starts by conceding that it is a religion of "salvation". But he asserts in the next breath that Buddhist "salvation" is the opposite of Christian "salvation" because it is based on a "negative enlightenment." Buddhist "salvation", he says, comes from "indifference to the world" while Christianity frees people "from the evil through the good which comes from God." This is quite in keeping with the centuries-old Christian propaganda that Indian religions are "pessimistic", "fatalistic" and "other-wordly"

Ram Swarup tells the Pope that in Christian history "this good included persecution and genocide of heathens and their conversion, it included Inquisition, burning of heretics in hundreds of thousands for their own good — burning their bodies in order to save their souls." On the other hand, the "negative enlightenment" of the Buddha means "negation of greed and hatred, negation of ego and delusion, negation of false views (*drishṭi*) — which would include negation of deluded ideologies and theologies, negation of infatuation with self-assumed roles like 'the white man's burden', or the 'divine mandate' of the missionaries to convert the world, negation of *da'wah* and *jihād*." Small wonder that those who have "no inkling of a higher life" find this Buddhist negation "unpalatable and call it 'negation of life', the only kind of life they know." In any case, it was not so long ago that "Christianity took pride in being *other-worldly*." Christian theology anticipated the "end of the world" at any time, and warned people that they would ensure eternal damnation for themselves if they remained preoccupied with this world.

The fact is that "negation is eminently a Yogic concept and it is regarded as necessary for self-exceeding and self-transcendence." Yoga teaches that "there is much in life which has to be negated so that life can be 'affirmed' in its more luminous aspects." There was no dearth of people who used to sympathize with the Buddha because they thought that he was leading a life of "deprivation". The Buddha used to tell them that "his life, his worlds, and joys were incomparable." It is wrong to think that "the worlds and life and joys of *nirvāṇa* are negative." *Nirvāṇa* is "not nothingness but fullness, *pūrṇam* of the Upnishads." The experience is "expressed in the language of negation" because there is nothing comparable to it in ordinary experience to which language is normally suited.

Coming to Christian salvation, Ram Swarup says that "there is near total silence on the subject. We are told that there is Resurrection and Judgement — and these are interpreted not as parables and morals but literally as events in the most physical plane. The man rises with his body and nothing is said about the regeneration of the soul. He rises with his old body with the same old desires and hankerings and infatuations. If he is an unbeliever, he is condemned and goes straight to hell or Fire, to a life of eternal punishment. But if he is a believer, he is 'saved' and sent to heaven. Muslim theologians have spoken of the joys of the 'saved' at length — untiring copulation and gourmandizing. Christian theologians have added some more. One of the greatest joys of the 'saved' according to them is that they would watch, from their balcony in heaven, unbelievers and heretics roasting in hell."

Christian missionaries have been taking credit for what the modern West has achieved by disowning Christianity. The Catholic Church in particular has been the greatest enemy of science. But the Pope repeats the big lie. He praises "Western Civilization" for its "*positive approach*" to the world and claims that the "achievements of science and technology" are rooted in "ancient Greek philosophical tradition and Judeo-Christian Revelation." Ram Swarup reminds him of the "relentless war" which the Church has waged on "Greek religion, sciences and freedom." The Pope should remember the "Inquisition which persecuted free enquiry and scientists throughout its career", of the "*Syllabus of Errors* (1864) which found everything wrong with science." The age-old struggle between science and Christianity is still continuing.

At any rate, it makes no difference whether Christianity claims to be this-worldly or other-worldly. Christianity lacks innerness and compassion, and both the claims amount to the same thing — both are projections of an external mind. "Under either name the nature and aims of the Church have remained unchanged, and it has continued to play a cruel and destructive role; it has taught and exercised hatred and enmity towards 'unbelievers', it has been making pretentious claims and has been assuming an egoistic and deluded role. Its whole approach is based on spiritual arrogance and deluded assumptions — on *anātma*, to put it in Buddhist language."

The Pope is mighty worried over the inroads which Hinduism and Buddhism, particularly the Yogas, have been making in the West. He warns against them in his present book. "It is not inappropriate," he says, "*to caution* those Christians who enthusiastically welcome *certain* ideas originating in the religious traditions *of the Far East* — for example, techniques and methods of meditation ... In some quarters these have become fashionable... First one should known one's own spiritual heritage well and consider whether it is right to set it aside lightly." This is in keeping with the warning issued in December 1989 by the Vatican's Sacred Congregation for the Doctrine of the Faith.

Ram Swarup discusses what Christianity has to offer as its "spiritual heritage". The Bible knows no meditation. The New Testament talks only of "sin, repentance, the expected end of the world." This view inspired scourging. Christians went in processions through the cities led by the Bishop. All of them scourged themselves. Those who did not, "were held worse than the Devil." Even today there are "Revivals" where "crowds of Christians weep over their sins." Then there was "speaking in tongues." But it was difficult to decide when the voice came from the Devil and when from the Holy Ghost. In due course, the Devil became the primary preoccupation of the Church. "He was busy everywhere but particularly in the monasteries and nunneries and in the Christian countryside. Here men and women made pacts with the Devil; women even copulated with him though without much satisfaction for his organs were icy cold." Millions of women were denounced as witches and burnt at the stake.

Today we hear a lot about "Christian mysticism". But Christianity has never known any mysticism on its own. Whatever mystics arose in medieval Europe were due to contact with Paganism, particularly Neo-Platonism. And they were invariably denounced by the Church as inspired by the Devil. The pope hounded out Scotus Erigena till the man died "pierced with the iron pens of the boys." Eckhart escaped the Inquisition by dying before he was discovered and denounced. "Practical minded Churchmen thought that contemplation gave more trouble than it was worth; others like Bousset saw danger of the dogmatic truth being obliterated by a 'cabal of mystics dominated by women'."

Now that Yoga and mysticism have become known in the West, Christian theologians have started talking of "experience" and "states of consciousness" — words which were never known to them earlier. Christian missionaries go about masquerading as "Hindu sannyasins" and establish "ashrams". The Pope also compares "Eastern mysticism" with "Catholic mysticism". He dismisses the former as "born of negative enlightenment" and hails the latter as "born of the *Revelation of the Living God.*" Ram Swarup draws our attention to the history of Christianity and tells us "how living and kicking this God has been — a veritable militant and even terrorist in the Church's cause." Eastern mysticism is based on Yoga — the technique of self-purification par excellence. Revelatory religions have no concept of the "forces that keep a man bound to lower impulsions and perspective, to a life of love and hate (*kāma-krodha*), ego and delusion." They are non-Yogic religions rooted in *rāga-dveṣa* — self-love and hatred of others. They project "narrow and impure Gods — egoistic Gods, hegemonistic Gods." Such Gods can hardly be called spiritual.

The Pope also attacks the New Age Movement in Europe. He sees in it a "return of ancient gnostic ideas under the guise of the so-called New Age." Ram Swarup tells us why "those who manage Christianity find it disturbing." The Movement "is based on no single idea but is made of various ideas and strands." What characterises it most is that its adherents "find the religion and culture of their birth narrow and unsatisfying" and have revolted against their Christian heritage. "They seek new sciences, more compassionate ways of living, holistic and non-violent systems of health." They are attracted by Taoism, Hinduism and Buddhism because they "find in them truths which their own deeper mind was seeking."

The Pope's identification of the New Age Movement with Gnosticism, however, has a whole history into which Ram Swarup goes in some detail. "To start with," he says, "Christianity was Judaic but as it tried to enter the Gentile world, it sought a new idiom. It made an alliance with Gnosticism which, in one way or another, was the real religion of the Graeco-Roman elite. It tried to give Christian apocalyptic beliefs a deeper meaning. Christianity gained immensely from this alliance." But when Christianity became the state religion of the Roman Empire, it denounced Gnosticism as a heresy. Gnostic literature, which was considerable at one time, was ruthlessly destroyed so that nothing was known about it till the discovery of fifty-two Gnostic texts at Nag Hammadi in Upper Egypt in 1945.

The Nag Hammadi texts tell us a lot about what the Gnostics thought of man and God, of Jesus and his suffering, of martyrdom, baptism, resurrection etc. Hindu-Buddhist influences had become operative in the Graeco-Roman world in the form of Gnosticism. Christianity which was a political movement of one God, one Saviour and one Church, could not tolerate a spirituality of pluralism and deeper search. So its struggle against Gnostic ideas became increasingly bitter till it succeeded in stamping out the rival root and branch.

The Pope cannot forget the old enemy who is raising its head again under a new name. And he is not alone in his hostility to the New Age Movement. Other denominations of Christianity have also noticed and denounced it as "age-old lies of Satan himself" and "the influence of Eastern religions" which "best represent the lies of Eden." "They say that the Devil does not expect Americans to become Hindus right away, but his strategy for the time being is to take them beyond the one true God and His Son, Jesus Christ." Pat Robertson says that the New Age Movement in America "is the same thing" as Hinduism. He calls for an offensive against it as the best defence.

Ram Swarup has also commented on the Pope's new approach to Judaism. An attempt is on to make people forget what Christianity did to the Jews for many centuries and prepared the theology of the Nazi Holocaust. Even now the Pope hopes "Judaism can find its fulfilment in Christianity." In like manner, the Pope flatters Islam to a certain extent but says at the same time that "Islam is not a religion of redemption" and that it "completely reduces Divine Revelation." Thus an effort is on to forge a united front of monotheistic religions, forgetting that mutual conflict and strife is inherent in the their very character. Each of them has its own prophet, its own revelation, and its own claim of superiority over others.

He goes on to show how the "dislike" of "alikes" arose. Judaism was the religion of a "special people" with a "special God". Christianity "embraced the Judaic God but denied his people." Islam also "embraced the Judaic God and the Judaic prophets but dropped the Jews." In all these religions "there is no concept of mankind and no concept of a universal God." Through Islam and Christianity, this God of a chosen people has tried "to become the God of all through conquest and slaughter." So the problem is not of "reduced revelation" as the Pope sees it. The problem is of "reduced spirituality" which the three revelatory religions share in common. "They have a reduced concept of Godhood, of man, and of their relationship." The God of the chosen people "refused to reveal himself directly to them." Man in these religions was reduced to a vital-mental being without a spiritual dimension. Finally, spirituality was "reduced to a narrow form of theism — monotheism, which in turn was reduced to monolatry and prophetry."

In the last chapter of his critique Ram Swarup deals with the claim of the Pope about himself, Church Rites, Hell, Ecumenism, world evangelization etc., and shows how Christianity has been and remains cruel or ridiculous. The Pope's book is die-hard Christian theology once again. It is the same old garbage about "God's great love for man so that he sacrificed his only son to atone for man's sin." What is, however, intriguing about the above, comments Ram Swarup, "how the Christian theologians know all these things. If they knew about themselves even a fraction of what they claim to know about God and his Sons and Grandsons and his purpose and plan in history, they would have done very much less mischief."

Science and Eastern influences have subverted Christianity. It has collapsed in its traditional strongholds. The Pope is only giving a pep-talk when he says, "Be not afraid." What he really means is: "Be not afraid of making claims for Jesus, for the Pope, for the Church. Be not afraid of claiming that the Christian God alone is true, that Jesus is his only and begotten son, that salvation belongs to Christians alone, that the Church alone knows the truth and is the sole custodian of salvation. Be not afraid if the statements sound like nursery tales. Brazen it out. Say them and repeat them with a straight face and you will pass through. They may sound preposterous and arrogant to your own ears but your faith is on trial. Don't fail. Allow no intellectual or moral scruples to come in the way of your faith."

Bibliography

Arun Shourie and his Christian Critic, Voice of India, New Delhi, 1995.

Bates, M. Searle, *Religious Liberty: An Enquiry,* New York 1945.

Barrett David B. et al, *Seven Hundred Plans to Evangelize the World,* Birmingham, Alabama, U.S.A. 1988.

Buchanan, Claudius, *Memoirs,* London, 1805.

Burke, Marie Louis, *Swami Vivekananda in America,* Calcutta, 1958.

Chuvin, Pierre, *A Chronicle of the Last Pagans,* Cambridge, Mass, USA, 1990.

Constituent Assembly Debates, Volumes III, V and VII, New Delhi 1947-49.

Das, Sisir Kumar, *The Shadow of the Cross,* New Delhi, 1974.

David, M. D. (ed.), *Western Colonialism in Asia and Christianity,* Bombay, 1988.

Dayananda, Maharshi, *Satyårthaprakāsha* in Hindi, Delhi, 1975 Impression.

Desai, Mahadev, *Day to Day with Mahatma Gandhi,* 9 volumes, Varanasi, 1968-1974.

Downs, F. S.,*Christianity in North East India: Historical Perspectives,* Gauhati, 1983.

Duboi, Abbe, *Hindu Manners, Customs and Ceremonies,* Fifth Indian Impression, OUP, 1985.

Gandhi, M. K., *Christian Missions, Their Place in India,* Ahmadabad, 1941.

Gandhi, M.K., *The Collected Works,* 90 volumes, New Delhi, 1958-1984.

Gandhi, M. K., *Hindu Dharma,* Ahmadabad, 1950.

Goel, Sita Ram, *Papacy: Its Doctrine and History,* Voice of India, New Delhi, 1986.

Goel, Sita Ram, *Defence of Hindu Society,* Voice of India, Third enlarged edition, New Delhi, 1994.

Goel, Sita Ram, *Catholic Ashrams: Sannyasins or Swindlers?*, Voice of India, New Delhi, 1995.

Goel, Sita Ram, *Jesus Christ : An Artifice for Aggression*, Voice of India, New Delhi, 1995.

Gopal, Sarvepalli, *Radhakrishnan: A Biography*, OUP, 1989.

Gospel of Sri Ramakrishna, The, Volume I, Madras, 1985 Impression.

Hinduism Today, monthly from Hawai, U.S.A., February, 1989.

Indian Chruch History Review, December 1967, July 1970, June 1972, December 1973, June and December 1981, December 1985, December 1988.

Ishwar Sharan, *The Myth of St. Thomas and the Mylapore Shiva Temple*, Second Revised Edition, Voice of India, New Delhi, 1995.

Jeevadhara, A Journal of Christian Intepretation, New Delhi, September, 1988.

Johnson, Paul, *A History of Christianity*, London, 1978.

Jyotirmayananda, Swami, *Vivekananda: His Gospel of Man-Making*, Second Edition, Madras,1988.

Keshavmurthi, *Sri Aurobindo: The Hope of Man*, Pondicherry, 1969.

Majumdar, R. C.(ed.), *The History and Culture of the Indian, People*, Volume II, *The Age of Imperial Unity*, Fourth Edition, Bombay, 1968; Volume X, *British Paramountcy And Indian Renaissance*, Second Edition, Bombay, 1981.

Mangalwadi, Vishal, *Missionary Conspiracy: Letters to a postmodern Hindu*, Mussoorie, U.P., 1996.

Mitter, Partha, *The Much Maligned Monsters*, Oxford, 1977.

National Christian Council Review, The, 1945, 1946, 1947 and 1956 volumes.

Nehru, Jawaharlal, *Glimpses of World History*, OUP reprint, Fourth Impression, 1987.

Neill, Stephen, *History of Christianity in India: The Beginn-ings to 1707 AD*, Cambridge University Press, 1984.

Panikkar, K. M., *Malabar and the Portuguese*, Bombay, 1929.

Panikkar, K. M., *Asia and Western Dominance*, London, 1953.

Panikkar, Raimundo, *The Unknown Christ of Hinduism*, London 1964.

Plattner, Felix Alferd, *The Catholic Church in India; Yesterday and Today*, Allahabad,1964.

Pope John Paul II, *Crossing the Threshold of Hope*, New York, 1994.

Price, Rev. J. Frederick et al (tr.), *The Private Diary of Anand Ranga Pillai,* 12 volumes, Madras, 1904.

Priolkar, A.K., *The Goa Inquisition* (Bombay, 1962), Voice of India reprint, New Delhi, 1991.

Ram Swarup, *Introduction* to D. S. Margoliouth's *Mohammed and the Rise of Islam,* New Delhi Reprint, 1985.

Ram Swarup, *Introduction* to Anirvan's *Inner Yoga (Antaryoga),* New Delhi, 1988.

Ram Swarup, *Ramkrishna Mission in Search of a New Identity,* Voice of India, 1986.

Ram Swarup, *The Word As Revelation: Names of Gods,* New Delhi, 1980.

Ram Swarup, *Pope John Paul II on Eastern Religions and Yoga: A Hindu-Buddhist Rejoinder,* Voice of India, New Delhi, 1995.

Report of the Christian Missionary Activities Enquiry Committee, Madhya Pradesh, 3 Parts, Nagpur, 1956.

Shiva Rao, B., *The Forming of India's Constitution,* 5 volumes, Bombay, 1967.

Singhal, D. P., *India and World Civilization,* Volume I, Calcutta, 1972.

Tagore, Rabindranath, *Gora,* A novel translated from Bengali into English, Calcutta, 1961 Impression.

Tambaram Series, Volume 3, *Evangelism,* London, 1939.

Temple, Richard, *Oriental Experience,* London, 1883.

Thirty-four Conferences Between the Danish Missionaries and Malabarins (or Heathen Priests), London, 1719.

Thomas, M. M., *The Acknowledged Christ of the Indian Renaissance,* Second Edition, Madras, 1976.

Thomas, P., *Christians and Christianity in India and Pakistan,* London, 1954.

Transfer of Power 1942-47: The Quit India, London, 1971.

United Nations and Human Rights, The, UNO, New York, 1984.

Vatican Council II: The Conciliar and Post Conciliar Documents, Bombay, 1988.

Vivekananda, Swami, *The Complete Works,* 8 volumes, Calcutta, 1985 impression.

Young, Richard Fox, *Resistant Hinduism,* Vienna, 1981.

Index